ERIK H. ERIKSON

The Growth of His Work

THE DA CAPO SERIES IN SCIENCE

OLIVE PIE

ERIK H. ERIKSON

The Growth of His Work

by ROBERT COLES

A DA CAPO PAPERBACK

Library of Congress Cataloging in Publication Data

Coles, Robert.
  Erik H. Erikson: the growth of his work.

  (The Da Capo series in science) (A Da Capo paperback)
  Reprint. Originally published: Boston: Little,
Brown, 1970.
    Bibliography: p.
    Includes index.
    1. Erikson, Erik H. (Erik Homburger), 1902–
  2. Psychoanalysts — United States — Biography.
  3. Erikson, Erik H. (Erik Homburger), 1902–   — Con-
tributions in psychohistory. I. Title. II. Series.
RC438.6.E75C65 1987   150.19′5′0924 [B]   87-593
ISBN 0-306-80291-0 (pbk.)

A substantial portion of the contents of this book appeared originally in *The New Yorker* in somewhat different form.

The author wishes to thank W. W. Norton and Company, Inc. for permission to use excerpts from *Childhood and Society, Young Man Luther: A Study in Psychoanalysis and History, Insight and Responsibility, Identity: Youth and Crisis,* and *Gandhi's Truth* by Erik H. Erikson; and Harcourt Brace Jovanovich, Inc. for permission to quote from "Burnt Norton," which appears in *Four Quartets* by T. S. Eliot.

This Da Capo Press paperback edition of *Erik H. Erikson: The Growth of His Work* is an unabriged republication of the edition published in Boston in 1970. It is reprinted by arrangement with Little, Brown and Company.

Published by Da Capo Press, Inc.
A Subsidiary of Plenum Publishing Corporation
233 Spring Street
New York, N.Y. 10013

TO CESAR CHAVEZ, who like Erik Erikson, if on different territory, has struggled to make things clear, but beyond that, to see what is right and important — and who at the end of a fast, at the end of a Mass of Thanksgiving celebrated in Delano, California, said these words, which do indeed speak to the ideals of the man this book is about:

When we are really honest with ourselves, we must admit that our lives are all that really belong to us. So it is how we use our lives that determines what kind of men we are. It is my deepest belief that only by giving our lives do we find life. I am convinced that the truest act of courage, the strongest act of manliness, is to sacrifice ourselves for others in a totally nonviolent struggle for justice. To be a man is to suffer for others. God help us to be men.

Contents

Preface

A PREFACE permits a book's author to tell where he stands, and unquestionably in so doing he runs the risk of self-centeredness if not self-display. Yet this is a preface to a book about the work of a man who has argued persuasively that sustained and cultivated anonymity on the part of historians and biographers, not to mention psychiatrists and psychoanalysts, can be dangerous. We owe it to ourselves and our readers to show something of our lives and our purposes, to indicate, as it were, the context out of which a particular book has emerged. I want, therefore, to do what I can right off to spell out some of the interests and involvements that have, I believe, had a direct and compelling part in bringing about this book.

In 1962 I visited three youths, three college students, in an old and crowded jail. Two of the students were black, one was white; and the jail was in Alabama. I was at the time living in Georgia, and studying school desegregation as it took place in New Orleans and Atlanta as well as in the smaller towns of North Carolina and Tennessee. I was also working with students like those three, students of both races who belonged to organizations called CORE or SNCC, who in the midst of school or on a leave of absence from school were confronting Southern sheriffs and store-owners and restaurant managers with — themselves, their willful, polite, nonviolent, determined, unyielding insistence that the time had come, the time for this nation to realize its ideals at last, the time for both races of a beleaguered region to sit and walk and talk as equals, to look right at one another, to affirm one another, to put away tired pieties and forge new allegiances.

Those years, 1960 and 1961 and 1962, marked a turning point in the nation's history. Because of the sit-ins, the various voter-registration projects, the freedom houses and freedom marches and freedom rides, the South would never again be quite the same, and neither would America's youth, who showed the rest of us that idealism need not be abstract and cloistered, but rather, actively tied to life's events. And so students who were reading novels and poems and plays and essays were also spending time in jails, and it was my task to visit them, to talk with them, try to enlist the prison's doctor on their side, try to carry news in and out of high and forbidding brick walls. Those youths were learning as well as doing; they were learning how history is made, how societies work, what politics is like, and not the least, how changes are made — in habits, in customs, in the way people think and feel. In and out of jail they talked about what they were learning, all night in unforgettable marathons. Through books they also summoned up the wisdom of others; in Louisiana or Mississippi, in Alabama or Georgia I would come across those books, a mixture of literature and theology and history and philosophy: James Agee's *Let Us Now Praise Famous Men*, W. J. Cash's *The Mind of the South*, William Faulkner's novels, James Baldwin's novels and essays, Richard Wright's novels and stories, Ralph Ellison's *Invisible Man*, C. Vann Woodward's history books that read like epics — and also, *Childhood and Society*.

I can recall quite clearly the visit I had with the three youths in that Alabama jail. We talked about their immediate difficulties and their long-range purposes; and because of the pressure of time our conversation had to zigzag sharply, had to be awkward and self-conscious and fumbling. As I was leaving, my eye stopped to look at a pile of books, three or four of them, on a table. There it was: that familiar yellow jacket with black letters that announce the author, Erik H. Erikson, and across the cover in red the words *Childhood and Society*. I remember moving toward the table, picking up the book, looking at it, putting it down, and asking the young black student how he liked it. "It's good, it's real good," he said, quietly but firmly, and with an accent out of the bayou country of Louisiana. I was asked if I knew the book, and I said yes I did, and then I was asked what I thought of it, and I said that I agreed, that it is indeed a real good book. Then he added something, as both of us edged toward the door, me to go, he to say good-bye and remain: "I can see where you'd have read it."

I wasn't quite sure what he meant, and he must have seen or sensed that to be the case. He amplified his remarks briefly: "A book like that has a lot to tell you, especially if you're going to be a psychiatrist. I'm not, but I learned a lot, too." Soon I was gone and driving back to Vinings, Georgia, where I lived at the time. I remember thinking to myself that in a way the visit to the jail had been far more important than I ever could have anticipated. I had been in and out of those Southern jails before (and I would be again) but for the first time I had left feeling a little less confused and sullen and sad and disgusted and guilty. Somehow the barriers seemed less formidable, less unyielding — between black and white, between one generation and another, between a Southerner and a Northerner, a college student like that youth and a professional man like me.

Those were the days when we all were singing "black and white together," though we wondered even then what assumptions we actually shared and how long our various purposes and hopes would continue to keep us "together." I had felt at that time particularly skeptical about my own purposes and hopes; and though I have gone into all of that at substantial length in volume one of *Children of Crisis*, it is I believe appropriate at least to repeat here the doubts and questions I had. What kind of medicine, what kind of psychiatry, what kind of child psychiatry, what kind of research was *this?* Of what use were all those "observations" to clinicians, whose job it is to understand the "pathological," treat the "sick"?

Yet, for all my worries about my professional "role," I had seen a copy of *Childhood and Society* in the possession of that black youth, the son of a sharecropper, a scholarship student at a college run by a Southern state so that he and his kind would hopefully learn "agricultural and mechanical" matters and no doubt keep in their "place." I had heard the youth say how grateful he was for having the book, and how important it was that *I* also know what such a book has to say. A historian who wanted to study American psychiatry and psychoanalysis of the fifties would not find the prominent journals and books of that decade full of concern with the way societies affect childhood — or for that matter, the way Luther or Gandhi can exert a psychological influence on millions of mothers and fathers and children, affect how they all think and feel and act. In an Alabama jail I had unwittingly discovered that such a book could have a very special meaning to a person apparently far removed from those "groups" of people more or less traditionally taken up with social science and in particular psychoanalysis. And as a matter of fact, over the next few years I was to see *Childhood and Society* in a number of Southern freedom houses and Appalachian "outposts." In a sense, I was to see something else: though not all doctors understood what Erikson was getting at, at least thousands of students did. They read him loud and clear, and told me so. They laughed at some of my hesitations, my professional "hang-ups," and often enough they "invoked," that is the word, *Childhood and Society*.

Of course, other books were also recommended by those youths: novels and collections of poetry, essays on history or politics, essays full of social criticism. Over the years one comes to witness changes in preference; a particular author gives way to another in the minds of idealistic young men and women always hungry for more views, a different kind of sensibility, a new and surprising summons. Over the years one also sees fads embraced: a certain book is "in," and God forbid if anyone has his reservations. And over the years something else becomes apparent, too: those who want to change a society are no more immune to despair and sadness and anger and a sense of futility than the rest of us. So, out of nowhere, it seems, new books appear: books saturated with pointless abuse and wild almost random hate and crazy suspiciousness; books that offer proposals or theories beyond comprehension; books that dote on murkiness and fantasy and, worst of all, contempt for everyone and anything, with only a small elite exempted.

Through it all, through the sixties, a decade of progress and heartache and disaster, I have tried to observe what I can about the way whites and blacks get along in the South and the North, about the way migrant farm workers and sharecroppers and the mountain people of Appalachia get along — live and struggle to grow, falter and lose all hope and die. My writings are an attempt to describe a decade of so-called field work among lonely, frightened children pioneering school desegregation; vigorous and unyielding youths confronting the South with their ideals; migrants moving up and down and all over America in search of harvests, in search of a livelihood; Appalachian miners working underground and Appalachian "subsistence-farmers" planting what they could up those hollows, all in order to stay in a region they love; and finally, black and white families trying to live "up North," which means struggling with uncertainty and pride and fear and distrust — in schools, on streets, in this neighborhood and that ghetto, places where mountaineers have settled reluctantly or Southern blacks have settled grimly or expectantly.

Before I began that work I was a resident in psychiatry and child psychiatry in the late fifties, just after *Childhood and Society* and *Young Man Luther*, like a breath of fresh air indeed, arrived at the door of a profession thoroughly respected, but by no means without its crustier, insistently dogmatic, and narrow-minded side. I recall a supervisor recommending *Childhood and Society* and telling us to take heart, to go forth, as it were, a little less intimidated by the bureaucracies of psychiatric and psychoanalytic organizations — which have not been immune to the sequence many organizations go through: a brisk, vigorous beginning, and gradually the onset of middle age, with its necessary consolidations, but also its brittle, self-protective and self-justifying ways.

I recall reading *Young Man Luther* in Louisiana, where I started my work with those four children whose court-ordered presence in two elementary schools (the year was 1960) so alarmed and aroused the sophisticated port city of New Orleans. I recall reading *Insight and Responsibility* in 1964, the year of the Mississippi Summer Project, the year when I worked with Dr. Joseph Brenner at Oxford, Ohio, where some five hundred students prepared to go South and spread all over the Delta and the hill country and the Gulf Coast of the Magnolia state.

Soon, even before all of us had left Ohio, three were killed; and later, during the summer and autumn of that year, a crucial turn in the "civil rights movement" began to take place: frustration and resentment and bitterness, so long denied or forgotten or ignored in the interests of a political effort, could finally be stayed no longer. Immediately after the destruction (by dynamite) of the McComb freedom house, in August 1964, I heard a black youth speak: "It is getting late. We cannot go along with the old assumptions — and believe that somehow in some way we will come through on the winning side. We've tried taking things for granted, going along with things as they are. Now is the time to stop and think; and I mean really think. I mean think about what we really do believe, whose ideas mean something, where we should be going. When this summer is over, if we're all alive, we ought to go read someone, someone who lights up our thinking, and we ought to stop and ask ourselves — we'll each of us do it differently — what this life is all about, and what we should do next with our energy."

In September of the same year I was attending Erik Erikson's undergraduate course at Harvard and enrolled in a seminar of his that concerned itself with "history and life-history" — that is, with

the manner particular individuals both go through their individual
lives and take part in a given society's development, its unfolding
history. In October of that year I wrote a review in *The New Republic* of Erikson's *Insight and Responsibility*, and by that time I
believe I had a *conviction* about what I had noticed in those jails
and freedom houses and had probably felt rather than known during
those years of training and more training: books like *Childhood and
Society* and *Young Man Luther* and *Insight and Responsibility*
teach people a lot, explain a lot of things, but more than that, do
what that black youth from McComb, Mississippi, said they should
do, namely, move people to examine their assumptions, examine the
broader social and historical forces at work even in the most cloistered of offices. I think it was about then, about 1964 or 1965, that
I began to study Erikson's various writings systematically. I had
decided that if I was going to write one book after another about
the various "children of crisis" I would meet and come to know,
I had better well look at the particular viewpoint I was using in the
course of my work, using to look at others and understand them,
to fathom their purposes, to comprehend their weaknesses and problems — and hopefully, their strengths, those strengths I for all too
long could not let myself even be aware of, let alone appreciate.

I had, in effect, decided also that for me and my work Erikson's
viewpoint was crucial, was illuminating, was (to use an old-fashioned word) edifying, and was necessary. In 1966, I even began
setting down on paper page after page of notes: thoughts, ideas,
opinions, impressions. I should not omit the fact that in 1963 one of
the first essays I wrote about my work in Georgia and Alabama
and Mississippi and Louisiana ("Serpents and Doves: Non-violent
Youth in the South") appeared in a volume entitled *Youth: Change
and Challenge*, edited by Erik H. Erikson. I remember the long-
distance call from a stranger asking whether I might want to set
down some "observations" for that book. I can still hear that voice
on the phone: the German accent, the straightforward use of good
and plain English. And not the least, I can still hear a sentence, a
reassuring sentence in reply to my stated fears that all that struggle
in the South would, through me and my writing, get turned into
one more aggrandizing, self-serving bit of "research." Yes, he could
see how I would worry about that, "but you can tell others what
you saw and experienced in the schools or the jails, no more and no
less. There's a little room for that in psychiatry." I wasn't so sure

then; if I am somewhat more sure now, I am also sure that books like *Childhood and Society*, *Young Man Luther*, *Insight and Responsibility*, *Identity: Youth and Crisis* and *Gandhi's Truth*, addressed to the general public, as Freud's books were, have had their effect on even the most protected and authoritative realms of American psychiatry and psychoanalysis.

I have no wish to go into an extended discussion of this book's character and purpose; either that will be self-evident by the last page, or alas, one more wasted effort will have to be recorded — in a field already cluttered with the obscure, with the banal dressed up as the original, and worst of all, with the peculiar arrogance "experts" can demonstrate in their writing. Still, I do not feel I am cheating when I ask the reader's indulgence for a brief series of disclaimers.

This book is not primarily a conventional biography of Erik Erikson; nor is it an attempt to fit his ideas into the larger framework of psychoanalytic theory; nor does it come near assessing and conveying the influence his work has had on disciplines other than his own — political science and history, not to mention anthropology and sociology; nor is it "objective" or "neutral"; nor, finally, does it aim to "analyze" the man, give the "reasons" he has become what he has, said and done what he has.

I am clearly not doing here what Erikson has done in *Young Man Luther* or *Gandhi's Truth*. I suppose if this book has to be classified, fitted into some category, it could be called an intellectual biography of sorts; I add "of sorts" because I find the term "intellectual biography" rather pompous. I would never have allowed this discussion to end up so, were it not that I think it fair, given my own profession and the profession of this book's subject, to make it rather clear at the outset what will not be forthcoming. I hope that the book itself will indicate why I believe this effort is of some value. And I believe the reader will recognize that this is only one of several books that could be written about Erikson and his writings. Like everyone else, a writer can be only himself.

In any event, I have tried to look at the psychoanalytic and historical research and the ethical reflections of a clinician and professor I know and admire. I have hoped to give the reader in this one book a sense of what is to be found in five other books, and in dozens of articles, monographs and essays. I have less thoroughly (again, one has to choose a central task, an emphasis) indicated something about the social and cultural history of psychoanalysis. God knows, a thorough intellectual history of the psychoanalytic movement needs to be done — by a historian free enough to be both sympathetic and critical. Perhaps the time is not yet ripe; or perhaps scholars have kept their distance from the subject, aware as they must be of the strong and conflicting historical and ideological claims that continue to press themselves upon the field of psycho-analysis. One can only hope that time will bring with it detachment and humor rather than yet additional bitterness and narrowness.

In April 1968, Anna Freud delivered the eighteenth Freud Anniversary Lecture ("Difficulties in the Path of Psychoanalysis"). The entire lecture is eminently worth reading; but at one point she contrasts with particular poignancy those who became psycho-analysts in the beginning and those who are now drawn to the field. She does not mean to be condescending or nostalgic. She knows that as psychoanalysis has become more advanced and influential as a discipline, a body of knowledge, a means of research and treatment, the demands upon it have increased and so have its responsibilities. In a way, she simply wants to point all of that out, remind her listeners that history (like psychoanalytic treatment) also affects the assumptions of people, affects the climate of a profession, even comes to determine who become analysts: "When we scrutinize the personalities who, by self-selection, became the first generation of psychoanalysts, we are left no doubt about their characteristics. They were the unconventional ones, the doubters, those who were dissatisfied with the limitations imposed on knowledge."[1]

But now "the dreamers" (as she calls them at one point) have given way to those "hardworking enough to wish to better their professional efficiency," because rather clearly "psychoanalytic training has become institutionalized and appeals in this stricter form to a different type of personality." I supposed it can be said, then, that this book is about one of those "dreamers" — though dreamers can also work hard and long to give their dreams the utterly understandable and summoning substance that sensible language can provide, as is demonstrated by Miss Freud's own articles and books, not to mention her father's. If a touch of the "romantic" comes across in this book, I have no apologies to offer: a life can, in fact, be romantic, be full of passion and enthusiasm, full of the doubts and unconventional brilliance Miss Freud had in mind when she gave her lecture. Freud looked upon himself as a conquistador, a rather romantic notion indeed for him to have had — except that it was true.

I have no interest in providing one more analytic "explanation" of the heroic and charismatic "personality." Some men live rather more astonishing or striking or fascinating lives than others — and manage in their words as well as their presence to convey not only the hard and serious work they have done, but again, their dreams and hopes, the drama of their minds and hearts. It is true, one can wrongfully "romanticize" a person, even in what is, predominantly if not exclusively, an intellectual effort to come to grips with his writing, rather than his personal life. On the other hand, "romantics" are not the only ones who distort "reality," give an inflated or imaginary view of things. By dwelling ruthlessly on theoretical details, by endlessly analyzing motives, by throwing buckets of icy-cold water on this or that "trait" of a person, or "position" he has argued — yes, it is quite possible in those ways to strip a man of his warmth, his humor, his liveliness, his infectious charm, the grace he has as a particular human being, and the grace to be found in his books.

Nor should anything I have been saying so far (or will say) be interpreted as "hostile" to the essential spirit of psychoanalysis. I am all too aware of the unwarranted purposes to which Erikson's writings have been put by some — who are always on the lookout for a way of ignoring Freud's hard-won psychological discoveries. I am also aware that as I write these words psychoanalysis is no longer of great interest to large numbers of young people, including many I work with and teach. Anna Freud mentions that same fact at considerable length in the essay just quoted. But I believe that the essence of psychoanalysis, its heart and soul, will live on indefinitely — or at any rate, as long as human beings manage to survive and keep their wits about them. At its best psychoanalysis has to do with man's effort to understand *and* get along with others; in that sense psychoanalysis is not only a means of private introspection, but is a social act. Nietzsche said, "It takes two to make a truth." Every day patients find that out in their analytic hours — and hopefully, so do their doctors. The whole thrust of Erikson's work is to show how *much* goes on in the unconscious. No one ought to imagine that he, of all people, will be of any help to those who want to see us as a bundle of reflexes, as social automatons of sorts. Each of us takes in the world, and then, prodded by our bodies and minds, does "our own thing" — as is obvious from what goes on in the offices of psychoanalysts all over the world every day: thousands of thoroughly different and distinct dreams and fantasies are discussed.

When a man builds on another man's work, as Erikson has on Freud's, he does not always have to repeat his predecessor's every single tenet or assumption. If it is true that one has to beware of those who want to dilute fatally the utterly precise and important discoveries of Freud, it is also true that those same discoveries can come to naught in other ways: "dilution" is a kind of drowning; but alternatively, in St. Paul's words, "the letter killeth." And that said, there is no point, really, in going on. Either it is all clear or it is not. I can only emphasize how sad many of us feel that rhetoric and rancor continue to plague a decent and honorable profession, psychoanalytic psychiatry. If some of the trouble has been a hostile, reluctant public, whose opposition has been one of hysterical flight or an ingratiating and misunderstanding kind of acceptance, then an additional source of trouble has been we, the doctors: we are human, and like all men and women, we can become worried, fearful, angry, nervous, devious, possessive, jealous.

Before turning to the book proper, I should like to thank the individuals I formally interviewed or spoke with in recent years about the life and work of Erik Erikson; in particular, I want to thank for their time and energy and help Peter Blos, Rudolph Loewenstein, Margaret Mead, Maria Piers, and Reinhold Niebuhr. I also wish to acknowledge a most helpful interview with the late Heinz Hartmann. I wish to thank Mrs. Lucy Hilgendorf, Mrs. Devorah Gilbert, Miss Martha Stearns, Lawrence Rhu, and Mrs. Pamela Daniels for the substantial effort and care they have given to this book's manuscript; and once again I am indebted to Peter Davison for his good judgment and assistance. I wrote this book while on the staff of the Harvard University Health Services and with the support of a grant from the Ford Foundation. A considerable portion of the book appeared in different form in several issues of *The New Yorker*. I thank that magazine's editor, William Shawn, for his kindness and tact. Several years ago he encouraged me to write much of this, and do it in my own way. We all of us in this world need — at certain moments *especially* need — sanction. And so much the better if it can come from a quiet and thoughtful man who wants to impose no particular and exclusive political or intellectual viewpoint, but rather encourage a wide range of observations and opinions. I also thank the editors of the *International Journal of Psychiatry* for permission to draw upon an article I wrote for them, "Erikson's Search for Gandhi," which appeared in July 1969. And finally, I could not have written this book without the cooperation of the Eriksons: Erik and Joan and their children; nor do I see how I ever could have done the work without my wife Jane's encouragment, or the presence of our children — who, like children everywhere, including the children I work with, have a way of making complicated and confused matters all of a sudden crystal clear.

ROBERT COLES

ERIK H. ERIKSON
The Growth of His Work

I

Philosophical Roots

I DO not think it is unfitting to begin this book with a few words about Søren Kierkegaard. In 1768 a boy of twelve named Michael Kierkegaard left the heath and bog country of Jutland for Copenhagen. His maternal uncle had built a modest success for himself in the Danish capital as a hosier. At that time hosiers did more than sell stockings; they were often from Jutland, where wool was produced, and they traded fabrics as well as ready-made clothes. Young Michael learned the business well; by the time he turned twenty-five he was on his way to a fortune in textiles. At forty, a childless widower, he retired to read heavily in philosophy and theology. Eventually he remarried and fathered seven children, the last of whom, Søren Aabye, was born on May 5, 1813.

The aging Michael took a particular fancy to his son Søren, the Benjamin of the family. As the boy grew into a frail and slender youth he felt the strong influence of his father's intensely religious and argumentative mind. Michael Kierkegaard lived until 1838, by which time Søren was twenty-five, and himself destined to die in only seventeen years. The two of them were for a while contemporaries of Goethe, Hegel, Carus, Schelling, and Schopenhauer, five German nineteenth-century philosophers who knew very well that the human mind was powerfully influenced by an unconscious — which, in fact, eighteenth-century writers such as Rousseau, Diderot, Hume, Kant, and Fichte had made mention of and discussed.

In the very year of Søren Kierkegaard's birth, Schopenhauer — heavily under Kant's spell — wrote his first book, *On the Fourfold Root of the Principle of Sufficient Reason.* He next worked on a massive study that was finished and published in 1819: *The World as Will and Representation*. In the chapter "On Madness," Schopenhauer takes the unconscious for granted, and describes it as a dynamic force capable of causing forgetfulness and even physical symptoms such as paralysis. It would be another half-century before the medical and psychiatric professions started studying systematically his intuitive and conceptual observations — and then only reluctantly, under the prodding of the Viennese doctor Sigmund Freud, whose fierce and brilliant "will" surely would have impressed the young Schopenhauer. (Schopenhauer's "will," in fact, was a complicated metaphysical concept in many respects not unlike Freud's "libido." And Freud eventually recognized the resemblance.)

Students of Kierkegaard such as Regis Jolivet and Walter Lowrie[1] give us little information about the Danish theologian's schooling. Michael Kierkegaard was a brooding but severely loyal worshiper. His son Søren was also moody, but a far more radical thinker. He filled his short lifetime with an unusually intense kind of introspection. He searched passionately for the sort of faith that by his own definition he could never knowingly possess. And he was a polemicist whose *Concluding Unscientific Postscript* (1846) contained a fierce attack on Hegel. Hegel was *the* rationalist, *the* dialectician, but he saw in human history not merely a "pattern" or an intelligible "plan," but the expression of God's will — something commonly forgotten today by those whose interests are strictly confined to the "material" events of this world. Kierkegaard foresaw accurately that later generations would find in Hegel the justification for a cult of "objectivity." To Kierkegaard, God is inscrutable, His intentions utterly mysterious. To know God, to approach Him, requires a "leap," a suspension of man's inevitable self-centeredness — which may take the form of a prideful effort to tuck the destiny of the universe into one or another intellectual scheme.

What we ought to do, according to Kierkegaard, is look at ourselves rather than at God's design or History's ultimate purpose. We ought to do this boldly and frankly — if we can summon the gall and faith to try. In *Either/Or* (1843), his longest and best-known work, the book which eventually made him both famous and notorious, he began to look at himself, at what today we might think of as the mind's various and conflicting dispositions. He was interested in what *happens*, happens to the "things of this world," to people and their feelings, rather than what *characterizes* them; that is, in method he was more dynamic than categorical, and in this respect very much like his enemy Hegel.

From 1843 until his death twelve years later Kierkegaard lived a secluded, feverishly creative life. In one two-year segment of that period he published fourteen books, which were all avowedly psychological and even explicitly clinical. The more he analyzed himself the more he jarred an age that could take speculation on anything, including the life of the mind — the precedent for that went back to Aristotle at least — but was hardly prepared to find the thinly disguised personal anguish of one man propounded as a "general" truth. The shock in Copenhagen was severe enough to cause in a generation the relative disappearance of the once common name Søren. "Don't be a Søren," children heard from their horrified parents, and generations of obliging children have made Danish intellectual life pay the price ever since. (No matter how scandalized Vienna was by Freud's ideas, the first name of Sigmund has remained a reputable one.)

Although in America existentialism followed psychoanalysis as an object of both genuine and faddish intellectual interest, historically it was quite otherwise. Kierkegaard, the first and most powerful of modern existentialists, died in 1855. In 1856 Sigmund Freud was born in Moravia, hundreds of miles south of Copenhagen. He also was a wool merchant's son, and in quite a different way he was destined to penetrate the same psychological territory Kierkegaard insisted on considering all-important. It cannot be said that the one influenced the other — they came from almost incompatible intellectual worlds — but the similar problems they each chose to confront, the incisive genius they both had, and the common century each struggled both to escape and to change, all combined to make their lives more alike than either might ever have dreamed possible.

Kierkegaard was the Christian tradition's first explicit psychologist. (Only in the eighteenth century did the word "psychologist" begin to appear in the English language.) He constantly insisted that man's duty to God required not confident prayer but self-analysis, and he followed his own advice to the end, leaving behind a virtual literature of observations, arguments, parables, and self-addressed admonitions — for the most part intentionally unorganized and written in a strikingly immediate style that fairly grabs hold of the reader in order to emphasize the urgency of what is being said. He saw the individual mind as a scene of successive battles, which become resolved only to be fought again and again for higher odds: the pursuit of pleasure, of the self in all its momentary but exciting possibilities, is resisted by the ethical responsibilities felt to some degree by most people; among those whose moral sensibilities prevail, the temptation toward self-satisfaction is often countered by the grim knowledge that God's relationship to man is arbitrary and utterly incomprehensible; and finally, for the man who would obtain the grace of faith, there is the distinct challenge that everything must be assumed lost and even meaningless before there can be the slightest chance of success — the redemptive kind.

If we put aside Kierkegaard's strictly religious speculations — and he often does so himself — we are left with an exceedingly canny and modern view of the mind. Instinct struggles with conscience. Society has its rules, but they vary, and there is no way of knowing their absolute value, if any. What appears to be the case may not be the case; indeed, the mind is contrary, devious, and hard to fathom. Moreover — Kierkegaard always insisted — each man's mind has its own particular history and destiny, just as history itself is not a uniform or predictable series of events but an endless number of trials between man and himself, always under the shadow of eternity, which for him was clearly more than just a period of time. Every psychological crisis is hard to explain and can turn out to be a moment of disaster or grace; one cannot be sure of an outcome because appearances deceive. A seeming victory can be a defeat, and vice versa.

Kierkegaard fought Hegel's orderly, scientific mind as only a tempted man can; he shared with Hegel a desire to perceive, to replace mystery and chaos with some kind of reliable vision. They differed not in their purposes or even in their methods, but in their interests. Both wanted to end the confusion between man's fate and God's design: Hegel, by finding in history its own laws, and only then — as a gratuitous afterthought, it has been argued — deriving them from God's infinite wisdom; and Kierkegaard, by showing once again that man's mind is not his soul, but in the long run may be the paradoxical scene of his most significant religious experience. The shift from the soul to the mind is doubly important: for one thing, a choice is offered, with man freed, so to speak, from a seat of built-in or necessary religious conflict; and in addition, man's thinking becomes a thousandfold more interesting and momentous.

Kierkegaard sees us as alone, naked and afraid. Nor will churches and prayerful gestures help; in fact, his contempt for religious piety was limitless. On the other hand, every thought and mood really does count — for keeps. We cannot bargain with God, or ingratiate ourselves before Him. He knows us as needy and greedy, and He sees us as we ought to try to see ourselves. That is, we have motives — which demand from honest ministers psychological analysis rather than hasty indulgence or pardon. I do not think Kierkegaard would be shocked at Freud's stubbornly agnostic *The Future of an Illusion*, let alone the substance of his psychoanalytic work. Almost as a matter of course Kierkegaard seemed able to find the religious in unconventional places.

In any event, the radical power of Kierkegaard's gloomy, suspicious mind was no match for nineteenth-century optimism. Freud admitted to a conscious avoidance of Schopenhauer's books. He was afraid that he would find that Schopenhauer had just about said it all. As for Kierkegaard's books, Freud probably found them far less threatening. In 1890 Kierkegaard was thoroughly unknown. It was not until 1944 that *Either/Or* was translated into English — barely in time, some would say, for a Western world that was about to accept genocide and hydrogen bombs as part of its political and technological "reality." Kierkegaard's moment of favor in this century's intellectual life has to do with his strongly moral, personal, and emotional tone, and his anti-institutional bias. Hegel would say that people who are so independent they need no faith in anyone or anything except themselves — their concrete, comfortable, fearlessly productive one-time lives — are bound to have a reactive panic and turn to a man like Kierkegaard when, for example, Germany's intellectual genius leads to Auschwitz, and America's matchless productivity makes for the possession of enough military hardware to eliminate from the face of this planet *all* panic.

Even so, it can be argued that without Freud, Kierkegaard would still be as ignored or misunderstood as he was in his lifetime. We are now rather used to the idea that almost from the beginning each of us has to face conflict and tension, regardless of how "healthy" or "well adjusted" we are, or how sensibly and considerately our parents treat us. Freud himself first saw anxiety as a very specific thing, a product of a particular conflict, and of the mind's tendency to deal with conflict by pushing it forcibly aside (repression). We live uneasily because we have paid the price of not knowing what ails us. Later Freud began to feel that anxiety is far more pervasive than he had ever dreamed, its presence an inevitable or developmental part of everyone's mental life: "It is not repression that creates anxiety; it is there first and creates repression." Once Freud had said that — and had been heard by a culture attentive to his ideas — the anxiety Kierkegaard repeatedly described could be acknowledged in a skeptical, "scientific" age as an utterly irreducible (hence existential) phenomenon. When all the antecedents of adult behavior are revealed, and all the progressively consolidated deceptions of the mind unraveled, there remains in any patient what Freud called a certain kind of "basic anxiety." Kierkegaard called the same thing "dread" or "fear and trembling" — and the choice of words matters very little. The point is that both men saw life as inevitably, necessarily painful: growth is painful; the world frustrates the individual and brings pain to him; and finally we each have the painful assurance that there must be a last heartbeat.

The thoroughly psychoanalyzed or "enlightened" but still (normally) anxious man is just the person Kierkegaard had in mind when he wrote *The Concept of Dread* (1844). He did not shirk looking into what Freud called "the psychopathology of everyday life." If Kierkegaard moved from philosophy and theology to psychology, Freud also had to make a move. Late in life his mind left his office to begin the task of placing what had been found out about patients into a perspective that accounted for the development of civilization. He became curious about the nature of normal and gifted thinking as opposed to the disturbed kind. He discussed the relationship of the individual to "the group": be it a group of neighbors, the people in a nation, or the sum of what is left of people now gone — who survive in personal memories or general traditions.

Kierkegaard saw the mind split between the alternatives of self-fulfillment, self-expression, and self-importance on the one hand and ethical responsibility on the other. He made categories of the two trends (the aesthetic and the ethical) and called them "stages," each with a contrasting philosophy, and each struggling for predominance over the other in every life. To him both stages lead nowhere, though clearly ethical sensibility is in itself an accomplishment, an advance. Man finds his destination in a third stage, the religious, but its characteristics are hard to define because no longer is the individual mind with its immediate life and experience at issue. Amid the religious stage a person confronts everything — a world so large that it can only be called (by an agnostic) eternity. Grace is ineffable precisely because the person who has it cannot by himself account for it — that is, either explain it or justify it solely on the basis of his own life. As a theologian Kierkegaard examined the psychology of man the believer and sinner in a new way — deeply, extensively and with enormous intuitive skill. What St. Augustine did through autobiography, Kierkegaard did as a solitary observer of others. He was a step removed from himself. In Kierkegaard's psychology, one finds the mind constantly up against the world. There is the neighborhood, with its churches, marketplaces and saloons, all ready to tempt, betray, or facilitate redemption. And there is a history that Kierkegaard refused to pin down; quite the contrary, he insisted that every human being has his own history and his own relationship to all of history. In spirit he was a clinician, sensitive to the particular, wary of the general, and allergic to Hegelian universals; but he was a clinician stubbornly unwilling to become captured by his own clinical instinct. Like Pascal, he saw "reason" elsewhere — in the heart as well as the mind, in the influence that others exert upon us, and of course in the other part of our selves, the unconscious.

Freud gradually worked his way from a neurophysiological laboratory to a study of Moses — thus meeting Kierkegaard more than halfway. He did so by stretching the confines of his own point of view, which is all anyone who has *created* a point of view can be asked to do. Nor could Kierkegaard, working as a theologian at a particular moment in history, systematically survey the mind's ground he instinctively knew to exist. That job had to wait for a man like Freud, and perhaps for his kind of language and thinking. Freud extracted from various observations the greatest achievement any scientist can wish to be his: a method, a manner of study that made the human mind, any willing or desirous human mind, accessible to investigation. Since he naturally did so within a specific scientific tradition, and at a particular moment in the history or development of that tradition, he, like Kierkegaard, could only fulfill the one destiny any genius has. He had to tread as grandly and nervously and unsystematically over the world *outside* the mind, the earth and the universe, as Kierkegaard did with the mind's *inner* world. A telescope makes the viewer feel too little, a man condemned to speculation about the distant; a microscope tempts the viewer with divinity, the sight of the invisible making everything else seem unimportant.

Both men had those very special followers who are much more

than followers. Karl Jaspers and Gabriel Marcel have taken Kierke-gaard's century-old work and shown its powerful relevance to modern psychological and philosophical problems. In doing so, they have been drawn not to exegesis but to the profound compliment of reliance and use: a man in Copenhagen long ago spelled out the pre-dicament of the Christian existentialist, and so it remains for each generation to take note of that predicament and once again prove its essential nature with the confirmation of new evidence. When Ga-briel Marcel[2] talks admiringly of Karl Jaspers as "following in the steps of Kierkegaard," the reader is meant to appreciate that an off-hand and even indirect acknowledgment can be more genuine than the most ostentatious devotion. Marcel, like Kierkegaard a passionate Christian existentialist, talks repeatedly about "creative fidelity." He even gave a book that title. What he calls "vivifying philosophical minds," like Kierkegaard's, enables the thinker of the next generation "to surpass himself as a simple *Fachmensch*, as a simple specialist." The debt to the past is acknowledged by an assumption of personal responsibility, by an effort of self-assertion worth a hundred sterile vows of obedience to the dead master.

Freud, too, generated a very special intellectual tradition — de-scribed by W. H. Auden as "a whole climate of opinion." Had he lived only as long as Kierkegaard, he would have died at forty-two, still the doctor who had studied the unconscious, learned the sig-nificance of dreams, and written some of what he had discovered in *The Interpretation of Dreams*, his masterpiece that was finished in his forty-third year. But Freud lived into his eighties, and unlike Kierkegaard saw his ideas become extremely influential all over the world. As early as 1902 a psychoanalytic study group called the Psychological Wednesday Society was formed: Alfred Adler, Max Kohane, Rudolf Reitler and Wilhelm Stekel started meeting every Wednesday evening in Freud's waiting room. When Kierkegaard lay dead in his coffin a group of students stood guard, fearful of the hostility they knew he had aroused. Freud died in exile, but at least in England and America his body and his books needed no such alarmed defense.

Actually, men like Kierkegaard, Darwin and Freud always gen-erate both dazzle and fear, so that it often takes a generation or more for their views to receive attention that is free of fearful hos-tility or stylish and uncritical acceptance. Freud not only lived long enough to attract followers; he freely admitted that he *wanted* them, so that his ideas would have wide institutional backing. And after the first followers came the innovators, some of them like Jung and Adler eventually rejected by Freud as hopeless deviants, others like Ferenczi, Abraham and Hanns Sachs welcomed as collaborators in a continued and exciting search.

Someday historians will be in a position to take a long look at what twentieth-century men, from Freud's immediate followers to thousands of others, "found" in psychoanalysis, which is at the same time a theory of the mind, a method of investigation, and a therapeutic technique. As I mentioned in the Preface, a social historian's view might be especially useful. He could suggest reasons why psychoanalysis took hold in one country and not in another, among some men and not others. He could note the changes in what has become, at least in America, a distinct profession, and try to explain those changes as logical outgrowths of a certain kind of psychological theory, or as subtle responses to a variety of social and cultural forces. Finally, he could select one or two unusually creative psychoanalysts and show through the development of their careers how stimulating psychoanalysis can be.

II

Personal and Professional Roots

B Y any measure — originality, excellence, productivity, influence, fame — Erik Erikson's work would warrant special attention from that yet-to-arrive social historian. Erikson's unusual career as a psychoanalyst shows how enduring Freud's influence has been — responsible years after his death for the kind of contagious achievement in another mind, which Marcel described. Historically, psychoanalysis could only come of age when it was no longer guarded by its first students, or pursued by Marcel's "specialists" — who always turn vivid, imaginative ideas into hard, thorny dogma. A genius has never achieved his purpose until he has given succeeding generations of men — as Marcel put it — the courage to "surpass themselves."

Of course Marcel's "specialists" are not born but made. Societies either want them or have no great interest in them. Parents urge upon their children a disciplined, obedient study of the era's reigning technology, or they set an example of opposition, indifference or nostalgia. They may teach their children to espouse the message of old poets. They may urge them to seek out the private vision of contemporary philosophers. They may encourage them to admire the stubborn individuality of artists who want to paint a world somehow (and more than somewhat) different. It is not possible to predict for sure what a child will choose to do with his life, but his place of birth, his time of birth, and his parents' values exclude more choices from later consideration than perhaps any of us — determined to be "free" — cares to know.

Whatever his future was destined to be, Erik Erikson's ancestry made it highly improbable that he would ever become the kind of narrow technician Marcel has described. Though he was born on June 15, 1902, near Germany's Frankfurt, which means near Germany's scientific and industrial brilliance, his parents were Danish, both reared in Copenhagen a short generation's time after Kierkegaard's death. (As a youth Erikson was told by his mother that during her pregnancy and his infancy she had read widely in Danish literature, including a number of Kierkegaard's books, and indeed, some nineteenth-century American writers such as Emerson also interested her.) Before Erikson was born his parents had separated, and his mother left Denmark for Germany to be near friends. Eventually, with Erik, she stopped to rest at Karlsruhe, where she knew a number of people. While there her son (at age three) fell sick and was seen by a local pediatrician, Dr. Homburger, who cured the patient and fell in love with the patient's mother. In a while they were married, and the boy Erik was given his stepfather's name.

And so the wandering Danish woman and the boy who reminded her of an earlier life came to live in a Jewish doctor's home in Karlsruhe, which is now a city of about two hundred thousand people, about thirty miles from both Heidelberg and Stuttgart. Karlsruhe's history goes back to 1715, when a minor nobleman, Karl Wilhelm of Baden-Durlach, built a hunting lodge on an elevated plain five miles east of the Rhine and on the fringe of one of Germany's famous forests, the Hardtwald. Like Erikson's mother, he is reported to have stopped there for a breathing spell, hence the name Karlsruhe, "Karl's rest." Between 1751 and 1756 a *Schloss* slowly rose, and in time streets began to radiate from the *Schloss* like a fan, so that the city became known as the "fan city." From about 1870 on, it also became known as an industrial center, with railway workshops and factories that turned out tools and machinery, watches, surgical instruments, furniture, gloves, cement, carpets, perfumes, tobacco and beer — a rather German combination of products. While the spokes of the fan became longer and longer, the center remained the same: a *Schloss* with a fine park around it, and facing them both a few fortunate homes.

In one such home Erik Erikson spent his childhood. His room was upstairs and overlooked the castle as well as the grounds around it. Right off the boy had a view — and one that was both lovely and stately. He also had ample space to walk, run, or play, and a solid, comfortable home waiting upon his return. Nearby was evidence of

Germany's technological genius; also nearby were fine secondary schools, or *Gymnasia* as they were called, and of course in cities only a few miles away, world-famous universities. The psychoanalyst whose book *Childhood and Society* shows how pervasively social institutions affect the child's growth, and later the adult's mind, would not want to exempt his own early childhood from the following analysis: he lived near beauty, but also near enterprise; in his own home he saw ill and hurt children being treated and cured; he lived in a country and a region that presented to its middle-class citizens a rich tradition of culture, solidly transmitted by its educational system.

Young Erik went to *Vorschule*, or primary school, from six to ten, and then until eighteen to the *Gymnasium*. His eight years in the *Gymnasium* were extremely important to him later; they were, in fact, his last really sustained bout — just that — with formal education. He went to a so-called classical *Gymnasium* rather than a "reform" one, the difference being somewhat similar to the difference between a high school that emphasizes classical languages and literature and one whose courses are mostly scientific and technical. He studied Latin for eight years, Greek for six, and of course German literature all along; in addition there were ancient history and art — in both of which he excelled. He was not a good student. He did not take to the strict and formal atmosphere but was interested in *Bildung*, what we would call "general education." And his mother, a doctor's wife, entertained many artists of the region. By the time he was ready to graduate he felt at a loss, out of place and out of joint. In the language of our time, he was "alienated"; but there is nothing new about feeling out of sorts so far as society goes. The Germans had a word for a young student who had his doubts about things: *Künstler*.

Instead of going on to college, he wandered through Europe with the same energy and determination that others of his age and background were applying to study. He would walk through the Black Forest and eventually work his way to the shores of Lake Constance, where for some months he spent most of his time reading, putting his thoughts down in a notebook he kept, and looking about the countryside.

After a year of such "escape," he returned to Karlsruhe, somewhat intent upon a career as an artist. He enrolled in an art school, the Badische Landeskunstschule, and for a year managed to accept the fact that an artist could learn something in a formal setting. But again he became restless, and left for Munich, where he studied briefly at another art school, the famous Kunst-Akademie. Yet he actually did most of his work by himself: enormous woodcuts which demanded a good deal of physical energy as well as artistic imagination. As in Karlsruhe, he continued drawing and doing woodcuts or etchings. His work was shown in Munich's Glaspalast, where he shared a room with Max Beckmann and Wilhelm Lehmbruck. Erikson's woodcuts and Beckmann's paintings covered one wall of the room, and in its center stood two of Lehmbruck's delicate, almost unbearably frail statues. Beckmann would, of course, go on to achieve fame as an artist; but for Erikson that exhibition in Munich was a high point.

After two years in Munich he went to live in Florence, a city he loved. While there he gave up sketching altogether and simply wandered through the streets and over the hills, perhaps trying to get from that Renaissance city an inkling of the "measure" of man, which he felt was threatened by the awful and ironic anarchy brought about by certain tight-knit political organizations — like the quick-stepping *fascisti* who then dominated Florence's old streets. To the Italians he was a not an unfamiliar sight: the young, tall, thin Nordic expatriate with long, blond hair. He wore a corduroy suit and was not seen by his family and friends as odd or "sick" but as a wandering artist who was trying to come to grips with himself, a not unnatural or unusual struggle — particularly in Germany. His friends in Italy were Peter Blos, the well-known American child psychoanalyst, then a writer, and the late Oscar Stonorov, a Philadelphia architect for a long time but then a sculptor. And Erikson remembers walks with Gaetano Salvemini, the fierce liberal whom Mussolini would soon exile to America.

Walter Z. Laqueur in *Young Germany*[1] gives a valuable account of that nation's youth movements. Their history goes back well into the nineteenth century, and their philosophical traditions have consistently reflected the self-conscious, romantic and introspective character of many middle-class Germans. At the very time Kierkegaard was denouncing the arbitrary restraints Hegel wanted to put on all history, many of Germany's youth were going through a phase of what was to be a century of "storm and stress," the almost mystical turbulence that writers like Goethe — and later Nietzsche

— took pains to celebrate. Young men from the upper bourgeoisie, steeped in classical education, in the virtues of thrift and industry, were urged by certain writers and teachers to throw off the restraints of family and school, to seek after "nature," the wildness or freedom in "life," the fulfillment that goes with assembly, exercise, singing and devotion to the nation, the fatherland. The emotional self-scrutiny Kierkegaard undertook was not at all the defiant self-centeredness paraded by German youth from 1850 to 1930, but common to both was a turning away from the world, an almost ecstatic embrace of what is actually elusive, but to youth eminently concrete, the "I."

Erik Erikson was not a member of the Wandervogel, an organization of German youths particularly wedded to the obscure (and potentially sinister) cult of national honor, group travel, vaguely defined "adventures" and folk song. He did, though, live at a time and in a country where the stroller, the apparently aimless but serious youth, was very much part of the scene, and could count on an occasional free meal in a simple *Gasthaus*, and lodging too, if a night under the stars was too cold. A psychoanalyst who later would write about the problem of identity — whether among contemporary American students or in a great German of the past, Martin Luther — at least was able to go through his own years of discontent and confusion without being especially singled out and thereby forced to defend behavior often best granted the limits of its own momentum.

Slowly the youth who had left Karlsruhe seemed headed back there for good. The stay in Florence was over, and at twenty-five, Erikson was living in his home town, both studying and preparing to teach art. It was at this point in his life that a letter came from a friend in Vienna, certainly one of the most fateful letters he would ever receive. It was from Peter Blos, one of his close friends from *Gymnasium* days, who also seemed to be drifting. While Erikson made his way through forests and around lakes, looking, reading, sketching, Blos was cultivating a strong interest in biology. But he did so like his artistic friend, irregularly and in a manner very much his own. Supposedly studying for a higher degree in science, he seemed to be looking for diversions, for opportunities to delay that final confrontation with the academy, let alone the world. While studying in Vienna he met Dorothy Burlingham, an American lady who had come there with her four children to see and eventually study with Freud and his youngest daughter Anna. (Miss Freud was then beginning what was to be a long and distinguished career as a child analyst.) Mrs. Burlingham was of an old New York family (her maiden name was Tiffany) and her husband was a well-known lawyer. She was not unlike a number of Americans who came to Vienna in the twenties to be psychoanalyzed. They were invariably well-to-do, well educated, and inclined to look relentlessly at themselves and their children. They constituted the vanguard of a far larger movement, whose influence would leave a mark on American social, cultural and intellectual history.

In the twenties Paris and London beckoned American expatriates who wanted to find (or lose) themselves as writers and artists, or merely as the inevitable hangers-on. In contrast, Vienna drew a different sort from the States: psychiatrists convinced that William James was right when he told Freud "the future of psychology belongs to your work"; educators whose minds had been awakened by men like John Dewey, and who were thus unable to settle for the strap and rote memory as the way to earn a child's trust; and just plain (or extraordinary) citizens who were troubled in mind or curious in spirit. Hemingway, Eliot and Pound, in the tradition of Henry James and Whistler, went abroad almost as a matter of course; their careers demanded it. Now Americans started going abroad almost in spite of whatever career they had. They went expressly to try a new and radically different kind of patienthood, in which ideas are not exchanged face-to-face over wine in a sidewalk cafe but spoken willy-nilly, as soon as they come to mind, and examined relentlessly by a doctor who is out of sight and seems most often a listener, sometimes a talker, and never the man of action that most physicians aim to be.

Mrs. Burlingham had four young children, and they needed schooling. She wanted them tutored privately, and in the course of events met and engaged Peter Blos to do the job in the sciences and in German. He lived with the Burlinghams for two years, and of course came to meet and know the Freud family, to which Dorothy Burlingham became increasingly attached. When Blos felt the time had come to move on — perhaps to finish his own education — Mrs. Burlingham and Anna Freud worked hard to prevent the loss of a brilliant and charming teacher. They offered the irresistible to the young, unhurried and idealistic Peter Blos: a school of his own, where he could continue to teach the Burlingham children, and in

addition work with other English and American boys and girls —
many of whom, along with their parents, were in analysis.

A building was secured — it stood in a garden that belonged to a
friend of the Freud family, Eva Rosenfeld — and about twenty
children were enrolled. Blos needed another hand on deck, and told
Miss Freud and Mrs. Burlingham of his friend in Karlsruhe: he was
a gifted artist; he particularly did etchings, and his subjects often
were children; he was widely read, an avid student of history, and
a stubborn individualist who was having trouble with his life; he
tended to meditate on his own rather than study assigned lessons;
and he had no really fixed future in store for himself. The two
women were interested, and suggested he be invited to Vienna.

In 1927, at twenty-five Erik Erikson gave up wandering. In Vienna he was quickly appreciated for the sensitive man he was — by
men and women who, after all, were no more interested than he in
living by outmoded or irrational social and psychological tenets.
He and Peter Blos were given full freedom to organize a curriculum
and teach it, a necessary gift from people who appreciated more
than many the importance of such freedom to both children and
teachers. The result was what I suppose could be called a progressive school, similar in certain respects to some American experimental schools. The children were not graded. They were taught as
individuals. They themselves were encouraged to teach, to share
in planning the day's activities and choosing the subject matter. If
there was conventional matter to be learned conventionally — languages, facts and axioms — there was also a good deal of the adven-
turesome to be met, and taken in not as something required, but
something chosen and enjoyable.

The children worked with both their minds and their hands. Herr
Erik, as he was called, taught them how to draw and paint, how to
put together a collection of poems and songs, or a yearbook. He
also taught them history, and not only German history. They read
about Eskimos and American Indians, and they poured their impressions into compositions and pictures. They also made a variety
of tools, toys and exhibits, so as to give each culture they studied
some flesh. They studied geography, ancient history, mythology,
and all the arts, classical and modern. Long lists of subjects were
posted, so that in *freien Arbeit* the children could choose a topic
of particular interest and eventually write on it as they pleased, at
length, briefly, formally or casually. Blos and Erikson wanted the

children to feel "free," that is, unafraid of school, and in many respects their own masters.

Yet the teachers did not overlook the need children have for a sense of order, for controls that make things work but don't senselessly intimidate. At that time few children were in danger of the excesses later committed in the name of "spontaneity" or a "liberal" education. Quite the contrary, all over Europe and in America the desirable child was thought to be a docile boy or girl who learned what the teacher taught, and did so quietly and efficiently. Few teachers worked on the assumption that children had either rights or desires of any kind — intellectual, social or emotional. Freud's ideas about the unconscious mind and the sexual conflicts it harbors were unsettling enough; but perhaps more shocking than anything else was his claim that children are full of passion, are driven by the same assortment of emotions as adults. Philippe Ariès in *Centuries of Childhood*[2] analyzes the social origins of the nineteenth-century middle-class family and demonstrates how the child was regarded as utterly innocent, indeed, without a will of its own, for the first decade of life. Children were to be sheltered, of course, but also strictly trained and regulated. They were in fact a special kind of property, alive and with a destiny no other property can have, but nonetheless owned, and pushed or pulled without consultation.

Peter Blos and Erik Erikson created a world of their own in the school they began, yet it was a world they insisted on sharing with their students. The responsibilities of equal citizenship were immediately made known to the children; the school was in fact founded to make possible those responsibilities. The school was also one of those frontier settlements that any living civilization periodically establishes. The children Blos and Erikson taught were also teachers who were giving analysts like Anna Freud a lot to think about.

Miss Freud was trying hard at that time to convert a psychoanalytic interest in the childhood of adults — as it is recalled by patients — to a concern with childhood itself. Under her leadership the new profession of child analysis was being born, a development that would eventually affect the majority of analysts who don't work with children. Psychoanalysis was bound to become an increasingly theoretical discipline so long as it relied upon dreams and associations, upon retrospective accounts by people who have reasons of their own for distorting what they do remember and forgetting what they most need to remember. When Anna Freud — who was first an elementary school teacher — started working with children, she immediately realized how much there is to *observe*, to notice, and take in. Growing boys and girls require watching, while the swift and various changes in their behavior require from the analyst a tentative and flexible theoretical point of view. In 1925 Freud's ideas were already becoming *beliefs*, pure and simple, to some of his followers, so that Anna Freud's interest in childhood as a new field of inquiry was bound to be an antidote to that development. The mystery of childhood was added to the mystery of the unconscious as twin challenges — for those interested in challenge rather than faith.

Any aspiring science needs men to pursue and modify its tenets. Speculative ideas have to be weighed against observations — and in the case of a field like psychoanalysis, which draws its life from lives in crisis, there are always the patients to be treated. In the twenties Freud was steadily gaining recognition all over the world, but by no means were doctors rushing into psychoanalytic training. The very fact that any psychoanalysts were being trained was itself a mark of the new field's success, though it had not been fully determined *how* they were to be trained by the time Freud died in 1939. Freud did insist upon one thing: to know psychoanalysis one must experience it. The intellect can make its formulations, but by definition the irrational side of the mind tends to hide itself from the intellect, and indeed use it for any number of purposes. Freud asked would-be analysts to go through what he himself had braved: relentless self-scrutiny, assisted — as he was not — by another's informed presence.

Some of the children taught by Blos and Erikson were the sons and daughters of future analysts. Some of the children were in analysis themselves, and eventually their teacher, Herr Erik, joined them. It all started on the Semmering, the highest mountain near Vienna, where one of those famous European spas was located and where the Freud and Burlingham families spent their summers. With a view, with bracing air and sunshine, with mineral water flowing from the springs, one could feel restored, cleansed, born again. It was at the Semmering that Erikson had first come to know the Freud family and to be judged a desirable candidate for psychoanalytic training. In those days one did not apply, but was chosen, and it was all done quietly, without endless "interviews" and "evaluations."

In town Anna Freud shared a waiting room with her father at Bergasse 19, the now famous building where the Freud family lived, and where father and daughter worked at analysis. Erikson began analysis with her, and there he went daily and became more and more involved in a process the obscurity and pain of which he could not have foreseen — particularly since at the time he knew very little about psychoanalysis and was not interested in a career as an analyst or even as a schoolteacher. In 1927 and 1928 he was still very much the artist; but as his teaching and his daily analysis continued, his eyes no longer tried to come to terms with the demands of the canvas. Instead, he was looking at childhood as it daily presented itself to him in the classroom, and as he recalled it while lying on Anna Freud's couch.

The years Erikson lived in Vienna — from 1927 to 1933 — have been described by Ernest Jones[3] as Freud's time of "fame and suffering." "The Professor," as Freud was called by his few local supporters and the increasing number of foreigners who came to study psychoanalysis in Vienna, struggled every day with growing age and a painful malignancy that eventually would eat away the roof of his mouth and hasten his death. Nevertheless he continued to see patients and write prolifically. His daughter Anna was in constant attendance, caring for him and helping him in his work. Together they were surrounded by an increasing number of students, patients and interested visitors from every continent. Once the theory of a single Viennese doctor, psychoanalysis in 1930 had turned into a widespread intellectual movement, with member societies in the various continents and with an Austrian publishing house that issued a succession of books, monographs and journals. Letters came to Bergasse 19 from everywhere, and from year to year Freud and his discipline gained more and more respect.

Inevitably a circle of friends, colleagues, students and patients developed around the Freud family, some of whom sent their children to be taught by the two young German teachers, one in analysis with Miss Freud. Despite the worsening political climate in Central Europe, the Freud circle, including its school, seemed an island of confidence and relative good cheer. Yes, there was wild inflation, and from the gutter strident political voices were making themselves heard as never before. But the study of psychoanalysis seemed to offer an urgent and valuable answer to such irrationality — if only enough people could understand themselves in a way never before possible. Then, and only then, said many of Freud's students, the madness that was gaining dominance over the market-places and parliaments of the West might be stopped.

So, amid falling currency and rising hate, a small colony of analysts and patients worked on, and a small number of their children went to a school full of adventure, inquiry and experiment. The atmosphere inside school and out was cordial and informal. Analysts did not go to great lengths to avoid their patients, and indeed the very nature of analysis was different than it is today: shorter, more relaxed, less expensive, and far less complicated. Young Erikson could see Anna Freud during the day to tell her about his childhood, and later in the day find himself joining with her in a children's affair and maybe even a swim in the Danube. In 1930 when Freud went to Berlin for medical treatment, his daughter could tell Erikson to come along. He would stay in the house of Freud's son, who was then living in Berlin, and continue his analysis. The psychoanalyst was not then some solemn, inscrutable, fleetingly seen person who for five years does little but listen, his every word a memorable occasion, his feelings seemingly nonexistent. (Freud himself was a man of strong, if controlled, emotions, something that was appreciated by all who made his acquaintance — visitors, colleagues, patients.) True, analysts in the twenties probed and listened, but they also talked about the ordinary events of the day — and they even felt free to offer advice on all sorts of problems. For one thing, professional ceremony had not set in; for another, psychoanalysts at that time labored to uncover the mind's hidden facts, then explain them, often enough rather volubly. Now the emphasis is on circumspect observation of what goes on between the analyst and the patient — which, naturally, can turn into a kind of overworked and oppressive self-consciousness.

When Erikson started his analysis he had no lengthy period of training in mind. He was on scholarship, so he paid only a token fee to Miss Freud. There was no long-range, highly structured commitment required; he simply taught school as before, and had his analytic hour each day. Even that schedule at times caused him to be apprehensive. The wanderer and artist was not yet ready to settle down and listen to others "free associate." He still wanted to draw and paint. He remembers telling Anna Freud in one session that no matter how much he had learned about himself, psychoanalysis as a profession was not for him. He had been an artist, and he would be one again. He also remembers Anna Freud's reply that psychoanalysis may need people who can make others *see*. That simple reminder was hard for him to forget — in fact, to this day he can recall her words. When I asked him how he began to build a bridge between art and psychoanalysis he said: "I began to perceive how important visual configurations were, how they actually preceded words and formulations: certainly dreams are visual data, and so is children's play, not to speak of the 'free associations' which often are a series of images, pure and simple — only later put into words."

As an artist he had worked with children; they were most often his subjects, and he had an understanding of them which he could bring to life in a drawing. In Vienna he was again with children, now teaching *them* art. Gradually he did begin to take theoretical courses in psychoanalysis, and see patients as well. At last the artist could be a pediatrician of sorts — which is what his stepfather was and wanted him to be. Under the supervision of August Aichhorn he began to be a clinician. But there was also the school, with its eager children, hungry for the same active, unsupervised, freewheeling study he himself liked; and there were vacations and summers, when German lakes and forests or Italian cities could again be enjoyed. Doctors choose a grave and confining world. If Erikson was going to become an analyst, one who day after day must sit and try to comprehend mental aberration, somehow his mind and heart would have to become committed as never before — so that the confinement and frustration every therapist must face would at least be tolerable to a young man whose childhood in a doctor's home had so far stimulated no apparent interest in healing.

During those years — the late twenties and early thirties — Herr Erik both taught and attended school; in fact he went to two schools, as if hedging his bets on his own future. He studied clinical psychoanalysis with August Aichhorn, Edward Bibring, Helene Deutsche, Heinz Hartmann, and Ernst Kris, a stunning group of teachers whose collective brilliance would slowly unfold in the next twenty years. He also studied with a Montessori group in Vienna, and was one of two men to graduate from the Montessori teachers' association, the Lehrerinnenverein. His later psychoanalytic studies were influenced by the Montessori education. He became interested in how children arrange various objects in a given space, such as a miniature room or a portion of a real room. A good Montessori teacher could help a child psychoanalyst work out the mechanics of that kind of research.

Certainly the nature of psychoanalytic education in Vienna at that time helped Erikson continue his training. He could feel free, open-minded and curious without making anyone particularly nervous. His teachers were those specially gifted and bold people who often take up revolutionary intellectual pursuits. Moreover, psychoanalysis was itself in a ferment, in the midst of a turmoil-ridden period of growth. Someone unwilling to foreclose many directions in his future could feel at home with a profession that was like June, "bustin' out all over." Freud himself was becoming increasingly preoccupied with applications of psychoanalysis to literature and art, to psychobiography, and to the general issues that face all civilized men: the alternatives of war and peace, the nature of education, the sources of religious faith. For example, while Erikson was in analytic training Freud wrote *The Future of an Illusion, Civilization and Its Discontents,* "Dostoevsky and Parricide," a letter to Maxime Leroy on Descartes's dreams, a postscript to his "The Moses of Michelangelo," and upon the award to him in 1930 of the Goethe Prize, a lovely acceptance speech (delivered by Anna Freud) that showed how akin he felt to the writer or the artist. The city of Frankfurt gave the prize, and Freud followed Stefan George, Albert Schweitzer and the philosopher Leopold Ziegler as a recipient.

In retrospect, one can find another reason for Erikson's growing desire to stay in Vienna and become a psychoanalyst. Not only an interesting job and his analysis kept the wanderer relatively rooted to one place. In 1929, at a Mardi Gras masked ball in the Laxemburg Castle, one of Maria Theresa's homes, he met a young woman, Joan Serson, of mixed Canadian and American background, and promptly fell in love with her. (He was dressed as a Turk, red fez and all; she as a heavily bejeweled dancer.) Some months later they were married, and by 1933, when he was to graduate from the Vienna Psychoanalytic Society, they had two sons, Kai and Jon.

The marriage not only encouraged him to settle down, but his wife's interests and background were very much like his. In retrospect one can see that both of them were struggling to establish a life rooted both in art and in science. Mrs. Erikson — a very beautiful, charming and gracious woman whom the Viennese called "Die Schöne," the lovely one — was far ahead of her husband in academic training. She had received a B.A. in education at Columbia, a masters degree in sociology at the University of Pennsylvania, and in addition had taught modern dance there and at Teachers

College. Eventually she became interested in the history and social origins of modern dance. She wanted to earn a doctorate in education at Columbia, and was in Europe to do research on the origins of the various schools of dance that proliferated in Germany after the First World War. Moreover, she too had been analyzed – by Ludwig Jekels, one of Freud's first followers.

The young couple was poor, and lived an almost rural life. Their home was in Lainz, an outlying district of Vienna, and was situated on a hill, Kuniglberg. The water they drank came from a well, and their cottage had no plumbing. Yet neither the couple nor the patients seen in the basement of the cottage saw anything unusual in a life idyllically simple but also given over to complicated analytic study.

Erikson's wife joined the school's faculty. She taught English, English literature and American history. When their first son, Kai, was born they carried him down the hill between them in a laundry basket and she nursed him during the school's recesses, which of course could be arranged as the need arose. The children would hear Kai crying and would exclaim "*Kai weint.*" His mother would call a halt to the class and tend to her child. In that school a mother who sometimes nursed her child and also loved to teach young children could only be considered a special asset.

The friendly, imaginative, straightforward atmosphere in the school had its counterpart in the psychoanalytic community which graciously received and entertained the young couple. Miss Freud and Mrs. Burlingham could visit them at home to no one's embarrassment or self-consciousness. Today Joan Erikson recalls her analysis with Dr. Jekels: "I remember one day noticing some lovely *Schneerosen*, roses of the Alps, as I entered his office. I remarked on their beauty, and later he got up, picked some and gave them to me. On other occasions he would remind me that a particular opera or play was in town, and tell me how much he enjoyed it – and how I would, too. A warm and yet naturally reticent relationship between analysts and patients – or students – was not then considered out of order. Quite the contrary."

It is no secret that things have changed, at least in America, where applications for psychoanalytic training are initiated by those who want it, and certainly processed more formally – perhaps with different criteria than Freud had in mind. Only doctors are allowed training by most psychoanalytic institutes in America, and the fees they pay their analysts for a "training analysis" average from twenty-five to thirty dollars an hour. Of course as psychiatrists the student analysts are themselves making sums like that, hour after hour each day. Gifted but unsettled artists no longer find themselves in analysis on scholarship while teaching at schools that defy the local educational customs in order to teach what children and instructors together find exciting. Nor would a young American lady expect the American analyst she was seeing to requite her fancy for flowers by gallantly plucking one or two of them from a window box high above the street. It would be "unrealistic" — a downtown office building is not an Austrian house — but worse, it would be "seductive," a break in proper "technique." And gallantry — what can it possibly be but a way of concealing something?

By 1930 those lively and informal Viennese days were numbered by events that no one in his right mind could possibly have predicted. The first blow was the American depression, which began to tighten the bank accounts of even the relatively well-to-do people who sought analysis in Europe. Germany and Austria were also having a rough time of it economically, and with less to fall back on than the United States. Both nations had recently lost a war, and thereafter made a shaky transition from monarchy to constitutional, parliamentary government. In Berlin and Vienna, socialists and communists fought openly with rightist groups. If Freud was becoming increasingly preoccupied with the violent, destructive side of man, it was not only a terrible world war and his own aging, ailing condition that brought out such gloom in him.

It is fashionable today to consider Freud the quaint prisoner of the nineteenth-century Victorian Hapsburg world to which he was born, and in the midst of which he made his major discoveries. His patients, we remind ourselves, were of a certain kind — middle-class, proper, no doubt sex-starved. He himself was strong-minded, and determined to make of what he found in a patient's mind the stuff of science, that is, science like physics or biology. No wonder he saw what he did, and talked the way he did. We of course — alive today — claim to know better. We know that as times change, new psychological problems arise and different ways of looking at those problems have to be sought. Since the patients Freud saw in 1900 are no longer around, it seems reasonable to ask why the theory he built to explain their behavior still remains very much with us.

In point of fact, Freud was much more sensitive to social and cultural forces than some of his critics allow. The First World War had a devastating effect on him, and not simply a personally devastating one because his sons went to war and his homeland suffered so. He felt moved to reconsider his whole view of man. He had always relied upon the mind's rational side to win any battle, given the slightest help from someone like himself. After 1914 he began to question his own optimism; and in the decade from 1920 to 1930 — like the sensitive sociologists and cultural anthropologists of our day — he let the fateful and threatening issues of his lengthening lifetime very much shape and modify his ideas. From the complaints of hysterical, sexually confused Viennese women, or nervously inhibited, fearful men, he turned his attention to a world that seemed literally falling apart. And always the willing theorist, he was prepared for just that eventuality: Thanatos, or Death, fights Eros, or Life — and no one can possibly predict the winner.

In *Civilization and Its Discontents* Freud saw man inevitably caught between his hurtful, vindictive or quarrelsome "self" and an equally significant need for companionship, affection and love. At the end of the book he made it clear that Europe's ominous political and economic difficulties had been very much on his mind as he wrote: "Men have gained control over the forces of nature to such an extent that . . . they would have no difficulty in exterminating one another to the last man. They know this, and hence comes a large part of their current unrest, their unhappiness and their mood of anxiety." Perhaps, he concludes, the better side of man will assert itself in such a struggle. "But who can foresee with what success and with what result?" Though *Civilization and Its Discontents* was published in 1930, the editors of the standard English edition of Freud's *Complete Psychological Works* make the following comment about the far from optimistic rhetorical question Freud chose for the book's ending: "The final sentence was added in 1931 — when the menace of Hitler was already beginning to be apparent."

Certainly in the early thirties Thanatos began striking at the psychoanalytic community in Vienna. One after another the German and Austrian analysts who made up the majority of Freud's intimates and followers began to leave. Scattered through the third volume of Ernest Jones' biography of Freud are references to what fascism would do to psychoanalysis: "the exodus to America was beginning" (1931); "the emigration to America was continuing"

(1932); and finally, "this year saw the flight of the remaining Jewish analysts from Germany and the liquidation of psychoanalysis in Germany" (1934). The year before, just after Hitler took office, Freud's writings had been given over to a bonfire in Berlin. It would take only five years for book-burning to occur in a Vienna no longer Austrian but German. Freud himself would then be seen going into exile, in his hand the manuscript of *Moses and Monotheism*.

By 1932 it was quite clear to Peter Blos and Erik Erikson that their school could not last much longer. Joan Erikson was teaching English not only to children but to analysts like Robert Waelder and Edward Bibring, who were getting ready to leave for America. Time was short, though it had not yet run out. Herr Erik had at last become as devoted a student of psychoanalysis as he was a teacher of children. He was preparing to graduate from the Vienna Psychoanalytic Society and was known there as an exceptionally bright and gifted candidate.

While still an analyst in training he wrote and had published three papers whose subject matter indicates how accommodating psychoanalysis could then be. The first one was read before the Vienna Psychoanalytic Society in April 1930 and published later that year in a journal devoted to furthering a relationship between psychoanalysis and education. In 1935, when Erikson was in America, the article was translated into English and published in the *Psychoanalytic Quarterly* as "Psychoanalysis and the Future of Education." It is an interesting paper, not only because it is Erikson's first published one, but also because in both style and content it foreshadows his later development.

He begins with a reminder that teachers are not analysts. What he calls the patient's "pitilessly selective life" must make itself known to a rather cautious and passive analyst who knows only too well the dangers of responding to patients as they variously and unwittingly desire. In contrast, the teacher has quite another job. He, too, will receive from children feelings that cannot help but spill over from home. If the child has learned to be rude and spiteful or meek and obliging with his mother or father, he may very well behave in the same way with his teacher, even when the teacher does not particularly encourage him to do so, or he may do exactly the opposite, namely, make sure he distinguishes his parents from his teacher in all sorts of ways. Freud called this "transference," a carry-over of attitudes from the nursery — and nurseries live on forever in our minds — to the world. In his paper Erikson pointed out that what the analyst has to look for, and later point out to the patient, the teacher has to *use:* "Although he is the object of transference, he cannot eliminate his own personality, but must play a very personal part in the child's life. It is the X in the teacher's personality which influences the X in the child's development." The teacher's duty is "to train, to present, to explain and to enlighten. Therefore he should ask himself not where his work touches on the work of the analyst or the worker in child guidance, but where and how it in itself gives him the opportunity to make use of his new knowledge of human instincts."[4]

Those words were spoken at the beginning of a heady decade, when psychoanalytic knowledge was about to be embraced as uncritically and inappropriately as it was formerly attacked. Particularly in America, social workers, teachers, ministers and others would use Freud's ideas to answer just about every possible question known to man. Some would want to leave their own work to take up the new and promising field — not in itself an objectionable decision, unless of course the decision was made for the very reason Erik Erikson warned against, a conviction that teaching or any other work that aims to help people is in fact merely an inferior version of or a mere adjunct to psychoanalysis.

The heart of the paper, significantly, was clinical, with theory kept to a minimum. The author showed himself to be serious, but also able to find light, ironic moments in his work. For example, he tells in detail how children can be made to think about the tensions and rivalries that must have plagued the people they read about — the Puritans, or historical figures like the explorer Amundsen. As a result of such training, the children he had worked with became much more aware of *themselves,* and dared to speak about what they had come to know and feel. The older children saw how they sometimes took out on the younger children what they felt they themselves endured at the hands of their parents or teachers. "They even discovered 'civilization and its discontents' in our little progressive school."

"Now of course, all this is very easily said," Erikson adds, "but the reactions following such talks are not as easy to predict. This was demonstrated the next morning when, for the first time in two years, two of the older boys fought. I was reminded of Chancellor

Snowden's remark at the London Conference: 'Another such peace conference and we'll have war again.' "[5]

Erikson's two other articles were published in the same journal that had received his first one. "Bilderbücher" and "Triebschicksale im Schulaufsatz" they were called; in literal English, "Picturebooks" and "Instinctual Vicissitudes in School Compositions." The reader is made to realize that children draw and write about things that have both an objective and a subjective meaning. Psychological "forces" influence the artist's various choices, the writer's subject matter; but art and literature are not "free associations" piled up one on top of another. Form, style, manner, sensibility — they are also "forces," and as far as the canvas and the writer's notebook go, are really decisive "forces." In 1931 the temptation to see only the subjective or emotional side of artistic effort was firmly resisted by at least one student of the unconscious.

By 1933 Erikson had finished his analytic training, just at the point that the school he and Peter Blos had founded was ready to close. On the evening of his graduation from the Vienna Psychoanalytic Society he was asked to step out of the room so that his record could be reviewed and his status as an associate member voted on and confirmed. When he came back into the room he was told by Paul Federn, the chairman of the society, that he would not be considered an associate member because it was decided to make him a full member — a decision that made it possible for him to leave right away for Denmark and eventually America.

To the north Adolf Hitler was in power, to the south, Mussolini. In Austria, Engelbert Dollfuss had taken over, perhaps on the supposition that the way to fight the spread of fascism abroad was to consolidate it at home. The Eriksons saw little point in banking on an imminent defeat of three dictatorships. Their first thought was a move to Denmark, but Joan Erikson's ancestral roots prompted consideration of America. In fact they did go to Denmark briefly, and before leaving Erikson was made a training analyst for that country, in hopes that he would enable others to enter the field. It proved difficult, however, to stay there: at the time of his adoption, Erikson had lost his Danish citizenship by becoming a naturalized German; and anyway, America, for all its own problems, seemed thankfully removed from an increasingly violent Europe. While still wondering whether to go to Denmark or America, Erikson heard that Hanns Sachs was in town. Sachs was a native Viennese.

In 1912, with Otto Rank, and under Freud's direction, he had founded the journal *Imago*, devoted to interpreting mythology, art, literature and religion from a psychoanalytic point of view. Sachs had first moved to Berlin and then to Boston, where he was an important and welcome addition to a growing psychoanalytic community. Though not a physician, he received the hospitality of the Harvard Medical School and the attention of a number of the city's doctors. A year after his arrival in America he returned to Vienna. Erikson tried to see him, only to be told that the visit was over and that Sachs was on his way back to Boston. Later that same day Erikson took one of his long walks — which marriage and a career as teacher and analytic listener had made a matter of hours rather than days. He stopped for coffee at a little restaurant near the end station of a streetcar line. There he saw Sachs alight from a streetcar, obviously perplexed. He had taken the wrong line! They talked, and Sachs told Erikson that by all means there would be a place for him in Boston. Erikson had been trained in both adult and child analysis, and indeed was one of the first analysts so trained. Were he to settle in Boston, he would come as the city's only child analyst, his arrival marking a first step in what Sachs believed was destined in later years to be a profession within a profession.

III

To America

SOON after the meeting with Sachs the Eriksons sailed for America. They had spent the summer in Denmark, and found the process of renationalization too difficult — in spite of the help of Marie Bonaparte, the French psychoanalyst, who was a princess of Greece and also a member of the Danish royal house. With him the young analyst carried a paper that attempted to explain the powerful attraction Hitler` exerted upon German youth. It was a first draft, written of course in German, and it had to be tentative because it dealt with history that was very much still in progress. On the boat he met a young American diplomat named George Kennan, at the time a member of his country's legation in Riga, Latvia. Together they translated the paper into English. They also gloomily speculated during the long voyage about beleaguered Europe, and in particular the two turmoil-ridden countries they knew, Germany and Russia.

By Christmas of 1933 Boston had its child analyst. His time and advice were quickly sought by a number of institutions in a city known for its academic and medical leadership. Like Sachs not a physician, and unlike Sachs without any degree at all, Erikson was nevertheless given a position at the Harvard Medical School and also at the highly regarded Massachusetts General Hospital — called by some Bostonians "*the* Hospital." He was asked to consult at the Judge Baker Guidance Center, a pioneering clinic devoted to the diagnosis and treatment of children's emotional disorders. He opened up an office on Marlborough Street, one of several addresses in Boston that qualifies as an equivalent of London's Harley Street.

Nearby were not only doctors of all sorts, but the city's small group of psychoanalysts. Since the intellectual roots of psychoanalysis lie well buried in nineteenth-century science and philosophy, it was fitting that men like Sachs and Erikson saw patients in the stately, solid, yet graceful Victorian buildings that one after another line the Back Bay's Marlborough Street.

Erikson lived across the Charles River in Cambridge and also worked there. He came to know Henry A. Murray and became associated with the Harvard Psychological Clinic. He enrolled at Harvard as a candidate for a Ph.D. in psychology, though in a matter of months it became clear that his mind still could not accommodate itself to formal, academic study. He had become a clinician, and he wanted to spend his time with people.

However, the Harvard intellectual community exerted an important influence on him. Though he would leave Cambridge after only three years, it was there that he first met people whose ideas helped shape the direction of his entire professional life: anthropologists like Margaret Mead, Gregory Bateson, Ruth Benedict and Scudder Mekeel, and psychologists and educators like Henry Murray, Lawrence Frank and Kurt Lewin. As a child analyst he treated troubled children of middle-class professional families; but at the Judge Baker Guidance Center he came across the American version of another sort of child, the poor and delinquent boy or girl who at ten or twelve is already in trouble with school officials and the police. At first the European analyst could hardly understand such children, but he asked them to play games with him, and he watched them carefully. Gradually he discovered what can be masked by the particularly stubborn silences of frightened children; and gradually his courage — and his reputation as a clinician — grew. At Harvard his research allowed him to see students who had no problems at all, at least none that prompted them to seek help. For the rest of his life he would follow a similar course, one that balanced clinical work with research, and one that kept him in touch with people who are not usually seen by analysts or for that matter many doctors — Sioux and Yurok Indian children and poor children treated in big-city pediatric clinics.

From 1934 to 1936 Erikson started his first research project, and in fact chose as his "subjects" ordinary (if they can be called that) Harvard students. He described his work in this way:

When the present writer, a psychoanalyst for children, and therefore in-
Harvard Psychological Clinic the development and character-formation
terested in the psychology of play, undertook to study with others at the
of a group of college men, it seemed of possible interest to place these
subjects in a play situation and observe what their adolescent imaginings
would do with it.[1]

Then, before he went into the more technical aspects of his
study, he had this to say:

Play that is of concern to psychology ranges from the first playful movements of the baby to the various manifestations of the need for play in
adults. Taking the most fascinating extremes of "play," the child's play
on the one hand and the productions of the artist on the other, we find
that in spite of the testimony of language, popular opinion tends to evaluate them as antithetic phenomena, finding "no sense" in children's play
but looking at the artist's play as burdened — and in modern times, over-
burdened — with conscious problems and meanings.[2]

In America only three years, the author could write straightforward English, and felt able to comment pointedly on the increasing
tendency in the United States of both psychoanalysts and the general public to see everything as a *symbol*, as an expression of this or
that unconscious striving. Today we may be bored by those who
continue to practice that kind of game, but in the mid-thirties our
culture's faddish preoccupation with psychoanalysis was just beginning. Both the vocabulary of the young science and its evident interest in what had been called "the psychopathology of everyday
life" were taken up by people who certainly lacked the humility
to be found in Freud's "The Creative-Writer and Day-Dreaming"
(1908) and "Dostoevsky and Parricide" (1928). In the latter paper
Freud spoke directly and sadly: "Before the problem of the creative artist analysis must, alas, lay down its arms." It was a tentative
surrender, though. He cautiously looked at *The Brothers Karamazov* as well as at Dostoevsky's personal life, and in a sense he emphasized more specifically the observations he had made in the
earlier paper on the creative writer: the writer's gift cannot be "explained"; instead the psychoanalyst can only show how children's
play, or the fantasies we all have (and most often admit to no one),
resemble at least in purpose if not form or style any number of artistic productions.

Erikson took precisely the same tack. In fact he set out to do what
Freud had suggested be done: study the way people continually

seek after expression by finding (or making) in daydreams, in a playground, in the library or in the theater the riddles and conflicts of their own mental life. He knew how his patients felt, but now he wanted to find out what Harvard students would do to the motley assortment of toys provided them — with the request that dramatic scenes be constructed, as "scenes from an imaginary drama." Again and again the students took the miniature human figures, the little animals, the small pieces of furniture, the toy cars and trucks, and arranged them to produce various kinds of accidents, usually involving automobiles. "Having asked our subjects for a *dramatic* scene," Erikson notes in the conclusion of a paper that describes the research, "we find a product of *traumatic* tension; instead of tragedy we find accident."

How does one explain such results? Erikson points out that the dramatic and traumatic both do something to the individual's sense of himself. In a drama the person portrayed is often representative, that is, more than any one individual in particular. In an accident the person risks losing himself, possibly for good. "Both are events which transgress the boundaries of the human ego, the first in widening it beyond individuation, the second in nearly extinguishing it." He had demonstrated that the toys and a chance to do something with them aroused old memories in the students, so that they did what they used to do in their childhood play — try to confront and master fears.

The investigator concludes by taking pains to set forth the limits of his work: "In describing these results we naturally do not describe or characterize individuals in their conscious and rational individuality, as little as a war correspondent in the trenches can describe the state of the country behind." When everyone seemed taken with the passion and force of the unconscious as a new source of truth, it seemed wise for at least a few analysts to declare the obvious: the mind is more than the drives or instincts that come to bear upon it. Indeed, each mind (hopefully) learns how to deal with the unconscious in its own way, a considerable achievement and one likely to be overlooked not only by those who observe and analyze conditions on the front line, where ego and id interminably clash, but by those in "the country behind" who want to make a particular conflict the cause or inspiration of everything under the sun.

In 1936, shortly before his research at Harvard was published (in the *Psychoanalytic Quarterly* and thereafter in Henry Murray's book *Explorations in Personality*), Erikson left Cambridge for New Haven. He had been offered a position in the Yale University Institute of Human Relations, with considerable freedom to pursue whatever research and study he desired. He was made an instructor in the Yale Medical School, and in a short time an assistant professor. Again, as at Harvard, he was in a medical setting, but in close contact with sociologists and anthropologists as well as psychiatrists. Again, he continued his analytic work with troubled children, but also took an interest in observations then being made at Yale on the normal growth and development of infants.

In 1938 the Eriksons gained another infant of their own, a daughter named Sue, who from the very moment of birth established a historical record as the Grace–New Haven Hospital's first "rooming-in" child. Joan Erikson had wanted to have her third child at home. In Vienna her two sons had been with her from the moment of birth on, and she disliked the prospect of not having it that way in America. However, just before she was due to deliver she came down with the mumps and was sent to an isolation ward of the hospital, where she gave birth to her daughter. The doctors had to do their work outside the maternity ward, and then they had to decide whether a baby whose mother had mumps should be allowed to stay in the nursery with other babies. The doctors' dilemma provided just the opportunity Joan Erikson eagerly was looking for anyway. She asked that her little girl be kept with her, and the doctors could not resist a chance to settle their problem. In later years, prompted by child analysts like Marian Putnam and Edith Jackson, "rooming-in" became an institution.

That same year, 1938, found Erikson making a trip in many ways as significant as the one he took from Vienna to Boston. At Yale he was becoming increasingly interested in the work of anthropologists. At seminars and informal discussions he began to realize that the kind of patients he saw in Vienna (and in New England) did not exist everywhere; quite the contrary, right in America, let alone in Africa and Asia, children grew up with hopes and fears very much like those of the children an analyst expects to see in his office on Marlborough Street, or at Yale University. When Scudder Mekeel told him of a good chance to observe the children of Sioux Indians living on the Pine Ridge Reservation in South Dakota, he made plans immediately to go west and see.

To reach Pine Ridge from New Haven at that time one had to take a train to Omaha, then proceed across Nebraska into the southwestern corner of South Dakota. Even though Topeka, home of the Menninger brothers, is about a hundred miles due south of Omaha, and only several hundred miles from such Dakota cities as Buffalo Gap, Custer and Pine Ridge, it is quite possible that in Erikson's trip psychoanalysis made its deepest penetration into rural America. Beyond question, graduates of the Vienna Psychoanalytic Society were not flocking to places like the Pine Ridge Reservation, Hitler's triumph over Austria notwithstanding.

The encounter itself must have been rather interesting. The European psychoanalyst, only four years in America, day after day came to know Indian mothers and their children, spoke with employees of the government's Bureau of Indian Affairs, and gradually got the feel of the prairie, of people living exceptionally close to their past because they have very little new history to make. Some of the Sioux, who like to give nicknames, immediately called him "Einstein" because his hair, now gray, stood up in the prairie wind. If Erikson's work with Harvard students showed him to be a young clinical investigator who was already interested in what lives below the surface of the sane and well-ordered mind as well as the sick one, his work with the Sioux Indians marked the beginning of a lifelong effort to demonstrate how the events of childhood are affected by the inevitable encounter with a given society, whose customs affect the way mothers hold and feed infants, and later on bring them up to behave. When a child psychoanalyst — there are still well under a hundred of them in America — leaves a busy Eastern professional life for an Indian reservation, he is by that very act saying something about how he sees neurosis as well as cross-cultural variations in growth and development. Mothers and fathers live in history. Their actions and thoughts as parents bear a relationship to their *citizenship*, to the nation (and, within it, the particular community) they call their own. While all this may sound a bit obvious, not everyone in either the medical or psychoanalytic world has always seen fit to dwell very long on the obvious, perhaps because it is just that.

In 1939 "Observations on Sioux Education" was published just as Erikson was getting ready to go even further west, to California this time, and not on a field trip but to take up residence. The paper has both breadth and focus, and it reveals a social scientist who knows how to use plain, direct, forceful language:

Once the Dakotas [Sioux] were the embodiment of the "real Indian." Organized in an elastic system of "bands," they followed the buffalo over the vast plains. Periodically they gathered in camps of light tepees, but always resumed the nomadic life on horses and with travois. Their communal activities (such as the collective buffalo hunt and the regular dance feasts) were strictly regulated; but constantly small groups, colorful and noisy, followed the impulse to radiate out: to hunt small game, to steal horses, and to surprise enemies. Their cruelty was proverbial; and it extended unsparingly to themselves when in solitary self-torture they sought a guiding vision from the "Great Spirit." . . .

Today on the now desolate plains, reservations like Pine Ridge provide the descendants of those romantic Sioux with central homesteads. . . .

The history of America shows what farmers can do under the poorest conditions, if their tradition has provided them with the memory of successful farming, the daily habits of a farmer, or a belief that a God will in the end reward with daily bread him who works hard. But the Indian's consciousness lacks the memories and aspirations of early settlers; his beliefs are built on the age-old abundance of game which became a legend overnight, vanishing too quickly for human comprehension.

In fact, it seems only yesterday, especially for the older Indians, that the three inseparable horsemen of their history's apocalypse appeared on their horizon: the migration of foreign people, the death of the buffalo, and soil erosion. Somehow they still seem to expect that tomorrow the dream will be over.[3]

The author draws from historical books such as Wheeler's *Buffalo Days* and Wellman's *Death on the Prairie*, and from Carl Sandburg's *The People, Yes*, as well as from Freud's *The Interpretation of Dreams*. He tries to indicate how the historical fate of the Sioux becomes for each generation of the tribe a living psychological force. Members of an Indian tribe suddenly deprived of space, of a sense of destiny, behave in subsequent years like helpless, petulant children, to the impatience and outrage of everyone else, namely the descendants of the white nation that subdued the tribe in the first place. The essential psychological problem Erikson noticed and tried to comprehend unfortunately still exists: the Sioux and other tribes are treated with special deference, yet in the white man's opinion remain bored, unambitious, and hopelessly uninterested in achieving agricultural and technological competence. "Forget about them and they'll *have* to survive," some say, while others look back in heavy guilt at what was done to tribe after tribe of people who, after all, were Americans. In any event, pity and the best of intentions from "us" so far have not made the Sioux and most other Indian tribes budge very far in the direction of self-sufficiency.

Erikson asks the central question that must occur to someone like himself under such conditions: "What experiences make certain maladjusted people unwilling to cooperate in their adjustment, except under unrealizable conditions?" He finds a number of answers. Right off, he emphasizes the very limited possibilities that confront both the Sioux and the white man who once conquered them and now so earnestly wants to "help" them. Victors have come to suffer with the vanquished. In the nineteenth century the Sioux were pushed aside by a nation bursting at its seams. The central plains were overrun by men who planted seed in the land, dug it for gold, covered it with roads and railroads. Now those plains are quiet, their wealth is the wheat and corn that "factory farms" produce. Yes, the Sioux own their land, their reservations, but to them this is the wrong land in the wrong place. As for other Dakotans, many of them have also had to struggle hard to make an adequate living.

What keeps the Sioux so tied to their painful history and their scarce land? To some extent the answer will be found in the swift and terrible experiences their ancestors suffered; they were left dazed and uncomprehending by the time the white man was through with them. Erikson goes to the very first days of Sioux childhood for additional answers. He notes that the Sioux actively encourage their infant children to be independent. Only when "strong in body and sure in self" is the Indian child subjected to the inevitable social forces and pressures any society brings to bear on the young. Quite a contrary state of affairs holds for other American children, and Erikson strongly emphasizes the importance of the distinction he makes: "In contrast, the dominating classes in western civilization have been guided by the conviction that a *systematic regulation* of functions and impulses in *earliest childhood* is the surest safeguard for later effective functioning in society." Only after a first condition of orderliness and compliance is established in our children do we urge upon them at least the ethic of individual assertion — though whether in fact our society today allows that ethic any substantial realization is quite another matter. In sum, the older a Sioux becomes, the more he has cause to dream wistfully of a golden age — his first few years; whereas the older we of the American middle class find ourselves, the nearer we get (so we hear) to *our* promised land — success.

The drift of particular lives thus differs — the Indian child's away from initial glory and toward increasing disenchantment, the white child's away from restraint and inculcation and toward widening power and influence. In a striking way, patterns of child care seem to make historical sense. The Sioux as a tribe, like Sioux children, once knew the freedom and contentment that go with plenty of food and no worry about the demands of neighbors. For many of them the Black Hills of the Dakotas were a sanctuary, one shared with thousands of buffalo, which provided not only meat, but material for clothes, shelter, boats, cups and spoons. Men made strings for their bows, and women made strings for sewing from the buffalo's skin. In dance and ceremony, in mythology and children's play, what we think of as an extinct animal was venerated as "Our Father, the Buffalo."

The historian Hiram Martin Chittenden estimated that in the year 1853 alone four hundred thousand buffaloes were killed. Slowly the Sioux got the point: their mainstay, something close to the bounty of Providence, was doomed by an invader. In a desperate effort to fend off the white men and the fate they imposed upon people merely minding their own business, the Indians, as Erikson put it, "tried three methods, all foreign to their nature and all unsuccessful: military warfare in the white sense, the signing of treaties as a nation, and a nationalistic movement of mystic character." By 1890 the Sioux had been subdued forever, and their children were left with an enduring inheritance: America's guilty desire to give back some small share of what had been taken away. A people whose own children in the natural course of events always had their best time at the beginning of life now became the forlorn wards of a busy growing nation with little time to spend on *its* past. The Indians had no choice but to accept the reservation as their literal and symbolic place in American society, and in turn the Bureau of Indian Affairs became for hundreds of thousands a protector and provider. Erikson writes of this development like a de Tocqueville come back to America a century later — and shows once again how helpful an outside observer can be to antagonists caught up in a struggle whose origins they themselves no longer understand:

The young American democracy lost a battle with the Indian when it could not decide whether it was conquering, colonizing, converting, or liberating, and sent successively representatives who had one or another of these objectives in mind — a historical doubt which the Indians interpreted as insecurity, much as children do when faced with their parents' vacillations. The discrepancy between democratic ideology and practice, furthermore, is nowhere stronger than in the hierarchy of a centralized bureaucracy. The older Indian especially, who has been reared in the spirit of hunter democracy, which leveled every potential dictator and every potential capitalist, has a good, if not malicious eye for the occasional anxiety for position and advancement among the powerful white officials. But ideologies are not logical systems; they cannot be weakened by the evidence of discrepancies nor reconciled by discussions.[4]

The critical question for a psychoanalyst who has learned enough social and political history to make that kind of observation must then be how Indian parents bring up their children in the face of poverty and dependence that are rooted in military defeat and territorial conquest. Today's Indians have been just barely kept from starvation by a society whose technological competence makes their traditional interests and skills irrelevant. What now happens to the children of people whose everyday lives continue to be defined by their historical past? For mere survival, one can feel more or less grateful; but perhaps emotions like rage and hate stir in mothers and fathers who are given handouts as a memorial to the failure of their ancestors.

Erikson reported carefully on the training of the Sioux child. From the very start his mother is apt to be more quiet and less nervous about child-rearing than her middle-class white counterpart. He is easily and freely breast fed. As a toddler he is allowed the same freedom his forefathers once unequivocally possessed. And by the time he goes to school he has learned how to meet (and resist) the outside and alien world of white teachers, nurses and missionaries.

In Scudder Mekeel, Erikson had with him an old friend of the Sioux, and thus was spared the reserve and suspicion that Indians consider a white stranger's due. Though committed as an analyst to a struggle against the psychopathological, Erikson could still appreciate those blessed times when things *do* work — in the mind and between minds:

The women showed throughout a healthy, intelligent, often humorous frankness, though their bashful smiles indicated that they would not have dared to bring up certain subjects had Mekeel not been able to throw details into the conversation which surprised them, coming from a white man, and which set their memories and critical powers to work. As is the case with children, they had never thought of certain vital details of their lives as being of any interest to other people or as having anything to do with the world contained in the English language.[5]

Throughout the long paper he wrote summarizing his work one finds a continuous discussion of normal childhood, growth and development, of education as it occurs every day in homes and backyards as well as in schools. The young teacher and analyst found in another culture not the odd and radically different, but a vivid reminder of those common tasks all parents (and later teachers) must help children accomplish. In point of fact Erikson's analysis of the Sioux was much more than a scholarly paper; it marked the decisive achievement of a very special style of writing and research, and it contained in their first form some of the concepts which were later to characterize his way of thinking. In his language, he emerged unashamedly strong, at times poignant and at times ironic and sharp. He favored clear, idiomatic English for whatever thinking he was trying to express, no matter how complicated or tentative its nature. (In this regard his wife Joan, a gifted writer, was a great help.) In his method of work, he demonstrated a keen ability to mix the field worker's vision with the analytic experience of the clinician, and to supplement even that rather unusual combination with the perspectives of social and economic history. His later work — with patients, with other Indians, with religious and political figures — and the theoretical formulations to come from that work would always pay attention to both the individual and society, and would always be historically sensitive. He took great care to show how one thing leads to another, both in Sioux history and in the childhood of each Sioux; and later he would not dwell single-mindedly on any problem, on any "period" of life. Every life, every "conflict," every nation has a background and a future.

IV

To California

THE Sioux had once enjoyed wandering, only to find themselves confined in reservations. In contrast, most analysts who left Germany and Austria were only too glad to be done with travel, to find themselves safe and at rest on America's eastern shores. To Erikson, though, travel has always been stimulating. For all the bleakness, poverty and disenchantment he found among the Sioux, his trip to Pine Ridge not only aroused his intellectual interests but prompted him to move once again. In 1939 he arrived in California, where he would stay for a decade. In San Francisco he resumed his analytic work with children, and in Berkeley he took up once again his interest in both anthropology and history. He became connected with the Institute of Child Welfare at the University of California, and in particular with a study of "normal" or representative California children going on at that Institute. The study was designed to continue for years, indeed for a generation, so that discrete observations and measurements made at this or that time in the life of one or another boy or girl could be put in some larger context of child development. Erikson devised "experimental play situations" which were meant to demonstrate the hopes and fears and struggles and triumphs and disappointments of growing children. His overall purpose was to understand, in his own words, "the main configurations in the life span already lived by these children and a prediction of their future course." He also went north to observe and gather information on another Indian tribe, the Yurok. With the onset of the Second World War he undertook several additional research projects — this time for the government and for

Erik H. Erikson

committees working closely with the government. The titles of the reports he wrote tell their own story: "On Submarine Psychology," "On the Feasibility of Making Psychological Observations in Internment Camps," and "Concerning the Interrogation of German Prisoners of War." (In his bibliography these papers appear suddenly like the war itself; they come after an article on "play disruption" in young children and in turn are followed by one on "play construction.") When the war's casualties began to return home he worked with them ("Plans for the Veterans with Symptoms of Instability"); and when the war continued because of desperate, suicidal Nazi opposition, he turned his attention to a Germany he perhaps could understand better now that he was no longer one of its young citizens, but a distant observer ("Comments on Hitler's Speech of September 30, 1942," and "Hitler's Imagery and German Youth").

The richness and diversity of this work requires the very same historical perspective that Erikson urged upon his fellow analysts. When Erikson was in analytic training Freud was making critical changes in psychoanalytic theory. In the beginning Freud had noted that his sickest and most contrary patients could in fact be understood if what they said and did was seen by the doctor as a reflection of an inner and unknown reality whose logic and purposes are at odds with the world's logic, the world's purposes. He was not really interested in describing symptoms or in attempting by one or another manipulative device to get rid of them. He wanted to comprehend their meaning, the reasons they appeared among the particular patients he was treating. What he essentially encountered and had the determined sense to pursue in a systematic way was the unconscious, whose presence and power, once established and clarified, proved all of us more helpless and blind than we may care to believe. It is natural for an explorer like Freud, who seeks out the unknown, to lose a degree of interest in the familiar land he leaves — in this case the land upon which schools and courthouses and factories and indeed all social or cultural institutions are built. And he worked alone, in near disrepute, during the last years of the nineteenth century, the first decade of this one. Only his stubborn, single-minded devotion to the process of discovery kept him from giving up and returning in penitence to the orthodoxies (and as he saw it, the superficialities) of his day.

As a result, psychoanalysis was concerned for many years with the "drives" that urge actions upon people or find expression in dreams, fantasies, conflicts, or symptoms. Victorian psychiatrists (like other Victorians) saw the mind as a willful, moral executive responsible for puzzling and reprehensible behavior in essentially rational human beings. Certainly they found nothing in madness which the rest of us might claim as ours also. Quite the contrary: the demented were perverse, cursed or condemned, and the job of the alienist (as the psychiatrist used to be called) was to judge patients and get them to change their behavior.

At no time did Freud ignore the power of the outside world to influence the human mind. He knew what conscience was, and as a father he helped his children one by one learn the virtues of obedience and conformity to the ideals and practices of his age, his nation, his particular class. He also knew as a grown man, and indeed as a skilled scientist, how much we slowly accumulate in our minds: perceptions, aptitudes, capacities, knowledge, experience, achievements, various kinds of competence. When he mapped out the mind and assigned names to the diverse forms of activity that together comprise mental life, he was quick to set against the instinctual id both a superego and an ego, so that in all there were three "agencies" (as some call them), each with its province and power.

Yet for a long time the struggle — and he saw everyone inevitably destined for it — was pictured as hopelessly uneven, despite the fact that in actual life it was quite clear how successfully (all too successfully) the id could be shaped or tamed. The id was described as a "seething cauldron," its energy (libido) in constant search of "objects" to have, to possess, and for a number of reasons to destroy. Just about everything we do and fail to do, or do but with a slip here or an accident there, was traced back to unconscious sources, to *desires* — which are finally expressed at whatever cost to the person and in the face of whatever prohibition by society.

No science — and certainly not one like psychoanalysis — can free itself from the restraints of language; moreover, the very nature of what we consider to be "science" changes from century to century as new ideas in turn stimulate new ways of thinking. When Freud wrote in 1895 or 1900, he tried hard to give his clinical observations the sanction of "hard" science, of physics, which served as a model for all the other sciences and supplied them with a world view of various forces and counterforces, all engaged in a struggle for invisible territory, things called molecules or atoms. Such imagery essentially suggests a conflict of the most basic kind, which turns everything else into the literally obvious and the merely apparent. In the laboratory one gets down to the "real" truth, to "fundamentals," and Freud had worked in laboratories long before he turned his attention to psychiatry.

Both an observer and a theorist, Freud took the evidence he had gathered — in itself a feat that took years — and gave a certain *form* to his many discrete observations, so that not only particular patients but the human mind itself could at last be better understood. Precisely because he concentrated so hard on the "deep down" it was possible for him to forget the "differences" among people and unite everyone as by the nature of things relentlessly *compelled.* Underneath everything that only *seems* to distinguish people from one another live the great universals: lusts within families; hates and envies; and an almost endless blend of the banal, the peculiar, the comic and the deadly serious, all, as it were, kept under wraps by our conscience and our common sense — the "civilization" that in growing up we each acquire as a sort of doubtful and unreliable inheritance.

But gradually Freud began to achieve some distance on the unconscious. He began to say what he always knew, that there is more to life than impulses sent and impulses received, thwarted, or disguised. In 1921 he published *Group Psychology and the Analysis of the Ego* and in 1923, *The Ego and the Id.* The ego, which for years had seemed a token concept, an acknowledgment by depth psychologists that the mind also has a surface, was now given its own authority and history. Psychoanalysts started paying attention to the normal in contrast to the abnormal, to the "adaptive" nature of all men as well as to the disordered mental life of patients. Though everyone shares with the sickest patient certain conflicts, each of us has his own particular way of dealing with those conflicts, and in fact what separates people is not only the content of their dreams, but the manner in which the agitation of a dream or a desire is put to rest or given expression by the part of the mind called the ego.

Freud saw the ego as also unconscious. We are not regularly aware of how we manage and resolve the various impulses that contend within us for satisfaction. While one person may deny a given desire, or attribute it to others rather than to himself, another person may turn the desire inside out, so to speak. We have all known people whose "kindness" seems sticky, effusive, unshakably persistent, and a bit too much. We have all seen people become guarded or strike out when in fact their affections have been aroused.

The fact is that for all practical purposes the ego in most cases achieves an armistice between the mind's conflicting psychological forces, and so its executive strength is considerable. What is more, the ego possesses qualities that in other ages people called "common sense," "intellect," "intelligence" and "imagination." It took a very shrewd and unusual man such as Freud to ask what lies behind our daily activities or thoughts. But in his later life he forecast the additional question his successors would have to ask. What goes to make up the very skills and traits that psychoanalytic theorists initially ignored in their single-minded quest for a confrontation with those raw and untutored and unconscious "drives"? If psychoanalysis was to remain a study of *conflict* — and unquestionably Freud looked at his work that way — the various protagonists needed equal attention, even if their relative strengths do vary from person to person.

In 1936 Anna Freud published *The Ego and the Mechanisms of Defense,* and in 1939 Heinz Hartmann's *Ego Psychology and the Problem of Adaptation* appeared. These two books changed psychoanalytic theory decisively by describing the particulars of the normal, daily effort each mind wages to achieve coherence, competence and sustained, useful contact with other people. Without in the least forsaking Freud's view of an unconscious powerfully grounded in biological "needs" and "drives," Miss Freud and Dr. Hartmann showed how we develop the energy, readiness and will to turn the child's insistent and impertinent urges into the grown-up person's reasonably sane and sensible state of mind. What happens, they said, is that we learn to see and take stock of the world, to use our eyes and ears, our developing ability to think and plan, to obey others and eventually to obey ourselves. While all that may sound rather obvious now, we again have to remind ourselves that a theory of the mind bent on exposing the hitherto *un*obvious could only later reverse itself and look at the most evident and undisguised — those skills, habits and customs that societies or institutions encourage in all of us.

The task was to achieve a reconciliation of somewhat divergent theoretical trends, and by 1937 (in "Analysis, Terminable and Interminable") Freud was quite clearly trying to do just that. He emphasizes the *individuality* of each mind. Each of us is different — in the intelligence we have, in the ability we have to perceive and make sense of the world, in constitutional strength. He had already noted in previous publications how significantly "groups" or "mobs" affect individual behavior (and vice versa); but he did not have time before his death to spell out what effect those larger groups we call societies or cultures have on the child's growth, on his psychological development.

By 1939, the year Freud died, and the year Heinz Hartmann's book on ego psychology was published, psychoanalytic theory had gone through a major overhaul — one that had taken a generation's time, the years between two world wars, to accomplish. Now clinical evidence was in demand as never before. A new *theory* desperately needed fresh *observations*. Common sense demanded that analysts see people as more than a bundle of wanton "drives" (libido) in search of "objects" (libido-cathexes). And, anyway, Freud's original vision had emerged from an almost exquisite mixture of pragmatic clinical work and abstract speculation. His patients — people driven and overwhelmed by forces they did not understand — inspired a theory that accounted for their predicament. But again and again psychoanalysts were telling one another that if their discipline was to be more than a body of knowledge about the sick, it would have to do more than assert the common humanity the sick share with everybody else. While it is true that all people have conflicts and suffer from this or that neurotic difficulty, it is also true that the nature and character of mental life vary, *and* that what makes for these variations requires the same careful analysis Freud gave to his patients when he wondered what brought on all their troubles.

Erikson was a young analyst, and an American, when Anna Freud and Hartmann published their books. In a sense they sanctioned in theory what he was beginning to do in practice. It is important to note that Erikson did not at first speculate on the conceptual relationship between psychoanalysis and anthropology or history. Instead he made a series of observations, direct observations of specific people living under particular and varying circumstances. One by one he studied both individuals and the conditions of life they faced, and in paper after paper he showed — concretely and specifically — how the various "drives" we all have in common in no way prevent the development of very different people on this planet. The id — with its restless hunger for nourishment, for "objects" to fix itself upon, for people to have, to be rid of, to possess fiercely, to consume — eventually learns the power of the ego, including the superego; learns, that is, how well (all too well at times) the neurones in the frontal lobes — with a boost from the institutions and cultures of the outside world — can match the "seething" appetites of the entire body.

In ten years, perhaps without knowing exactly what his overall purpose was, Erikson gradually gave psychoanalysis enough clinical information to achieve the very theoretical connection his book's title announced when it was published in 1950: *Childhood and Society*. As one looks back now at the history of psychoanalysis it seems more than lucky that Freud was determined to see analysts practicing all over the world. The American West is a long way from Vienna, and although there is plenty of libido in both places, no one who has traveled from one to the other can forget that he has done so — moved halfway around the world, to a very different society.

In California Erikson immediately resumed his earlier studies. Once again he wanted to see how blocks or toys or dolls are arranged in space — this time by boys and girls of eleven, twelve and thirteen rather than by college students. Naturally, as a child analyst he used toys every day in his office to help young children express their troubles, and to discover, on the basis of what they did with playthings, what might be going "wrong" at home or school. But in Berkeley, he had as mentioned come upon the Institute of Child Welfare, where important research headed by Jean Macfarlane was under way — described by her as "a twenty-year cumulative study dedicated to the investigation of physical, mental and personality development." As he had at Harvard, Erikson could extend his clinical observations to "normal" children, and he did so rather ambitiously by drawing upon 79 boys and 78 girls of age eleven, 80 boys and 81 girls of age twelve, and 77 boys and 73 girls of age thirteen. Since the majority of children were asked to make three "constructions" with the various toys, 468 separate "scenes" were observed. While the children tried to oblige Erikson's request that they construct on a table "an exciting scene out of an imaginary moving picture," he sat at his desk, took notes, and also sketched the "stages" of progress made by the child. The artist who fifteen years earlier had made woodcuts of German children's faces now drew pictures of the work done by American children. In a paper describing the study, a touch of the artist's unwillingness to "explain" his work can be found in remarks like the following:

In general none of the simpler explanations of the motivations responsible for the play constructions presented could do away with the impression that a play act — like a dream — is a complicated dynamic product of "manifest" and "latent" themes, of past experience and present task, of the need to express something and the need to suppress something, of clear representation, symbolic indirection, and radical disguise.[1]

He noted a distinct difference in what boys and girls did, and thus presumably have on their minds:

It will be seen that girls, on the whole, tend to build quiet scenes of everyday life, preferably within a home or in school. The most frequent "exciting scene" built by girls is a quiet family constellation, in a house without walls, with the older girl playing the piano. Disturbances in the girls' scenes are primarily caused by animals, usually cute puppies, or by mischievous children — always boys. More serious accidents occur too, but there are no murders, and there is little gun play. The boys produce more buildings and outdoor scenes, and especially scenes with wild animals, Indians, or automobile accidents; they prefer toys which move or represent motion. Peaceful scenes are predominantly traffic scenes under the guiding supervision of the policeman. In fact, the policeman is the "person" most often used by the boys, while the older girl is the one preferred by girls.[2]

He was studying children on the verge of adolescence, and his findings showed how quietly yet distinctly the boys knew they were destined to be men, the girls sensed their future as women:

The most significant sex differences in the use of play space, then, add up to the following picture: in the boys, the outstanding variables are height and downfall and motion and its channelization or arrest (by policemen); in girls, static interiors, which are open, simply enclosed, or blocked and intruded upon. In the case of the boys, these configurational tendencies are connected with a generally greater emphasis on the outdoors and the outside, and in girls with an emphasis on house interiors.[3]

In a sense that study enabled him to demonstrate in a planned way how he looked more generally at human beings. The emphasis is on both the biological and the cultural. The bodies of his subjects were developing, creating for them challenges and the need for responses. How they chose to respond would depend upon where they lived and when. The approach is configurational. That is, recurrent patterns of behavior are looked for, then described. Every effort is made to be suggestive, and to call upon all plausible explanations for what is seen. The children are watched — when they approach the table where they will work, when they play, when they leave. The style of work done by a boy or girl is considered as important as the product that finally emerges: attention is given to *where* work gets finished, *how* the blocks are fitted together, *what* is meant to happen. Psychological themes — what the child says he is up to, what he can be seen doing and experiencing — are related to "spatial configurations," namely, objects and forms that exist in a world outside the mind. The mind in turn uses those objects or forms to express and reveal its wishes, fears and conflicts. Towers, closed or open spaces, all lend themselves to the mind's imagination. Again and again the reader is reminded that universal biological differences inspire a variety of customs and ideas in different societies:

Cultures, after all, elaborate upon the biologically given and strive for a division of labor between the sexes and for a mutuality of function in general which is simultaneously workable within the body's scheme and life-cycle, meaningful to the particular society, and manageable for the individual ego.[4]

It did not take Erikson long to seek out in California societies other than the particular one (upper middle class, intellectual) a psychoanalyst can all too easily come to think of as universal. Among the Sioux he had found children taught to ignore property because at any moment one might be asked to move. At Berkeley he learned from Alfred Kroeber — then virtually the dean of American anthropologists — about another group of Indians, the Yurok, who did things differently, who taught their children to keep and to store whatever they were given, whatever they earned. Kroeber agreed to accompany Erikson in an old Ford roadster up the foggy coast to the home territory of the Yurok, and much later in a series called the "University of California Publications in American Archaeology and Ethnology" there appeared a monograph titled "Observations on the Yurok: Childhood and World Image," by Erik Erikson. It opens as follows:

Some two hundred miles north of San Francisco the Redwood Highway (U.S. Highway 101) enters the area from which its name is derived. Here the Pacific's humidity — creeping inland as fog, or beating coast and mountains with rains — permits evergreen forests at sea level. Before reaching the Oregon border, the highway crosses the elaborate estuary of the Klamath River and enters the town of Klamath. Here is the center of the ancient Yurok territory. The Yurok lived, and still live, on lagoons and at the mouths of small streams down the coast to Trinidad Bay and up the coast to Wilson Creek (about forty miles in all), and on ancient river terraces for about thirty-six miles upstream along the ever-narrowing, densely forested Valley of the Klamath just beyond its confluence with the Trinity River.[5]

A vivid prelude actually emerges as a fundamental proposition: the Yurok, like everyone else, live in a particular region, and what some might call facts of geography, history and economics are for Erikson critically important matters in child development. Where a Yurok lives, what he eats, how he manages his land and water, how he looks at neighboring territory, all combine to influence his daily moods, his thoughts, his attitude toward his children and their behavior. But more specifically, the Yurok are above all fishermen along a salmon river, and their children have got to know that, and eventually become fishermen themselves.

As he did with the Sioux, Erikson emphasizes both history and geography. The Yurok lived on salmon, as the Sioux once did on buffalo. Both have grimly learned to live with the power of the United States, but the Yurok could do so more easily because their present work — farming, lumbering and fishing — is useful as well as familiar to them, and their values in many ways resemble those of the white men, who of course are everywhere around. In Erikson's words:

The observing white man, however, who is at first repulsed by the Yurok's money-mindedness and suspicious compulsiveness, cannot escape the final insight that his relations with the Yurok lack alleviating romanticism because the Yurok and white man each understands too well what the other wants, namely, possessions.[6]

The effort is to show parallel developments — or divergences — rather than to apply knowing labels (learned, after all, in one culture) to events that take place among "primitive" people. In this regard a most touching and instructive moment occurs when Erikson describes an encounter with a Yurok shaman:

One of the first Indians to whom the writer was introduced was in a certain sense a colleague of his. F. called herself, and was called by others, a "doctor." So far as she treated somatic disorders or used the Yurok brand of physiological treatment, the writer could not claim to be her professional equal. However, she also did psychotherapy with children, and in this field it was possible to "exchange notes." She laughed heartily about psychoanalysis, the main therapeutic principles of which, as will be shown presently, can be easily expressed to her in her terms. There is a radiant friendliness and warmth in this very old woman; if melancholy makes her glance and her smile withdraw behind the stone-carved pattern of her wrinkles, it is a dramatic melancholy, a positive withdrawal, not the immovable sadness seen in some faces of other Indian tribes.[7]

What did she teach the analyst from San Francisco? For one thing she gave him firm reassurance. Only in the beginning was the anthropologist Kroeber there to interpret and intercede. Erikson writes, "On the second day I noticed that he was absent from the room for some time, and I asked where he had gone. The old woman laughed merrily and said, 'He give you chance to ask alone. You big man now.' " The more they talked — as equals — the more Erikson could learn about Yurok children as well as about the doctor who cared for them. When he describes her work he shows how sensitive he believes her to be, how responsive she is to the guilts, angers and passions that all parents not only have, but in various ways share with their growing children. She is a healer; she knows her work; she is not pompous but realizes fully the special position in society that goes with that work. She succeeds!

Like her, cultures try to succeed, try to mediate between the individual and his environment, between the individual and all other individuals, between those now dead, those alive, and those yet to live. Erikson tried to learn from the shaman and from other Yurok informants how a particular culture gives content to the thinking of adults and establishes a certain style of child-rearing. The Sioux were militant wanderers, and prepared their children for that fate; the Yurok were above all standpatters, a secluded and steadfast people who lived in valleys hidden from the rest of the world by high trees and mountains. The way they talk and think, the imagery they use, the myths they have developed, together reflect what they — like all people — see happening in the world about them and in their own bodies. The Yurok are a people who above all have to depend upon a river filled once a year by salmon who come "home" and are caught by people who live there only to avoid hunger. And so the Yurok regulate themselves and their children in the ways of cleanliness, supplication and earnest, cautious hoarding. It is almost as if everyone must learn to hold his breath psychologically — and wait for the one dramatic moment of the salmon's return. When nothing can be taken for granted — even biologists do not quite know how to account for the salmon's relentless and ironic habits — then everyone has to be on guard, or in T. S. Eliot's words be "cautious, politic and meticulous."

From the moment of birth Yurok children had to learn to deal with fearful, hedging parents. The birth of a child is another one of nature's inscrutable occasions, and ceremonial caution is most certainly required. Until the child's navel heals, both parents abstain from deer meat and salmon. While she delivers her baby the mother must keep her mouth shut. For ten days the newborn is not breast-fed, but is offered a soup specially prepared from nuts and served in a tiny shell. The child is then given all the milk he wants and can take — but only for six months, when in Yurok language "forgetting the mother" takes place. The child is very much encouraged to creep and walk, to be on his own. Later, as if to make sure that the first experiences are remembered, the boy or girl old enough to understand directions is made to eat slowly, gratefully and with evident restraint. Not only must utensils be handled in a prescribed and formal way, but the child's mind is urged to match his behavior: certain thoughts — having to do with money and salmon — are to be summoned and carefully mulled over. As a result there is strict silence during meals.

At other times, when talk is allowed, the children hear stories which, like all fables, convey the values the elders uphold — among the Yurok warnings of the dangers that go with lack of self-control. Erikson tells one such story, about a hungry bear married to a blue jay. The pair made a fire one day and the bear told the blue jay to go get some food. She returned with one acorn, and the bear scornfully asked, "Is that all?" The blue jay became angry and threw the acorn into the fire, whereupon the acorn popped about, became semiliquid, and splattered all over the ground. The bear lapped it all up and became gravely ill. Some birds came and sang for him, but to no avail. He seemed beyond help, until finally a hummingbird came and said, "Lie down and open your mouth." He did, and the hummingbird zipped right through him, taking with her the awful mess of burnt acorn. That is why a bear has such a big anus, and can't hold on to his feces.

By the time he becomes a grown-up fisherman each member of the Yurok tribe has learned to live in subdued, prayerful *expectation:* there is a future, a time of fulfillment, a moment when salmon will be everywhere, filling up nets cast exuberantly about the waters of the life-giving Klamath River. It is then, for a few days, that all the puritanical bonds are broken; it is then that an exultant tribe reminds itself that life, after all, has its moment of confirmation; it is then that every bit of earlier penury or cunning seems worthwhile, and every virtuous sacrifice earns its reward. Salmon, red salmon steak are suddenly everywhere. No wonder that at such moments the Yurok become freewheeling, indulgent and carnal.

Erikson takes pains to show that the thrift and circumspection the Yurok culture chooses to emphasize are not signs of pathology, of "group" — in this case, tribal — sickness. Nor does he want to postulate a "national character," and then analyze it — something all too commonly done about twenty-five years ago. Instead he puts it this way to his eagerly categorical Western readers:

One has to see the Yurok among themselves — adults dancing through a night after the mourners have been paid off and the old treasures have been produced for exhibition by the dancers; or Yurok children at play — in order to visualize the pervading harmony and decency that can ensue from the cultural elaboration of mechanisms which we, as members of a different culture, or of a psychiatric subculture, are used to meet only in pathological isolation in "queer" or "malicious" individuals.[8]

The analyst who wrote those words about the Yurok was obviously learning as much about his own assumptions as he was finding out about the "world image" of the Yurok. And indeed, by giving his paper the title "Observations on the Yurok: Childhood and World Image," Erikson indicated that he was an observer first, an observer particularly interested in how children get along and grow up, an observer who wants to fit his own behavior, his own assumptions, as well as the behavior of the children he observes, into a perspective that encompasses geography and history, religion and politics — in sum the whole world.

In the early forties psychoanalysts would have seen among the Yurok evidence of widespread "anal-neurosis." Freud and his co-worker Karl Abraham had noticed how frequently people who tend to be annoyingly tidy and methodical to a fault are also suspicious and miserly. They traced back such "character traits" to the excessive concern that parents can have about the toilet habits their children develop. The longer the analysts listened to the thoughts, fantasies and dreams of certain patients, the more they saw how compelled some children are to regulate themselves, to become fearfully punctual. Control is the task of early childhood, control over the body's various urges and rhythms; and parents can make the achievement of that control just about the only task their children face. The child's response, in turn, to an arbitrary and punitive world — bent on making him do this or that, here or there, now or later — is to worry obligingly about every fine point that life has to offer. The child comes to see grown-up people as timekeepers and marauders, ready in an instant to demand yet another duty, and to complain about anything done of its own accord or at the prompting of the body's insides. And such a child all too often turns into the kind of parent he or she once had.

Freud's clinical genius enabled him to explain the seemingly random characteristics of his grown-up patients by making a formulation which in essence derives later behavior from earlier trauma — in Thomas Mann's phrase, the "disorder and early sorrow" of childhood. Put differently, Freud gave to symptoms a *history*. From the first, a baby has to be fed enough to live, and fed in such a way that he feels comfortable. Freud and other analysts traced clinical problems or symptoms they saw — such as food phobias and rituals and obesity — to difficulties that take place between troubled mothers and the hungry children whom they must feed and often frighten or frustrate in the process. And so the concept of the so-called oral character was devised — to describe a person who shows in his behavior, in his cravings, his tight-lipped stability, his asceticism, his overindulgence in food or drink or tobacco, consistent evidence that what happened in his mother's arms or in the high chair meant enough in the past to persist in the present as an "attitude" or even as a whole way of life. The gourmet, then, is possessed of an "oral trait" or "oral character," and the alcoholic is plagued by "orality" — a kind of "remembrance of things past" with a vengeance.

The essential psychopathological nature of this way of seeing child development was a natural outgrowth of psychoanalytic work: unhappy, hurt men and women complaining of specific fears or vague but intensely felt anxieties were seeking — with the help of analysts — the first "events" or antecedents which paved the way for an eventual neurosis, or, if you will, a manner of getting along in the world. One has to keep mentioning that Freud was a nineteenth-century scientist, and looked always for causes and effects, for specific beginnings to concrete endings, though he had enough irony and humor, and was enough of a poet (even on occasion a mystic) to speak of his "mythological theory of the instincts." He was also a physician, and a German-speaking one at that, so he found a categorical and historical mode of thinking both congenial and imperative: one moves from the "oral" to the "anal" stage, and then one comes to terms with sex, first inside the family during the "phallic" period, and later in the outside world when "genitality" is secured or found wanting.

Only in his later years did Freud naturally try to make his ideas more broadly relevant — to more than a few patients, and Viennese bourgeois patients at that. Though he did not undertake any first-hand anthropological studies, he saw how important it was for a psychoanalyst to locate the roots of contemporary behavior in historical incidents and social practices. His book *Totem and Taboo* (1913) shows how "primitive" people suffer psychological problems very much like ours, and indeed solve those problems in not so different ways. In a little-known paper ("The Claims of Psychoanalysis to Scientific Interest") written for the Italian periodical *Scientia*, Freud emphasized his interest as an analyst in theories of education, in aesthetics, in history and in sociology. He also revealed himself to be no determinist, helplessly caught up in the workings and demands of his own theoretical system:

Psychoanalysis has fully demonstrated the part played by social conditions and requirements in the causation of neurosis. . . . A constitution and a set of childhood experiences which, in other cases, would inevitably lead to a neurosis will produce no such result where this compliance is absent or where these demands are not made by the social circle in which the particular individual is placed.[9]

He never meant to have words like "oral" or "anal" attached willy-nilly to the everyday actions of ordinary individuals or to the "character" of nations. Rather he was interested in using his method of study (which is what psychoanalysis is, after all) to understand from a new vantage point *some* of the reasons people have the beliefs they do, treat children the way they do, work at what they do, eat as they do, or love when and in the manner they do.

Not all psychoanalysts have been quite so willing to consider the mind as critically rather than superficially affected by social and cultural institutions. After Freud's death in the autumn of 1939 (Erikson had just arrived in California), a number of psychoanalysts began to accept without reservation the ideas of "the master," as he was affectionately called by some analysts. This or that theoretical interpretation was claimed to be the standard or authorized one, an essential step in the development of an ideology. Rival "schools" or "institutes" developed, emphasizing different aspects of psychoanalytic theory, and Freud's heirs showed themselves capable of petty bickering as well as sharp, strident competition for his mantle. Many of them, in fact, behaved exactly as those who caricatured them said they did. Everything was "interpreted," given a name, and attributed derivatively to the "oral" or the "anal" stage of libidinal development. The analyst A. A. Brill has described the enthusiasm with which life itself, as a flow of daily events, was submitted to such scrutiny:

> We made no scruples, for instance, of asking a man at table why he did not use his spoon in the proper way, or why he did such and such a thing in such and such a manner. . . . We had to explain why we whistled or hummed some particular tune, or why we made some slip in talking or some mistake in writing. But we were glad to do this for no other reason than to learn to face "the truth."[10]

"Truth" meant the drive-bound unconscious, inevitably forcing its way up first against the strictures of a person's conscience or superego and then against the ego's peace-making efforts aimed at achieving a tense but viable state of live-and-let-live between the body's urges and society's demands. Again, no one can deny explorers the enthusiasm they feel when new territory is found; but by 1940 the discoveries that prompted the kind of behavior Brill described had been made nearly fifty years earlier, and deserved not literal-minded devotion but a kind of open, critical respect.

When the analyst leaves his office and takes a look at "ordinary" people (who are not patients) or "different" people (who live in other nations or regions), he may well be brought up short: everyone has to contend with his drives, but what happens to those drives varies from culture to culture, and even within cultures. What separates us is the particular way each of us comes to terms with the universal and inevitable consequences of mental conflict. In the beginning, psychoanalysts were taken up with documenting that conflict and its sources, rather than its outcome. The "ego psychologists" among the analysts — Anna Freud, Heinz Hartmann, Ernst Kris, Rudolph Loewenstein — began to stress the significance of the ego in *settling* conflict, and Erikson began to give both them and himself the clinical and cross-cultural evidence, the hard, concrete facts that are necessary if a theory is to be more than an expression of intellectual virtuosity.

From his studies of the Sioux and the Yurok Erikson learned that style is not superficial. When Buffon said, "Le style c'est l'homme même" (Style is the man himself), he was suggesting what has been forgotten by some members of the "psychiatric subculture" Erikson mentioned in his paper on the Yurok. Indeed, toward the end of the paper, for the first time he set for himself the major task of overhauling the imagery used by that "subculture." He was trying to prevent his profession from abandoning Freud's views to rigid veneration. He wanted to amplify and reinterpret those views, so that they would be more suggestive and useful.

So Erikson refused to call the Yurok an "anal" people. Once he had denied himself that all too prevalent satisfaction, he had to account for the quality of Yurok psychological life in another fashion — or else leave both himself and his readers unsatisfied:

No student of psychoanalytic literature could avoid the impression that many of the Yurok "traits" correspond to the "anal character" as described by Freud and Abraham. . . . In the psychoanalytic observation of adult patients it has been emphasized that it is hard to reconstruct orality because in retrospect one finds it buried under a layer of traits and fantasies developed during the anal period. The archeological picture used here, as so often, is too static to do justice to the nature of developmental facts.[11]

The gauntlet was thus thrown — to himself and to his profession. Either the facts were to be put into a new "picture," or the old "static" one would have to stand, in many respects telling us less about the Yurok than about ourselves — the "subculture" of white, middle-class Americans who have taken to psychoanalysis as if God Himself were the author of its various tenets.

V

Building a New Point of View

FROM the time of his arrival in California, in 1939, to the publication of his first book, *Childhood and Society*, in 1950, Erikson worked at creating his new "picture." The book, in fact, *is* that picture, and the book's title tells what the picture is about — "being-in-the-world," to use Heidegger's term. The "mechanisms" of the mind had to be put into a three-dimensional frame of reference. The hydraulic images of force and counterforce, of energy flowing and being bottled up, had to be given a context, a place in man's social and cultural life.

To do so Erikson had to put his own professional "being" into a "world" outside the strictly psychopathological one, outside his private office and outside his office in a medical school. He had to seek a world elsewhere — one that eventually would include Indian reservations, the halls of the University of California, the compact space of a submarine, the rooms in a clinic for the rehabilitation of troubled war veterans, and the guidance department of the San Francisco public school system. He also had to develop his own tools, his own way of thinking, even his own language and symbols — not in order to contradict Freud's ideas, as other analysts have done, both wisely and to no great effect, but rather so that he could do what he had to do, turn what had become "static" into something again forceful and compelling.

His tools were concepts — either taken from biology and from Freud's psychoanalytic writings or developed on his own — such as epigenesis, modes and zones, identity. His method was direct observation of a particular (configurational) kind, followed only later by theoretical formulation. A review of his various articles and papers, both published and unpublished, shows how gradually those tools were fashioned and put to use. It is almost as if the method (of observation and self-observation) made the tools, rather than the other way around. Again Freud was being built upon or extended, rather than done away with or done in! The method was his, the psychoanalytic one — today as useful as ever. For that matter, historically the method may well outlive any of the particular theories it prompted. If that proves to be the case, Erikson will deserve more credit than he takes in the very last paragraph of *Childhood and Society*, a book which certainly helped make an "encompassing psychological theory" out of psychoanalysis, and a book which perhaps more than anything written since Freud's death linked twentieth-century knowledge to a theoretical system undeniably born in the nineteenth century and by 1950 badly in need of a new orientation:

The "psychoanalytic situation" is a Western and modern contribution to man's age-old attempts at systematic introspection. It began as a psycho-therapeutic method and has led to an encompassing psychological theory. I have emphasized in conclusion the possible implications of both theory and practice for a more judicious orientation in the unlimited prospects and dangers of our technological future.[1]

That paragraph also is noteworthy for the historical context it supplies to psychoanalysis. It is quite possible to read some psychoanalytic texts and find nowhere even a hint that, after all, Freud's method grew out of a Western intellectual tradition, and specifically out of an encounter between a Western man, a nineteenth-century Viennese doctor, and his middle-class, German-speaking patients. It may be that California — so far west of Vienna — provided at least enough physical and cultural distance to produce the historian's perspective in a willing psychoanalyst.

Erikson became an American citizen in California, just before war broke out for the first time between America and an Asian country, not to mention Germany and Italy. It was hard for him to ignore the fact that his new homeland was fighting his old one. His work with the Sioux had shown him how much the mind is influenced by social and historical change. But if he had any doubts in the matter he could always consider his own life and the events that one by one "happened" to him in such a way that an uncertain artist from Karlsruhe, Germany, should in fifteen years become a San Francisco child analyst – who knew more about Indian tribes than the overwhelming majority of Americans, and spent a good deal of time treating war-weary American soldiers.

Immigrants to this country have several possible alternatives: they can huddle together and cling to earlier and familiar values and ideas; they can abandon them promptly and become very much what they at least believe to be "American"; or they can try very hard to keep the beliefs and customs they brought here, but also make significant changes in them – changes inspired by life in a new nation and by changing historical conditions. Erikson wanted very much to be an American psychoanalyst; but he did not want to stop being a psychoanalyst who was trained in Vienna at a time when an artist, an introspective wanderer, and a schoolteacher could be welcomed by Sigmund Freud and his co-workers as a valuable and necessary addition to a community of psychologists and psychiatrists. Because Erikson kept Vienna inside him but loved America and found California so stimulating, he became in succession a translator, an innovator and a discoverer, as some do who straddle worlds and make of that very experience a new world.

And so, by merely asking, in connection with the Yurok, what "criteria" justify labeling an activity "oral" or "anal," Erikson was making a very important intellectual statement – which might be put like this: words such as "oral" and "anal" were first used to describe what happens to a lot of energy or "drive" in the body. The infant goes through a period when he not only eats, but gets a kind of continuing pleasure out of sucking (the breast, the bottle, toys, his own fingers) that in a way corresponds to the sensual excitement lovers feel with one another. Certainly when an adult lies on his back and says out loud whatever comes to mind, a good deal of his imagery and recalled memory can be called (or subsumed under the word) "oral." That is, he will think of food and drink, or recall times of hunger or dissatisfaction at the table. He will wish he once again had little to do but sit back, or lie down and take the world in – perhaps on a Caribbean beach, in the form of sun, gin and tonic, calypso music and exotic women. In more gloomy and spiteful moments the tiger in him may come out, in dreams or fantasies that tell of people being devoured or banished by hungry machines, vengeful accidents, consuming illness. All this life of the mind Freud saw, and tried to explain as the persistence in later life of significant childhood experiences — in this case the physical and psychological ones that specifically have to do with feeding, and more broadly with nourishment or care, like being held, caressed, and given a good deal of attention.

Unfortunately some analysts tended to forget what Freud had in mind — namely, an explanation for what he observed every day in his *office* — and instead began to circumscribe wide arcs of behavior found to some degree in all people as "oral" or "anal." It is true that Freud and Abraham, as Erikson mentioned, showed how a certain kind of childhood preoccupation with bodily wastes can live on, so that a grown man will be guarded, worried about disorder or dirt, very tight about money and his feelings — indeed, about anything that requires giving up what is owned or possessed to the outside world. On the other hand, they mean — or should have made clear that they meant — to describe certain trends in certain patients, their particular patients from the middle-class world of Vienna. They did not want to describe everything, all occupations, all interests, all activities as "oral" or "anal," though it has come to that among some literal-minded analysts and their followers. Stamp collectors and coin collectors are disguised hoarders, still worried about their losses, about what it means to flush the toilet. Painters are always messing things up, smearing canvases, then trying to straighten them out or tidy them up. And, in this view, neither gourmets nor alcoholics have ever been able to forget or take for granted food and drink.

Many intelligent people could always laugh at such thinking; but in the thirties and forties the psychoanalytic literature — not to mention a considerable body of literary criticism — was quite taken up with what Erikson has since wryly called "originology," a word he explains and defines in this way:

In its determination to be sparing with teleological assumption, psychoanalysis has gone to the opposite extreme and developed a kind of *originology* — a term which I hope is sufficiently awkward to make a point without suggesting itself for general use. I mean by it a habit of thinking which reduces every human situation to an analogy with an earlier one, and most of all to that earliest, simplest and most infantile precursor which is assumed to be its "origin."[2]

Labeling the Yurok "anal" people would have been rather easy for him and exciting for others. Why should the Yurok be spared what various people, including a number of authors and characters in their books, were getting all the time from analysts and analytically "oriented" literary critics? Anyway, if not the Yurok, there was always Hitler to be labeled. Left and right he was being called psychiatric names, and around 1940 perhaps outraged Americans could do little else. In 1942 Erikson published a paper called "Hitler's Imagery and German Youth," in which, again, he shunned the temptation to throw around psychiatric terms, this time at the German leader. In point of fact Erikson said at the very start of this paper that Hitler *was* that, a leader, a German leader, and an adventurer on a grand scale. Any psychoanalytic discussion of a political figure would have to start with an acknowledgment of what he has *done*, what he means to others around him. Children, especially children, also deserve whatever "cool" a parent or observer or theoretician can possibly muster. Who knows *how* they will "turn out"? Who can dare label them for sure? Before he left Yale, Erikson wrote (in 1940) for *The Cyclopaedia of Medicine, Surgery and Specialties* an article called "Problems of Infancy and Early Childhood," which later on seemed prophetic even to him.[3] In simple, strong language he sets out to clarify some of the major psychoanalytic concepts about childhood. (Indeed, as one reads him, one can feel him trying to do it for himself, to say nothing of the reader.) By the time the paper is finished, interpretation has given way to commentary — including a new way of looking at the behavior of both individuals and national groups. The article is one of a threesome that marks the most decisive point in Erikson's intellectual development, the other two being his papers on the Yurok and on Hitler. They all were published between 1940 and 1945; they all deal with *both* the individual and society — in fact, three societies, the Yurok, the German, and the middle-class American; and each one makes a major reformulation of psychoanalytic theory by taking a fresh, flexible look at childhood — in child-conscious America's middle class, among the Yurok, and in the life of a historical figure who changed Germany and for a while, it seemed, the course of world history.

In his paper on infancy and early childhood, Erikson takes up the same issues he had to confront among the Yurok. Should a child psychoanalyst leave his office and his patients and speak sensibly about the "normal" growth and development of "ordinary" children? Is there anything psychoanalysis has to say about the grown-up mind that is not, finally, an assertion about childhood? What accounts for the critical differences in people — the conflicts and anxieties they experience with their parents, and a wide variety of biological, social and cultural influences that many psychoanalysts have to be reminded not to forget? What do psychoanalytic concepts have to offer the suburban mother who is confused about the swiftly changing "advice" she receives, much of it a result of the attentive ear we have all given to Freud's ideas? Can a psychoanalyst rightly talk about the immense ambiguity of life — what William James called its "big, blooming, buzzing confusion" — and then go on to deny that very ambiguity by resorting to categories and simplifications of one sort or another?

Without apparently meaning to answer such questions, Erikson never for a moment stops asking them of himself, so that after a while the reader also feels curious rather than glibly knowledgeable, and most of all wary of yet another set of psychoanalytic "prescriptions." In this regard, it may be useful to quote from Anna Freud's book *Normality and Pathology in Childhood* (1965). She is writing about the "psychoanalytic education" for children that several generations of eager parents fervently sought: "The attempts to reach this aim have never been abandoned, difficult and bewildering as their results turned out to be at times. When we look back over their history now, after a period of more than forty years, we see them as a long series of trials and errors."[4]

She proceeds with a summary that is a striking historical document, and a vivid, pointed reflection upon Western, middle-class culture:

At the time when psychoanalysis laid great emphasis on the seductive influence of sharing the parents' bed and the traumatic consequences of witnessing parental intercourse, parents were warned against bodily intimacy with their children and against performing the sexual act in the presence of even their youngest infants. When it was proved in the analyses of adults that the withholding of sexual knowledge was responsible for many intellectual inhibitions, full sexual enlightenment at an early age was advocated. When hysterical symptoms, frigidity, impotence, etc., were traced back to prohibitions and the subsequent repressions of sex in childhood, psychoanalytic upbringing put on its program a lenient and permissive attitude toward the manifestations of infantile, pregenital sexuality. When the new instinct theory gave aggression the status of a basic drive, tolerance was extended also to the child's early and violent hostilities, his death wishes against parents and siblings, etc. When anxiety was recognized as playing a central part in symptom formation, every effort was made to lessen the child's fear of parental authority. When guilt was shown to correspond to tension between the inner agencies, this was followed by the ban on all educational measures likely to produce a severe super-ego. When the new structural view of the personality placed the onus for maintaining an inner equilibrium on the ego, this was translated into the need to foster in the child the development of ego forces strong enough to hold their own against the pressure of the drives. Finally, in our time, when analytic investigations have turned to earliest events in the first year of life and highlighted their importance, these specific insights are being translated into new and in some respects revolutionary techniques of infant care.[5]

A little further on she remarks on the great hope and faith that was involved in all this: "In the unceasing search for pathogenic agents and preventive measures, it seemed always the latest analytic discovery which promised a better and more final solution of the problem."[6]

Yet hope and faith can give way to disappointment:

Above all, to rid the child of anxiety proved an impossible task. Parents did their best to reduce the children's fear of them, merely to find that they were increasing guilt feelings, i.e., fears of the child's own conscience. Where in its turn, the severity of the super-ego was reduced, children produced the deepest of all anxieties, i.e., the fear of human beings who feel unprotected against the pressure of their drives. . . . It is true that the children who grew up under its influence were in some respects different from earlier generations; but they were not freer from anxiety or from conflicts, and therefore not less exposed to neurotic and other mental illnesses.[7]

While such things were *actually going on*, Erikson spoke like this to doctors, who presumably were his main audience:

But today the practitioner, turning to established psychologies to learn what a child is, still finds himself confronted with strange pictures — which either depict an aggregate of psychological mechanisms in the state of pathological insurrection, or synthetic robots reconstructed from single isolated reflexes, instincts and growth patterns. Each robot functions only in terms of its own terminology, and without a complete mastery of this terminology the way back to the problems of the living child is often far from clear.[8]

He then takes note of the "inhibitory fatalism" that some scientific theories generate — so unnecessarily, because "the individual child is rarely as good or as bad as the tests show him to be; there is a large field of balance and chance provided by human contact." And indeed the purpose of the essay — and of much of Erikson's subsequent work — is to show how children grow and become able (or unable) to take advantage of those "balances" and often enough those "chances."

In the beginning, we grow in almost dramatic steps, or as embryologists put it, the fetus develops epigenetically. One by one the various organs of the body have their day — so that it seems as though each of them for a while commands all the energy in at least one microcosm of the universe. For a time the fetus is preoccupied with its nervous system, then its lungs, then its heart, and these "concerns" have a sequence, with one organ or "system" invariably developing before or after another. When the infant is born his body has gone through a series of "stages," each related to the other in a very definite way. If anything goes awry — due to the mother's illness or accident — while a particular organ is about to achieve developmental prominence or is enjoying it, that does it: never again will there be a second chance. What is more, other organs will pay a price, too. We grow, then, in a progressive hierarchical fashion, each part of our body being very much related to all other parts. The critical words are "rate" and "sequence," critical in embryological theory and critical to Erikson as he considered the infant — who is after all the miraculous product of such delicate timing. In sum, for us to be born whole (or "normal") each part of our body needs to have been allowed its proper rate of growth. (Time is very much tied to quality and quantity here, as the word "stunted" implies.) In addition, that rate of growth must have taken place in a certain desirable sequence, neither ahead of nor behind what is ordained by God, nature, fate, the genes, whatever.

Erikson emphasizes that birth is really a *further* step in development: the infant continues to grow "by developing not new organs, but a prescribed sequence of locomotor, sensory and social capacities." Psychoanalysis can fit into a developmental psychology: "Psychoanalysis has added . . . the understanding of the less normative, often seemingly less normal and always more individual 'habits' of strong positive or negative emotional tone."[9]

Clearly he was insisting upon a number of propositions. First of all, there is in childhood a sequence of biological development that sets the stage for the behavior given various psychological names by psychiatrists and psychoanalysts. To Erikson the "oral stage" is evidence of a simple, universal, yet complicated truth about human growth: for many months the mouth *is* the critical area of the body. Sensations constantly arouse it. Mothers have known for centuries that the child's frustrations, his hunger, his unfulfilled craving for the world of another person, are mediated through his smacking lips and his open mouth, able to send forth impatient, unnerving and commanding cries. Why, then, should older people be saddled with the mark of "neurosis" because they show to eager students of psychopathology continued evidence of "orality"? As we grow up we acquire and discover a number of other interests and obligations, but none of them make eating, talking or kissing less necessary or desirable.

It is true that people can be somewhat distinguished by how much they eat or talk or like to kiss, just as some infants have a better time than others with food or in making themselves and their wishes clear to their parents. It is also true that some infants die at four or six months, or become sad and withdrawn because they have not been fed enough food, or because they have not been touched and kissed and held enough. Far less extreme and more common variations occur, and no matter how they are described psychiatrically, the variations can be pretty well boiled down to this: each child is born with his own constitution, a particular body and nervous system; at the same time each mother has her own style of motherhood, a result of her own life as it has progressed in a given society and at a specific moment in history.

Here is how Erikson describes the matter:

While it is quite clear, then, what *must* happen to keep the baby alive (the minimum supply necessary) and what *must not* happen, lest he die or be severely stunted (the maximum frustration tolerable) there is increasing leeway in regard to what *may* happen; and different cultures make extensive use of their prerogative to decide what they consider workable and insist on calling necessary. Some people think that a baby, lest he scratch his own eyes out, must necessarily be swaddled completely for the better part of the day throughout the greater part of the first year; but also that he should be rocked or fed whenever he whimpers. Others think that he should feel the freedom of his kicking limbs as early as possible, but should "of course" be forced to wait for his meals until he, literally, gets blue in the face. . . . What then, is "good for the child," what *may* happen to him, depends on what he is supposed to become, and where.[10]

The mouth, then, is the territory where the infant first meets his future tribe or nation, his class or caste. As in all encounters, there are nuances as well as the more obvious and strenuous dealings. In Erikson's words, the mouth is a "zone," a place of highly charged and continuing significance; and how we use it is a "mode." Infants not only wait expectantly with their mouths open as birds do, but use their jaws and gums to close down on what they want, to get things more surely or actively, to get a grip on things. Infants also throw up and spit out. They tighten their lips and retain what they have inside themselves, even as they or others want them to let go of this or that (dangerous) object. They even use the entire head and the neck in vigorous, assertive gestures toward the mother, as if they were directing themselves right at and into her.

This view of the infant's first months can naturally be extended in time to encompass other developments. With increasing awareness the child learns to coordinate his eyes, his ears, his voice, his arms and legs. Always he is learning, even though mothers (thankfully not self-conscious) think of him or her as "simply" living, getting along from day to day, and growing. Erikson points out how very much is learned in the first months and years, and does so by using the strong words of a language he himself learned in later life: "To our great relief, therefore, we can at this point take recourse to some of the simplest English words instead of inventing new Latin combinations."[11]

He shows how the child learns to *get*, to receive and be grateful for what is given, and later to get in the sense of fetching: "One may say (somewhat mystically, to be sure) that in thus *getting what is given*, and in learning to *get somebody to do* for him what he wishes to have done, the baby also develops the necessary ego groundwork to *get to be* a giver."[12]

Later the child learns to take and hold what he eyes and desires. And inevitably, he learns that he can't always win. He loses things or sees them taken away. As the child acquires new skills and tastes, he gradually surrenders his old ways. Nostalgia is born — as children move ahead, then go wistfully back, then ahead again. For Erikson all this action in the first years of life has a final outcome — different for each child, for groups of children and for the children of particular regions or continents. The child grows with a *basic sense of trust*, or on the whole he feels somehow empty, cheated, at a loss, ill at ease with others and himself, and so is plagued by a *basic sense of mistrust*. It is not meant that "trust" and "mistrust" become new measurements or standards for a nervous American middle class to dwell upon obsessively. The intention is to describe the possible directions, to indicate the forces at play, to emphasize the *tone* that can emerge from what is both a struggle and a natural, wonderfully inevitable experience — growing.

By the age of two and three, children can walk and talk and eat by themselves. They have already learned what they can eat and how they ought to eat. Their bodies then take over and extract from food the vitamins, minerals, protein, fat, energy and water that keep life going. Once that has been accomplished in the stomach and upper intestine, the body is done with what it has taken in, and the child has waste products to give back to the outside world. Freud not only offended the delicate sensibilities of "civilized" Vienna by taking sex so very seriously; he even had to take up the whole matter of the toilet, of what people find "clean" or "dirty" and why. He insisted that everything matters, that sex matters, and that how we come to regard those private bathroom duties also matters. There is no doubt about it, he eventually angered a surprised, blushing world by repeatedly discussing what was vaguely known but kept strictly unmentionable.

As mentioned, Erikson refused to dub the Yurok culture "anal," but instead worked hard to go beyond labels and capture the *experiences* that Freud the clinician had tried to comprehend. In "Problems of Infancy and Early Childhood," the issue of "anality" naturally comes up, this time in connection with us, not the Indian: "bowel and bladder training has become the most obviously disturbing item of child training in wide circles of our society." He agrees with Freud that as children grow (say, at two or three) they become very much aware of and sensitive to "the whole procedure of evacuating the bowels and the bladder." He emphasizes the biological facts:

Two developments gradually give these anal experiences the necessary volume: the arrival of better-formed stool and the general development of the muscle system which adds the dimension of voluntary release, of dropping and throwing away, to that of grasping appropriation. These two developments suggest a greater ability to alternate withholding and expelling at will.[13]

Then he takes up the matter of "culture" as it affects childhood: "As far as anality proper is concerned, at this point very much depends on whether the cultural environment wants to make something of it." He reminds his middle-class American readers — who live in clean, sanitary, hygienic households — that others do things differently, let older children slowly and casually teach the toddler about the use of the bushes:

Our Western civilization, however, has chosen to take the matter more seriously, the degree of pressure being dependent upon the spread of middle-class mores and of the ideal image of a mechanized body. For it is assumed that early and rigorous training not only keeps the home atmosphere nicer but is absolutely necessary for the development of orderliness and punctuality.[14]

So again the child faces a crisis, and again a part of the body is charged with both neurophysiological and psychological meaning, in turn made more or less urgent by the "attitude" of the world, its values and customs, not to mention the personal qualities (and worries) of each mother. The new zone also has its primary modes: keeping in and letting go. The mind's tendency to put the body's functions to symbolic use guarantees that any body opening (not only the mouth) will stimulate in dreams and fantasies notions of "getting," or "taking in," or "moving against" and "inside." Pediatricians know how children want to explore themselves, how they do not confine themselves to the mouth (swallowing) when it comes to experimenting with straws or little sticks. It is all part of learning what properly are the body's limits, what is foreign, what belongs to the "outside."

All this may seem — especially to sensitive mothers — an unnecessarily complicated or deterministic analysis of what in fact occurs rather imperceptibly and even by virtue of chance. And indeed there are very practical reasons for the psychoanalyst to keep in his mind that any behavior, no matter how stylized, no matter how apparent its antecedent forms, can have its origin in a great variety of accidental or random experiences. The point is that psychoanalytic description, like any other kind, ought to supply the proof that comes with sustained observation. Why, then, did Erikson not find the Yurok "anal-neurotic"? When he answered that question he did so on his own terms as an observer: "What is called anal often seems to fit the Yurok personality," but on close inspection, "the main body zone emphasized in Yurok child training is the oral-nutrition one; the modes stressed are reception and retention."

The way the Yurok live, how they see the world, what they do about money or work or recreation all have to do with their experience as people who inhabit a particular region, with its own (ecological) rhythm of life. If the Yurok are fussy about contaminating a river, or if they save here and scrimp there, deny themselves this and distrust that, they are doing so for *their* reasons. In Erikson's last words on the subject:

> They seem to express the general idea that by being a good warden of his nutritional system and a good warden of the river, and by guarding strength and wealth, the Yurok is clean enough to perform the miracle of existence, namely to eat his salmon and have it the next year, too.[15]

The man who made that statement had to estimate the psychological "strength" of a people. The remarks imply that somehow the Yurok child learns to trust, and then to become an agile and unashamed, though appropriately cautious, fisherman. Yurok children, like other American children from different homes, learn to feel that "inside" they are good and deserve self-respect, even as others have given them encouragement. Or they learn to feel ashamed of themselves and doubtful about how they stand in relation to the world. If children are given what they need as infants; if they are encouraged to rely upon their increasing neuromuscular ability to control themselves; if they are presented with sensible, matter-of-fact requirements, rather than rigid and arbitrary rules; then by the time the children are three or so parents find themselves with reasonably confident boys and girls. They have their whims and moods, their whiny setbacks and stubborn or doubtful moments, but on the whole they feel "good," they feel in control of themselves, and they act so. In Erikson's words, they have *autonomy* and are not persistently or overwhelmingly plagued by *shame* and *doubt*.

By the end of the third year children have won a number of battles: they walk confidently and unselfconsciously; they speak; their hands and eyes are truly, efficiently coordinated; they are incessantly on the move, wanting to go everywhere, enter everything, and pry into all secrets. It is about this time that children become aware of the feelings they have. In most middle-class Western homes children live intimately with two parents, who are constantly around. Often the young child knows few others for any length of time. It is a commonplace to assert the mother's love for her babies and their reciprocal devotion to her; yet when Freud simply pointed out some of the psychological implications of those feelings he stirred up not boredom, amusement, thoughtful disagreement, or even dismay, but outrage — some of it vindictive and accusatory enough to be unprintable. He was scorned and isolated in Vienna, denied the professional rank he wanted and deserved, refused referrals by other doctors, and generally treated like a moral monster.

His first and perhaps greatest book, *The Interpretation of Dreams*, with its discussion of the so-called oedipus complex, was ignored, not reviewed by a single scientific publication. Only a book review in the *Berliner Tageblatt* had good words for it. As a result, in 1901, scarcely a year after the book was published, Freud shortened it and had it published again with the title *On Dreams*. For the rest of his life he would write clear, nontechnical prose and direct it at the general public, the cultured reader, with the conviction that his cause was at least not hopeless among people who knew already — from Sophocles, Shakespeare, Diderot or Dostoevsky — what he was then writing in a more systematic and explicitly "psychological" way.

Today many people, perhaps including a few of Freud's most avid followers, fail to appreciate what he was actually talking about and trying to express when he used words like "libido" or invoked legendary heroes like Oedipus. From his patients, from the self-scrutiny he relentlessly pursued, from what he observed to be the everyday events of the nursery, he affirmed what mothers know, and anthropologists have documented all over the world: children at four or five are very much interested in their bodies, in how boys differ from girls, men from women. Children get excited by their parents, physically excited. In primitive societies they are often seen imitating the sexual play they have observed among their kin, and in our society they are more concerned with what their parents do in the bedroom than some of us are willing to acknowledge publicly, no matter what we know privately — because of our experiences as parents.

Erikson very much wanted the psychoanalytic theory of "infantile sexuality" to be understood as something actual and natural, rather than the bizarre product of mixed-up, grown-up minds. He also wanted his colleagues to distinguish between on the one hand a child's devotion to his mother and on the other a grown man's fantasies — which in turn are hastily labeled "oedipal" by a doctor who hears them expressed by a patient. Here is how he takes up the subject:

The third way station finds the child able to move independently and vigorously. . . . More immediately, he can now associate with his age mates and, under the guidance of older children or special women guardians, gradually enter into the infantile politics of nursery school, street corner, and barnyard. His learning now is intrusive; it leads away from him into ever new facts and activities; and he becomes acutely aware of the differences between the sexes. This, then, sets the stage for infantile genitality and for the first elaboration of the intrusive and inclusive modes.[16]

Young children, of course, are not wordy; they are not interested in putting their feelings into declarations, let alone concepts. They feel, and then they act what they feel, or express what they feel with their bodies, their gestures: eyes excited and radiant, face downcast, neck turned in curiosity, arms tense, feet wriggling and impatient. In strong and allusive language Erikson points out that boys are forever on the move and "on the make," and in contrast girls learn *to* make. They each are taking on their future "roles," as our society has defined them: active, assertive boys become vigorous, effective men; and quiet but comely and pleasing girls become attractive, exciting women.

At home, in school or in the child psychiatrist's office the behavior that adults conceptualize and argue about, children simply demonstrate. They want to marry their mothers and fathers, or their teachers. They fight with one another for the attention of their favorite adult, and in a painting or a game reveal almost flagrantly sexual interests. They know perfectly well how nervous and shy their parents are when it comes to talking about certain things, but still the questions are asked, one after the other, and reveal the most precise or the most outrageous assumptions about sex, about the mystery of creation and birth. Indeed, if children don't become a bit taken with sex, if they become models of propriety, restraint and containment, the price paid is high — and easily noticed by the most determined "anti-Freudian." Children can become young caricatures of very old and tired people who fear *any* step or move as possibly the last one. The more one talks with boys and girls who so "behave," who worry about almost everything and conjure up in their minds the most outlandish fears, the more one sees that if nursery school children are to grow, to be curious and bold, they must come to feel that the passions and affections they feel toward their parents are quite ordinary and unsurprising and legitimate.

Eventually, the child must settle within himself the yearnings and rivalries he feels at home, and turn his energetic mind elsewhere. All of which means that a third emotional struggle takes place. Erikson describes the child's developing *initiative*, first toward parents, then toward other people, places and things. Hopefully that initiative becomes more than a match for the child's inevitable sense of disappointment and *guilt* — because in some final way the home is not his, and to have wished otherwise means to have wanted what is increasingly comprehended as impossible, "wrong" or "bad."

When he was finished, Erikson called his effort a "restatement of the theory of infantile sexuality." To explain himself he used a chart, a diagram that emphasized the step-by-step or progressive nature of the mind's development, and stressed the ways (or modes) that the body's sensitive zones (openings, organs) work. (See Figure 1, below.) All along he had emphasized that "cultures, in various ways, underline and utilize the child's larger social potentialities" — as they gradually become available. He tried to show that a succession of bodily sensations was also a sequence of social experiences. He wanted to outline certain critical "periods" that children must face and either survive handily or fail somewhat. Failure means becoming at least in some respects hurt or limited.

It is quite clear from his various writings that he worried about what would come of his own search for clarity and precision once literal-minded readers got the message. In talking of the chart and

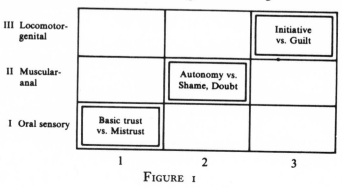

FIGURE 1

the stages described in it, he noted that though his "method of developing the chart was *additive*, as if at each stage something entirely new was emerging, the whole chart should now be reconsidered as one that represents a *successive differentiation* of parts all of which exist in some form from beginning to end, and always within an organic whole, the maturing organism."[17]

We do not, that is, "solve" our "oral problems" or go through the "anal stage" successfully or reach the "oedipal period" because we have said a final and conclusive farewell to the earlier "periods." We do not "acquire" trust and forever rid ourselves of mistrust or "achieve" autonomy and thus spare ourselves continuing doubts and hesitations. However bold and assertive we become, whatever initiative we develop — as explorers or home builders — there will be moments when we hesitate, when we feel ourselves to be wrongdoers, somehow at fault or to blame for something. Erikson had tried to put into mere words no less a phenomenon than life itself, as it unfolds and achieves for each person a distinctive quality; and he knew all too clearly the problem his words would pose for a public eager to convert a psychological formulation into a creed or a catechism:

> Because of historical habits of defining cause and effect according to older physical theories, we again and again find ourselves trying to decide what in a given case one factor (i.e., in society) did to another factor (i.e., in the individual) or how one item (i.e., in the body) is a function of another (i.e., in the mind). Yet we are never able to isolate pure factors and one-way functions.[18]

He goes on to emphasize that "only he who enters the child's world as a polite guest and studies play as a most serious occupation learns what a child thinks when he is not forced to adapt himself to the verbalized and classified world."

The intention, then, was to show the trends in early growth, and to show that each child grows simultaneously in mind, in body, in a society, in history — and does so in such a way that what was once experienced and learned (to the good or the bad) lives on, continually significant and influential. After Erikson has finished his discussion of "infantile sexuality" (and made clear just how important it is to have the two words in quotes) he makes the following wry remark: "The chart is now completed. To many, it will seem an all too stereotyped way to account for the phenomena of early life. Such stereotypy may, indeed, be the result of the origin of the schema in clinical observation. Now, the question is how much further such schematization can lead us."[19] He knows from experience that a field worker studying people like the Sioux or the Yurok needs some method, some framework to give a number of discrete observations at least initial coherence — presumably the purpose and justification of all theories and charts. Hopefully, what one gains is appropriate perspective rather than dogmatic conviction. The Indian child's psychological behavior makes sense not because it happens to confirm a particular psychopathological theory, but because Indian boys and girls are *children*, and like all children they are growing, developing, changing — in markedly different and stylized ways, in regular and consistent ways.

In addition to the clinical and cross-cultural uses of the chart, one further application is possible:

There is another reason for proposing the schema's further discussion which I am not competent to make explicit, namely, my feeling that the relation of modes and zones points to a biological and evolutionary principle. Konrad Lorenz expressed this when in a meeting of the World Health Organization in Geneva he exclaimed: "What irks me about the diagram which Erikson has just shown us demonstrating these differences is that it can be applied, with very little or no change to animals which do not have, never have had, and never will have either a penis or a vagina. So the zone-theory certainly does not hold for these animals, but the principle of the diagram does."[20]

The principle Lorenz had in mind was exactly the one that prompted Erikson to develop the chart: life unfolds in an observable sequence. At various moments or points in time there are critical events. Achievements are won, or failures occur, and the future is to some extent better or worse for it. What is won can later be lost — and rewon. The body (and in the case of humans, the mind) is not irrevocably set or determined by any one thing — genes, the mother's "behavior," the so-called environment — but by a combination of everything and everyone, both within and outside the flesh.

For most of his professional life Erikson has, so to speak, studied *life:* unfolding life, confusing life, life as a series of encounters, struggles, victories and defeats, life as a history that is gradually made — and felt by others. And since he "restated" the psychoanalytic theory of infantile sexuality, logic required one more step forward, one more look at one more part of "life," one more effort — a formulation of "adult" sexuality that did justice to clinical experience without making it the sole arbiter of everything that ever happens.

"A system must have its utopia. For psychoanalysis the utopia is 'genitality.' " After that lead-off he defines what "genitality" presumably means: the sensual pleasures (and addictions) of childhood somehow fit in with (but do not deter) "genital orgasm." Love and sex are compatible with one another, and sex does not become an obsession that precludes effective and productive work, children, or indeed all other interests.

The modes shown at work in childhood obviously persist throughout life, and are called upon by people every day — in bedrooms, at work or at play. Each person's sexual life can be shown to have its individual "tone," to some extent a reflection of how strongly each person continues to be under the spell of one or another earlier experience. Some lovers want to give, others to get, others to take. One person holds back in love, and another pours out to his or her beloved. Though men intrude and women receive, predominantly, there is nothing that prevents, or should prevent, men and women from wanting to share with one another a variety of bodily experiences, even if some of them have been labeled by psychopathologists as "passive" or "aggressive" or "oral" or "pregenital." For Erikson the really important (and demanding) test is how it all comes together. He wants to know the constituent parts — both ordinary and bizarre — so that they can be fitted into something larger, the person's life. The issue is not really whether a person likes to kiss or hug or squeeze or scream or whatever while making love. The issue is whether the person *does* make love, love that can be shared and that will not only be a refuge from the world but will enter it: through the children that love brings, through love's ability to stimulate and inspire and inform a person's daily life. Like everything else, if love (or what is called "genitality") is to be judged, the criteria must be social as well as psychological, the two in fact being inseparable. This is perhaps why Erikson insists on putting the word "genitality" in quotes. What "genitality" is to describe cannot be conveyed by a word so literal and limited; and besides, since Freud's essential vision was correct — childhood does indeed constitute a decisive experience for both the body and the mind — psychoanalysts today have to keep in mind what he *saw*, rather than the particular way he chose to *say* what he saw. There comes a time when words — like theories — can defeat their own purpose.

When Erikson applies his "modes" to the life of the intellect, he is wary of developing the same theoretical rigidity he found so prominent in the psychiatric literature. He does point out types, but in a vivid and concrete way:

Some grasp at knowledge as avidly as the cartoonist's goat who was asked by another whether she had eaten a good book lately; others take their knowledge into a corner and chew on it as on a bone; again, others transform themselves into storehouses of information with no hope of ever digesting it all; some prefer to exude and spread information which is neither digested nor digestible; and intellectual rapists insist on making their points by piercing the defenses of unreceptive listeners.[21]

"But," he immediately adds, "these are caricatures." He does not want any concept or generalization (even his own) to get in the way of the large and important point he is making: even where caricatures or complexes hold up best (in a particular person or "patient") they are not the whole story. To do justice to a *person*, a particular man or woman, requires a level of abstraction, a style of description, a method of evaluation, that takes into consideration more than excesses and distortions, and even more than "agencies of the mind," including the most individualistic of them, the ego. Widely known as a leading "ego psychologist" among psychoanalysts, Erikson says that the ego "is not 'the individual,' nor his individuality, although it is indispensable to it." Always his aim is to provide a context so that he can take very seriously what he wants to define and explore without becoming in the process domineering.

Freud once and for all proved the adult adult still in many respects a child. Erikson said yes, that is true, and so true that it also works the other way: children have within them forecasts and forebodings of the future. They have "libido" and strong (possessive or angry) feelings toward their parents; but they also have what grown-up people have — an ear for what the neighbors believe or oppose, an eye for how one ought to dress, a sense of what should be done with the hours of the day, a feeling for people and places.

When the child goes to school he is particularly ready in many respects to be "grown-up." Psychoanalysts have stressed that the child has by then felt strong passions, and seen (or sensed) the futility of trying to give those passions anything but disguised expression. The "latency period" to Freud provided large-scale evidence of man's inventive persistence in the face of frustration and disenchantment. Freud had a dramatic as well as a fiercely logical mind. He had no intention of leaving boys and girls stranded at the age of five with something as unsettling (and by name demonic) as an "oedipus complex," or an "electra" one. The child who cannot have (his) mother or (her) father goes underground — and ironically, deeper "instincts" or "drives" come to the surface. The imagery — always hydraulic or cloak-and-veil — may get a bit confusing here, but the gist of the operation goes like this: energy toward a parent gets the child nowhere, is frustrated, or meets up with the presence of the other parent, not to mention any brothers and sisters around; besides, desire outstrips the physical capacity to do something about it; so, there is a solution that children of five or six find — they put away useless wishes and take on what Erikson describes as the very serious work of play, the achievement of "new stages of mastery."

Adults mean by play "recreation," but children mean business in the backyard or the schoolyard. Freud saw how much of their energy once was directed elsewhere, within the family. Erikson added that it is not merely the "sublimation" of the "latency period" that accounts for the reappearance of that energy. It is true that children like adults find ways of dealing with broken love affairs. If there is not a he or a she, there is work and study and exercise and one or another absorbing interests. On the other hand, a child of five is not only contending with thwarted devotion, fancied or real rebuff, disappointment and guilt. His mind is moving along, awakening, making more and more observations about the world. His body is bigger, and he has real, reliable control over it. The grown-up world expects new things of him, and has begun to teach him some of its secrets and rules. In Erikson's words, he has "the new status and stature of 'one who can walk,' with whatever connotation this happens to have in the coordinates of his culture's space-time — be it 'one who will go far,' 'one who will be able to stand on his own feet,' 'one who will be upright,' or 'one who must be watched because he might go too far.'" The child (if all goes well in body and mind) feels more confident than ever before, as well as defeated, the loser in a love affair, a family struggle. He becomes convinced that he is "learning effective steps toward a tangible future, and is developing toward a defined self within a social reality" — or he fails to have any such conviction.

Again we have a "restatement" of psychoanalytic theory — not a "revision" but an expansion, not an abandonment, but an almost "orthodox" insistence that not merely the letter but the essential spirit of Freud's vision be preserved. And again there are the alternatives, the polarities that define the best outcome and the worst that can happen: a child can learn to be *industrious* and feel competent, in the way his particular world defines the word, or he can feel increasingly useless, moody and out of sorts, *inferior* to others around him. By no means is it only the oedipus complex and its vicissitudes that prompt the intense curiosity and agility of the school child:

In all cultures, at this stage, children receive some *systematic instruction*, although . . . it is by no means always in the kind of school which literate people must organize around special teachers who have learned how to teach literacy. In preliterate people and in nonliterate pursuits much is learned from adults who become teachers by dint of gift and inclination rather than by appointment, and perhaps the greatest amount is learned from older children. Thus, the *fundamentals of technology* are developed, as the child becomes ready to handle the utensils, the tools, and the weapons used by big people.[22]

During the Second World War, Erikson's work made him more than ever aware that a child can grow into a very sturdy young man, in spite of all the problems a psychoanalyst might observe in him at any given age; and conversely, that even the most "normal" of grown-ups can falter under stress, and become overwhelmingly childish, almost in caricature of the worst moments any child occasionally has. He felt an increasing need to formulate the conflicts we all have in such a way that their outcome would come as no surprise — How did so-and-so ever manage to do so well, and without analysis! — but rather would be expected as much by the psychoanalyst as by the ordinary man, whose common sense tells him that regardless of what doctors find hidden in dreams or fantasies, large numbers of people manage to work, to love, to make a go of it from day to day. Nor was he quite willing to accept even the revised and up-dated versions of psychoanalytic theory, which held everyone to be more or less neurotic, differentiated only by where they "put" how much "libido" or which "mechanism of defense" they use to deal with their unconscious strivings.

Perhaps the first evidence in print of the theoretical direction he was to take in the postwar period appeared in "Problems of Infancy and Early Childhood," the article he wrote for doctors in *The Cyclopaedia of Medicine:*

Small differences, jealously guarded, preserve the virtues and the latent panic of generations, classes, nations: they are symbols of status, of identity, and to many, especially in times of change in the structure of society, identity becomes as important as food, security and sexual satisfaction.[23]

The word "identity" catches the eye of any present-day reader of that passage, written a quarter of a century ago. No word is more closely associated with Erikson's name; and none of his concepts has at once commanded so much attention from him, yet plagued him through its misappropriation by an all too interested public. The work he did in California — and later at Austen Riggs Center in Stockbridge, Massachusetts — very much had to do with "identity," a word he used to formulate certain clinical experiences. Though many people have latched on to "identity" as a faddish replacement for some of Freud's nineteenth-century terminology, Erikson has said that he gradually came to use the term during a generation of "conceptual living." I do not believe that he is particularly interested in *defining* "identity." What he would like is a wider understanding among his readers of exactly why and under what circumstances he resorted to that word, and to others such as "identity crisis" and "moratorium." To gain it, to comprehend the purpose that led him to invoke new terms, construct the chart we have discussed, become increasingly interested in historical figures and in the makings of political conflict and social unrest, one must keep in mind that he was above all a pragmatic clinician who developed concepts as a response to real-life experiences.

And so in the *Cyclopaedia* article, which was written for doctors, we can find modes of thinking which undoubtedly brought a concept like "identity" to Erikson's mind. He reminds his audience of physicians that habits and fears cannot simply be spotted or judged; they have to be seen for what they mean to "others," to the society and culture in which each of us lives. When we are tired, scared or ill, old troubles come back, not to haunt us, or cause us to be called "neurotic," but because we have within us what we *were* as well as what we *are,* and what we hope to be or fear becoming. Erikson asks when a disturbed child is merely misbehaving, and when, in contrast, the word "abnormal" ought to be used. (That kind of question, natural though it may seem, still does not always occur to psychiatrists.) The answer he gives to himself shows the struggle he was then (in the early forties) having:

The easiest answer to this question is given by the voice of tradition; if this voice fails, great anxiety arises. It is as if everybody felt that tradition (as long as it is part of a living culture) establishes channels of mutual self-regulation between body and mind, adult and child, individual and culture — poles of existence which are hard to comprehend rationally.[24]

In that same vein he draws his remarks to an end by looking at the psychological problems of parents in a rather interesting way. What really keeps the generations in lively touch with one another is each parent's "ability to face his children with the feeling that he was able to save some vital enthusiasm from the conflicts of his childhood." In other words, problems generate a good deal that is valuable. They are not to be avoided (Who can do so, anyway?) or worried over or even analyzed except under very special circumstances. In fact, surprising though it may be to some, there are children on this planet who have problems that are not at all essentially psychological: "It must be kept in mind that some of the conflicting and unreasonable demands made on infants are not mere signs of adult malice or ignorance, but are an outgrowth of historical habits and socio-economic goals."[25]

He illustrates his remarks by calling to mind how high a premium we Americans put on "minute reliability" and "mechanical precision," among other things. Such "virtues" are taught our children from the start; and to some American parents they are virtues that are threatened by everything from "unselective immigration" to the "boisterous free-for-all" that may be found in younger or more "alien" nations. The nation as a whole may well be abandoning its emphasis on those virtues, as one group after another becomes authentically American, yet remains interested in its own values and own way of bringing up children. The search is for the "more in clusive identities" that make the people of many regions, ancestries and groups feel very much on common ground without having to behave exactly alike, and treat their children identically. Ironically, "certain groups" want psychoanalysts or social scientists "to replace the nation's search for more inclusive identities with any suggestions that could be rationalized with new terminologies." Delicately — the country's upper middle class was then at the height of its romance with "child psychology" — the point is made: psychoanalytic concepts are no more immune to mechanistic exploitation and punitive use than other intellectualizations and creeds, and some people can even set themselves apart as, of all things, a smug, all-knowing elite of analysands.

Indeed, what Anna Freud had the unfortunate job of describing in 1964 had been forecast by at least one of her students two decades earlier. Analytic tenets became for a certain kind of American parent (and doctor and social worker) a means of becoming self-satisfied and even contemptuous of the way "others" get along — with one another and as parents. Certain mothers and fathers rushed to be done with "puritanism," only to become psychological-minded with an exuberance that never completely concealed the underlying pedantry and arrogance. Some Anglo-Saxons once looked down on Mediterranean immigrants, and the "irresponsible" or "wild" ways they had with their children, but it is quite possible that America's new snobs are those highly educated, self-conscious (and of course "progressive") people who never cease to be amazed at how much they have learned, and how little others know — among other things, about how to handle babies, feed them, "properly" train them, and teach them.

While Erikson was making his observations on middle-class America he had cause to think about the nation he left to become a teacher and student in Vienna and later an immigrant to the United States. Though he first used the word "identity" in the article he wrote for American doctors, the development of the concept was very much stimulated by the war and its effect on his work — and life. On the boat that first brought him to the United States, he and George Kennan had spent days talking about Germany, and in particular German youth, whose susceptibility to Hitler and his henchmen had become all too obvious by 1933. It was hard for Erikson to put these ideas aside; world history brought them continually to mind — and by 1940, with the fall of France, no one could overlook the significance of Adolf Hitler and his young, eminently successful warriors.

In 1942 an article of Erikson's called "Hitler's Imagery and German Youth" appeared in *Psychiatry*, one of the more intellectual (as opposed to technical) and broad-minded of the many publications read by psychiatrists and psychoanalysts. Though by 1942 he had published a number of articles and monographs and was working on or planning still others, this particular one is the most decisive he has ever done: it marked his emergence as a psychoanalyst who knew how to use the theoretical tools of both history and political science as well as anthropology; it revealed how far he had gone in formulating the relationship between childhood experiences and national or tribal customs; it showed how unwilling he was to see "youth" as but an inevitable expression of certain early psychological events; it disclosed his intention to make his "identity" concept useful to both clinicians and historians; it demonstrated his firm control of the English language, his capacity to employ it with force and grace; and finally, it indicated for the first time his interest in the leader, the man of charisma, the individual who is a historical figure — and who needs from psychoanalysts particular understanding rather than gratuitous and easily summoned generic labels. Very little that Erikson would do for the next two decades was not in some respects foreshadowed by this paper — which his colleague Rudolph Loewenstein, a leading psychoanalytic theoretician, has called "a unique and memorable contribution."

Erikson takes his lead from a passage in Hitler's *Mein Kampf:*

In this little town on the river Inn, Bavarian by blood and Austrian by nationality, gilded by the light of German martyrdom, there lived, at the end of the eighties of the last century, my parents: the father a faithful civil servant, the mother devoting herself to the cares of the household and looking after her children with eternally the same loving care.[26]

He starts the analysis this way:

The syntax promises a fairy tale, a myth — and indeed, as myth-making we shall evaluate what Adolf Hitler has to say about his childhood. . . . A myth blends fact and fiction in such a way that it "rings true" to an area or an era, causing pious wonderment and burning ambition. The people affected will not demand truth and logic; the few among them who cannot help doubting will find their reason paralysed.[27]

He is going to look at Hitler's images and themes as expressions of something more than his one triumphant and diabolic life: "This paper . . . is intended to be a contribution to the question of what the *common symbols* are that make all Germans one people and one danger: the fiery leader as well as the obedient follower; the indif-

ferent onlooker, as well as the paralyzed rebel and the romantic de-
serter."[28]

He explicitly declines an interest in doing a psychiatric study of
Hitler. Instead he compares Hitler to an adventurer, an actor — a
man who undoubtedly has his problems, but knows how to exploit
them. Anyway, they were problems that did not deter him from becoming the Chancellor of the Third Reich:

Hitler knows how to exploit his hysteria. . . . On the stage of German
history Hitler senses to what extent it is safe to let his own personality
represent with hysterical abandon what lives in every German listener
and reader. Thus the role he chooses reveals as much about his audience
as about himself; and precisely that which to the non-German looks
queerest and most morbid becomes the Brown Piper's best tune for German ears. It is the tune, not the man that I intend to analyze.[29]

Erikson emphasizes his purpose by pointing out how openly
Hitler blends talk of country and talk of family in *Mein Kampf*.
Germany is called the "beloved mother," who has a "tragic alliance"
with Austria, an old sham state. One might speculate that Hitler's
parents were counterparts to Austria and Germany. His mother
was twenty-three years younger than his father, and the father
was known to be a drunkard and a tyrant. Why not say that a son
who loved his mother and badly wanted her for himself had to
suffer (and would never forget) her humiliating attachment to a
decaying brute? While that may be true, and even suggestive, there
is something about such leaps that must be resisted, and for very
good reasons:

Such a sequence of themes easily — too easily — lends itself to a psychoanalytic interpretation of the first chapter of *Mein Kampf* as an involun-
tary confession of Hitler's *Oedipus Complex*. This interpretation would
suggest that in Hitler's case the love for his young mother and the hate
for his old father assumed morbid proportions, and that it was this conflict which drove him to love and to hate, to save and to destroy beyond
reason people and peoples which really "stand for" his mother and his
father. This implication, while correct as far as it goes, is a generality
underlying too many types of action to offer a fruitful approach to any
given public performance. To be meaningful, it must be formulated in
its relation to the course of history. Only thus will we know whether the
striking use of parental images in *Mein Kampf* constitutes a neurotic confession — or shrewd propaganda.[30]

Speaking of the "course of history," a certain progress had come to psychoanalysis when such a demurrer could be made, particularly in the face of the obvious temptations that Hitler's life and his own words provided. Erikson was not looking for confirmation of clinical constructs in the historical arena, nor was he trying to attack or make light of Hitler by showing him to be "ill" or an absurd and disturbed "neurotic." In fact he was doing something quite different, something he would develop in his later books (*Young Man Luther* and *Insight and Responsibility*). He knew, for instance, how demeaning it is for psychoanalysis — which at least aims at being a scientific method of observation — to be used punitively or moralistically, even against an Adolf Hitler. He knew that Freud used descriptive words to convey what he saw, and that the last thing he expected was that his followers would take them over and make of them pejorative labels, epithets to be used against this or that person, especially those who have different ideas or are seen as "opponents." First Erikson had said that there is more to a life than its early conflicts, and now he was saying that there is more to history than the tidy sum of childhood "traumas" experienced by various leaders.

He was looking for what he called an "inner affinity" between Hitler's childhood (or the legend of his childhood that the Führer propagated in his autobiography) and "whatever patterns can be described as characteristic of pre-Nazi German childhood," a task of correlation that is described very openly as "most difficult." In fact, it cannot really be done, at least not precisely or with the confident assurance of a "scientist." Instead, "what follows is an impressionistic version" of middle-class German family life — "representative in the sense in which blurred composites of individual photographs are representative."

To begin with, there are German fathers and mothers — whom Erikson well knew:

When the father comes home from work "even the walls seem to pull themselves together" (*nehmen sich zusammen*). The mother — although often the unofficial master of the house — behaves differently enough to make a baby aware of it. She hurries to fulfill the father's whims and to avoid angering him. The children hold their breath, for the father does not approve of "nonsense," that is, neither of mother's feminine moods nor of the children's playfulness. . . . The little boy comes to feel that all the gratifying ties with his mother are a thorn in the father's side, and that her love and admiration — the model for so many fulfillments and achievements — can be reached only without the father's knowledge, or against his explicit wishes.[31]

Mothers sometimes betray their sons. A naughty child can be turned over to the father for a licking. "Sons are bad, and punishment always metaphysically justified," or so German fathers seem to think and feel. The mother's weakness and betrayal do not endear women to the boy. Nor is the father without clay feet. He can be a swaggering bully at home, but will cower before his bosses and exude foolish sentimentality when drunk among friends.

But there is love, too — and a good deal of genuine respect — between parents and children. Erikson has no wish, even in 1942, to make a caricature out of the home life of millions of Germans. He is not even sure "how much of this culture pattern on this impressionistic level, could be called primarily 'German.'" There is, however, a certain kind of stormy German adolescence that Goethe knew — and perhaps Erikson, too: "It leads to a crisis with the alternatives of open rebellion, cynical deviousness, actual flight from home, or of a submissive type of obedience which breaks the boy's spirit once and for all." He believes that much of what he described has "traditional antecedents" and tends "to have a climactic character and a specific tension related to the totality of that which is German."

One can feel an artist struggling not for an exact definition or a sweeping conclusion, but for something that is suggestive, that evokes a sense of both familiarity and surprise: "As a culture pattern, it always happened to happen, although it was, of course, not 'planned.' Indeed, some fathers who had resented the pattern during their boyhood would have preferred avoiding it — an intention which, however, traumatically failed them in periods of crisis."[32]

He shows himself to be a critic who will not countenance facile psychoanalytic speculation. "What, then, makes this conflict in father and son so fateful? What differentiates — in an unconscious but decisive way — the German father's aloofness and harshness from similar traits in other Western fathers?" Somehow the German father's authority does not ring true; the son is unconvinced that he owes the father real respect, for all the noise and bravado in the household. Needless to say, "everybody can think of German regions, of confessional and professional groups, and of individual homes where the German father's inner authority seemed deeply justified, founded as it was on old rural and small urban *Gemütlichkeit;* on urban *Kultur;* on Christian *Demut;* on professional *Bildung;* or on the spirit of social *Reform.*"[33] Yet somehow all that never assumed "an integrated meaning on a national scale." Erikson draws on Max Weber to show how nations like England, France and America went through social and political upheavals that united them psychologically — gave a degree of coherence to *citizenship,* as it is experienced in everyday life. Germans never felt their political institutions really sovereign. They never could proclaim themselves *Germans* — at least not with the same quiet pride and conviction that the English and French could assert their nationality.

Does the quality of a nation's political institutions affect the lives of individuals? Erikson shows how the adolescent conflicts of German youth reflected their country's political uncertainty. A country not quite sure of itself *as a country* contained millions of young people who ironically could take one tradition for granted: the obligation of rebellion. There were "bands of intellectual cynics, of delinquents, of homosexuals, and of race-conscious chauvinists; and there were the *Wanderbird,* often led by professional youth leaders. The common feature of all these activities, however, was the exclusion of individual fathers, and the adherence to some mystic romantic entity: *Natur, Kultur, Genie, Rasse.* While it was sometimes assumed that the mother openly or secretly would favor, if not envy, such freedom, the father was considered its foe. If he failed to manifest sufficient enmity, he would be systematically provoked: his opposition was the life of the experience."[34]

The "social and political vagueness" that characterized much of this activity all too closely paralleled Germany's struggle for some enduring and intelligible sense of itself. In the individual the revolt led nowhere, or rather back to its starting place:

In intricate ways, treacherous *Fate* would finally make a Bürger out of the boy — a "mere citizen" with an eternally bad conscience for having sacrificed genius for mammon, for a mere wife and mere children. . . . This split between precocious individualistic rebellion and disillusioned, obedient citizenship was a strong factor in the political immaturity of the German: *for the adolescent rebellion was an abortion of individualism and of revolutionary spirit.*[35]

As if psychological conflicts were not enough trouble for many German families, military defeat came in 1918 and economic ruin a few years later. We are not allowed to forget how intimately the mind lives with the world:

The inflation endangered pensions earned in lifetimes of servile toil. On the other hand, the groping masses were unable really to anticipate the role of a free citizen or of a class-conscious worker. It is at this point that the psychological interpretation of the rise of Nazism meets political and economic ones. Only a combination of the two explains why Hitler's images immediately convinced so many and paralyzed so many more.[36]

What did Hitler's particular troubles as a child and a rebellious youth have to do with the charismatic power he exerted over Germans? Even the most cynical student of the various economic and political intrigues that flourished during the Weimar Republic's short and ill-fated life would have to acknowledge Hitler's unpredictable, mercurial rise as a leader who was in a class by himself. He confounded both the right and the left, and indeed the whole world. And he cannot only be considered an eccentric, a madman, or on the other hand, an ordinary German whose troubles merely mirrored those of many millions. Erikson puts the matter this way: "It frequently happens in history that *an extreme personal experience fits a universal latent conflict so well that a crisis lifts that experience to a representative position.*"[37] He saw Hitler's writing as an autobiographical statement and a piece of clever propaganda, and he saw Hitler as one German who could tell other Germans what went wrong (or was about to go wrong) in their lives. They had betrayed their own revolt, screamed the Führer; they had surrendered to an assortment of fathers, employers, emperors and presidents. Hitler again and again summoned German youth to "shape its own destiny." In tirade after tirade he denounced as "senile fools" tired and corrupt leaders. Erikson calls him "an adolescent who never gave in . . . an unbroken adolescent who has chosen a career apart from civilian happiness and 'peace'; a gang leader who keeps the boys together by demanding their admiration, by creating terror, and by shrewdly involving them in crimes from which there is no way back . . . a ruthless exploiter of parental failures."[38]

How did Hitler do it? He stood before his countrymen, assembled by the thousands amid pageantry, music, guns, and shouted *Germany, Germany, Germany*. By his saying it over and over again the word became real: Germany once and for all pure; Germany united; Germany inviolate. Erikson devotes a major part of his paper to Germany's search for unity and for *Lebensraum*. He is not going to fall into the obvious trap:

The mere impressionistic comparison of a nation's familial imagery with her international attitudes easily becomes absurd; it seems to lead to the implication that one could change international attitudes by doctoring a nation's family patterns. Here the psychologist has to call on the historian. He has to ask him to consider a few statements which psychology alone could neither make precise nor prove.[39]

Here is how an analyst who can also be a contemporary historian deals with the subject of *Lebensraum:*

It would be impossible to approach American mentality without characterizing the development of the American family in its relation to such large-scale patterns as "the shifting frontiers," "islands of settled isolation," "waves of immigration," and the orientation toward the Atlantic and the Pacific. It is equally impossible to characterize what is German without relating Germany's familial imagery to her central position in Europe. This position established *encirclement, Lebensraum,* and *inner division* as overall national concepts — and this, of course, increasingly so with the rise of the ideas of political units and of national greatness.

The power of spatial images, which denote a nation's general setting and her feeling in her setting, should not be underestimated. Tragic examples of recent military history, such as the "Maginot Line" or "Singapore," illustrate how national policies with untold strategic and economic details are staked on a "spatial slogan" which does not yield to reorientation, even in the face of intelligent criticism. This has to do with the necessity of even the most intelligent groups to orient themselves and one another in a relatively simple subverbal, magic design. Every person and every group has a limited inventory of such historically determined configurations. They dominate and narrow imagination. When they become rigid, they may lead to temporary high distinction or they may invite extinction.[40]

An America now preoccupied with military phrases such as "nuclear deterrent" and "antimissile missile," not to mention essentially territorial ones, such as "hemispheric solidarity" (guaranteed by the Monroe Doctrine) and "domino theory" (a justification for our Asian involvement), will perhaps understand that Erikson intended his observations to have universal implications. In fact, one of his main points is that what sounds "real" and convincing to one nation may seem absurd or illogical to another. He shows how even Max Weber — certainly no ordinary chauvinist — can feel the pull of his own country's imagery when he says, "Our destiny has decreed that Germany alone of all countries has as direct neighbors three great land powers and the greatest sea power." Weber talks of "destiny," not geography or history, and Erikson does not quote him in order to be critical. Be he a Yurok fisherman, a Sioux hunter, an American businessman, a German intellectual, or a child of any culture who is merely playing with his toys, the human being lives with a sense of space — his own immediate space and his "people's" space. Historical facts — invasions, conquests, battles — give substance to ideas like *Lebensraum*, even as childhood experiences give rise to later goals or fears.

Adolph Hitler's appeal was made up of many things, as was the echo he found in millions of Germans. Germany has been exposed to foreign values as well as to foreign armies. In fact, "one may say that no young nation of similar *size, density* and *historical diversity of population*, with a similar *lack of natural frontiers,* is exposed to *cultural influences as divergent* in their nature and as *disturbing in their succession* as the influences emanating from Germany's neighbors." Nevertheless, *no one* of those items should be dwelt upon and called a specifically German problem. It is rather "the *mutual aggravation*" of them all that makes the "German problem" so uniquely distressing.

So, Germany became a great, strong nation but nevertheless felt fatally vulnerable. In response to the pressures from "outside," Germans tended to become either narrow or cosmopolitan. Some of them accepted the influential neighbors who everywhere surrounded them, and even made a virtue out of a predicament by becoming exemplary, worldly Europeans. Others turned their backs with a vengeance on anything "outside." All foreign tastes, ideals and enthusiasms became suspect; worse, they were seen as a vicious and dangerous attempt by enemy nations to kill and dismember Germany — a nation with a special, fragile and enviable "soul" that others could only want to have for themselves. In effect, many Germans reasoned like this: what I fear to be a possibility becomes for my neighbor a desire, an intention — or so I believe; of course, he may well want just what I say he does, but he may not either, and his aims might not be the consuming passions I believe them to be.

All nations have their freethinkers, their men of catholic tastes and worldwide concerns, and all nations have their parochial, narrow-minded citizens, who want to obey rather literally any rule, any law, any custom — and punish those who don't follow suit. What made Germany different was its political — in contrast to military or industrial — weakness. As a nation it lacked the coherence that inspires a certain solidarity in all citizens, regardless of their psychological makeup or social background. Max Weber pointed out that German intellectuals lived in a world "without political or economic passion." In like manner, the constricted, illiberal burghers — or aristocrats — felt only regional attachments, or else a purely mystical devotion to much more but much less than a country, to *Germany*. In daily life they were as apolitical, as cranky, critical and reserved about the Reich as their "internationalist" fellow citizens.

Erikson points out how two ostensibly divergent groups can pursue an essentially similar line of thought. After 1918, the "too wide" German gained ascendancy in Weimar. Among the most cosmopolitan types, "political immaturity and intellectual escapism combined to create a myth of a strange, almost hysterical fervor." *Fate* had sent defeat to Germany in order to choose her from among the nations. *Fate* wanted her to be the first great country to accept voluntarily both defeat and moral blame, to demonstrate a capacity for *hubris*. *Fate* had brought about a war and caused millions to die so that Germany would be elevated to a place of intellectual greatness, of spiritual *Lebensraum*. Such self-debasement was quickly followed by its opposite, the angry defiance of a clenched fist extended toward all of Europe and indeed the world. Now the Germans wanted a very worldly kind of *Lebensraum*: "The too-narrow German, in bitter hiding since defeat," came to the fore, and nothing less than an Aryan world could put him to rest.

Before Erikson discusses Aryanism — the polarity between Nordic and Jew — he devotes a section of his paper to the subject of the German adolescent. For the first time he writes at length about the psychological problems faced by young people who are fast growing up but are not yet parents:

As the clinician looks back on Germany's defeat and its "resurrection" in Hitler's imagery, he is forcefully reminded by an analogy from his daily work: it is as if Hitlerized Germany as a whole could be likened to a certain kind of adolescent who turns delinquent. Gifted, ambitious, proud,

Erik H. Erikson

he is possessed by conflicting drives, is inconsistent in his social ideas, unsure of his ideals, and morbidly suggestible. During a period of rapid growth, increasing strength, and consequent unbalance, he suffers a severe humiliation. He disavows his primitive tendencies and attempts to adjust abruptly to his neighbor's standards. His personality, however, is not ready to sustain the change; nor is his "environment" decent or prudent enough to back him up. He "overadjusts," debases himself. Anxiety within, disappointment without, are the result. Soon the adolescent finds that he has relinquished his old self without either gaining a new self or sustaining social recognition. He begins to mistrust the values which he had just begun to share with his neighbors. At this point he meets a leader and a gang who proclaim that the neighbors are senile imbeciles, that adolescence is always right, that aggression is good, conscience an affliction, adjustment a crime. He seems to throw off his conscience. He closes up against the people he had loved and the values he had recognized. There is only one goal: to be himself, even if there is little he can call "self," and even if this means utter dependence on the gang and its leader. He is seduced into acts of defiance which he can only justify before himself by further acts of defiance. He must constantly act, or else his conscience will depress him. He must defy and conquer, lest he feel isolated — and become ready to surrender again.[41]

The analogy can be pressed but must tactfully be dropped at the right moment. Yes, Germany's neighbors can to some extent be compared to the parents of a delinquent adolescent. They are at a loss. They don't know whether they should punish him or pour upon him all the love they feel (or feel they should feel). They don't know whether to curb his appetites or allow him more rein than ever before, on the theory that he will get it all out of his system and then behave. They don't know whether they should disregard him or pay him every bit of attention they can muster. "But beyond this," Erikson says, "the analogy fades out, and not only because analogies always do." Germany's neighbors in fact cannot be called "adult," because their behavior was childishly self-centered and deceitful. The rich and the powerful (whether nations or classes) looked upon the weak or the needy as dangerous children — to Erikson a persistence of the "decaying imagery of feudalism" — and the result favored "fascistic-adolescent movements." If only Germany's neighbors *had* been "adult," and if only the greedy and wealthy *had* felt the responsibilities of parenthood! In any event, the analogy does have its point: delinquents do not rise out of thin air, but in some degree emerge from (and give expression to) the vanities, the blind spots and the wrongdoings of their elders.

Almost every bit of delinquency, and worse, murder, that Hitler set in motion was somehow tied to the Jews, to their dangerous presence — which required an unusual and then a final "solution." What did the Jews "mean" to Germans? Erikson accepts the obvious psychological explanations of anti-Semitism, but he also refuses to be content with a strictly psychological or psychoanalytic analysis of Hitler's remarkably effective political use of the Jews. Yes, people often need scapegoats, and the Jew is a handy one. Yes, the Jew was called names that the German feared he himself might deserve. Yes, the "Jewish problem" could divert the masses from other, more sinister social and economic issues — and give hungry people at least the bread of hate. Yes — as Oswald Spengler of all people pointed out — the Jew has been familiar to Germans because they have accepted and fought against their own "Jewish" inclinations for years. Somehow all these "truths" seem like conventional wisdom — and do not quite do justice to the passions, the hysteria, the vengeful abandon that swept through a great nation, an intelligent people.

"It is no coincidence that at this crucial moment in history the most encircled and the most dispersed nations should find themselves in extreme juxtaposition," Erikson notes. Once again history, geography and politics are to be included in a psychological analysis, and once again the concept of "identity" helps the psychoanalyst leave his office for the world outside:

Whoever and whatever can be identified today as Jewish contains in its identity the extreme (but variably intense) opposition of two trends favored by centuries of dispersion, namely dogmatic orthodoxy vs. relativistic adaptability. We think here not so much of types as of attitudes and symbols, yet there is the extreme role of the religiously dogmatic, culturally reactionary Jew, to whom change and time mean absolutely nothing: the Word is his reality. And there is his opposite, the Jew to whom geographic dispersion and cultural multiplicity have become second nature: *relativity* is *his absolute*. While in many respects he blends with his environment (so much so that on occasion he comes to represent a purist version of contemporary absolutes), his talents and compulsions remain associated with a deep sense of the relativity of values. He is the trader of goods, the critic and interpreter in the arts and sciences, the healer of inner conflict, the mediator and the artist in cultural change. His balanced sense lies in a responsible sense of relativity.

This sense of relativity can turn to relativism. Critical insight lends itself to a more or less subtle devaluation of the absolutes of majorities which cannot be defeated by other means; and it can lead to morbid self-devaluation (often a conflict between disguised orthodoxy and opportunism). These are the Jew's dangers, keenly felt by himself.

Where the understanding of relativity is mated with genius, single Jews with lonely moral courage expand human experience to include new dimensions which make all that is visible and knowable relative to a more inclusive order.[42]

He spells out those "dimensions," those contributions — the establishment of a universal ethics which linked this world to a Beyond, and earthly empires to the Kingdom of God, and the studies of Marx, Freud and Einstein, three German Jews who formulated "redefinitions of the very ground man thought he stood on," so that physical, mental and historical "reality" became forever different. Yet a gifted person or nation — no matter how dispersed — can threaten as well as enlighten others:

Strong peoples — peoples whose sense of identity is enhanced, not endangered, by redefinitions facilitating progress — can assimilate strong Jews. In times of collective anxiety, however, the very concept of relativity is resented — and this especially by those classes which are about to lose prestige, status, and self-esteem. Trying to find a platform of conservation, they cling with grim single-mindedness to traditional absolutes which freedom had made them relax, defeat remember.[43]

In the desperately troubled Germany of the late twenties and early thirties the Jews stood out as a convenient and sore reminder of another people's precarious destiny. Jew and German alike have faced the "desperate alternative of living in encircled provinciality or of becoming over-extended in cosmopolitan identifications." Yet dispersion actually seemed to help the Jew become more Jewish. He seemed to succeed in making relativism a means of self-preservation. To Hitler, this phenomenon called for the assumption of a Jewish pact with fate, an especially devious chauvinistic arrangement — such as many Germans dreamed of accomplishing when despairing of their country's military destiny.

So, it is envy that hard-pressed Germans felt toward Jews, the kind of envy that is found among people who share similar worries and fears, who have similar crosses to bear. To Erikson "these psychological considerations do not explain anti-Semitism. But they are indispensable to an understanding of its variations." This was a

rather modest way of putting it, when compared to some of the
sweeping psychoanalytic "interpretations" of prejudice some of his
colleagues were then offering.

In sum, Hitler was a leader. He sensed Germany's mood, and
provided desperate Germans with an answer that meant something
to them and gave them hope and a chance to express their bitterness. Moreover, Hitler enabled Germans — whom Nietzsche called
"the multiple people of the center" — again to arm, again to fall
back on the soldier. And Hitler's imagery was particularly appealing to the young. What seemed to foreigners like a shrill, mad voice
fell upon native ears long sensitive to plaintive cries and fits of fury.
Nor can Hitler be dismissed as a cunning liar. His own imagery
allows him, while he talks or writes, to believe what he says. At this
point in the discussion Erikson reveals an interest that eventually
would lead to studies of both Luther and Gandhi:

For in his imagery no actor and no redeemer is really independent or can
dare to be original: his originality must consist in the courage and singular concentration with which he expresses an existing imagery — at the
proper time. If he does so, however, he is not only convincing to himself
and to his followers, he also paralyzes his adversaries. For insofar as they
unconsciously partake in his imagery, they will hesitate, become insecure,
and finally surrender.[44]

It was Hitler's genius to see the young German soldier as a rally-
ing point for a confused and terribly shaken nation. The image of
the soldier would summon a people — to become an intact, powerful nation: "His enemies, inside and outside Germany, shrugged
their shoulders. It seemed unthinkable that someone would spend
civilization's busiest time with the redemption of an image."[45]

Hitler was no lucky fool, but once in power he fooled others,
those who thought him a psychiatric case or a willing, accommodating emissary. In military expansion he found the solution a stag-
nant economy needed; but to understand his frenzied efforts to
marshal German youth into a Wagnerian, apocalyptic struggle with
the entire world one must, in Erikson's words, "look through the obsessive and see the ingenious." For a long time Germans felt something special about their soldiers; even the humanistic Thomas
Mann (in *The Magic Mountain*) glorified them. Erikson could
speak what millions of Germans must have felt but not necessarily
thought about that soldier: "He represents the 'Watch on the

Rhine'; the human wall replacing Germany's lacking natural frontiers. In him unity through blind obedience proves itself, aspirations to political freedom defeat themselves."[46]

What about the German army, made up of all those bricks in that long human wall? An aristocratic elite became in the days of the Weimar Republic an army of specialists and technicians. Hitler added a spirit of bravado and daring, and asked for the energies of youthful conscripts, who were exhorted again and again by a man who knew exactly how to reach them and make them listen. Erikson quotes a Nazi writer, Wilhelm Backhaus, to show how the new German army, the army of fast-moving machines, of blitzkrieg, fitted in with the interests of young people: "The instinctive pleasure which youth finds in the power of engines here divines the expansion of mankind's limitations which were so narrow from the start and, on the whole, have not been widened by civilization." And so, "it would be fatal to brush such Nazi mysticism aside." In order to defeat Hitler's motorized German youth, the youth of other countries would have "to learn like modern centaurs to grow together with their fighting machines into new restless beings of passionate precision." The effort would not be easy or without built-in dangers:

It is not yet known what the imagery of an age will be that experiences a *motorized* world as *natural;* maybe the image of a totalitarian "state-machine" obedient to one brain has affinity to it. However, American youth has grown up with machines as no other national group has; it is probable that it can identify with machines without losing its head.[47]

The last paragraphs of the essay look to the future. Erikson is worried about the German children who grew up with Nazi ideals everywhere proclaimed and enacted. He is worried about a postwar world in which a new Germany might well have the same unsettled and unsettling position in a still conflicted continent. In 1942 — when vengeance was very much on almost everyone's mind and when no one could take victory against Hitler for granted — he wrote as follows:

As far as one can dare to envisage a post-war world, many interests seem to demand the only psychological solution: a supranational Europe, with a social order based on culturally defined regions and an economic order comprising the whole continent. Only a logical and lasting European order will free the Germans — and their neighbors.[48]

In 1950, well after the war, he had to observe (in a revision of his paper on Hitler's imagery published in *Childhood and Society* under the title "The Legend of Hitler's Childhood") that again Germany was split, defeated, divided, vulnerable — and potentially vengeful. And in 1963 he added a footnote in the second edition of the book:

By some eerie historical logic, there exists again in our nuclear age a simple wall concretely dividing Germans from Germans. On the other hand, the new economic empire of Europe includes one part of Germany. Neither her newly reinforced division nor the new field for her organizational genius seem to settle the problem of Germany's national identity or that of her hegemony over the continent of which she is the center.[49]

During the Second World War Erikson put to use the knowledge that enabled him to analyze Hitler's imagery. He consulted with a number of government officials on a variety of problems. He scrutinized Nazi propaganda. He looked at the material obtained from interrogation of German war prisoners and prepared an advisory memorandum that examined in detail the reasons why — but under what conditions, and with what legal limitations — observation of war prisoners would be useful. He did studies for the U.S. Navy by talking casually with officers and sailors. He went to the Library of Congress and read the international conventions that presumably determined the way prisoner of war camps were set up. He went aboard a submarine and experienced one of its dives. In what other way could he get to know how German crews and American crews lived — and risked death? He monitored Hitler's speeches over short-wave radio. And later he wrote up his "conclusions." As one goes through those old unpublished manuscripts, the clinical investigator who wrote them seems familiarly like the one who went to study the Sioux and the Yurok: appreciative as well as analytic, an observer of action as well as one who listens to free associations, the relaxed (and at times vastly amused) participant, who only later mulls things over and makes recommendations.

His work on submarines prompted him to marvel again at what works: "We have the paradox that men who live in the greatest danger and in the smallest space have by far the best morale." He found little evidence of psychopathology among the submarine crews and he wondered why. He did what he could: made observations and tried to answer his own questions. The men were paid more than others. A submarine was a sort of "open ice-box": anyone could eat the best food anytime. The submarines were called the "dungaree navy." Nobody had to wash and shave unless he wished to do so. Griping was permitted, and the men could call the boats "pig boats," "ashcans," "sewer pipes." The boats were kept as comfortable and clean as possible and — very important — the commander shared his plans and information with the crew.

As the war came to an end, and American soldiers and sailors started coming home, many of them complained that they felt bewildered and unable to resume the lives they had left to go fight a war. Erikson spent much of his time working with such veterans; they were being "rehabilitated" in hospitals and clinics. He tried to learn what the veterans felt, what they put aside for the sake of war, and what they expected to find when they returned to their families and jobs. He refused to submit the worries and fears of those men to various kinds of psychiatric or psychoanalytic classification. In fact, the more time he spent with returned soldiers — anxious, badly shaken, often for the first time moody and introspective, yet not "sick" — the more he realized how important it was for a psychoanalyst like himself to understand the vicissitudes of normal life.

In 1945, *The Psychoanalytic Study of the Child* first appeared. From the very beginning it was a scholarly, literate and imaginative periodical — an annual that clearly intended to remain unattached to any particular version of conceptual orthodoxy. Since those who work with children have a hard time becoming set in their ways — as either therapists or theorists — they are unlikely to pay for dogma on a subscription basis once a year. In the first two volumes of the new publication Erikson contributed a long account of the work he had done with American Indians ("Childhood and Tradition in Two American Tribes") and his first systematically theoretical paper on the ego, on identity, and on the relationship of the mind as psychoanalysts see it to social and historical changes as people experience them ("Ego Development and Historical Change").

The paper on Indian tribes puts his earlier observations in summary form, and then goes a step further by contrasting the lives of Sioux and Yurok children with those of middle-class American boys and girls. The last section — dealing as it does with changes in American life — really belongs to the second essay on the ego and historical change, and in fact may be considered its prelude. It is as if the Sioux, the Yurok, dozens of Navy men and veterans, not to mention many healthy, reasonably untroubled children, had somehow all come together, elected Erikson one of their spokesmen, and charged him with the responsibility of making their cause known to a profession that on the whole seemed to care little about their particular lives.

The first sentences of "Ego Development and Historical Change" were strong and challenging:

Men who share an ethnic area, an historical era, or an economic pursuit are guided by common images of good and evil. Infinitely varied, these images reflect the elusive nature of historical change; yet in the form of contemporary social models, or compelling prototypes of good and evil, they assume decisive concreteness in every individual's ego development. Psychoanalytic ego psychology has not matched this concreteness with sufficient theoretical simplicity.[50]

He goes on to emphasize that psychoanalytic theory, too, has had a history: "Freud's original formulations concerning the ego and its relation to society necessarily depended on the general trend of his analytic argument at the time and on the sociological formulations of his era." To Freud, man's neurophysiological "drives" or "instincts" (called the id) pushed upon the ego from one direction; and from another direction the ego had to deal with pressures exerted by vague, nondescript entities like "the masses" — non-Marxist masses that most likely were composed of sober Viennese professional men and shopkeepers, or more colorfully, *boulevardiers*. In Erikson's words:

The ego, the individual center of organized experience and reasonable planning, stood endangered by both the anarchy of the primeval instincts and the lawlessness of the group spirit. One might say that where Kant gave as the coordinates of the moral burgher "the stars above him" and "the moral law within him," the early Freud placed his fearful ego between the id within him and the mob around him.[51]

And then there was the matter of conscience:

To take account of this encircled ego's precarious morality Freud substituted within the ego the ego-ideal or superego. The emphasis, at best, was again on the foreign burden which was thus imposed on the ego. The superego, so Freud pointed out, is the internalization of all the restrictions to which the ego must bow. It is forced upon the child (*von aussen aufgenoetigt*) by the critical influence of the parents, and later, by that of professional educators, and of what to the early Freud was a vague multitude of fellow men (*die unbestimmte Menge der Genossen*) making up the "milieu" and "public opinion."[52]

So the poor child is caught betwixt and between. As an infant and young child he is rather innocently wrapped up in himself. He indulges himself unselfconsciously, when he can. He wants to eat and sleep and play fondly with his family, all of whom he likes, or indeed grows to dislike or fear. Slowly he learns that if he is to gain acceptance and peace, both at home and abroad — in school, in the neighborhood — he must watch his step and obey the rules of the game as society enforces them through the mediation of mothers and fathers. In other words, the child develops a conscience, a superego.

In Freud's last work, *An Outline of Psychoanalysis*, published posthumously, a decided theoretical shift was in evidence. The superego was declared far more than something private, or even familial:

What is operating (in the superego) is not only the personal qualities of these parents but also everything that produces a determining effect upon themselves, the tastes and standards of the social class in which they live and the characteristics and traditions of the race from which they spring.[53]

Freud's self-initiated revisions were not lost on Erikson. He took note of them, but did not allow them to preclude elaboration:

Instead of emphasizing what social organization denies the child, we wish to clarify what it may first grant to the infant, as it keeps him alive and as, in administering to his needs in a specific way, it seduces him to its particular life style. Instead of accepting the oedipus trinity as an irreducible schema for man's irrational conduct, we are striving for greater specificity within this scheme by exploring the way in which social organization predetermines the structure of the family.[54]

Then, for the first time he goes into a theoretical discussion of the two concepts, "group identity" and "ego identity" — though, as always, he draws upon both clinical practice and field work to achieve the unmistakable concreteness that characterizes his essays. The Sioux, the Yurok, and indeed the American middle-class family living in, say, Pennsylvania or Ohio, have distinctive ways of caring for children. We "bring up" children to become members of what we consider "the world"; and clearly there are thousands of such worlds on the planet. From the very beginning an infant is fed, handled and cared for in a way that affects what *we* call his "ego," the part of his mind that will among other things give coherence to his experiences and feelings as they happen, or as they are recalled (consciously) or remain influential (in the unconscious). The Sioux, then, have a "group identity." Together they share a very definite past, present and future. Erikson would have no trouble explaining his ideas to William Faulkner, Tolstoy, or even Kafka; but some of his colleagues found (and continue to find) his concern with traditions, customs, frontiers and the land "irrelevant" to the psychoanalyst's concern. The sense of "space-time" he mentions in connection with Indians or indeed contemporary Americans is what Faulkner wanted to describe about Yoknapatawpha County: the Delta with its cotton plantations to the south; Memphis, the urban, trading center to the north; Old Man River to the west; and to the east and up beyond, those miles and miles of land that could only lead to a mortal enemy and accuser, the Yankee. In novel after novel, indeed in many of his complicated, tortured sentences, he wanted to show how utterly bound we are to time, to *all* time rather than one or another of its segments, such as a given century or a given age, childhood. We are also bound to the space, territory or turf we call our own, be it the black earth and scrubby pineland of Mississippi, a ghetto block in Harlem, the Russian countryside, or the mysterious but suggestive landscape that the office buildings and courthouses of Prague dominate.

To the novelist, even the one most absorbed with symbolism, everything is grist for the workings of the mind. Who can set apart the reasons for my particular "feelings" toward my mother from the tradition of motherhood that gave a whole style of behavior to my mother as her birthright, and in turn mine? Who can separate the "private" workings of the ego, as it deals with individual lusts or with the rules of the home or the nursery, from all that makes any ego a member of a neighborhood and a nation, or a participant in the events of a given century?

In short, group identity helps each person obtain a sense of his own identity. Each of us must come to terms with both the relatively private and the obviously public: "Ego identity, then, in its subjective aspect, is the awareness of the fact that there is a self-sameness and continuity to the ego's synthesizing methods and a continuity of one's meaning for others." If by "personal identity" I mean that I am aware that I have a reasonably intact and persistent existence — one that other people can see and that I know they can see — then by "ego identity" I mean some comprehension on my part that under any number of circumstances the mind I have has a certain recognizable quality or character, both all its own yet in some measure thoroughly shared with others.

Erikson quotes from memory the German words once used by Freud ("von einer uebermasessigen Gedruecktheit durch einen gewissen Mittelzustand zu einem erhoehten Wohlbefinden") to describe "a certain in-between stage to heightened well-being — and back" that moody people experience. Then he asks whether such moments of "happiness" or "contentment," when a person is reasonably animated and cheerful, deserve to be ignored, or defined only by the *pathology* that is *absent*. He asks what psychiatrists have to say about an Indian, a California doctor, or indeed anyone who is simply being himself, going about "the daily chores of the year's cycle." Suppose a person does have the ups and downs that psychopathologists are quick to notice. What about his "normal" or ordinary days, the kind Freud described as characterized by "heightened well-being"? Can't we do better by those days than stating that "Neither a maniac nor a depressive trend is at the time noticeable, that a momentary lull exists on the battlefield of the ego, that the superego is temporarily nonbelligerent, that the id has agreed to an armistice?"

With quiet irony, Erikson draws on his own wartime experience to indicate the substantial inadequacy of the psychoanalytic imagery of conflict: "This writer had an opportunity to make a few observations on one of the more extreme milieus of human endeavor, namely life on submarines. Here emotional plasticity and social resourcefulness are put to a high test."[55] He describes the tact and good sense he found in crew and captain, whose relationships to one another constituted a working alliance, despite all the subtle tensions a psychoanalyst might notice. True, the men become a sort of gang, and they loved to eat all day long, and felt better for doing so. But does that mean they had "regressed to a primal horde," or into a state of "oral" lethargy? The fact is that "if we ask why men choose such a life, why they stick to it in spite of incredible monotony and occasional nightmarish danger, and above all why they function in good health and high spirits, we do not have a satisfactory dynamic answer." Then he makes his point by indicating exactly what any number of psychiatrists might have to say about submarine crews, or about a hundred other kinds of work: "In discussions we not infrequently end up by suspecting — on the evidence of mere analogies — whole units, crews, and occupational groups of being regressive, or motivated by homosexual or psychopathic tendencies."

He was touching upon that curious American marriage of psychoanalytic theory to secular, punitive moralism. Though at first glance psychoanalysis would seem a natural enemy of our middle-class pietistic allegiances, quite the contrary proved to be the case. Among many of us Judeo-Christian imagery has yielded to the psychiatric kind, and we continue to suffer the vulgar results. If I like someone or approve of what he is doing, then he is "mature," or his drives are well "sublimated." If I dislike a person, I can summon a battery of psychiatric terms and concepts to call him all sorts of things — passive, hostile, a latent this or that. Some analysts may deplore such tactics, but they are resorted to every day, and not only by the so-called uninformed public. Erikson has repeatedly mentioned the problem, protested the behavior, and tried to show how revealing it all is: that psychiatric and psychoanalytic concepts emerge from and become very much suited to a particular society — which exerts its (moral, puritanical) influence on everything, even the most complicated, rarefied and "objective" of abstractions.

He insisted that the sailor doing his job in a submarine, the Sioux hunting, the Yurok fishing, the American man enjoying himself at work, or his wife taking care of their family, or their children simply growing up to be "healthy" or "sound and solid" persons, all share Freud's "in-between state"; they are human beings "who feel at one with what they are doing when and where they are doing it." For such people at such moments a terminology devoted to illness or combat is inappropriate at the very least.

The rest of "Ego Development and Historical Change" — and in a sense, all of Erikson's subsequent work — centers on the social and historical forces that make for the ego's weakness and its strength. Clinical illustrations are generously offered: a bombardier's son who suddenly abandoned his quiet, babyish ways to become a violent fire-setter; a rebellious child of a German émigré family who defied all authority — when it was asserted by Americans. The effort is to show how children accept historical figures, regional values and political ideologies as prototypes of good and evil. Parents, teachers, neighbors — we all let our sons and daughters know what really matters, what really counts in this world. Any child can spot the things that command our favor or inspire our disgust. Especially in moments of social and economic crisis parents are likely to fall back upon "old" values — and earlier problems in their own lives. Their children find them suddenly worried or anxious, and not only about national or international events. Dormant fears or abandoned symptoms appear as if out of nowhere, and demand that the psychoanalyst appreciate how contemporary world events can revive the earliest of memories and stir up apparently "resolved" problems.

Again and again the emphasis is on broadening the mind's life to include something more than impulses and defenses against impulses. Here is how Erikson sees Bruno Bettelheim's well-known ordeal in a Nazi concentration camp:

In an outstanding document Bruno Bettelheim has described his experiences in a German concentration camp of the early days. He reports the various steps and external manifestations (such as affectations in posture and dress) by which the inmates abandoned their identity as anti-fascists in favor of that of their tormentors. He himself preserved his life and sanity by deliberately and persistently clinging to the historical Jewish identity of invincible, spiritual and intellectual superiority over a physically superior outer world: he made his tormentors the subject of a silent research project which he safely delivered to the world of free letters.[56]

Erikson was not only *describing* social stereotypes or traditions; as a psychoanalyst he wanted to explain how they take effect in the mind:

the ego, in the course of its synthesizing efforts, attempts to subsume the most powerful ideal and evil prototypes (the final contestants, as it were) and with them the whole existing imagery of superior and inferior, good and bad, masculine and feminine, free and slave, potent and impotent, beautiful and ugly, fast and slow, tall and small, in a simple alternative, in order to make one battle and one strategy out of a bewildering number of skirmishes.[57]

Moral and sexual problems may thus become converted into racial or religious ones, or indeed vice versa. And because psychoanalysis is so much a part of America's culture, the imagery Freud used to describe certain clinical events also gets summoned. One can hear black and white Southerners talk about the various forms of "repressed sexuality" that are the "real" or "ultimate" cause of racism and segregation — when, of course, they are no such (unequivocal) thing. What the mind often finds impossible to resist is some — *any* — abstraction or abridgment that simplifies the confusing ebb and flow of life into a few, easily available alternatives. Is it any wonder, then, that we all have our instant likes and dislikes, or snap judgments and sudden outbursts, our decisions that come "out of the blue" and often enough command an unquestioning commitment of energy and faith?

Erikson saw the sexual and moral dilemmas of the growing child as inextricably class-bound and race-bound — which any school-teacher who looks carefully at children's play or drawings certainly knows. I remember being shown a picture of a rather battered school building with a woman standing beside it. A seven-year-old black girl in New Orleans made the drawing, and when I asked her what was happening in it, she replied tersely, "New Orleans is in trouble." I was puzzled, and I asked her how the picture showed that fact. "Well," she said, "there are bad people shouting outside school, and they want to tear it down. I didn't draw them, but they're on the sidewalk outside the school. And my mother, she got a bad appendix and they took her to the hospital."

That particular black child was *not* one of the handful who endured the mobs that plagued New Orleans when its schools were desegregated. She was the daughter of a well-to-do black doctor — and her life seemed to all appearances uneventful. In point of fact she was having her (ordinary, normal) troubles, as was her mother, who was indeed sick. The child's mind sees no point in dividing "trouble" into some of the categories adults find convenient, useful and indeed mandatory. To that girl life was harassing. Her mother was being harassed in the hospital, and she felt harassed at home — as harassed as was another little girl who appeared on television as she struggled past her white, racist tormentors in order to enter a school building.

Psychoanalysts must learn to ask about almost everything: "It is essential to correlate a patient's childhood history with the history of his family's sedentary residence in prototypal areas (East), in 'backward' areas (South), or in 'forward' areas (Western and Northern frontier), as these were gradually incorporated into the American version of the Anglo-Saxon cultural identity."[58] Religion, class and caste are not only sociological concepts but terms that describe what for children are a succession of deeply felt experiences. Erikson offers in example a series of partial case histories and prefaces them with the following comment — in which the language and style as well as the message are particularly and tellingly his:

Often when a psychoanalysis seems immovably bogged down, one encounters in the patient's memories the picture of a proud grandfather, whether it is a blacksmith of the old world or an engineer of the new one; an as yet proud Jew or an unreconstructed Southerner. What these grandfathers have in common is the fact that they were the last representatives of a world as yet more homogeneous in its feudal values, masterly and cruel with a good conscience, self-restrained and pious without loss of self-esteem. It is the world that invented the machine, and still considered it a gigantic plaything, not apt to challenge the social values of the men who made it. When we are forced to indicate to the patient how much he fears the future and that his ego must learn to make the best and the most of its development within fast-changing concepts of reality, these grandfathers rise from their graves and challenge us. Their clearer design for living always has stood behind and above the father's ethnic feebleness and the mother's driving harshness. In the following I shall sketch this background for a number of cases from various regions of this country.[59]

For a man barely ten years in America — whose profession was child psychoanalysis, as it was then defined — the paragraph was no mean achievement. Entire books have managed to say less about this nation. Nor have all psychoanalysts been quite so able (or willing) to indicate — as Erikson then proceeded to do — exactly how those so-called socioeconomic factors are in fact a part of the very core of psychoanalytic work:

Patients of psychoanalysis repeat in their transferences and their resistances abortive attempts at synchronizing fast-changing and sharply contrasting remnants of national, regional and class identities during critical stages of their childhood. The patient weaves the analyst into his unconscious life plan: he idealizes him (especially if he is European-born) by identifying him with his more homogeneous ancestors; or he subtly resists him as the enemy of a brittle and tentative ego-identity.[60]

The final segment of a crucial theoretical declaration offers a *tour de force* in the sense that — the year is 1946 — a psychoanalytic clinician uses the subtitle "Ego Strength and Social Pathology." The author very much wants to give his audience (Some of whom he calls "psychopathological writers"!) an idea of what money, a job and a sense of self-respect mean to people — yes, way deep down inside their "minds." He shows how, step by step, children need from society a sustained opportunity to exercise whatever skills and aptitudes they learn at home. To give his ideas concrete expression he discusses in turn the childhood of American blacks, the special problems of American adolescents, and the difficulties that American veterans faced upon their return home from the Second World War.

His remarks on black children are extremely significant. They were written a quarter of a century ago, when even the most socially minded psychoanalyst might have been forgiven his lack of interest in a people so decisively without — among other things — decent medical and psychiatric care. They were also written at a time when Congress was unable to agree on an "antilynching" bill. That is, liberals were struggling for some guarantee that blacks could take life itself for granted; and so it may well have been "premature" for Erikson to look into the *quality* of that life.

"Consider our colored countrymen," he asks the reader.

Their babies often receive sensual satisfactions which provide them with enough oral and sensory surplus for a lifetime, as clearly betrayed in the way they move, laugh, talk and sing. Their forced symbiosis with the feudal South capitalized on this oral-sensory treasure to build up a slave's identity: mild, submissive, dependent, somewhat querulous, but always ready to serve, and with occasional empathy and childlike wisdom. But underneath a dangerous split occurred. The humiliating symbiosis on the one hand, and on the other, the necessity of the master race to protect its identity against sensual and oral temptations, established in both groups an association: light-clean-clever-white; and, dark-dirty-dumb-nigger. The result, especially in those Negroes who have left the poor haven of their Southern homes, is often a violently sudden and cruel cleanliness training.[61]

He described three "solutions," three identities that a black person can fall back upon: the "mammy's child," who is tender, expressive and rhythmical; the clean, restrained, always friendly but always sad "white man's Negro"; and finally, "the bad nigger," the angry and violent man who respects nothing and nobody, black or white.

When faced with so-called opportunities which only offer a newly restricted freedom but fail to provide an integration of the identity fragments mentioned, one of these fragments becomes dominant in the form of a racial caricature; tired of this caricature, the colored individual often retires into hypochondriac invalidism as a condition whch represents an analogy to the ego-space-time of defined restriction in the South: a regression to the ego-identity of the slave.

I know of a colored boy who, like our boys, listens every night to the Lone Ranger. Then he sits up in bed, dreaming that he is the Ranger. But alas, the moment always comes when he sees himself galloping after some masked offenders and suddenly notices that in this image the Lone Ranger is a Negro. He stops his fantasies. While a child, this boy was extremely expressive, both in his pleasure and in his sorrows. Today he is calm and always smiles; his language is soft and blurred; nobody can hurry him, or worry him, or please him. White men like him.[62]

In America the so-called adolescent is also set apart, an object of mixed curiosity, envy and derision to a "youth-conscious" people who nevertheless have become an aging example for literally dozens of newer, younger nations. In the forties the psychiatric and psycho-analytic literature was full of talk about "rejecting" and "schizoid" mothers, whose sons and daughters have any number of discernible "problems." Erikson wanted to look beyond the relative handful of patients whom he and his colleagues see. He constantly wondered whether clinicians like himself weren't tempted to call a youth "sick," a mother "disturbed," even though their behavior actually was prompted by a long social tradition. Furthermore, there are strengths and extraordinary capacities in some of the people psychiatrists sweepingly describe with this or that clinical word. The issue for Erikson was not how "schizoid" a youth (or his mother) is, but how and why that particular kind of person became so prevalent — that is, under what social, economic and historical conditions. Characteristically, he describes young Americans whose ego identity is well defined, as well as those who for various reasons are having trouble finding out what in themselves works, makes sense, and is dependably *there:*

The family is Anglo-Saxon, mildly Protestant, and of the white collar class. This boy is tall, thin, muscular in his body build. He is shy, especially with women, and emotionally retentive, as if he saved himself for something. His occasional grin, however, indicates a basic satisfaction with himself. His goals are defined. Before the war he wanted to be an athlete; during the war, an aviator or pilot. . . . As for the mother, who shows a certain contempt for male weakness, her bark is worse than her bite. She has a male ideal, usually derived from her father or grandfather, and she indicates to the son that she believes in his ability to come close to this ideal. She is wise enough (sometimes lazy or indifferent enough) to leave it to him whether he wants to live up to this ideal or not.[63]

He then speculates on whether such a mother is not more than a product of our Puritan tradition. Perhaps the nation's history required mothers who wanted sons to look ahead rather than back to some blissful and indulgent past. Perhaps a nation of migrants and wanderers, explorers and assorted conquerors needed men who were not quite content, who believed that there is always a chance and a choice — ahead. Perhaps the dangerous frontier could not tolerate thoroughly satisfied and unthreatened children, naive and weakened "sissies" or "suckers" who cannot handle suffering and loneliness. Collective habits with children, or attitudes toward them, may reveal outmoded virtues as well as contemporary vices; and in any case, no family ought to be judged out of its own cultural and historical context. In other words, both the middle-class, patriarchal Austro-Hungarian family and the American one deserve a better fate than one that makes them measuring rods or bludgeons against one another.

And finally, we meet the veterans of the Second World War. Many of them were destined to be short-lived conquerors. They came home safe but soon began to suffer continual anxiety and gloom, cutting headaches and episodes of forgetfulness. One after another they sought out hospital clinics, complaining of vague aches and pains or unsettled "nerves." They asserted a loss of sleep, a loss of appetite, a loss of interest in life — in sum, a loss of "themselves." Moreover, because they no longer felt "right" about who they were and what they were doing, they had started for the first time to put their feelings into questions (Who am I and what am I doing?) that the rest of us feel are appropriately asked only by professional philosophers or boys and girls who are growing up and discovering how confusing and ambiguous "life" can be.

Erikson listened to them, former soldiers in trouble. He tried to account for their heightened vulnerability, their susceptibility to almost anything — to what he called "the gradual grind of a million annoyances." He looked into each man's past, and into the world of postwar America they all found so hard to accept:

In their struggle to gain access to the nonreversible escalator of free enterprise, their traumatized ego fights and flees an evil identity which includes elements of the crying baby, the bleeding woman, the submissive nigger, the sexual sissy, the economic sucker, the mental moron — all prototypes the mere allusion to which can bring these men close to homicidal or suicidal rage, ending up in varying degrees of irritability or apathy.[64]

He noted that in their attempt to find out what ailed them — and in their drive to give the psychiatrist the information he seemed to want — many former soldiers made both themselves and their childhood experiences seem improbably bad. They had learned how to be patients, and indeed the willingness of these men to seek help from psychiatrists was itself a historical event — and one that generated its own particular hazards. For one thing, as noted, suddenly troubled men might be seen by determined psychopathologists as unquestionably "ill" — at the very least "latently" so. For another, both patient and doctor can easily dwell on symptoms to the exclusion of what so often brings them about: the very real forces in the world. After all, American soldiers and sailors had come home to an already changed and still-changing nation. Our economic and political institutions were struggling to keep up with our new prominence as the world's strongest, most influential people. Whole continents cried out to us for help — while at home doubts and accusations of one sort or another filled the air. The psychotherapist who overlooks what such events can mean to people is "apt not only to miss the specific dynamics in contemporary life-cycles; he is apt also to deflect (or to serve those whose business demands that they deflect) individual energy from the collective tasks at hand."

In other words, when improperly used, psychoanalysis can become a very convenient political weapon. At the core of psychoanalytic theory one finds easily corruptible concepts, like the "reality principle." Whose "reality" does the analyst have in mind when he strives to help his patient? Here is one answer to that question: "The reality principle, in theory and therapy, has taken on a certain individualistic color, according to which that is good which the individual can get away with by dodging the law (in so far as it happens to be enforced) and the superego (in so far as it causes discomfort)." To this day psychiatrists talk about a person's "good social adjustment" and "poor social adjustment." Clearly a doctor has to estimate how well his patient comes to terms with the conventions and values of his society; but by the same token the conformist and the rebel present psychiatrists with a number of very real ethical and philosophical problems. Shall the conformist be called "healthy," though he is profoundly dull and spiritually dead — that is, if the therapist finds the society in serious trouble and saturated with evils? Shall the rebel be called "sick" or "sociopathic" or a "borderline" personality with a "severe character disorder" — that is, if the therapist thinks the society is in fine shape and not in need of serious change?

These are still vexing issues, and the many questions they inspire have yet to find satisfactory answers. To Erikson it was unthinkable (again, back in 1946) that the analyst overlook what joblessness or racism can do to the mind — yes, to the "deepest layers" of the unconscious. Nor could he ignore the uses to which his profession can be put — either by dogmatic analysts or by a social order that wants one or another justification for the "reality" of its existence. The Soviet Union rather quickly outlawed psychoanalysis as an "idealistic" and "pseudo-scientific" doctrine that supposedly ignores the all-significant "material" forces of social struggle in favor of futile introspection. America gave Freud's ideas and those who practiced them quite another reception, though of course a fashionable embrace can make for a special kind of tyranny — dazzling, glutting and eventually stupefying. Would America be quite so taken with psychoanalysis if more analysts emphasized how men are psychologically enslaved not only by unconscious drives, but by social and economic conditions that exert commanding power over the thoughts and deeds of people?

With the publication of "Ego Development and Historical Change" Erikson had reached a critical point in his intellectual development. As is often the case with creative men, he probably did not realize at the time that he had staked out and even rather precisely defined his future work, but the books and articles destined to appear in the coming decades expand upon the interests, intentions and convictions he declared in 1946 at the age of forty-four. For several years thereafter he disappeared from psychiatric and psychoanalytic journals. In the midst of a busy analytic career he kept one day a week to himself, and used it to write and work on what he had already written. He did this in the empty beach house of a friend. He was "working on a book"; but he certainly was in no rush to see it appear in print. He had the ideas; he wanted to make sure that his writing did justice to them; that is, he wanted as much as possible to be understood correctly.

Ideas gain energy and become active through words; and in psychoanalytic practice words — or the silences that conceal them — are all-important. Freud appreciated the value of clear, pointed language. And his reasons were not merely aesthetic or "literary." If — as seems obvious — psychoanalysis has made explicit what generations of men have known, from Sophocles through Shakespeare to Kierkegaard and Dostoevsky, then Freud's "style" as a writer was an indispensable part of his genius. He had the ability to put into words what others vaguely sense — or allude to in novels and poems. He also had the ability to wait, to sit still with an idea until it is crystallized and ready for the eyes of other people. It took him years to go from recognition to expression — and he was well into his forties when the transition was made final.

There are forces at work in this country that resist the slow ripening of knowledge. In the academic world, and in the medical and psychiatric world too, the emphasis is on production — so that professors and doctors are not as removed from the "commercial orientation" of our society as they sometimes suppose or insist. Professional journals multiply, and never seem to want for "material." Rather often that is what the reader finds, piece after piece of raw, undigested material — scorned, even by the owner, who has obviously not taken a moment of time to live with and reflect upon what he insists others try to comprehend. The result is not the dense prose that men of real ideas sometimes find walling them in, but the sloppy, hurried prose of men on the make. And all the while there are the tasteless readers, growing in number, willing and eager to swallow anything and feel stronger and better for it. Some have become so used to a certain kind of language — to long-winded, idiotic sentences — that anything direct, simple (and God forbid, eloquent) evokes first distrust, then contempt. It is as if the purpose of "science" is to make things complicated, rather than deal with complexities. Perhaps the fear is that one's observations will be found unsurprising or merely reasonable and sensible.

In the four years that Erikson took to sharpen and amplify his views, then put them into a carefully written manuscript, only once did he go into print, and then to write a eulogy for the great anthropologist Ruth Benedict, who died suddenly on November 4, 1949. The Viking Fund sponsored a memorial meeting in New York City, and in addition to Erikson, Alfred Kroeber, Cora DuBois, Clyde Kluckhohn, Robert Lynd and Margaret Mead spoke. Their remarks were put into a booklet, whose frontispiece was a portrait sketch Erikson had done of Mrs. Benedict shortly before her death.

Sometimes moments of tragedy can be as redemptive as the Bible says they by rights should be. Erikson's eulogy was filled with the gratitude he owed Ruth Benedict and other anthropologists, who had given him their eyes, even as he had given his to them. His remarks possess something more, though. It was as if he were telling a fallen comrade that she has not died in vain, that the effort and sacrifice she made were enough to free her ideas from herself, from the limitations of life itself. In a sense, then, the eulogy was not only respectful but reassuring — as if the man who wrote it knew from what he himself was doing how successful the influence of Ruth Benedict had been. Perhaps the eulogy was literally a prelude, a statement by a distinguished psychoanalyst to a grieving audience of social scientists that in a coming book the work they had all done side-by-side for so many years would receive full account and full justice:

I am very grateful for the privilege of joining you in this testimony of Ruth Benedict's living and unique image. Each of us, who knew her, knows that it will be with him as long as any vision remains. But what can we say to one another to share our common possession of that image?

Shall I speak of the relation Ruth Benedict had to my field, psychoanalysis? She accepted psychoanalysis as a major humanistic critique of the discontinuities which our civilization forces upon its children. She accepted it concretely, and worked assiduously in her cultural studies to uncover data the relevance of which had become clear through Freud's work. Her acceptance was intuitive, not systematic and argumentative. Of systems and creeds, Ruth Benedict was merely tolerant. As a humanist, she warned against the biologizing of human behavior, be it in the crude form of racism or the refined projection of "human nature." She showed how every step in the unfolding of physiological potentialities in the human child carries with it the experience of a cultural continuity or discontinuity; a sense of being at home, or a sense of being one's own worst enemy. . . .

But it is not along these lines that I can express what to me is most important about Ruth Benedict. Permit me, for a few minutes, to tell you of more personal things. When I saw Ruth last June, in California, I asked her to sit for a sketch. She was the fourth person in a year or so who had evoked in me — a dealer in words — this irresistible urge to document a face by drawing it. As I sketched Ruth I thought of the others.

The first had been an old Jewish woman from Mt. Carmel in the State of Israel. Visiting California, she had impressed us all with the new sense of dignity and identity which her work had given her: the work of tending her grandchildren, freeborn Jews in their own State.

The second was a grand old woman of the pueblo community of San Ildefonso in the American Southwest. In perfecting her black pottery she has given new life to one of the oldest arts.

The third was an old skier in the Sierras who as a youth had come from his native Finland to the then lonely country around Lake Tahoe, to range the snowbound trails between the early power stations.

Before Ruth came I had asked myself why I had wanted to sketch these people. Was it easier to draw old people because of the depth and finality of their facial lines? Or was I getting old, and looking for people who seemed to make aging worthwhile? Ladies and gentlemen, I would not steal this time to discuss autobiographic items with you, were it not for the fact that I found an answer to my question when I sketched Ruth Benedict; and what more can we say of any human being than that, by his mere being, he becomes to us not a question, not an argument, but an answer?

I wish the sketch itself could, as it should, convey what I mean. Let me try to say it.

Here was a person who was not vitally healthy anymore. Yet she was not sick. She seemed so calm that to ask whether she was happy in any conversational sense would have seemed incongruous.

Here was a friend, who was deeply alone, who had, in fact, stopped fighting loneliness. She had begun to befriend death, without in any way inviting it or being demanding of it.

Here then, was a consciously aging woman, who looked as much like a young girl, as she looked like a man, without being in the least juvenile or mannish.

Here was a woman who had been denied motherhood, but who had encompassed with motherly care her experiences, her observations, and her thoughts. She did not argue. But when she wrote she dealt with thoughts as a mother deals with impatient children, reconciling content and form until they befriended one another.

Here was an American who had learned to live beside and beyond boast and achievement. In her poetry she had struggled to find words for that other pole, which seems to signify the inner crisis of the observant American. She had gone so far as to call it "faith in failure." For to her victory was to be only a means to a mature end. . . .

Above all, here was a scientist, who had focused her analytic gifts on the differences between people and people, not in order to forge weapons of discrimination nor even of "scientific" manipulation, but in order to understand the crowning purpose of being individual and of being different: achievement of a particular style of simplicity and serenity.

In doing so, she herself acquired what I now saw was the common good of these four old people, Ruth's as well as the Palestinian's, the Finn's, and the Indian's: some of the beauty and simplicity, some of the faith and serenity, announcing clearly and indestructibly the near fulfillment of a life cycle which has found accord with the moral and esthetic realization of its community.

There is tragedy here, we know. Ruth was too young to be completed and detached. What the personal, or if you wish, clinical, reasons for this were, I did not make it my business to know. Let us not forget that she lived in the thick of an intellectual battle, which puts living on the defensive; and that it literally takes strength to fight and to feel, all the time.

What I have said I have not said in Ruth's praise. I have said it because we owe it to ourselves to think it and to remember it, for the sake of our personal fortunes as well as for the focus of our further work. . . .[65]

VI

Childhood and Society Achieved

ERIKSON'S "further work" was published the next year by
W. W. Norton, and I doubt that any other book by a student
of Freud is as well known over the world. *Childhood and Society*
was immediately published in England and has since been translated
into Japanese, Swedish, German, Spanish, French, Hebrew, Finnish,
Dutch, Italian, Norwegian and Danish. For thirteen years it sold
steadily in a hardback as well as in a paperback edition, until finally
in 1963, a second edition, revised and enlarged, was issued. In a
recent study, 140 approved (three-year) psychiatric training centers
were asked to submit reading lists given to young residents. Out of
twenty-eight hundred books recommended at least once, eighteen
were universally used — basic texts, as it were. *Childhood and Society* was one of the eighteen. It is also a familiar sight in many
university bookstores over the nation — and in other places, as I
indicated in the Preface — where undergraduates, graduate students,
medical students and law students as well as psychiatrists and psychoanalysts seek out the book.

In a foreword Erikson establishes his style and method — as a
psychoanalyst, artist and writer. He is gathering together years of
clinical work: the study of anxiety in young children, apathy in
American Indians, confusion in veterans of war, arrogance in young
Nazis. As an analyst he has understood psychological conflict, but as
an investigator he had steadfastly refused to arrive at the "easy
conclusion that our relatively advanced knowledge of neurosis permits us to view mass phenomena — culture, religion, revolution — as
analogies of neuroses." He pointedly adds, "We will pursue a different path."

The path was in fact one he himself had made by pressing forward into territory claimed by neither doctors nor sociologists, territory where the child's ears meet up with the world's sounds. What helped him clear the path and avoid any number of pitfalls? Perhaps this way of going about things:

Neither terminological alignment with the more objective sciences nor dignified detachment from the clamoring of the day can and should keep the psychoanalytic method from being what H. S. Sullivan called "participant," and systematically so.

In this sense, this is and must be a subjective book, a *conceptual itinerary*. There is no attempt at being representative in quotations or systematic in references. On the whole, little is gained from an effort to reinforce as yet vague meanings with seemingly conscientious quotations of vaguely similar meanings from other contexts.[1]

A little further on he writes more personally:

I came to psychology from art, which may explain, if not justify, the fact that at times the reader will find me painting contexts and backgrounds where he would rather have me point to facts and concepts. I have had to make a virtue out of a constitutional necessity by basing what I have to say on representative description rather than on theoretical argument.[2]

Childhood and Society is divided into four parts. The first section introduces and illustrates the clinician's method, the case history, and then applies that method of study — as a psychoanalyst uses it — to the "normal" child. The author wants to see how children grow and become the various adults they do. He is interested in using what he has learned in the clinic to understand what starts in the delivery room of the hospital and goes on in the nursery, the backyard, the school. He wants to convert a theory of psychopathology and metapsychology into a closely documented view of child development. He wants to make Freud's theory of "infantile sexuality" more, rather than less, relevant by giving it a place in something larger and more universal than the accumulated and catalogued memories of middle-class American and European neurotics. He wants to be concrete, biological, physiological, but also symbolic, as we all are when we dream or worship or sing or merely have a "thought." He wants to show how similar and yet different the children of this world are, and why. It is as if he has said to Sigmund Freud: I am not here to "change" or "revise" your suggestive and hard-won theories — which I know you yourself respected enough to change constantly; nor am I here to quibble and haggle with your words, to draw implications from them that you never intended, or to put meanings into them that succeed in making you narrow, boring, or cruel. I want your ideas as companions, to whom I can turn for advice and help while I walk my own way — in a direction you seemed to have set for yourself toward the end of your life, when you turned your attention to historical figures, religious problems and social events as subjects for psychoanalytic inquiry. I will go about my work in your manner, because psychoanalysis in the most profound sense of the word is a *style* — of looking at the world and of ordering various facts and feelings. On the other hand, I will pay you the respect of working hard to bring whatever ferment I can to your ideas. You once called yourself a "conquistador." If we are to emulate you, we will have to be more than slaves or literal-minded acolytes of yours.

Most of the book's first part had already appeared in the articles already discussed. The theory of zones and modes is presented, as is his earlier study of the way "normal" boys and girls play — and thereby give expression to their fears and desires. The book has Erikson's charts, meant to show *him* — as if on a canvas — the "steps" that children take in body and spirit as they move along the years. His "epigenetic" view is spelled out, and used as a means of linking what psychoanalysts see in the office to what is more generally required or forbidden in a particular society.

In the second part of the book the reader is asked to look not at patients or at children who are struggling with problems that (later on) they might recall if they should become patients, but at Indians. Again Erikson draws on work published, his two monographs on the Sioux and the Yurok. The man who wrote those two long papers was in the midst of discovery, in the process of finding out what he believed the bounds of psychoanalysis to be, but the author who sent the chapters "Hunters Across the Prairie" and "Fishermen Along a Salmon River" to his publisher knew exactly what he had been doing and why.

In his introduction to part two of the book he notes how little attention many anthropologists have paid to the quality of care received by children: "Even anthropologists living for years among aboriginal tribes failed to see that these tribes trained their children in some systematic way." Boys and girls simply grew up — or so it was assumed. What is more, childhood in Africa or Asia was either scorned as "animal-like" or heavily romanticized.

In contrast, Erikson learned that "primitive societies are neither infantile stages of mankind nor arrested deviations from the proud progressive norms which we represent." Like all groups of people, Indians (and other "backward folk") try to deal with the world they know, and bring up their children to do likewise — which entails developing the same complicated customs and ritualized actions that we assume to be part of "civilized" life. He found among both Sioux and Yurok "a complete form of mature human being" and even a "homogeneity and simple integrity" that may well be called enviable. He also saw the terrible and apparently insoluble vicissitudes that those tribes had to confront year after year. The Sioux are a conquered, brutally plundered and sequestered people; and their mere survival can be viewed as a lesson in the hazards of endurance. They avoided doing "just what our analogistic thinking would have them do." They did not become "a community of wild eccentrics, infantile characters or neurotics." They became a people with little "future" — as we define the word — but with a very real and coherent past. Under such circumstances the hope and the promise of the past live on, against great odds — all of which goes to show that nations like individuals try to do the best they can, try to make whatever sense they can of the world. Even when the world (or the home) fails them miserably, they continue to struggle for any coherence, any "sense of identity and idea of integrity" they can possibly find.

In other words, an anthropologist or psychoanalyst has to do more than take notice of behavior and then label it either "primitive" or "advanced," either "infantile" or "mature." He has to understand, as a social historian would, what possibilities are available for an individual or nation and why out of any number of possibilities a particular one makes most sense. How else, for example, can I as a psychiatrist comprehend the behavior of a marine corpsman who charges into a nest of enemy mines—to an almost certain death? I certainly cannot call him "suicidal," as I would a patient of mine who had been depressed for a long time, and finally decided to end it all with a bullet, a leap, or some pills. Instead I think of the marine as brave, courageous — a hero. Why the difference — if both men are knowingly embracing death? To answer such a question the psychiatrist has to take note of the values and norms that nations, churches and communities provide. As the man whose job it is to know the intentions of people and heal their difficulties, the psychiatrist also has to remember that one man's virtue can be another's weakness, something entire psychiatric systems of diagnosis have disregarded.

In part three of his book, Erikson moves to the ego, to the psychological side of what happens when children become (or fail to become) reasonably honorable and competent members of given societies. Again he writes an introduction that sets forth his main ideas and makes clear the continuity of both the book and his lifework. And again he thinks like a historian. He repeats what he has said before in a number of ways. In the beginning the id was all; it was felt to be the *real* force that prompted man:

The id is everything that is left in our organization of the responses of the amoeba and of the impulses of the ape, of the blind spasms of our intra-uterine existence, and of the needs of our postnatal days — everything which would make us "mere creatures." The name "id," of course, designates the assumption that the "ego" finds itself attached to this impersonal, this bestial layer like the centaur to his equestrian underpinnings: only that the ego considers such a combination a danger and an imposition, whereas the centaur makes the most of it. The id, then, has some of the pessimistic qualities of Schopenhauer's "will," the sum of all desire that must be overcome before we can be quite human.[3]

Next comes the superego, the conscience that children slowly acquire, the world's do's and don't's that they learn. Again, Freud's initial imagery made the ego appear to be vulnerable, put upon by the insistent id and the punitive superego. There are parallels in life to the merciless way we sometimes learn to take ourselves to task:

In moments of self-reproach and depression, the superego uses against the ego methods so archaic and so barbaric that they become analogous to those of the blindly impulsive id. So, too, in the cruelties of religious or political inquisition, it is hard to see where mere sadistic perversion ends and an all too hearty form of piety begins.[4]

Caught between these two "agencies" (they are abstractions meant to give a convenient order to certain psychological events and developments), the ego as originally formulated was hopelessly pinioned. As mentioned earlier, it was a virtual weather vane, at the mercy of this or that gust of wind, or at best it was a sort of negotiator, who must endlessly placate, bribe, cajole, importune, and in general live out a hand-to-mouth existence through guile and persuasion.

Anna Freud's book *The Ego and the Mechanisms of Defense* changed all that. She declared the ego to be a significant part of the unconscious, with its own territory and in particular its own, self-sustaining "mechanisms." Written in the thirties, when "defense" was very much on everyone's mind, her book showed how adroit and steadfast we can be — often unwittingly — in the face of enormous pressures. The ego could be seen as a sort of Maginot Line, studded with various protective devices, some of which go "deep down." In a way the analogy holds not only for the Maginot Line of 1936 (the year Anna Freud's book was published) but the one that was overwhelmed in 1940. In periods of great or unusual stress the mind collapses, overwhelmed by a rush of destructive, greedy passions, a flood of self-recriminations.

Yet the ego does more than defend itself. All during the forties Erikson had been saying that we can be inventive, creative, constructive, ingenious and resourceful as well as exceedingly well guarded. We do more than walk on tightropes. We conceive the *idea* of a tightrope. We see the act of walking on one as a *symbol.* In other words, we have an intellect, and in its service our minds can be willful advocates of more than "peace at any price." Finally — and very important — we are urged on or discouraged by events that take place "outside." The ego does indeed steer its way around "inner" hazards or forces; but the ego also learns *lessons* and *skills.* And anyone's ego has to learn how to survive very real external dangers. In part three of *Childhood and Society* Erikson wants to show how the ego grows — until a child quite "automatically" knows the "facts" of work and play, of friendship and love, of money and power, of frustration and sickness.

He begins the section with a clinical experience. First comes the patient, a sad and frightened girl whom he once treated. She is very much alone, very moody, very excitable, and very "difficult." Erikson makes no claim to have "cured" her; rather one gets the impression that she would never be quite "right," that when he first saw her, at the age of six, far too much had already happened, or had not happened. She was — he uses quotation marks — "schizophrenic." She pulled away from people with an almost desperate intensity. She seemed at once appealing, almost soulful, and frantic. What could possibly have happened to her?

Though this "case" is given only thirteen pages, and is not the most essential link in Erikson's theoretical argument, the discussion reveals something about him as a clinician. The girl is given the name Jean, and is described as having "beautiful dark eyes which seemed like peaceful islands within the anxious grimace of her face." He describes her "mad rush" through his home, her frantic behavior during their meetings. At a time when "rejecting" mothers and "schizophrenogenic" mothers were all the rage in psychiatry and were asserted to be the cause of an astonishing range of complaints, Erikson said no: the very word "cause" requires quotation marks. He insisted that labels and names, no matter how grim or scientific their sound, cannot supply the answers to what was then — and still is — a riddle: What specifically makes for the behavior we call "schizophrenia"? He is willing to consider any number of "factors"; but when very little is known he refuses to be a partisan of any "explanation," even the "psychodynamic" one that his own colleagues so frequently assert. Genes may be responsible. Somehow the child may be born a quiet, distant baby — call the reason his or her "temperament" or "disposition." Anyone who works in a maternity ward knows how widely infants vary, from the first moment of birth. A baby "by nature" slow to respond may be the child of a mother who is nervous for her own reasons, or indeed made nervous by her child's actions, or lack of them. Things don't work between them, or work only intermittently — and soon *do* work to the mutual pain and sorrow of both mother and child. What is more, an illness may occur, an accident happen, a crisis intrude — making the mother or the child or both not what they otherwise might be.

The point Erikson wants to make is that the clinician, of all people, cannot allow himself what he may feel most anxious to have, the certainty that words and catchy phrases provide. Furthermore, he clearly had sensed the peculiarly moralistic, punitive and vulgar way those phrases are too often used. Rather than appreciate the enormous complexity of the problems at hand, doctors who should know better summon answers, and just as important, they fail to ask the necessary and puzzling questions. In his own words he is "not trying to isolate first causes," but to show how even the sickest child lives amid more than the fantasies and habits with which he tries to build his own, private world.

He wrote about the child Jean in such a way that the heroic efforts of her mother (and her therapist) become quietly evident. Yet in spite of everything, Jean's mind repudiated her own body and its needs as well as the world's wish to do well by her. Often she closed her eyes, held her hands over her ears, hid here and there. In an illness like Jean's, the intact ego we can take for granted (in ourselves and in our children) reveals its fragmented, distinct parts. The outside world is misjudged, and the inside world is mistrusted. What is more, the senses and the intellect are misused or sorely neglected — so great is the person's fear, or for some reason, his incapacity. The worries and desires some of us feel and manage to fend off or indulge in a reasonably sensible and effective way devastated Jean, who knew vividly from overwhelming experience the disorder and confusion that challenge the ego of anyone's mind.

Jean's grim fate reveals, as sickness often does, how many things an unimpaired mind does without knowing it. Her relationship with her therapist, with all its ups and downs, is also edifying:

Such improvements seemed most rewarding. They were usually interrupted by crises which led to emergency calls. I would visit the family and talk with all the members of the household until I had ascertained what was going on in all their lives. A whole series of difficulties arose in this one-patient sanitarium. One can live with schizophrenic thought only if one can make a profession out of understanding it. The mother had accepted this task, which demands a particular gift of empathy and at the same time the ability to keep oneself intact.[5]

Characteristically, Erikson moves from sickness to health. After Jean we find a "more reassuring chapter" (titled "Toys and Reasons"), which takes up the play and work of children, and the growth they demonstrate, year by year. The heart of *Childhood and Society* may be found in this section of the book, and particularly in the way Erikson uses the following passage from *Tom Sawyer*:

He took up his brush and went tranquilly to work. Ben Rogers hove in sight presently — the very boy, of all boys, whose ridicule he had been dreading. Ben's gait was the hop-skip-and-jump — proof enough that his heart was light and his anticipations high. He was eating an apple, and giving a long, melodious whoop, at intervals, followed by a deep-toned ding-dong-dong, ding-dong-dong, for he was personating a steamboat. As he drew near, he slackened speed, took the middle of the street, leaned far over to starboard and rounded to ponderously and with laborious pomp and circumstance — for he was personating the *Big Missouri*, and considered himself to be drawing nine feet of water. He was boat and captain and engine-bells combined, so he had to imagine himself standing on his own hurricane-deck giving the orders and executing them:

. . . "Stop the stabboard! Ting-a-ling-ling! Stop the labboard! Come ahead on the stabboard! Stop her! Let your outside turn over slow! Ting-a-ling-ling! Chow-ow-ow! Get out that head-line! *Lively* now! Come — out with your spring line — what're you about there! Take a turn round that stump with the bight of it! Stand by that stage, now — let her go! Done with the engines, sir! Ting-a-ling-ling! *Sh't! sh't! sh't!*" (trying the gauge-cocks).

Tom went on whitewashing — paid no attention to the steamboat. Ben stared a moment, and then said:

"Hi-*yi! You're* up a stump, ain't you! . . . You got to work, hey?"[6]

Tom had been told to whitewash a fence on a fine spring morning, and as if that were not enough, Ben Rogers had to come along and play a *game*. Here is how Erikson speaks of Ben and Tom:

He [Ben] takes care of the body by munching an apple; he simultaneously enjoys imaginary control over a number of highly conflicting items (being a steamboat and parts thereof, as well as being the captain of said steamboat, and the crew obeying said captain); while he loses not a moment in sizing up social reality when, on navigating a corner, he sees Tom at work. By no means reacting as a steamboat would, he knows immediately how to pretend sympathy though he undoubtedly finds his own freedom enhanced by Tom's predicament.

Flexible lad, we would say. However, Tom proves to be the better psychologist: he is going to put Ben to work. Which shows that psychology is at least the second-best thing to, and under some adverse circumstances may even prove superior to, ordinary adjustment.

In view of Ben's final fate it seems almost rude to add interpretation to defeat, and to ask what Ben's play may mean. I presented this question to a class of psychiatric social-work students. Most of the answers were, of course, of the traumatic variety, for in what other way could Ben become accessible to "case work"? Ben must have been a frustrated boy, the majority agreed, to take the trouble to play so strenuously. The possible frustrations ranged from oppression by a tyrannical father from whom he escapes in fantasy by becoming a bossy captain, to a bedwetting or toilet trauma of some kind which now made him want to be a boat drawing nine feet of water. Some answers concerned the more obvious circumstance that he wanted to be big, and this in the form of a captain, the idol of his day.

My contribution to the discussion consisted of the consideration that Ben is a growing boy. To grow means to be divided into different parts which move at different rates. A growing boy has trouble in mastering his gangling body as well as his divided mind. He wants to be good, if only out of expediency, and always finds he has been bad. He wants to rebel, and finds that almost against his will he has given in. As his time perspective permits a glimpse of approaching adulthood he finds himself acting like a child. One "meaning" of Ben's play could be that it affords his ego a temporary victory over his gangling body and self by making a well-functioning whole out of brain (captain), the nerves and muscles of will (signal system and engine), and the whole bulk of the body (boat). It permits him to be an entity within which he is his own boss, because he obeys himself. At the same time, he chooses his metaphors from the tool world of the young machine age, and anticipates the identity of the machine god of his day: the captain of the *Big Missouri*.[7]

In those four paragraphs the clinician does not forsake his interest in "pathology," but he certainly sees more than "deep" conflict slyly masquerading as this or that "symbolic" act; and the use of quotation marks around the word "meaning" virtually warrants an essay in itself. Erikson is trying to show how the ego comes to terms with the body, the mind, and what some people call "social processes." Yet he is aware — and wants to remind the reader — how misleading any phrase or concept can be, necessary as they both are. When we talk about this "meaning" or that "explanation" we usually single out or concentrate upon one aspect of something much larger and more complicated — all well and good unless we forget what we are doing, in which case human behavior begins to sound like chemical elements at work in a solution: this "causes" that; this "means" that; this can be "traced back to" that. In one sense the chief purpose of *Childhood and Society* is to free both its author and the major truths of psychoanalysis from the kind of mechanistic, "cause-and-effect" thinking that does scant justice to either the "nature" or the "destiny" of man.

From Tom Sawyer, Erikson moves to play — first the adult variety, then that of children. When grown-ups play they do not work, at least at a "job" or to make money. (There is, of course, the danger of "going professional.") Somehow we choose rather than feel obligated, and we feel "free" or entertained. We are on vacation from what must be done, though play can also become an obligation or a moral necessity. In other words, the puritan mind can turn sport into a body-building or soul-strengthening exercise. However, Erikson quotes Schiller, who certainly was no puritan: "Man is perfectly human only when he plays." He also notes that "in its own playful way" play tries to "elude definition." He *could* have offered one, a definition all italicized and underlined, but at the cost of giving offense to everything he was trying to do. Instead he describes and he analyzes:

Take *gravity:* to juggle, to jump, or to climb adds unused dimensions to the awareness of our body. Play here gives a sense of divine leeway, of excess space.

Take *time:* in trifling, in dallying, we lazily thumb our noses at this, our slave-driver. Where every minute counts, playfulness vanishes. This puts competitive sports on the borderline of play: they seem to make concessions to the pressure of space and time, only to defeat this very pressure by a fraction of a yard or of a second.

Take *fate* and *causality,* which have determined who and what we are, and where. In games of chance we re-establish equality before fate, and secure a virgin chance to every player willing to observe a few rules which, if compared with the rules of reality, seem arbitrary and senseless. Yet they are magically convincing, like the reality of a dream, and they demand absolute compliance. Let a player forget that such play must remain his free choice, let him become possessed by the demon of gambling, and playfulness vanishes again. He is a gambler, not a player.

Take *social reality,* and our defined cubicles in it. In play-acting we can be what in life we could not or would not be. But as the play-actor begins to believe in his impersonation he comes closer to a state of hysteria, if not worse; while if he tries, for purposes of gain, to make others believe in his "role" he becomes an impostor.

Take our *bodily drives.* The bulk of the nation's advertising effort exploits our wish to play with necessity, to make us believe, for example, that to inhale and to eat are not pleasurable necessities, but a fanciful game with ever new and sensuous nuances. Where the need for these nuances becomes compulsive, it creates a general state of mild addiction and gluttony, which ceases to transmit a sense of abundance and, in fact, produces an undercurrent of discontent.

Last but not least, in *love life* we describe as sex play the random activities preceding the final act, which permit the partners to choose body part, intensity, and tempo ("what, and with which, and to whom," as the limerick has it). Sex play ends when the final act begins, narrowing choice, dictating tempo, and giving rein to "nature." Where one of the preparatory random acts becomes compelling enough to completely replace the final act, playfulness vanishes and perversion begins.[8]

The reader is next introduced to children's play. He is reminded that playboys and gamblers do the unforgivable — play all the time

— for which they are envied and resented. Most of us work and work and work — so that play is an interlude at best: "Therefore, to be tolerant of the child's play the adult must invent theories which show either that childhood play is really work — or that it does not count. The most popular theory and the easiest on the observer is that the child is *nobody yet,* and that the nonsense of his play reflects it."[9] And, of course, there are scientists who talk about "surplus energy," or in the case of some psychoanalysts, "cathartic energy": we have pent-up feelings, based on past frustrations, and we use play for "instinctual expression" or "gratification" or "sublimation."

In contrast, Erikson looks at the purposes and achievements that children find in play. What we call "child's play" often consists of a boy struggling to make sense of the world, bring it under control, come to terms with it and with himself, not to mention his parents. Like a poet, a dreamer or a day-dreamer, the child packs into a few gestures, a few words, a few repetitive motions, all sorts of doubts, fears or assertions. He presents to himself a problem, and tries to find its answer. He has an answer, and tries to find it convincing by doing something over and over again until it all feels "right" or "good." He has a life, a small one whose meaning his play can somehow encompass, and he tries to tame that life, or give it the rein he feels desirable.

Games can have their own meaning, and need not be seen as anything but what they are, a way to fill up the child's time, energy and interest. Games are also social occasions, when children can meet to share feeling and display skill. Yet there are times when a game becomes a very personal thing, an expression of what is most on a child's mind. For Erikson *all* these considerations are important. It is not a matter of going from a "superficial interpretation" of play as "mere" activity or as stylized social behavior to a "deep interpretation" of play as an outpouring of unconscious energy, symbolically directed. Rather the child's development, his progressively diverse involvement with people and things, sets the stage for his activities, fun and games included. What is really superficial is the use of vertical polarities like "deep" and "superficial," conscious and unconscious, when growth itself is gradual and our lives increasingly lateral — as we reach out and meet new people and new situations.

Children begin to play before we notice it. They repeat sounds, move themselves about with surprise and delight, and a bit later do all kinds of things to see what mother will or will not do. The mother's face, her arms and breasts and shoulders are the "child's first geography." Erikson calls George Santayana in witness:

Far, far in a dim past, as if it had been in another world or in a pre-natal condition, Oliver remembered the long-denied privilege of sitting in his mother's lap. It had been such a refuge of safety, of softness, of vantage: You were carried and you were enveloped in an amplitude of sure protection, like a king on his throne, with his faithful bodyguard many ranks deep about him; and the landscape beyond, with its messengers and its motley episodes, became the most entertaining of spectacles, where everything was unexpected and exciting, yet where nothing could go wrong; as if your mother herself had been telling you a story, and these pictures were only the illustrations to it which painted themselves in your listening mind.[10]

Later comes nursery school — with its world of other children and other grown-ups, who sanction or forbid. For a while young children treat others as things. They are to be "inspected, run into, or forced to be 'horsie.' " When in doubt or fear there is always solitary play, "an indispensable harbor for the overhauling of shattered emotions after periods of rough going in the social seas." For the seriously troubled there is even "therapeutic" play — when a child can talk through dolls or toy cars, speak with crayons or paints, and indicate feelings through one or another game. In sum, "the child's play is the infantile form of the human ability to deal with experience by creating model situations and to master reality by experiment and planning." Later, in the laboratory, on the stage, at the drawing board, we again do — in a more precise, relevant and useful way — what we once learned to do, that is, redeem the past and give form to the future. Erikson says that "no thinker can do more and no playing child less," and then gives William Blake the last word: "The child's toys and the old man's reasons/Are the fruits of the two seasons."

His work with children taught Erikson how useful a game could be when the analyst and the young child are getting to know one another; but he also realized that adults dismiss as "games" or "fun" or a "stage" what children experience as the very essence of living and growing up. Somehow he managed to see the child's view of what we call society, and in so doing show what the child's activities mean to the child, in contrast, say, to the man who observes children. So *Childhood and Society* is not a book about "child de-

velopment" or "the psychopathology of childhood." The significance of a child's activity cannot be understood by calling upon a
graph that tells when things are done and how; nor can an activity
only be seen as the resolution or expression of "conflict," or as an
adaptation to "reality." Something as universally learned (and "natural") as walking means any number of different things to children,
depending not only on who the child is and who his parents are,
but where and when they live. We may want to know whether a
child walks at one or one-and-a-half, or whether walking has become associated in his mind (or his mother's) with any number of
psychological "problems" or "developments." But most of all we
should take an interest in how children begin to feel that what they
do makes sense and feels good and fits in with what others do.

At times Erikson has trouble putting in words what he is trying
to convey. He resists the temptation to make "precise" what is necessarily highly complicated, though also marvelously simple and
direct, for example, the way physical agility, psychological competence and — from others — *acceptance* or *welcome* all come together
and make for a sturdy, lovable child:

> Children cannot be fooled by empty praise and condescending en-
> couragement. They may have to accept artificial bolstering of their self-
> esteem in lieu of something better, but their ego identity gains real
> strength only from wholehearted and consistent recognition of real ac-
> complishment — i.e., of achievement that has meaning in the culture.[11]

He sees many of us belittling the very real efforts of our children
to stand alongside us — as indeed they can be seen doing in certain
"primitive" cultures, where they work with their mothers and
fathers, become their allies and companions, yet still manage to be
"children." In contrast, what we often do is give our children a
lavish make-believe world whose absurd irrelevance they easily detect. No wonder they gratuitously destroy "expensive" gifts and
search out their own (militantly secret) amusement. In a society
whose machines make even adult labor progressively unnecessary —
or so specialized that many know very little about the purpose of
their work, or think very little of its value — our children, too, face
the prospect of becoming "a speciality called 'child,' who must
play at being big because he is not given an opportunity to be a
small partner in a big world."

Play is serious business for the child; and for Erikson destiny begins to take shape as we play, not because "psychic conflicts" are expressed, but because we hopefully have begun to discover what to *do* with ourselves — with our energies, enthusiasms and disappointments. No wonder that on Erikson's chart showing "the eight stages of man" (see Figure 2 on page 137) Identity — and what happens if it is somehow not achieved — follows Industry. The industrious child who at eight or ten feels like a reasonably capable person and acts like a reasonably resourceful one is on his way to something more than a job.

Even today many psychoanalytic texts and articles still grant the struggles and achievements of adolescence or the later years little respect that can be called their own. Youth, middle age and old age are studied, true, but always in terms of the "problems" they inspire — in minds whose essential character is considered already established. To a friendly critic who would acknowledge that all sorts of psychological changes do occur throughout life Erikson would say no: the issue is whether one sees the structure of the mind, its very nature, largely completed as childhood ends, subject of course to later modifications, or whether the mind itself is given a life — *to be lived.* Here imagery determines outlook. If I think of a "psychic apparatus" that is essentially and solidly "made" by the time a child is five or ten I will see later life as a sort of "environment," able only to exert pressure on that "apparatus," modify it, or elicit one or another "latent" quality from it. On the other hand, if I see the mind as never really developed, but always developing, in its *essence* developing, I will think of old age — let alone life at age fifteen or twenty-five — with the same clinical interest and theoretical devotion, the same mixture of bewilderment, surprise and unyielding attention that the oedipal drama ("family romance") obtains from me, the psychiatrist. That is, I can think of life as progressively unfolding, with its direction essentially fixed in the first few years by what happens between the child and his parents, or I can think of life as a series of steps, with plateaus and precipices that do far more than reveal the direction set by the first few steps — in which case only when a person's last breath has been taken can his biographer draw psychological conclusions.

As for youth, there is more to deal with than the formidable past. There is a present and a future:

In their search for a new sense of continuity and sameness, adolescents have to refight many of the battles of earlier years, even though to do so they must artificially appoint perfectly well-meaning people to play the roles of adversaries; and they are ever ready to install lasting idols and ideals as guardians of a final identity.

The integration now taking place in the form of ego identity is, as pointed out, more than the sum of childhood identifications.[12]

The ego's ability to deal with the id or the superego now becomes tested by new friendships, new obligations or new restrictions. The youth sees a job forthcoming, a career awaiting; or he knows that no matter how satisfactorily he settles things with mother and dad, the sheriff will reward initiative or self-reliance with jail, or worse. Anyway, black or white, rich or poor, he is a youth, more than a child, not quite (in his own mind) a man:

Young people can also be remarkably clannish, and cruel in their exclusion of all those who are "different," in skin color or cultural background, in tastes and gifts, and often in such petty aspects of dress and gesture as have been temporarily selected as *the* signs of an in-grouper or out-grouper. It is important to understand (which does not mean condone or participate in) such intolerance as a defense against a sense of identity confusion. For adolescents not only help one another temporarily through much discomfort by forming cliques and by stereotyping themselves, their ideals, and their enemies; they also perversely test each other's capacity to pledge fidelity. The readiness for such testing also explains the appeal which simple and cruel totalitarian doctrines have on the minds of the youth of such countries and classes as have lost or are losing their group identities (feudal, agrarian, tribal, national) and face world-wide industrialization, emancipation, and wider communication.

The adolescent mind is essentially a mind of the *moratorium*, a psychosocial stage between childhood and adulthood, and between the morality learned by the child, and the ethics to be developed by the adult.[13]

The last section of *Childhood and Society* is devoted to those youths, to "youth and the evolution of identity." It is as if the author of a book about childhood wants to remind us that children are going somewhere, and know it, even in the beginning of life. They are headed, for instance, toward *others*, with whom new bonds can be established. Intimacy becomes the challenge of the twenties or early thirties. To whom — if anyone — will we give whatever sense of identity we have secured? Among American middle-class men and women a sense of identity as Erikson defines it (or better, describes it) can be an end rather than one more beginning. Competence and success at work or play are pursued and obtained — but shared with no one. The person becomes shut off from others and from a good part of himself. He lacks friends. He shuns strong commitments or lasting associations. The vicissitudes of human relatedness both plague and inspire us throughout life, but at no time more critically than in late youth and early middle age, when all that we have achieved as sensual, skillful human beings is tested for its depth and plasticity.

Nor does love and marriage bring to an end the mind's evolutionary progress. A kind of unforgiving self-centeredness can gradually emerge in a person of thirty-five who has secured everything (including psychological strength) for himself, but wants to share it with nobody, not even his wife and children. Not all self-regarding persons stay unmarried, nor do egotistical and self-indulgent people remain childless. Parents can have many, many children, yet show no real care for them, no real interest in them as more than "offspring," objects of self-congratulatory pride. When Erikson writes of "generativity" and "stagnation" as alternative "states," he has in mind subjective, not objective, considerations — and considerations which are by no means exclusively or even primarily sexual.

In the forties any concern at all with middle and old age on the part of an analyst was rare, and even more unusual was talk about "generativity" and "stagnation" or about "ego integrity" and "despair." The postwar "existentialist" literature was just beginning to affect America — and for some was a convenient excuse to drop one fad (psychoanalysis) and take up another one. At the same time there were very good reasons for analysts to look at themselves and their (existentialist) predicament rather more closely. As mentioned, with Freud's death many of his followers closed ranks around his ideas, and actually turned them into an impasse. Either one believed, or one doubted. For those who dared dissent there were rebukes, penalties, and finally, expulsion from the "society" or "group." And as for everyone else, the twentieth-century men Camus was then describing, they all became subject to a kind of psychoanalytic "morality." Not only were there the "normal" and the "abnormal," the "mature" and the "sick," but whole styles of social as well as psychological behavior became approved or condemned by psychoanalysts *as* psychoanalysts. The lonely and "eccentric" genius, the unmarried nurse or teacher, the childlike philosopher who is also childless — they all have their "problems," their "sublimations."

Conspicuously absented from such difficulties — even, it would seem, from the need to have their sublimations analyzed — are the so-called well adjusted. They are married, have several children, and are moderately (but not too) successful. They are not rebels; they don't question things too closely — or at least don't get into "trouble" for doing so. They are generally quiet, and if they do become restless they become patients rather than political agitators or social non-conformists. As for the agitators — political, philosophical or otherwise — they are rather easily assigned psychoanalytic labels, which they have received over and over again. American puritanism — the need to condemn and exorcise — has found in psychoanalysis yet another ally.

The text of *Childhood and Society* is both existential and analytic. The reader is reminded how much the older generation needs the younger one — by an analyst who knows that the child's "dependency" is only half the story of human relatedness and need. The reader meets no narrowly based, slyly punitive judgments. Psychoanalytic concepts are not used pejoratively — so as to confuse the socially conventional with the psychologically "normal." We are not told to suspect individuals who, "through misfortune or because of special and genuine gifts," become generative not as parents, but as workers, artists, builders of one sort or another. And sex can give way to Care or Charity without the whole thing being called God-knows-what name:

Even where philosophical and spiritual tradition suggests the renunciation of the right to procreate or to produce, such early turn to "ultimate concerns," wherever instituted in monastic movements, strives to settle at the same time the matter of its relationship to the Care for the creatures of this world and to the Charity which is left to transcend it.[14]

As we approach the end of life, an idea like Charity either means something, or indeed means absolutely nothing. In Erikson's eighth stage, Maturity, the individual either does or does not find at least a degree of purpose and coherence in his life — hence, in all life. Hopefully the mind accepts itself and comes to value what has been, rather than dwell upon what will soon no longer be. Life is seen "as an experience which conveys some world order and spiritual sense, no matter how dearly paid for." As usual, we get no bland optimism. "Integrity" in old age does not mean that one learns to whistle in the dark. Despair is there, will be there — for everyone, no matter how much he has accomplished, how many years he has been analyzed, how "realistic" he has trained himself to be. The issue is not either/or; it is both/and — with tone or emphasis all-important.

Significantly, in his struggle to say what he means about "ego integrity" or "despair" Erikson draws upon two European writers, and lets them speak in their own words as well as through his translation. When he emphasizes how life is lived in history, how each of us makes a psychological "adjustment" not only to our parents, or even our "society," but to particular decades of a particular century, he says, "The style of integrity developed by his culture or his civilization thus becomes the 'patrimony of his soul,' the seal of his moral paternity of himself ('. . . pero el honor/Es patrimonio del alma': Calderón)."

As for despair, we all feel it, and it can be devious indeed: "Disgust hides despair, if often only in the form of 'a thousand little disgusts' which do not add up to one big remorse: 'mille petits dégoûts de soi, dont le total ne fait pas un remords, mais un gêne obscure.' " The man quoted is Edmond Rostand. Erikson believes that somehow in some people those inevitable "little disgusts" fail to smolder or turn into overwhelming "remorse" or regret. Instead in a circular way the end becomes the beginning, even as "In my beginning is my end." He notes that Webster's dictionary defines trust, the first of his "ego values" as the "assured reliance on another's integrity." The generations need one another, and hopefully can find in one another's presence the reassurance that makes life bearable, and sometimes much more than that.

In sum, we have a second chart (Figure 2), a second effort to apply "epigenesis" to what Erikson increasingly called "the life cycle." Yet, he is wary indeed of literal-minded readers. He knows how people crave the appearance of order, not to mention anything that lends itself to ritual and faith. "But a chart is only a tool to think with, and cannot aspire to be a prescription to abide by, whether in the practice of child-training, in psychotherapy, or in the methodology of child study." He has specific but limited purposes for his charts and for the concepts they contain. When he talks about "wisdom" and "renunciation" as qualities present in a certain kind of person — who has fought his way to an uncluttered honesty about himself that is in a particular way childlike — he does not refer to "achievements," secured as it were for life at age one or five or twenty-five or sixty-five. On the contrary, he is trying to indicate the unremitting tension that is the very essence of life:

	1	2	3	4	5	6	7	8
VIII Maturity								Ego integrity vs. Despair
VII Adulthood						Generativity vs. Stagnation		
VI Young adulthood					Intimacy vs. Isolation			
V Puberty and adolescence				Identity vs. Role confusion				
IV Latency			Industry vs. Inferiority					
III Locomotor-genital		Initiative vs. Guilt						
II Muscular-anal	Autonomy vs. Shame, Doubt							
I Oral sensory	Basic trust vs. Mistrust							

FIGURE 2

The personality is engaged with the hazards of existence continuously, even as the body's metabolism copes with decay. As we come to diagnose a state of relative strength and the symptoms of an impaired one, we face only more clearly the paradoxes and tragic potentials of human life.[15]

He is trying to weave melodies, some that work and make good music, some that don't, and in fact are noise or worse. I suppose his "method" could be called contrapuntal — or in a way, Hegelian, in as much as it displays a certain dialectic, a certain progressive momentum. What we are emphatically refused is a schedule of "traits." He knows all too well the risks he is taking when he uses words like "trust" or "hope" or "competence." He persists, but he also tries to explain himself:

In giving to these strengths the very designations by which in the past they have acquired countless connotations of superficial goodness, affected niceness, and all too strenuous virtue, I invited misunderstandings and misuses. However, I believe that there is an intrinsic relationship between ego and language and that despite passing vicissitudes certain basic words retain essential meanings.[16]

The chart is not intended to offer all sorts of sweeping generalizations.

If the chart, for example, lists a series of conflicts or crises, we do not consider all development a series of crises: we claim only that psychosocial development proceeds by critical steps — "critical" being a characteristic of turning points, of moments of decision between progress and regression, integration and retardation.[17]

One can sense a man struggling to make his case, to use the chart as a means of highlighting his views (for himself as much as anyone else), yet all the while fearing the very fate some of Freud's ideas came to have. Erikson knew — and wanted to say — how much his chart did not, could not, take into consideration. He knew that people want to *believe*, to believe in ideas, and make of them competitors or warriors as well as objects of devotion. He persisted in developing his charts — and in formulating the stages to which the charts give visual representation — because he felt he had achieved a concrete, coherent point of view that would stimulate in others what he called "thinking and rethinking." In paragraph after paragraph he tried to make sure that he was getting across no more and no less than what he had in mind. Perhaps Kierkegaard's phrase "stages on life's way" summarizes what Erikson wanted to study. Certainly, like Kierkegaard, he saw life as far more than the sum of any or all descriptions. Nevertheless, a psychoanalyst, no less than a theologian, has the obligation to try, to make the search for whatever understanding he can find. Erikson shares Kierkegaard's fear of the twin temptations, intellectual arrogance and willful ignorance — each of them evidence of the worst sin, pride, and each a poor alternative to the other.

Childhood and Society emphasizes the significance of time. The epigenetic viewpoint in some respects comes down to what T. S. Eliot said in "Burnt Norton":

> *Time present and time past*
> *Are both perhaps present in time future,*
> *And time future contained in time past.*

If that is the case, childhood (or any other "period" in life) deserves more than its own analysis. What comes after childhood may well be part of childhood, not because early experiences are endlessly determining, but because we are always what we were, and we always can become what we once were or once might have been. Many in psychoanalysis unequivocally invoke "the shadow of frustration which falls from childhood on the individual's later life." Erikson can put it that way, but go on to find sunlight, too:

In this book we suggest that, to understand either childhood or society, we must expand our scope to include the study of the way in which societies lighten the inescapable conflicts of childhood with a promise of some security, identity, and integrity. In thus reinforcing the values by which the ego exists societies create the only conditions under which human growth is possible.[18]

He not only wanted to pursue childhood over its life-long existence; he wanted to show how achievements as well as problems have a history — one that goes back to childhood. Wordsworth saw a kind of innocence in childhood, and Freud found in childhood the soil of neurosis. To Erikson childhood is the scene of man's beginning *as man*, the place where our particular virtues and vices slowly but clearly develop and make themselves felt. Psychoanalysis may have uncovered "a timeless elite of brooding neurotics" in men like Oedipus, Hamlet and the Brothers Karamazov, but the profession at its best ought to and does feel its kinship to Greek tragedians, English playwrights and Russian novelists — who saw suffering as not at all incompatible with heroism.

To reveal how heroism — or ordinary "goodness" — comes about, Erikson ends *Childhood and Society* with chapters on a nation, a political leader and a writer. Their common theme — once again we meet it — is the influence exerted by social and historical forces on childhood. In essence three nations are discussed: America, Germany and Russia, one through its youth, one through its demonic leader, Hitler, and one through a great writer, Maxim Gorky.

The chapter "Reflections on the American Identity" is rather well known. Its author had been in the country only a little over fifteen years, yet here is how he put into words the mixture of hesitation, curiosity and fascination he felt about his adopted land:

The point is that it is almost impossible (except in the form of fiction) to write *in* America *about* America *for* Americans. You can, as an American, go to the South Sea Islands and write upon your return; you can, as a foreigner, travel in America and write upon taking leave; you can, as an immigrant, write as you get settled; you can move from one section of this country or from one "class" of this country to another, and write while you still have one foot in each place. But in the end you always write about the way it feels to arrive or to leave, to change or to get settled. You write about a process of which you are a more or less willing, but always pleasurably harassed, part, and your style soon runs away with you in the high gear of dithyrambic or outraged expression.

The only healthy American way to write about America for Americans is to vent a gripe and to overstate it. This, however, calls for a delicate gift and for a particular intellectual ancestry, neither of which is easily acquired.[19]

Erikson may not have written about America in the "healthy American way," but he did so with enough discretion and sensitivity to prompt the inclusion of "Reflections on the American Identity" in a contemporary prose reader (*The Personal Voice*), whose editors include Albert Guérard and John Hawkes, and whose contributors range from Agee to Yeats. He speaks about young people and his adopted country, America, as if he were constantly aware that his own destiny had been decided by the way he spent his youth and by the character of the nation he eventually chose. And with particular poignancy he describes America's former and present ambiguities: "open roads of immigration and jealous islands of tradition; outgoing internationalism and defiant isolationism; boisterous competition and self-effacing cooperation." While small children are developing their oedipus complexes they are also learning about the kind of life they will live: migratory or sedentary, individualistic or heavily standardized, predominantly competitive or significantly cooperative, religious or secular.

Actually children do more than merely notice which Main Street is theirs, how large a bank account their father has, and how many cars move along the road. An endless number of assumptions become shaped by very ordinary (called by some people "nonpsychological") experiences. The "deepest" layers of the unconscious are permeated with imagery that prosaic and impersonal shopping centers provide. The child learns his lowliness or his self-assurance near the fireplace and in front of the grocer or druggist. At night he dreams what he has learned, and day after day he consolidates what he has learned into what we, of necessity, have to call something — his ego.

As an American child he learns how Americans move from place to place, satisfy their hunger and thirst, choose their husbands and wives, pick the home on the street they do or do not come to enjoy and call a "neighborhood." As an American child living in the sixties and seventies, he has a certain kind of mother, a "mom" who talks and dresses unlike many other mothers all over the world, and a "mom" who brings up her children in a very particular way.

In point of fact Erikson insists that just about *everything* is relevant to the child's psychological growth. He goes into an analysis of what is popularly called "momism" in American life, but he also shows what a ballad like "John Henry" and music like jazz and "old-time love songs" can tell us about childhood in this country. And the footnotes to his discussion tell their own story. Anna Freud's *The Ego and the Mechanisms of Defense* shares company with Alan Lomax's *Folksong U.S.A.*, A. H. Lewis' *Wolfville Days*, and *Colonel Crockett's Exploits and Adventures in Texas*.

It is all done tactfully and without condescension. Nor are psychoanalytic formulations used to attack people or their customs. Erikson acknowledges that "there is in much of our psychiatric work an undertone of revengeful triumph, as if a villain had been spotted and cornered." He is referring to the fate American mothers have encountered; they are called rejecting, dominating, sadistic, masochistic, schizophrenogenic, and all the rest by doctors who seem a little too casual with labels, a little too eager to use them: "No doubt both patients and psychiatric workers were blamed too much when they were children; now they blame all mothers, because all causality has become linked with blame."

The way Erikson looks at American mothers and fathers comes as no surprise to the reader of *Childhood and Society*, who has been prepared by some three hundred earlier pages for the following kind of psychoanalytic writing:

"Mom," of course, is only a stereotyped caricature of existing contradictions which have emerged from intense, rapid, and as yet unintegrated changes in American history. To find its beginning, one would probably have to retrace this history back to the time when it was up to the American woman to evolve one common tradition, on the basis of many imported traditions, and to base on it the education of her children and the style of her home life; when it was up to her to establish new habits of sedentary life on a continent originally populated by men who in their countries of origin, for one reason or another, had not wanted to be "fenced in." Now, in fear of ever again acquiescing to an outer or inner autocracy, these men insisted on keeping their new cultural identity tentative to a point where women had to become autocratic in their demands for some order.

The American woman in frontier communities was the object of intense rivalries on the part of tough and often desperate men. At the same time, she had to become the cultural censor, the religious conscience, the aesthetic arbiter, and the teacher. In that early rough economy hewn out of hard nature it was she who contributed the finer graces of living and that spirituality without which the community falls apart. In her children she saw future men and women who would face contrasts of rigid sedentary and shifting migratory life. They must be prepared for any number of extreme opposites in milieu, and always ready to seek new goals and to fight for them in merciless competition. For, after all, worse than a sinner was a sucker.[20]

When he moves his discussion from the frontier back to the puritan middle-class towns he does not let himself become puritanically antipuritan: "This much maligned puritanism, we should remember, was once a system of values designed to check men and women of eruptive vitality, of strong appetites, as well as of strong individuality." And what of those towns where fearful but sturdy parents fought hard to teach their children a believable and commanding ethical code — which we much later on call "puritanism"? It probably went something like this:

Towns, too, developed their sedentary existence and oriented their inward life to work bench and writing desk, fireplace and altar, while through them, on the roads and rails, strangers passed bragging of God knows what greener pastures. You had either to follow — or stay behind and brag louder. The point is that the call of the frontier, the temptation to move on, forced those who stayed to become defensively sedentary, and defensively proud. In a world which developed the slogan, "If you can see your neighbor's chimney, it is time to move on," mothers had to raise sons and daughters who would be determined to ignore the call of the frontier — but who would go with equal determination once they were forced or chose to go.[21]

No wonder that mothers tried to make sense of all the stormy movement in American life, with its immigrants, migrants, émigrés, refugees, cowboys, frontiersmen, and transplanted peasants hurrying to sweatshops and factories. In Erikson's words, "The post-revolutionary descendants of the Founding Fathers forced their women to be mothers and fathers while they continued to cultivate the role of freeborn sons." To this day, even though the old-fashioned frontier is gone, Americans are brought up to look around, to move around. Mothers may "dominate" their children for a while, but eventually sons and daughters by the millions move on to other villages, cities or regions. Homes are bought, sold, left behind, and sought out in astonishing succession — and not only by people who *have* to do so, but by those who *want* to move on, who have grown up expecting just that kind of freewheeling life — up and doing, quick on the trigger, on the go, on one's toes and snappy.

In *Childhood and Society* all these "social" or "historical" developments are also looked at as psychological events. Again and again we are reminded that children are taught to understand and join the world of their parents. Again and again we are told that as the child's ego takes on a particular shape from year to year, the mother's psychiatric "problems" or the father's "difficulties" are not the only "forces" at work. Again and again we are made to remember that from the first days of life a boy finds out whether the eight-hour day or the afternoon siesta dominates the country of his birth. The time-conscious American mother — so anxious that her children be regular, punctual and orderly — obviously lives in an industrial society that can only applaud her cooperation.

We often have to be made aware of the obvious. We simply don't think of connecting factory life with infant care, and even less do we stop to consider the historical sources of contemporary psychological behavior. Perhaps we lack the words and concepts that encourage us to do so. In a sense Erikson's use of "identity" was a pioneer act — in which theory is made to chase after and come to terms with "life." He gives the title "Adolescent, Boss, and Machine" to one section of the essay on American identity so that what only appears unrelated may be tied together. Certainly analysts writing about adolescence rarely bring up the industrial and technological forces that make "bosses" direct continuations of "domineering mothers." Like John Henry, whose stubborn triumph over the constricting power of the machine illustrates a fragment of American identity, Erikson seems to be saying that as a psychoanalyst he will try to ask his own questions and supply whatever answers to them he can find — no matter how severely others object. John Henry feared one kind of mechanistic regimentation ("And befo' I'd let that steam drill beat me down"), and in today's America, Erikson sees that professions also have bosses and dominating organizational machinery.

The title *Childhood and Society* indicates the author's intention, and in taking on American youth, their wandering ancestors, their diverse energies and enthusiasms, he showed he meant business. "The American Dream" required the same psychoanalytic attention that any patient's dream received; and so did Hitler's Germany and Gorky's childhood, the subject matter of the book's last two chapters. He wanted to do more than declare himself influenced by New England and California. Step by step he was trying to build a theory that would acknowledge all kinds of things — work, sports, citizenship, schooling — as extremely significant psychological experiences. To do so he, again, needed evidence, concrete examples and illustrations. He refused to make speculation an activity in itself. Every one of his theories is rooted in clinical work, in the observations of an attentive ear and a responsive eye. And from the start he realized there was more to see and hear in this country than the upper middle-class intelligentsia of Cambridge, New Haven and Berkeley provides, and more to the world than Vienna, London, Hollywood and New York City. So he called upon the prairies and the Dakota hills, and upon wayward Germany and imperial Russia.

His paper on "Hitler's Imagery and German Youth" became in *Childhood and Society* "The Legend of Hitler's Childhood," a companion piece to "The Legend of Maxim Gorky's Youth." After the Second World War he had become a consultant to what was called the Columbia University Research Project in Contemporary Cultures. Russia was one nation studied — by a group that was headed by Margaret Mead, and included among other social scientists Geoffrey Gorer and Nathan Leites. On one of his trips to New York (in March 1948) Erikson saw a film (produced in 1938 by a Soviet writer, Mark Donskoi, for the firm Soyuztetfilm) portraying Gorky's childhood. The picture was irresistible to a man who writes words but is still an artist, a man who first sees, and then responds with written thoughts. By 1948 he was rather skilled as an anthropologist and social historian, and *Childhood and Society* was about finished. The years given to carefully editing qualified assertions were over, and the book was allowed to include not only precise formulations but admitted impressions and moments of honest lyricism. Gorky's life offered a chance to work with a wide range of ideas, in the hope that they would not pin down a powerful Russian writer's life, but merely illuminate some of its qualities.

Erikson was after the moving picture's imagery — as he had been in the case of Hitler's *Mein Kampf*. He had tried to understand Hitler, the disappointed boy, the distant cause of an unspeakable national tragedy. In the film on Gorky he saw another legend, another effort to make a particular life representative — for a nation and a moment of history. In certain respects the two legends resembled one another. Each treated of a child struggling hard against more than usual or ordinary odds. Each boy was stubborn. Each fought the will of an old, arbitrary and unsympathetic father (in Gorky's case the man was his grandfather) and both youths paid for their rebellion with moodiness and bewilderment. Gorky as well as Hitler was an intellectual proletarian for a while, known to the police as a weird ideologue, a minor, ineffective troublemaker.

Hitler *became* Germany; Gorky for a while was one of the great idols of Russia, a literary hero to political heroes like Lenin and Stalin. He wrote for the Russian people and they saw themselves in his books and indeed in his life. Erikson contrasts Gorky with Tolstoy and Dostoevsky. Unlike his two great predecessors, Gorky always tried to keep his readers harnessed to everyday life, which he described carefully and vividly. He was not interested in universal problems, in apocalyptic confrontations, in the inscrutable workings of God and History. He was loyal to the Russian peasant's concrete life, his earthly mysticism, his boredom, his warm, animated, affectionate disposition, his dreary surroundings, and his narrow-minded, superstitious and cruelly intolerant world. Hitler the German politician felt vulnerable and wanted, wanted, wanted. Gorky the Russian writer claimed almost defiantly that his country already had everything and needed only the courage to deal with itself.

Erikson starts his analysis in these words:

The film is an old one. At first it makes impossible demands on American eyes and ears. But in content, it seems easy as a fairy tale. It flows along as a loose and sentimental narrative apparently designed to bring the hero, little Alyosha, close to the heart of audiences who recognize in it all their native Russia and their childhood, and who at the same time know that this Alyosha will some day be the great Gorky. In the Russians who saw the picture with me it left only nostalgic pensiveness, and no aftertaste of political controversy. The legend is its own propaganda.[22]

His eyes follow the camera and linger with it on the land, the Russian *mir*, the village that is so much and means so much. "Even death is good if you are in the *mir*," the peasant says, and no doubt tells his children repeatedly. Once more the psychoanalyst looks at empty plains and a holy river; once more he hears folk music and sees people brought together by the ritual of dance; again he confronts the land, the community, the child, and the particular kind of world that day by day "enters" the child's mind, eventually to "live" in it as a whole series of assumptions, attitudes, susceptibilities and inclinations.

The film is described by a man who writes like a veteran critic:

The family is then seen marching up the center of the street tramping heavily in compact closeness, like a procession of pilgrims, or maybe a band of prisoners — or both. Undercurrents of hostile gossip become louder. . . . Now we see this large family at home, crowded into a small room and immersed in a sequence of strange moods. A balalaika suggests tentative tunes of misery and nostalgia. . . . Then we see Gypsy dance the squatting dance.

Gypsy is young and handsome; and as he loosens his sleeves, pulls his shirttails out, and generally "unties" himself, he gives the most relaxedly vigorous performance of the whole picture. He leaps in the air, slaps his heels, and kicks his legs out from under him. The whole crowded room responds, as if in a gay earthquake. The furniture rocks, dishes jiggle, even the water in the decanter sways. . . . These vigorous scenes mark a happy beginning, or rather the reference to a happy past. As Westerners we had better prepare ourselves for the fact that there is no happy ending in this movie: no love story, no success story. What we see at the beginning is the remembrance of things past; at the end there will be a future of which only one thing is certain: it will be bitter. "Gorky" means "bitter."[23]

What about young Gorky's life? Who are his grandparents, his parents and cousins and friends and neighbors? Alyosha (who is Gorky) has to do what children everywhere do: make *himself* out of an assortment of "influences," some of them antagonistic, some all too cumulative. His grandfather is miserly and suspicious. His grandmother knows only how to give and to endure. The father is a provincial functionary, his weakness clothed in a uniform. The mother somehow could not measure up to *her* mother. She left her husband, and seems to have given her son just enough so that he always wanted more. Later in life Gorky would have fits of sadness. Once he would try suicide, and always he would be prone to nostalgia, tinctured however with feelings of doubt and uncertainty.

There are other people in the child's life — because he was a *Russian* child. If both Gorky and his readers never forgot that above all he was Russian, why should a child analyst overlook that fact, consign it to a peripheral sphere of importance, or call it a "derivative" of some sort? Erikson takes note of a decisive, eye-to-eye confrontation between grandfather and grandson and compares it to similar events that regularly occur in Russian literature. Gorky himself described Tolstoy as "with sharp eyes, from which neither a single pebble nor a single thought could hide itself." In "The Russian in Lenin" Trotsky notes that "when Lenin, his left eye narrowed, receives a wireless containing a speech he resembles a devilishly clever peasant who does not let himself be confused by any words, or deluded by any phrases." Whatever we mean by a peasant's "shrewd" glance or the "soulful" eyes of a Russian, their origin probably has to do with the way a nation's culture becomes, for the individual child, a distinct manner of looking, and even more, responding.

As he always does, Erikson draws on history as well as on contemporary writers, artists and political leaders to round out the point of view he is asserting. He begins with a careful survey of Russia's tsardom from its very beginning to its calamitous end. We are not going to have a picture "analyzed" the way all too many lives are, the way books, plays, and historical figures are: there is a mother and a father and a child; they live in a vacuum and they "interact" in one fashion or another; they love one another and hate one another; there is envy, rivalry, and secret admiration; the oedipus complex is obvious, or evident through insistent disguise; and all in all, this comes from that, whereas that means this; so there they are, quite summed up — Gorky, Russia and the movie.

The alternative is to ask questions and supply answers that are suggestive — openly speculative rather than categorical. What happens to a people psychologically when they cease being nomadic and defenseless in order to take up a new life of stabilized indenture? Was the tsar's control of serfs a matter of brute force exerting itself over the generations, or can something more ironic, complicated and even sinister be seen at work? Russia's kings were, after all, holy leaders. The veneration they commanded from the most downtrodden of Europe's peasantry requires more than a passing nod of recognition, particularly in view of the way history has repeated itself in the idolization of Lenin.

More than anything else, Erikson was questioning the relation-

ship between the leader and the led, as it is molded by history and
given expression in political life. He is interested in neither psychological nor economic determinism, but in some plastic combination of psychological analysis and historical perspective that
does justice to the way money and power exert their daily, hum-
drum leverage on both individuals and social institutions such as
schools, churches, the police and the courts. The rural poor become
the urban proletariat. Leaders change their style of rule, and followers change, too. Technological advances are accompanied by dramatic breaks with old values or religious traditions. It is, perhaps,
futile to argue which causes what. Individual men have drastically
affected whole continents, but social and economic changes have
been the necessary prelude to any number of tyrants, kings or presidents. Perhaps as well as anyone Tolstoy described the riddle of history: Do individuals make events, or do a series of events inevitably
produce a certain kind of leader? Did Napoleon settle the fate of
Europe for so many decades, or was Europe bound to have its
Napoleon, given the state of affairs that existed in England, France,
the German states and Russia around 1800? Historians, psychologists and economists sort themselves out when they try to answer
such questions, and Erikson's work can be characterized by the
way he chooses to reply.

In the first place he is candid: "The mysteries of prehistory are
as deep as those of early childhood. They both force us to mythol-
ogize in order to gain the beginning of an understanding." As he
did with American Indians and with Germans, he tries to show
what the Russian peasant does to his children that enables them, in
turn, to become yet another generation of peasants. Settled farmers,
after all, in contrast to wanderers, learn to stay put on the soil and
work it, subdue it, turn it into a reliable provider, and take from it
— but also take care of it and not plunder it so greedily that nothing
is left for the future. Somehow, Erikson postulates, nomadic parents
became peasant fathers and mothers, and in so doing changed psychologically. They had a different world, they saw a different
world, and they set a different example for their children. They
worried about different things, and their prayers changed in content
and style. More subtly, they treated their children differently. They
even shaped their own memories to fit their new desires or values.
If I am on the move, my son's ability to walk and run will not
strike me as just another "step" in his growth, but as an utterly cru-

cial development. If I till the earth, take food from it yet also expect it to come across with food once again a year later, I might be more interested than other people in the child's cycle of demand and surfeit, hunger and eating. Some people, that is, can take food for granted; to others, producing food is a life's job — which means that fears and anxieties associated with taking advantage of the soil and gaining its products inevitably become important enough to help determine the atmosphere a growing child learns to consider his own.

The cycle of planning, working, expecting and gathering up in reward is reinforced in customs, rituals and celebrations. The seasons take on a particular meaning, as do religious holidays and indeed growing up itself. There are long periods of work and restraint, in which anticipation grows out of mingled fear and hope. If all goes well the harvest is good, the fates and Almighty God are found generous after all, and the individual feels somehow congratulated — and for a moment "free" to be wildly, ecstatically grateful. Though sin and expiation, death and redemption are universal opposites, the peasant experiences an intimacy with them that is first of all concrete, but in time symbolic. More generally and abstractly: the mind takes everyday, workaday experiences and uses them as its eyes, so that what we see and find significant varies not only from person to person, but from country to country.

Gorky's life did not tempt Erikson to assert *causes;* once again he claimed only to study psychological variations as they are related to historical events and the circumstances of class, race, nation and culture. He cannot know exactly when or why the Russian nomad stopped exploring the steppes and settled down; nor can he know what then happened in the minds of millions of people. To that extent, as he admits, indeed insists, he has to be "mythological." He has to take what he observes now, among Russians and others, and travel back in time — in the hope of finding at best a presumptive "explanation" that seems to make sense, that is plausible and suggestive, that sheds light.

He does his work by thematic analysis. In Gorky's childhood, as the movie showed it, a number of representative themes do occur — incidents and events experienced by large numbers of Russian children, in contrast, say, to what American or English children go through. One of the children in the film has a lively, spirited temperament, yet incongruously enough his legs for some reason "are not alive, just there." Gorky and the other children want to make him a carriage, a mechanical device that will "free" him, make him no longer subject to his "condition" or situation. To Erikson the scene suggests something else: Russian peasants swaddle their babies, keep them bandaged tightly up to the neck for most of their first year. At the same time the infants are exposed to a remarkably warm and sensual home life, full of talk and vivid, emotional outbursts. Eventually, of course, the swaddled child is set permanently free — though by that time many have to be taught to crawl.

This cycle of restraint and liberty, of physical tightness and psychological exuberance, seems to fit in with what anthropologists have observed about the actions and moods of grown-up Russians. Moreover, the people Russian novelists describe are often both restrained and effusive, detached and suddenly at one with the whole world. Their periodic outbreaks of violence and spirituality, of passions and "fevers" of one sort or another, are notorious and have prompted some observers to talk of the Russian soul as a "swaddled soul" — quiet for stretches of time, but full of desire and turmoil all along.

Erikson carefully states the purpose of his analysis:

However, in order to evaluate the significance of an item of child training such as swaddling in the totality of a culture's configuration, it would be necessary to assume not a single one-way chain of causality in the sense that Russians are the way they are — or like to appear or to picture themselves — because they have been swaddled. As in our discussion of other cultures we must rather assume a reciprocal amplification of a number of themes.[24]

He goes on to stress that swaddling is a universal and practical way of dealing with children, a way especially useful to Russian mothers. ("What other way was there to carry a baby and to keep him warm through a Russian winter?") What has to be studied is the lasting, psychological significance (if any) that the experience of swaddling has — that is, the degree to which a particular experience is but a long and forceful prelude to many others that are in various ways similar. This Erikson does:

We observe a configurational affinity between these facts of Russian tradition. 1. The compact social life in a lonely stockade isolated in the rigors of the central plains and its periodic liberation after the spring thaws; 2. The long periods of tight swaddling alternating with moments

of rich interchange of joyous affection at the time of unswaddling; and
3. The sanctioned behavior of wooden endurance and apathetic serfdom
on the one hand, and on the other, periodic emotional catharsis achieved
by effusive soul-baring.[25]

If Russians had to be serfs, they managed also to keep themselves
intact, and with a "soul." The film (and much of Gorky's writing)
helps us understand what happened more recently when peasants
became industrial workers and as a consequence childhood in Russia
became quite different. The child Gorky turned away from the
land and from a whole climate of feeling, very much as Western
peasants have done in past centuries. With that change came a new
way of living, a new emphasis on doing things, going places, becoming systematic and analytic. The Puritans turned away from
the sensuality they associated with the medieval Church, and Russians like Gorky (who called writers "the engineers of society") lost
all interest in what Erikson describes as "the enchantment of God
as a spirit that enters through the senses as the light of the stained
windows, the fume of the incense and the lullaby of the chant."
No Soviet man loses himself in the Mass, in the tsar, in Holy Russia. Soviet children are not brought up to be still, patient, suffering.
On the contrary, like Americans, Russians are on the move — away
from villages, up from poverty, toward this goal or that "level of
production." Everything important moves — machinery and planes
and cars; and everyone must go along, move along — or be judged
by his "peers" or his bosses or his neighbors or his competitors or
his "congregation" or indeed his own conscience, which now stands
alone, or in the company of mere men. God is not immanent and
sins cannot be confessed and forgiven, or viewed in the perspective
of an unfathomable eternity. Instead sins persist in our *minds*, to
plague us and worry us and drive us on; and children must learn to
feel plagued, to worry, to drive themselves — all of which the
young Gorky learned, an older Gorky wrote about, and a movie
portrayed.

Ironically Erikson would soon move from Gorky to Martin
Luther, from an analysis of Russia's belated Protestantism to a study
of the first and greatest of Protestants. The concluding pages of
Childhood and Society in a way prepare the reader for this outcome. Great stress is put upon the historical tradition that enabled
psychoanalysis to take hold in the Protestant West, where man for
several hundred years had assumed the lonely responsibility of self-

scrutiny. Mention is made again of the treacherous yet inviting terrain that both separates and connects the individual with the political leader and the "man of the hour." There is no summary, though, no prognosis, no final comprehensive theory: "Here I must concede that whatever message has not been conveyed by my description and discourse has but a slim chance of being furthered by a formal conclusion. I have nothing to offer except a way of looking at things."[26]

But a particular vision he did have, and one which possessed a continuity and direction of its own. From children and society he was moving to youth and history. To do so he had to ask briefly whether the shift would lead to anything of value, and to do so he also had to take a brief look at the qualifications and obligations of the professional man (himself as psychoanalyst) who would make the attempt.

It is all very simple and very complicated. As he puts it: "Every adult, whether he is a follower or a leader, a member of a mass or of an elite, was once a child." To some extent, again, we are always children. The mind does not forget, and the many years we are small, vulnerable and dependent are not wiped out by a few inches of height gained in adolescence, or even by a few degrees and a career. It is a commonplace that men (and nations) constantly size one another up, take measure of who is bigger than whom, who has more than whom, who can beat whom in what. Though we often seek to rationalize or justify the reasons we do so — call them "practical," or more specifically, social, political and economic — the ancient Greeks or the prophets and disciples whose words we read in the Bible knew quite clearly what the issue is. *Hubris* or pride is inescapable; it is — in the terminology of contemporary psychology and psychoanalysis — "developmental," or inevitably tied to man's condition, his fate as a slow-growing, potentially anarchic animal who yet can become able to plan and create all sorts of things and ideas. Child psychoanalysts see pride and arrogance every day: children cannot help being frightened and anxious, and in reaction, overbearing and self-important, no matter how careful and attentive their parents are. As children get older they must learn to control themselves, so that anger and covetousness are modulated enough to keep "society" reasonably safe. Yet the very "taming" that makes a child capable of being a "civilized" man guarantees that for the rest of his life he will know what it means to be coerced, to be confronted with forceful persuasion. In that sense, then, the child *is* the man.

Whether Freud believed in God, or not, he had a biblical view of man: no psychological maneuver, no social institution, can make us into something we are not — without sin, or without a certain amount of fear, a certain amount of anxiety. Nevertheless, there are grounds for hope, too. Fear can be reasonable, in so far as it is based on what is actually or potentially dangerous. Yes, we may experience a certain kind of panic that has no validation in the outside world, but rises out of the anarchy or disorder of the mind. But a good deal of what most people call "anxiety" is in fact fear, or anxiety based on very real and frightening situations or past experiences. And certainly an analyst doesn't even want to reduce certain fears: fear of idleness, bombs, polluted air or racism. It is true, though, that a number of psychoanalysts have cultivated an air of detachment that makes one wonder whether Armageddon itself would prompt from them anything but a raised eyebrow. They look at the substantial and concrete and very real fears that people have as further occasions for finding the irrational, the pathological, the "unreal." They are appropriately calm and even-handed in their offices, but they seem to be suggesting something more, an attitude of almost limitless circumspection that can rather easily turn into political apathy and a withdrawal from the world — as if social problems too needed the neutral quiet of a consulting room rather than aroused, active attention.

In any event, at the end we hear from Erikson what all along his book was demonstrating. Because doctors study symptoms, they cannot afford to detach the "minds" of their patients, the "problems" they have, from the lives they live as people, as citizens. Nor are *variations* in behavior to be confused with or called one or another form of psychopathology — particularly since "we have only begun to study the combination and elements which, in a given case, would have resulted in an interesting variation of, rather than a neurotic deviation from, human functioning."

The psychoanalyst not only has to consider his patient's particular social background clinically "relevant," or watch any tendency he has to label people "sick" who in fact are nonconformists; he has to look hard at his own position in a country like America, where "a new system of 'scientific' superstitions" can be the ironic gift that a generation of psychoanalyzed parents bequeaths to its children. Psychoanalysts, like other people bent on making discoveries, run the risk of making their world the whole world. Theoretical constructs meant only to clarify thinking — or indeed enable it — become "the real thing." Since men who build theories also have needs, also want a universe that is understandable and under their control, they turn hypotheses into certainties and make a "design for living" out of their ideas. The result, in the case of a young and aspiring science like psychoanalysis, can be one more secular faith, with all the ritual and dogma that faith inspires in even the most hardheaded and practical of human minds. Erikson's last words in *Childhood and Society* deal with that development, among others, in the history of psychoanalysis:

Much has been said and is being said about the therapist's moral detachment from the multitude of patients who bring to him varieties of conflicts and solutions: naturally, he must let them find their own style of integrity. But the analyst has gone further. In analogy to a certain bird, he has tried to pretend that his values remained hidden because his classical position at the head of the "analytic couch" removed him from the patient's visual field. We know today that communication is by no means primarily a verbal matter: words are only the tools of meanings. In a more enlightened world and under much more complicated historical conditions the analyst must face once more the whole problem of judicious partnership which expresses the spirit of analytic work more creatively than does apathetic tolerance or autocratic guidance. The various identities which at first lent themselves to a fusion with the new identity of the analyst — identities based on talmudic argument, on messianic zeal, on punitive orthodoxy, on faddist sensationalism, on professional and social ambition — all these identities and their cultural origins must now become part of the analyst's analysis, so that he may be able to discard archaic rituals of control and learn to identify with the lasting value of his job of enlightenment. Only thus can he set free in himself and in his patient that remnant of judicious indignation without which a cure is but a straw in the changeable wind of history.[27]

Childhood and Society was published in October 1950, and immediately received an enthusiastic reception from a large number of social scientists who by then had come to know the book's author through his various articles. Some other analysts — Géza Róheim and Abram Kardiner in particular — had also been trying to combine analytic ideas and anthropological observation. Some other analysts had tried their hand at literary criticism or political analysis. Some other analysts felt keenly aware of history, and some others were quite willing to grant adolescence or middle age their own hazards and their own psychological dignity. Yet it is fair to say that no other analyst has taken up *all* those relatively unusual professional interests and fitted them together so elegantly into a broad and sensible point of view.

Unquestionably Erikson can be charged, indeed charges himself, with going his own way and to a degree ignoring the work of others. ("This is and must be a subjective book, a *conceptual itinerary*. There is no attempt at being representative in quotations or systematic in references. On the whole, little is gained from an effort to reinforce as yet vague meanings with seemingly conscientious quotations of vaguely similar meanings from other contexts."[28]) But perhaps he can be forgiven. His own way in fact encompassed many ways, and his aim was not only to wander and explore, but to pull things together or synthesize them. And for his efforts he has earned the gratitude and respect of the leading members of his profession. Heinz Hartmann emphasized to me how successfully Erikson as an analyst has worked with other disciplines:

The danger is always that the result will be a paint job, very superficial; that analytic concepts will be applied here and there but not much will be learned, either by us or the anthropologist or the historian. Erikson has really helped *integrate* psychoanalysis with history and anthropology, and that's a very hard job and an important achievement.[29]

And Rudolph Loewenstein agreed: "He has a feel for things some of us don't know much about. He has broadened analysis very much."[30]

Only gradually would a worldwide audience be reached. The book appeared at the start of a decade that was not to be the most relaxed period in our history; indeed while the manuscript was in press its author became involved in a struggle between the professors of the University of California and its Board of Regents, who in May 1949 had added a loyalty oath to the regular oath of office taken by every teacher. For years the following pledge had been enough: "I do solemnly swear that I will support the Constitution of the United States and the Constitution of the State of California, and that I will faithfully discharge the duties of my office according to the best of my ability." The Regents wanted something added to the oath: "I do not believe in and am not a member

Erik H. Erikson

of nor do I support any party or organization that believes in, advocates or teaches the overthrow of the United States government by force or violence." On April 21, 1950, that loyalty oath was changed into a contractual clause that had to be signed and affirmed every year. The old pledge now had a new section: "and I also state that I am not a member of the Communist Party or any other organization which advocates the overthrow of the Government by force or violence and that I have no commitments in conflict with my responsibilities with respect to impartial scholarship and free pursuit of truth."

Erikson was one of about ninety members of the Academic Senate at the university who refused to sign the contract, and he stuck to his decision even when, one by one, two-thirds of the initially reluctant yielded to the Regents' demand. He and others in the Academic Senate were given a warning. He and others were reappointed because they had declared themselves non-Communist. But a number of colleagues refused to declare themselves anything and were dismissed — whereupon Erikson resigned and wrote out a statement (on June 1, 1950), which eventually was read to the members of the American Psychoanalytic Association at a midwinter meeting, and published in *Psychiatry*:[31]

Dear Sirs:

I deeply appreciate the privilege of a free hearing before a committee of colleagues. With you I shall not play hide-and-seek regarding a question which must be implicit in what you wish to ask me and which must be explicit in what I shall have to say: I am not and have never been a Communist, inside "the party" or outside, in this country or abroad.

Because of my sincere appreciation of the position which I now hold, I shall state (as freely and as briefly as I can) what considerations and feelings have made it impossible for me in good conscience to acquiesce in the latest form of "alternative affirmation" which has been demanded.

I shall not go into matters which carry over from the issue of the special oath. But I may say that the constitutional oath still seems to me to cover admirably and fully my obligations to country, state, and job. I still resent being asked to affirm that I meant what I said when I signed the constitutional oath. One could accept such an additional affirmation wherever and whenever it might seem effective in a special emergency. To me, this contract is an empty gesture toward meeting the danger of infiltration into academic life of indoctrinators, conspirators, and spies. For a subversive person need not have a party card; a conspirator is not bound by declarations; a party member may be unknown to any but a few; a would-be commissar would not ask you for a hearing; and a fanatic indoctrinator may not feel that he lies when he says that he represents objective truth.

One may say, then, why not acquiesce in an empty gesture, if it saves the faces of very important personages, helps to allay public hysteria, and hurts nobody? My answer is that of a psychologist. I do believe that this gesture which now saves face for some important people will, in the long run, hurt people who are much more important: the students. Too much has been said of academic freedom for the faculty; I am concerned about certain dangers to the spirit of the student body, dangers which may emanate from such "compromises" as we have been asked to accept.

For many students, their years of study represent their only contact with thought and theory, their only contact with men who teach them how to see two sides of a question and yet to be decisive in their conclusions, how to understand and yet to act with conviction. Young people are rightfully suspicious and embarrassingly discerning. I do not believe they can remain unimpressed by the fact that the men who are to teach them to think and to act judiciously and spontaneously must undergo a political test; must sign a statement which implicitly questions the validity of their own oath of office; must abrogate "commitments" so undefined that they must forever suspect themselves and one another; and must confess to an "objective truth" which they know only too well is elusive. Older people like ourselves can laugh this off; in younger people, however — and especially in those most important students who are motivated to go into teaching — a dangerous rift may well occur between the "official truth" and those deep and often radical doubts which are the necessary condition for the development of thought.

By the same token, the gesture of the contract will not allay public hysteria. I know that the general public at the moment indulges (as it always does when it is confronted with change) in a "bunching together" of all that seems undefinably dangerous: spies, bums, Communists, liberals, and "professors." A few politicians always thrive on such oversimplification, some out of simplicity, some out of shrewdness. But who, if the universities do not, will lead the countermove of enlightenment? Who will represent, in quiet work and in forceful words, the absolute necessity of meeting the future (now full of worse than dynamite) with a conviction born of judiciousness? If the universities themselves become the puppets of public hysteria, if their own regents are expressly suspicious of their faculties, if the professors themselves tacitly admit that they need to deny perjury, year after year — will that allay public hysteria?

If the Regents and the President had asked the faculty to join in a study of what Communism is — abroad, in this country, and on this campus — a study of what we need and can do about it, and what we need and can do against it; we all would have participated to the limit of our competency. Instead, the faculty was taken by surprise and hopelessly put on the defensive, in this most vital matter. This is a thoughtless, and if stubbornly pursued, a ruthless waste of human resources.

I realize that the University of California is a big place, with many purposes. In many departments the danger which I have outlined will not interfere with the finding and teaching of facts. Mine is a highly specialized place in an area of knowledge still considered rather marginal to true science. My field includes the study of "hysteria," private and public, in "personality" and "culture." It includes the study of the tremendous waste in human energy which proceeds from irrational fear and from the irrational gestures which are part of what we call "history." I would find it difficult to ask my subject of investigation (people) and my students to work with me, if I were to participate without protest in a vague, fearful, and somewhat vindictive gesture devised to ban an evil in some magic way — an evil which must be met with much more searching and concerted effort.

In this sense, I may say that my conscience did not permit me to sign the contract after having sworn that I would do my job to the best of my ability.

ERIK H. ERIKSON
Professor of Psychology and Lecturer in Psychiatry
Berkeley, California, June 1, 1950

VII

Back East

WHEN it became obvious that Erikson's position at the University of California was in jeopardy other institutions began to bid for him. (In 1968 the same university offered him an honorary degree.) He knew doctors at the Menninger Clinic because he had often lectured there. One of them, Robert Knight, had left to become medical director of the Austen Riggs Center in Stockbridge, Massachusetts. When Dr. Knight heard about the impasse between his friend and the California Regents he immediately suggested Riggs as an alternative home — and after much deliberation the offer was accepted.

So again there was a move, a trip back across the continent toward the East, this time to an old New England village surrounded by the Berkshire hills. Dr. Knight was making Austen Riggs into a leading center for psychoanalytic training and research; moreover, its location and buildings allowed the staff to take care of seriously troubled patients without locking them up or confining them to the crowded isolation and abandonment of wards in state hospitals. If the setting was idyllic, and beyond the reach of most people, the small number of doctors and patients could at least try to learn together what is possible, given the best of facilities and psychiatric care.

The ideal patients for such an ideal place are young men and women whose problems are severe but not intractable. For a long while psychiatrists hesitated to say very much about adolescence because it seemed to be by definition a circumscribed period, relatively quick to pass by, and "normally" filled with turmoil and unhappiness. Youth was viewed as a sort of afterthought to childhood, a time when earlier conflicts — for a while stabilized during the "latency" or early school years — become newly assertive and influential as a result of the added biological ("instinctual") energy that exerts its presence upon the mind. In other words, the three "agencies" of the mind have reached a settlement of sorts by the time the child is seven or eight. The libido at the disposal of the id has its various "objects" or avenues of expression, though under the surveillance of a fairly well-developed superego. Meanwhile, the ego is still, as always, trying to reconcile what is wanted and what is forbidden with what is possible, useful and workable "on the outside," the world. It goes without saying that such a state of affairs is changed by physiological adolescence: the id receives new supplies of libido; the superego has a challenge it never thought possible; and the ego is at a loss to know how the whole, disconcerting, eruptive business can be settled to the satisfaction of the particular youth and his society, which can and will take "only so much."

In 1950 such a trinitarian model of mental life badly needed amplification, not only because it gave short shrift to any number of historical, social and cultural forces that every day become authoritatively psychological ones, but also because the model has a stubbornly deterministic air — as if whatever comes after the age of five may only be a repetition or variation of the same old struggle. In the electrical engineer's words, the input may vary, but the circuits are established. Of course, life does indeed have certain common or universal qualities to it, grounded in the unavoidable needs of the body that persist from the start to the finish of the cycle, Erikson's "life cycle." We may be mere waves of consciousness, suddenly here and quickly gone, but for the few years we have (or "are"), a series of inevitable and recurring experiences make us particular men and women: we eat and drink — that is, we take things in and later rid ourselves of water and solids; we sleep, dream, and make love; we fall sick and see others die; we watch our own bodies change, grow, and then begin to weaken; we see and feel; we talk and we listen; we move about, stay still, adjust ourselves to the actions of others; we also adjust to night and day, to the seasons and what they bring. Erikson did not think that his cyclical view of life was original, but he could hardly fail to notice how totally absorbed some of his colleagues were in the first years of the cycle, and as a child analyst, whose job demands watching children as well as listening to adults recall childhood, he must have known how treacherous the mind's leap back in time can be. In any event, we crave first causes, final explanations, decisive reasons, and without God the earliest years of childhood will have to do for people who, like others before them, have turned bits of useful or compelling imagery into cosmic answers to riddles that will probably always be with us. Does life unwind or unravel itself from some intricate "core" that is rather quickly constructed in the first few years? Is life a series of steps, each with one before it and after, and each person's set of steps very much beside and connected to those that belong to others? Are we essentially what we are by the time we start asking questions like these, or are we so many things that it is impossible from moment to moment to say what we are — because the nature of the moment itself "determines" or conspires to bring out what is "inside" us as "potential" or "latent" or "possible"?

Of course a man like Freud was not even trying to answer such questions. He was a clinical investigator, and he made his observations. Nor can he be blamed for dwelling on them; they were his. As few men have done, he discovered one of the chains of cause and effect that bind us all together. He did not make his line of thought and his discovery the entire story; that would be done by those who came after him. Geniuses are self-centered almost by definition, and spend their lives in one or another pursuit; the rest of us are hungry for direction, and quite prepared to find it in whatever ideas we find congenial.

Perhaps only a very special kind of person can follow the leader and yet resist the temptation to idolatry. Some intellectual geniuses want more than attention, more than the acceptance of their ideas; they are chiefs, and they want faithful believers. Should leaders — dogmatic or otherwise — be held accountable for the susceptibilities of their uncritical supporters? Freud wanted his observations recognized for the truth they contained; but unquestionably he was also a law-giver. By his own admission he once dreamed of a career in politics and the law. His ideas challenged those who studied with him in two ways. Could the ideas be accepted on their own merits, no matter how threatening and indeed revolutionary they were? At the same time could they be accepted for what any scientist's ideas are, a tentative, historically suitable way of putting facts or perceptions together and making sense of them?

Ideas, like lives, have a cycle to go through. The pioneer makes his mark on the world; supporters and enemies alike rush toward him. His farsighted vision runs the risk of becoming stupidly attacked, or virtually enshrined and hence subject only to the most decorative or insubstantial of changes. Yet men do come along who are not antagonists or pupils, but students who want to appreciate someone's theories by really using them, that is, finding them valuable here, outdated there, but above all a contagious means of achieving even more discoveries. In Freud's case professional isolation eventually gave way to international fame. Inevitably dissidents appeared, men who weren't happy with this, or objected to that. Men became uncompromising defenders, too — even when the teacher showed himself quite willing and able to modify his own ideas, change them drastically, or abandon them. In turn, some of the critics justified the need for a "defense"; they lingered interminably on what they could not accept, and allowed their objections to be their cause. If it is a pattern that seems very familiar and very human, it is also one that can lead to endless quibbling, squabbling, and worse.

Under such circumstances a man who possesses Gabriel Marcel's "creative fidelity" is desperately needed. A theoretical system has become to a large extent turned in on itself. Growth at best is restricted to cautious modification. Day in and day out a kind of prayerful elucidation goes on. Ideas are called tenets and interpretations are aggressively pronounced — or for that matter, denounced. Around one or another issue "schools" have developed, institutions that by definition aim to preserve and cherish ideas rather than allow them to lead where they may. Worst of all, discussion has become converted into highly personal argument, with the "problems" of the various advocates analyzed as frequently as the problems of clinical practice or research. What is to be done? Will the assumptions that initially inspired a particular method of observation remain the only possible ones for those who want to use the method, or will the method take on a life of its own and be found suitable to a variety of purposes?

From the beginning of his career Erikson seems to have realized that in science and in history what is called "truth" constantly changes, since no "fact" is immune to new information. What remains much longer is a viewpoint or a manner of inquiry. In the case of psychoanalysis it already was quite clear before Freud's death that Freud, like anyone, could be and had been wrong. He himself knew that, and took pains at the end to "reduce" his life-work to a few "essentials," as if to say something like this to those who would claim his mantle: Do not get bogged down in details and factional fights. If I have done anything it is to recognize the importance of childhood, its persisting existence as a state of mind. If I have learned anything it is how to find and comprehend the child in all of us — by listening, by following thoughts and tracking them down, by noticing what happens in me and in the patient as we talk day by day and together slip back in time, as do all people when they become "close," when they are reminded of those first ties, those first "entanglements" or "dependencies" that apparently impress themselves on us forever. Pay attention to *that*, to how we go about our clinical work, to the trouble we meet in doing it, to the larger vision we have of the mind — its capacity to hold secrets, to remember by forgetting, to struggle with the body, the world and the stars themselves.

In *Childhood and Society* Erikson showed how the mind lives in the body and the world, in worlds outside the Viennese consultation room and its equivalent in New York City and Los Angeles. To do so meant thinking of mothers and fathers as quite often different from those Oedipus had. To do so meant ignoring the interminable argument over which of the two is more "influential" — the body's "drives" or the "environment." To do so meant thinking of both mind and body as inevitably headed for a certain kind of historical fate, in which each man's survival, endurance and character depend upon everything from the water and food he does or does not reli-ably obtain to the kind of care and education he may or may not receive.

After all, if I am a psychoanalyst and studying children in Africa, China, or even many parts of America, I cannot assume that a child is not adequately fed or clothed because his mother has a psycho-logical problem of one sort or another. Nor can I assume that what makes a crucial difference to the parents of a two- or three-year-old boy is his ability to control himself and use a bathroom. Kind and generous mothers, who wish their children very well, may have to "deny" them what in fact is not to be had, food. Similarly, children may have to grow up in a home that has no running water, and their parents may get nervous about hunger, not cleanliness. For that mat-ter, grandparents, or brothers, sisters, and cousins, not to mention neighbors, may take care of children and get along with them in ways *we* reserve for the "mother" or the "father" — in which case the child will have his envies and jealousies, but they will not necessarily be part of some "family triangle," or even rectangle or hexagon.

All this Erikson tried to say, and say in such a way that he did not attack what had been discovered simply because it could not account for new or different circumstances and problems. No one can expect Sigmund Freud to have been a cultural anthropologist or a sociologist or a historian. Presumably no one would want to deny Freud (through his views) access to such scholars — who also study what happens to the minds of various men and women on this planet.

Yet it is one thing to be broad-minded, or advocate being so, and quite another to figure out how to go about integrating a given language and method of study with different "fields" or disciplines. Freud himself was very guarded in the way he looked psychoanalytically at artists and writers and in the way that he approached political and historical problems. He made clear what he did not know and what he felt he would never be able to know. He admitted his prejudices, and called a guess a guess. When writing about Dostoevsky he was more the literary critic than the psychobiographer; that is, he analyzed the theme of parricide in *The Brothers Karamazov* but refused to link up Dostoevsky's gifts, or any novelist's literary ability, with this or that psychological problem. When writing about Leonardo da Vinci he disavowed any interest in turning an exceptional man into one more neurotic, driven by his "problems" to what we call "greatness." As if anticipating (in 1910) what would later happen in the name of psychoanalysis he made his position clear:

Let us expressly emphasize that we have never considered Leonardo as a neurotic or as a "nervous person" in the sense of this awkward term. Whoever takes it amiss that we should even dare apply to him viewpoints gained from pathology still clings to prejudices that we have now justly given up. We no longer believe that health and disease, normal and nervous, are sharply distinguished from each other, and that neurotic traits must be considered as proofs of a general inferiority. We know today that neurotic symptoms are substitutive symptoms for certain repressive acts, which must result in the course of our development from the child to the civilized man, that we all produce such substitutive formations, and that only the amount, intensity and distribution of these substitutive formations justify the practical conception of illness.[1]

By no means have all psychoanalysts respected those words. "Applications" of psychoanalysis to the study of history, the art of biography, and the field of anthropology have taken the form of gratuitous labeling: this man was an obsessive type, and his writing shows how fastidious he was, how worried about dirt; that culture is "predominantly oral"; lawyers are working out "superego problems" by struggling with the law, whereas surgeons are "sublimating" various aggressions. If that all sounds — at last — absurd, one need only dip into contemporary professional journals, let alone earlier books and articles, to see how stubbornly such simple-minded and heavy-handed "explanations" persist.

Erikson had literally tried to complicate things, and stop the wholesale transfer of psychoanalytic concepts to Indian tribes or German politicians or Russian novelists. At Austen Riggs — starting in 1951 — he would do more: discover a way of thinking that would enable him and others to use psychoanalytic theory far more sensitively than ever before possible in historical, biographical and anthropological studies. What he had struggled to accomplish in a series of individual instances he at last managed to formulate systematically — so that future investigators could start at a point it had taken him years to reach.

The critical concept is *identity;* by using it over and over again and working for years to give it a particular kind of meaning, Erikson in fact gave real body and strength to the descriptive outline he had made earlier of the stages in the life cycle. It can be said that through his writings on the subject of "identity" he accomplished the single most important shift in direction that psychoanalysis required if it was to become at all useful for other disciplines.

For years psychoanalytic theorists (or the best of them) had struggled with time, had tried to look back yet somehow do justice to man's continuing development, his day-to-day growth — which in fact constitutes his life as a person. The concept of identity is in essence a statement about the past, the present and the future, all three of them abstractions that try to encompass every hour ever spent. A sense of "ego identity" emerges; it is an "accrued confidence" that starts from the very first moment of life but in the second or third decades reaches a point of decisive substance, or indeed fails to do so. Confidence about what? Confidence that somehow in the midst of change one *is;* that is, one has an "inner sameness and continuity" which others can recognize and which is so certain that it can unselfconsciously be taken for granted. The emphasis is on what has taken place that enables what is to continue to be.

And everyday expressions can sometimes make a point far better than more formal explanations: "One can observe a youngster 'become himself' at the very moment when he can be said to be 'losing himself' in work, play or company. He suddenly seems to be 'at home in his body,' to 'know where he is going.' "

Erikson has always liked this passage from William James: "A man's character is discernible in the mental or moral attitude in which, when it came upon him, he felt himself most deeply and intensely active and alive. At such moments there is a voice inside which speaks and says: '*This* is the real me.' " James noted that such experience always includes "an element of active tension, of holding my own, as it were, and trusting outward things to perform their part so as to make it a full harmony, but without any *guaranty* that they will."[2]

James and Erikson both struggled hard to make clear what they knew could only be — but had to be — suggested. Erikson knows when a definition has gone as far as it can. Perhaps the artist in him spared the concept of identity what so many other concepts have had to endure: interpretation, commentary, explanation, and exegesis to the point that an initially whole idea becomes an absurdly splintered and dissected one. For him psychological "elements" or "mechanisms" can amount to much more than the sum of their parts, as anyone knows who has used words or applied brush strokes to a canvas. By definition no analyst can refrain from turning coins over, looking below the surface, and linking contemporary actions to forgotten experiences. But the analyst also has to have a frame of reference, a coherent perspective that enables him to see whole lives as well as defenses and drives. One need not be religious to say we are something more than what our id urges and our ego and superego do in response, or even on their own; in fact one need only be a psychoanalyst — who sees patient after patient, each of them so very different, even if the "problems" they all have and the solutions they manage are for the experienced clinician depressingly predictable.

So it is once again a configuration that we are asked to see, and one that grows over a lifetime. Identity has to do with everything Erikson described in *Childhood and Society*. Hopefully, the infant is held and feels held, craves food and finds his appetites satisfied, looks and sees in return his mother's eyes. The child learns his name, and finds his way about the house and the street. He learns what to wear, how to talk, and how to act in any number of situations. He also learns how others regard him, address him, and respond to him — teachers and neighbors, playmates and classmates, store clerks and relatives. The child feels, and grows to recognize in himself, emotions like desire, anger, hate and envy. He wants people and things; he wants to do away with people and things. He learns what he can do, what he must do, what he wishes he might do; and he also learns what others do in response to his various needs. In fact, it can be said that the child learns, period. At home and at school he takes in information and discovers how to use it. He gains command of his body, begins to feel a certain authority over his immediate world. He can count and read. He lives in 1970, in suburban America — or indeed lives elsewhere and at another time. He can talk and persuade, or plead or give vent to his anger or frustration. He can make known his obedience and his defiance. He can act, and increasingly he can act with the consequences in mind.

When the child becomes what we call an adolescent his mind continues to "develop," to learn and struggle and adjust and make do. Erikson saw adolescence as more than a time of trouble, or of old turmoil newly awakened. Again and again in the years between 1950 (when *Childhood and Society* was published) and 1958 (when *Young Man Luther* appeared) he tried to express what his clinical experience (as well as his work with anthropologists and educators) urged him to take into consideration. The occasion might be the thirty-fifth anniversary institute of the Judge Baker Guidance Center in Boston (1953) or the midwinter meetings of the American Psychoanalytic Association in New York (1953). He might be delivering a lecture to the American Academy of Arts and Sciences (1953 and 1958) or the World Health Organization (1958). The papers had titles such as "The Problem of Ego Identity," "Wholeness and Totality," and "Identity and Totality: Psychoanalytic Observations on the Problem of Youth." For the Children's Bureau of the U.S. Department of Health, Education and Welfare an article called "Ego Identity and the Psychosocial Moratorium" was written. The eleventh annual congress of the World Federation for Mental Health meeting in Vienna heard an address on "Identity and Uprootedness in Our Time."

In a long paper published toward the end of 1956 in the *Journal*

of the American Psychoanalytic Association the issue is stated directly to an audience of analysts:

In a number of writings I have been using the term *ego identity* to denote certain comprehensive gains which the individual, at the end of
adolescence, must have derived from all of his preadult experience in
order to be ready for the tasks of adulthood. My use of this term reflected
the dilemma of a psychoanalyst who was led to a new concept not by
theoretical preoccupation but rather the expansion of his clinical awareness to other fields (social anthropology and comparative education) and
through the expectation that such expansion would, in turn, profit clinical
work.[3]

The author knew he was taking on a lot — something so real and
yet pervasive that it can make a reader or a speaker feel exceedingly
self-conscious, and a man of words up against a mountain of life
itself. In addition, Erikson had to face professional opposition. He
was asking his colleagues to go much further than many of them
were prepared to go at that time. Three leading psychoanalytic
theoreticians (Heinz Hartmann, Rudolph Loewenstein and Ernst
Kris) had just written as follows:

Analysts too are aware of differences of behavior caused by cultural conditions; they are not devoid of that common sense which has always
stressed these differences, but their impact on the analytic observer tends
to decrease as work progresses and as available data move from the
periphery to the center, that is, from manifest behavior to data, part of
which is accessible only to an analytic investigation.[4]

Erikson felt keenly that the relationship between the mind's "inner processes" (the dreams and fantasies psychiatrists try to comprehend) and the "outside world" was central and not peripheral.
He objected to the implications of the phrase "from the periphery
to the center" — as if psychoanalysts would someday find some
"level" of mental activity that is ultimately "deep" and, as it were,
sui generis, that is, removed from the social and cultural "conditions" that strike both analysts and nonanalysts of common sense
as important. He did not find the mind's continuing effort to deal
with social or political realities either a peripheral or superficial preoccupation. The ego, the very ego Freud had described and in his
later years increasingly studied, has no task more "central" than
learning to know where it stands in the eyes of others and in the
light of history. Again and again during childhood the mind comes

to terms with what nature has ordained and a given life in a given society must find important. To his colleagues Erikson put it this way:

From a genetic point of view, then, the process of identity formation emerges as an evolving configuration — a configuration which is gradually established by successive ego syntheses and re-syntheses throughout childhood; it is a configuration gradually integrating *constitutional givens, idiosyncratic libidinal needs, favored capacities, significant identifications, effective defenses, successful sublimations, and consistent roles.*[5]

He was not willing to ignore the need that psychoanalysis has for a concept like "ego identity." Nor would he hesitate approaching what he called "the subject matter of identity" from several angles. He would speak as a clinician, a student of social systems, a teacher, and, not the least, as a man interested in the lives of significant literary and historical figures. He would make reference not only to "ego synthesis," but to "continuity of personal character," to an "inner solidarity" with a surrounding neighborhood or region or nation, to a "sense of individual identity," or indeed to a "worldwide public identity" — such as a man like George Bernard Shaw worked so very hard to achieve.

Always sensitive to artists and writers, Erikson chose Shaw as an ally when the time came to speak most directly and carefully to the psychoanalytic community. At seventy Shaw had prepared a preface to the two volumes of fiction he wrote in his early twenties. The novels were published only because Shaw had become the world-famous G.B.S., and Shaw knew it. He decided to use the event to reminisce, and in fact he came up with an honest, revealing account of his childhood and youth. As always he was ironic and sarcastic — even with himself. He managed to set forth an extraordinary self-analysis and then conceal it with an inimitable and disarming mixture of guile and charm.

G.B.S. — a "public identity" if there ever was one — describes the young Shaw as an "extremely disagreeable and undesirable" fellow who was trying to find his "natural place" in society. He recalls the exceedingly difficult emotional experience he faced: "Behold me therefore, in my twentieth year, with a business training, in an occupation which I detested as cordially as any sane person lets himself detest anything he cannot escape from. In March 1876 I broke loose." He left home, left Ireland, left a comfortable job to which he apparently seemed well suited. During the next "light years of solitude" he tried to make a new life for himself as a writer. He wrote and wrote and wrote; he condemned himself to fill five pages of paper every day, "rain or shine, dull or inspired." He dreaded failure, but he also feared success, at least the kind that would lead him away from his self-imposed exile and isolation. He wanted fame, but he knew that he first had to achieve a certain victory over himself before he could win over everyone else.

Erikson shows how he did both, found the person he wanted to be and gained for that discovery recognition from others. In the course of analyzing Shaw's essay Erikson adds a few observations of his own. He refers to Shaw's "identity crisis," and calls the long period of lonely, introspective writing a "moratorium," an "interval between youth and adulthood" when someone tries to achieve an inner and outer coherence — work that can be enjoyed, self-respect, and the support, the loyalty of others. He also shows how one gifted man did in a dramatic and brilliant way what the rest of us do (or fail to do) every day — pick and choose without quite knowing it from our own past in order to fill up the future with a life that we can call ours.

He carefully traces the origins of Shaw's later characteristics: the snob, the noisemaker, the diabolic as well as brilliant and eccentric playwright and critic. Shaw himself had referred to his "family snobbery mitigated by the family sense of humor." He had also described the incessant music his young ears heard. Members of his family played trombones and violins, harps and tambourines, and they sang all the time: "When I look back on all the banging, whistling, roaring and growling inflicted on nervous neighbors during this process of education, I am consumed with useless remorse." The family also had its "problems": Shaw's father drank much too much, and his mother was a sad and frustrated woman, who could not help her husband and shied away from her three children, one of whom at an early age started writing by making up his own prayers: "literary performances for the entertainment and propitiation of the Almighty." In a religious sense the boy was a devil. Later he would perfect his technique until he became both impish and wrathful, and above all his own unmistakable person.

Shaw said, "I work as my father drank," but Erikson systematically points out how the sensitive and whimsical child turned both the virtues and vices of his parents into a life that was not theirs, yet of them, a life that belonged to no one else, yet in ways resembled many lives. If one asks how it is done, Shaw replies equivocally. He can be willful: "I had to become an actor, and create for myself a fantastic personality fit and apt for dealing with men, and adaptable to the various parts I had to play as author, journalist, orator, politician, committeeman, man of the world and so forth." In contrast he can be fatalistic; he can talk of being "born literate" and born with his political views, his sly and exuberant iconoclasm. To Erikson the paradox is exactly the point: we are not the inevitable products of genes and early childhood experiences, though they strongly influence us. In adolescence we begin to make a series of decisions which reflect what is now possible as well as what once happened. Perhaps the analyst was telling his colleagues that if a very cynical, shrewd and hardheaded critic could live with the ambiguity of human "choice" or "free will" then so could (or should) they.

Since "The Problem of Ego Identity" was written for clinicians, the life of Shaw had to give way to the lives of patients — in this instance young men and women who seek out psychiatric "help" for a series of "troubles," which Erikson considers elements in a clinical picture of "identity diffusion." He draws on cases seen at Austen Riggs, where he was a member of the senior staff from 1950 to 1960, and at the University of Pittsburgh's Western Psychiatric Institute, to which he regularly commuted. At Riggs he saw well-to-do young men and women who had to leave college because they were extremely upset, moody, anxious, paralyzed, and unable to decide what they wanted to "be," or where they wanted to "go." In Pittsburgh he saw the children of workers and of would-be workers who were jobless. He joined the staff of the Arsenal Health Center, worked with Dr. Benjamin Spock, and watched how relatively poor mothers — many recent immigrants — handled their children. He spoke with young men whose fathers worked in the steel mills and with youths who saw little use in a high school education and whose worries did not include a sense of uncertainty about graduate school education. He was interested in the relationship between "the environment" and the mind, and he did not intend to forget that by and large psychiatrists see patients who come from a particular (middle-class) kind of environment. While at Yale he had traveled to see the Sioux. While in California he had left Berkeley — and also the Mt. Zion Hospital and the San Francisco Psychoanalytic Institute — to spend time with the Yurok. In the same vein, he left the little town of Stockbridge, Massachusetts, every two weeks for Pittsburgh's different world.

What he saw all over America and during several decades of observation he described at great length in his explicitly clinical papers on identity. He was talking to doctors about a "syndrome of disturbances" and he spelled the disturbances out, one after another. In a state of "acute identity diffusion" the young individual may feel isolated, empty, anxious, and unable to make any number of choices or decisions that he himself (let alone his parents or teachers) feels pending. He feels threatened by what he senses to be close at hand: the possibility of intimacy, the chance at last to choose a career or find a job, the presence of others, who are seen as competitors, as somehow "better" or less "troubled." He finds himself at a loss, and he fears that the world is breathing hard down his back — ready to restrict him, type him, define him, and thus close him off from any number of possibilities he still finds attractive. He wants "out," he wants to be away, he wants "time" to think and decide and only later act.

It is not all so very pathological. True, plenty is "wrong" — and felt to be wrong by the suffering young man or woman. He or she may seem to be going backward rather than forward. In fact, a retreat to early childhood seems like a happy alternative to any job, any career, any involvement with another human being. Yet the apparently stalemated youth may have found a method in a madness that is more apparent than real. He may be buying time and putting it to the busy use of waiting, testing, trying.

Nevertheless some stumble and go awry, badly so; unlike Shaw they cannot find their own way, and in Erikson's words "they come, instead, to psychiatrists, priests, judges and (we must add) recruitment officers in order to be given an authorized if ever so uncomfortable place in order to wait things out." In the list of people he mentions as helpers or authorities a good deal is implied. One's background determines the person to be approached for advice, and indeed the style in which time is bought — by joining the army, or by getting into trouble with the police, or by going into a morbidly introspective seclusion in which ideas are worked to death and a psychiatrist regularly consulted.

Perhaps more than anything else the hazards of closeness or intimacy challenge young people — and all of us, who so often become "grown up" by escaping from feelings rather than confronting them. Erikson's chart in *Childhood and Society* indicated that the struggle for a sense of identity becomes in time a struggle to live with others, significant others. In effect a young person's struggle for identity constantly forces him to set himself off, to know himself by the company he keeps or chooses to ignore and even flee. Eventually he will find somebody he wants and considers *his*, or he will find no one. At twenty he is wan and aloof, afraid to go very near anyone; and that is recognized as "part of growing up." If at thirty he still shuns people, all people except strangers and the most casual of acquaintances, we begin to think of him as a loner. If he could talk about himself we would hear how hard it is for him to "give himself" to others, to feel close to them, to accept from them or feel accepted by them, to feel *himself* in their presence.

Nowhere is Erikson more pointedly and comprehensively descriptive than in his attempt to convey the sense of what he means by "identity." Since he does not want to settle for yet another psychiatric category, he has to apologize for going "all over the map," but it is a map he knows well and covers in fine detail. We really get to know the youth who is all mixed up, who feels like a child and like an old man, who can do nothing for very long without hating both his work and himself, who seems to turn on himself with a vengeance and become everything he was brought up not to be, who feels like a wanderer, a drifter or an outcast — at once eager to obey slavishly and repudiate violently.

The youth who seeks "tentative forms of playful intimacy in friendship and competition, in sex play and love, in argument and gossip" fears that for reaching out he or she will be slapped down, and thus lose whatever it is that is him or her. No wonder "a tense inner reservation, a caution in commitment" seems at least prudent if not altogether desirable. On the other hand, there are times when at any cost the youth "wants to be an apprentice or a disciple, a follower, sex mate or patient," anything to belong. Conflict seems to touch every minute of the day, every look into the future, and "portents of missed greatness and of a premature and fatal loss of useful potentials are common." There is a "decided belief in the possibility that time may bring change, and yet also a violent fear that it might." The patient, the young man or woman, seems slowed up, "as if he were moving in molasses." He finds it hard "to go to bed and to face the transition into a state of sleep, and it is equally hard for him to get up and face the necessary restitution of wakefulness; it is hard to come to the hour, and hard to leave it." On the brink of life, he or she seems determined to quit, to give up and retire for good from the impossible burden of the self.

There are other signs of "identity diffusion," of an "identity crisis." One minute the individual may not be able to concentrate at all, the next he seems lost in thought. Often there is "an excessive awareness as well as an abhorrence of competitiveness." To all outward appearances the person may have been doing fine — "successful in office work, in scholastic studies and in sports" — when suddenly he seems unable to work, to exercise, to get along with people. He is at the mercy of "formless fantasy" and vague but persistent anxiety. In some instances — perhaps the most obvious and publicized — another tack is taken:

A scornful and snobbish hostility [develops] toward the roles offered as proper and desirable in one's family or immediate community. Any part aspect of the required role, or all parts, be it masculinity or femininity, nationality or class membership, can become the main focus of the young person's acid disdain. Such excessive contempt for their backgrounds occurs among the oldest Anglo-Saxon and the newest Latin or Jewish families; it easily becomes a general dislike for everything American, and an irrational overestimation of everything foreign. Life and strength seem to exist only where one is not, while decay and danger threaten wherever one happens to be.[6]

For clinicians there are a number of examples to be had, fragments from case histories that illustrate what Erikson is getting at. A young man was plagued by his own critical voice; whatever he did was "phony." On the way from his home to his college he went through the poorer sections of several cities, and felt that "life really existed in those places and that the campus was a sheltered, effeminate place." There are those who one after another seek out everything they have been told is "wrong." They not only sweat and tremble themselves; they flirt with the law, and tease the police — just enough to worry their parents, but not enough to get into serious trouble.

In some, failure is sought out openly and vigorously, to the point that the youth feels he would rather "be nobody or somebody bad, or indeed, dead — and this totally, and by free choice — than be not-quite-somebody." Erikson describes such an attitude as a "rock-bottom" one, an almost deliberately negative search for the self, done with "devastating sincerity." A patient put it this way: "That people do not know how to succeed is bad enough. But the worst is that they do not know how to fail. I have decided to fail well." He could fall back on nothing but doubt, nothing but failure, both to be realized on a grand scale.

Young people are struggling to find the rituals, habits and assumptions that the rest of us take for granted and call (perhaps only if asked to think about it) a "way of life" or "everyday existence." In a ghetto or the wealthiest suburb they ask "why?" I once heard a black youth in the Mississippi Delta put the matter of identity as follows: "I don't know how it came that I'm here, and not someplace else, where if I was there I guess I would be different. And I keep asking myself if I'm going to be like my folks, or if I'm going to be different. And I don't know because you never can tell what will happen to you these days of trouble, and what you'll do when it does happen, I guess." He knew without "knowing it" what Erikson was trying to formulate.

For that matter, all too many psychiatrists fail to consider the issue of their own identity — and how their own training, their own analytic experience affects the view they have of themselves. Patients (including young psychoanalysts in training, hence in treatment) not only fear to learn certain "facts" about themselves; they may fear that the price of self-knowledge, the price of a "successful psychotherapeutic relationship" will in fact be that "the analyst, because of his particular personality, background or philosophy may carelessly or deliberately destroy the weak core of the patient's identity and impose instead his own." That is, a person in treatment may do more than "resist" insight or deny to himself the particular kinds of emotion that psychoanalysis again and again brings forth. He may feel that something more profound and critical is at stake, his dignity, his right to be himself — analyzed yes, but himself and not a stereotyped product of a "system," even if it be a system of psychiatric practice or "technique."

In the mid-fifties Erikson was mentioning — almost as an aside to his larger concern — an issue that would become much more significant a decade later: psychoanalytic training, too, can become rigid, doctrinaire, and insistently ideological. Young people covet something to believe, to believe totally and without reservation, even as they also dread the surrender that all faith asks. And among

young people one may find physicians who want to be psychoanalysts, and patients who have — besides "neurotic" problems —
all sorts of ethical, religious and philosophical needs and doubts. For
that matter, "it stands to reason that a communal setting such as a
hospital is characterized not only by the identity needs of those
who happen to be the patients, but also of those who choose to become their brothers' (and sisters') keepers."

So the last part of "The Problem of Ego Identity" makes a vivid
summary of the convergent themes of identity and ideology by trying to bring the reader, the professional reader, back to his own life,
as a person who has become a physician and a psychoanalyst.

In order to approach this whole matter psychoanalytically, it may well
be necessary for the individual psychoanalyst to ask himself what particular configuration of drives, defenses, capabilities, and opportunities
led him into the choice of this ever-expanding field. Some search in this
area may clarify the fact that some of the most heated and stubborn
answers to the question of what psychoanalysis *is* or *is not* originate in
another question of great urgency, namely: what psychoanalysis must be
(or *must remain or become*) to a particular worker because a particular
psychoanalytic "identity" has become a cornerstone of his existence as a
man, a professional, and a citizen. I am not denying here the necessity,
in a suddenly expanding and unexpectedly popular field, to define the
original sources of its inspiration and the fundamentals of its specific
morality. Yet, psychoanalysis, in its young history, has offered rich
opportunities for a variety of identities: it gave new function and scope to
such divergent endeavors as natural philosophy and Talmudic argument;
medical tradition and missionary teaching; literary demonstration and
the building of theory; social reform and the making of money. Psychoanalysis as a movement has harbored a variety of world images and
utopias which originated in the various stages of its history in a variety
of countries, and this as a result of the simple fact that man, in order to
be able to interact efficiently with other human beings, must, at intervals,
make a total orientation out of a given stage of partial knowledge. Individual students of Freud thus found their identity best suited to certain
early theses of his which promised a particular sense of psychoanalytic
identity, and with it, an inspiring ideology. Similarly, overstated an-
titheses to some of Freud's tentative and transient theses have served as
bases for professional and scientific identities of other workers in the
field. Such identities easily find elaboration in ideological schools and in
irreversible systematizations which do not permit of argument or
change.[7]

Then a little further on, Shaw is asked for help:

"I was *drawn into* the Socialist *revival* of the early eighties, among Englishmen *intensely serious* and *burning with indignation* at very *real* and very *fundamental evils* that affected *all the world*." The words here italicized convey to me the following implications. "Drawn into": an ideology has a compelling power. "Revival": it consists of a traditional force in the state of rejuvenation. "Intensely serious": it permits even the cynical to make an investment of sincerity. "Burning with indignation": it gives to the need for repudiation the sanction of righteousness. "Real": it projects a vague inner evil onto a circumscribed horror in reality. "Fundamental": it promises participation in an effort at basic reconstruction of society. "All the world": it gives structure to a totally defined world image. Here, then, are the elements by which a group identity harnesses in the service of its ideology the young individual's aggressive and discriminative energies, and encompasses, as it completes it, the individual's identity. Thus, identity and ideology are two aspects of the same process. Both provide the necessary condition for further individual maturation and, with it, for the next higher form of identification, namely, the solidarity linking common identities. For the need to bind irrational self-hate and irrational repudiation makes young people, on occasion, mortally compulsive and conservative even where and when they seem most anarchic and radical; the same need makes them potentially "ideological," i.e., more or less explicitly in search of a world image held together by what Shaw called "a clear comprehension of life in the light of an intelligible theory."[8]

The word "ideology" as Erikson uses it is not all bad, or nearly as sinister as any number of ideologues have given us cause to believe. He is trying to show that to some extent we all have a "world view," a distinctive set of persuasions, convictions, opinions, or articles of faith. Even fads and crazes bear a relationship to what is old and staid. One person's last word may be someone else's idea of nonsense, but everyone has at least an implicit notion of what life is and ought to be about.

Ideologies and values change, though, and Erikson has given his later life to the study of how particular individuals (Luther and Gandhi) take the lead in bringing about those changes. The young need to sort out what is believable. Sometimes they make a show of scorning what they quietly accept only a few years later; but sometimes they look in vain for an inspiring institution. They may be alive at a moment in history when collapse or decay threatens their society, and thus be particularly sensitive to whatever "new" ideas or actions appear. A man, a slogan, a deed, an event gets them going. Psychologically hungry — and maybe in need of real food, too — they start marching, or praying, or shouting. They and their newfound leaders have found an answer, a different direction to take, a revolutionary program.

Historians and political scientists take note of what happens, of deeds done and corners of history turned, but they usually fail to analyze how leaders engage with followers, how men of ideas summon youth bent on action. But who is a "great man"? He is an individual who becomes for his own reasons a public force — because conditions in the world make it possible. He is the kind of individual Erikson found himself able to study through the formulation of concepts like *identity*, *identity crisis*, and *moratorium*. Here is how he began to connect the leader and the led, political or social movements and the mass participation they command:

Ideologies seem to provide meaningful combinations of the oldest and the newest in a group's ideals. They thus channel the forceful earnestness, the sincere asceticism, and the eager indignation of youth toward that social frontier where the struggle between conservatism and radicalism is most alive. On that frontier, fanatic ideologists do their busy work and psychopathic leaders their dirty work; but there, also, true leaders create significant solidarities. All ideologies ask for, as the prize for the promised possession of a future, uncompromising commitment to some absolute hierarchy of values and some rigid principle of conduct: be that principle total obedience to tradition, if the future is the eternalization of ancestry; total resignation, if the future is to be of another world; total martial discipline, if the future is to be reserved for some brand of armed superman; total inner reform, if the future is perceived as an advanced edition of heaven on earth; or (to mention only one of the ideological ingredients of our time) complete pragmatic abandon to the processes of production and to human teamwork, if unceasing production seems to be the thread which holds present and future together.[9]

Of course he knew that larger ideological "movements" or systems can never really exclude islands of resistance or deviation. Within any society there are those who choose to say no rather than yes — and join cliques, gangs, mobs, rings or circles. Some are called criminals, some eccentrics, some "elitist" individuals who comprise a "formation" or a "set." What, in fact, makes us consider one person or one group "dangerous" and another "stimulating" or "challenging"? Can anyone study either individuals or societies with a "frame of reference" — as one hears it put — that is "value-free" or "culture-free"? Erikson was trying, perhaps hopelessly, to free himself of a hazard he and his fellow analysts constantly face and had better at least acknowledge: clinical categories can become pejorative, moralistic, partisan words. He was aware, for instance, of the dangers his own use of the term "negative identity" could generate. He insisted that he was not judging a person "negative," but describing the consequences of a psychological response that inevitably takes a certain social form. Indeed, the commentator, the man who sees, analyzes, and narrates, has the right — perhaps the obligation — to state his own social views, some of which may make him want to call a particular person's "negative" identity "positive," even though the "facts" — of money, power, caste and class — make it impossible to do so, at least if society's judgments are considered significant. At the end of a very long paper Erikson takes note of the problem, as if anticipating that his terms, too, can be used to pinion youths rather than help understand both them and the particular commitments they either make or strenuously avoid:

If, for simplicity's sake or in order to accommodate ingrown habits of law or psychiatry, they diagnose and treat as a criminal, as a constitutional misfit, as a derelict doomed by his upbringing, or — indeed — as a deranged patient, a young person who, for reasons of personal or social marginality, is close to choosing a negative identity, that young person may well put his energy into becoming exactly what the careless and fearful community expects him to be — and make a total job of it.[10]

As one reads the sentences above, or indeed any of Erikson's attempts to grapple with the exceedingly elusive yet enormously suggestive and by now celebrated concepts of identity, there is always the temptation to invoke the psychoanalyst's option — some would call it an indulgence — and ask *why*. Why did he preoccupy himself with such a problem, such "subject matter"? And why did he do it so persistently, elaborately, singularly and vividly? Why has his work, in a way his struggle, rung so many bells with so many people, both within and without the psychoanalytic profession — and especially in America?

Because in many of his first papers on identity one can almost feel him there, though he takes care to hide himself behind a relatively impersonal and scholarly but lively text, I asked Erikson about his own life, his own youth. He responded in this way:

Yes, if ever an identity crisis was central and long drawn out in somebody's life it was so in mine. Let me tell you some of my marginalities. To begin with I never knew my father. Both my parents were Danish, but they were separated when I was born and my mother first raised me among strangers, in Germany. Eventually, she married my pediatrician and I grew up in Karlsruhe in Baden. He was Jewish. I was blond and grew tall and the Jewish boys nicknamed me "the goy." In school, I became a German superpatriot to live down my Danishness (the Danes wanted to steal Schleswig-Holstein, you remember) and then found that my Jewishness was too much for the patriots, and their anti-Semitism too much for me. In adolescence, I was morbidly sensitive but luckily also gifted enough to become a plausible artist of the wandering type, then in Europe a sort of transitional beatnik. And I did wander, in the Black Forest, the Alps, and in Northern Italy. This made me sturdy physically and balanced in a sensory way: drawing is a good way to become observant. Later psychoanalysis added a certain inner sturdiness; but I often wonder whether this prone and wordy procedure is good for people who have not been ambulatory and generally curious first. Maybe, because of all of this, I recognized in maladjusted children and youths the need to move and to be moved and not just feel driven and to reflect on it. At any rate, in formulating all that, I found my style and professional identity, which must be one explanation for the impact of *Childhood and Society*. But a condition for my effort was, of course, the fact that the Freudian circle in Vienna were hospitable to an occasional non-physician and provided full training.

Then I met Joan, who was studying European schools of dancing. She is Canadian and the daughter of an Episcopal minister. We married and came to this country. That meant I had to acquire a new language in my thirties, while of all things German certainly the language had become most part of me; but luckily the German "Humanistische Gymnasium" had also provided me with a good foundation in Latin and Greek.

In the American Psychoanalytic Association I was probably the only member who had not completed any kind of college. But, being a fully trained psychoanalyst, I received only support. Only, when made a training analyst, I could train no one but physicians. In the meantime, Harvard, in 1934, had found a place for me on the Medical School Faculty. You can see, I had to strive doubly to become a reliable professional man, without sacrificing my privilege to roam and to observe.

You rightly ask about the Jewish part of my background as an identity issue: my mother's family was Jewish, but in Denmark baptism and intermarriage are old customs, so one of my ancestors (so she told me) was chief rabbi of Stockholm and another a church historian and pastor in H. C. Anderson's home town.

I have kept my stepfather's name as my middle name out of gratitude (there is a pediatrician in me, too) but also to avoid the semblance of evasion.

But I think that one's sense of identity should not be restricted to what one could not deny if questioned by a bigot of whatever denomination. It should be based on what one can assert as a positive core, an active mutuality, a real community. This would force fewer people to become (because they try too hard not to become) radical and religious caricatures. It would also force a new standard on communities: do they or do they not provide a positive, a nonneurotic, sense of identity? Jewishness as such has meant little to me, although I would consider some of the Jewish elements in psychoanalysis ancestral in my work. What some genuinely Lutheran elements in Christianity have come to mean to me is indicated in my book on young Luther.

So, it is true, I had to try and make a style out of marginality and a concept out of identity-confusion. But I also have learned from life histories that everything that is new and worth saying (or worth saying in a new way) has a highly personal aspect. The question is only whether it is also generally significant for one's contemporaries. That I must let you judge. But let me add that a concept of identity is only as good as the conception of the life cycle of which it is nothing but a stage, if ever so crucial. Obviously, there is a core to each man which transcends his psychosocial identity. I hope to get to that . . . but first, men on this earth owe each other something like what I call identity.

Erik Erikson as a youth took a long time and had a hard time coming to terms with himself and with the Danish-German "world" in which he grew up. Erik Erikson, the American psychoanalyst, teacher and writer, had a second "identity crisis" or struggle in the decade from 1950 to 1960, years that were for the most part his as well as the twentieth century's fifties. His thinking, both programmatic and fluid, became increasingly influential and he must have been tempted at forty-eight to sit back and do nothing but let his reputation slowly build. *Childhood and Society* was, after all, the culmination of many years of work; and its message, its style, its tone were almost desperately needed at the time it was published. Psychoanalysis was in danger of becoming a stuffy, obscurantist field — at once removed from medicine as well as from the universities of the West — and very much a piece of property, to be possessed or partitioned by all sorts of mutually suspicious and antagonistic cliques. Erikson's ideas offered a way out of, a way around, hair-splitting conceptual and methodological arguments;

and though his book did not put a stop to rancor and narrow-mindedness in the psychoanalytic "movement," he and his viewpoint did become a rallying-ground for younger psychoanalysts and psychiatrists, not to mention interested laymen. He was neither an "orthodox" Freudian, nor a "neo-Freudian," and certainly he was not "anti-Freudian." In fact he was trying very hard to follow Freud's example rather than his every word, to bring Freud's ideas up to date, to fit them into new historical knowledge. And in so doing he did not use hindsight to attack and discard early psychoanalytic formulations. Quite the contrary: he tried to show what Freud had done, and why, at a particular moment in the development of both neurophysiological and psychological knowledge.

Though his psychological and biographical essays on Hitler, Gorky and Bernard Shaw are well known and his book *Young Man Luther* even better known, relatively little attention has been given to Erikson's several efforts to comprehend Freud's life. In all he published three papers on Freud between 1954 and 1956, years in which he was also studying Luther's life. A psychoanalyst could therefore say that Freud was very much on Erikson's mind for a period of time, or that "for some reason" Erikson "had" to write about Freud at that point. Of course there were "external" reasons to "explain" each article: "The Dream Specimen of Psychoanalysis" (1954) was first given as two lectures at the San Francisco Psychoanalytic Institute. "Freud's 'The Origins of Psychoanalysis' " (1955) was written as a long book review for the *International Journal of Psychoanalysis*, and "The First Psychoanalyst" (1956) was originally delivered in German at Frankfurt to a combined audience from the universities of Frankfurt and Heidelberg on the occasion of Freud's hundredth birthday. Yet Freud's ideas and words dominate the thinking of *all* psychoanalysts, so that in looking at these three articles — in many ways one long statement — one has to ask exactly what about Freud so pointedly absorbed Erikson's attention at that particular time.

Actually, Erikson was beginning to look at Freud as a social historian might. He was a man who had fathered a new intellectual tradition. Psychoanalysts justly revere him, and every day learn what he enabled them to learn. Yet who *was* he? That is, what kind of person, from what kind of social and cultural background? Even more important, how did it happen that he did what he did, strike out so forcefully and boldly on his own? And how is it that his personal and intellectual struggle became so significant and so influential — for certain people in certain countries? By reading Freud's writings with these kinds of questions in mind, Erikson was in fact enlisting help in his own effort to forge ahead and not only add to an existing (psychoanalytic) edifice, but build a new one, adjacent and very much similar in appearance, yet designed for different purposes.

The contents of Erikson's essays do not lack Freud's analytic attitude, his ability to elevate the concrete and specific into the realm of the universal, and his literary skill. I believe that Erikson's essays on Freud bear the same relation to *Young Man Luther* that Freud's "Three Contributions to a Theory of Sex" do to *The Interpretation of Dreams*. In each case essays become satellites, the offspring of major works. Once Freud had delivered himself of his book on dreams he went on to discuss in a very theoretical way the source of dreams — in the sexual conflicts and tensions man never really shakes off. While Erikson was working on Luther's life (the book carries the subtitle "A Study in Psychoanalysis and History"), he also had to find and give expression to a theory that would enlarge the scope and relevance of his observations. And like Freud he had to call on others. Freud had invoked Shakespeare and Sophocles, and even his contemporary, Wilhelm Fliess, to justify and sanction his discoveries. Perhaps for the same reason Erikson turned to Freud. As one reads, say, "The Dream Specimen of Psychoanalysis" the message to Freud can be read, even though the author never puts it into these words: I am not only learning from you, and practicing a profession you founded; I am moved by a spirit you knew so very well, an urge to explore new territory, not in defiance of you, or to "revise" your ideas, but to honor you, a very creative man, by following suit the best I can, with whatever energy and originality I can summon. Of course, to do so requires some nod from you — and I mean *you*, not any self-appointed heirs who claim to be the authoritative guardians of your every word. So I am going back to your most vigorous, dissenting and productive years, when you stood alone and began to speak thoughts that could earn you only the criticism and rebuke of conventional and compliant colleagues. If I am to follow the example of those years, perhaps I should let my convictions lead me where they will, and I will be glad to let others quibble about what is or is not the prevailing orthodoxy of the day.

So in 1954 Erikson went back to the beginning, the unsettled and confusing beginning. He called it an "attractive task" to return to the dream Freud first interpreted, now called the Irma Dream. The dream took place in Freud's mind, but Erikson was not going to go over once again the infantile and neurotic conflicts that "produced" such a dream, or "caused" the dreamer to have it. He wanted rather to look at "the moment in Freud's life when it was dreamed — the moment when creative thought gave birth to the interpretation of dreams."

Freud himself wrote that perhaps one day the dream he had about his patient Irma would be commemorated by a tablet that would adorn his summer home and proclaim to the world: "In this house, on July 24, 1895, the mystery of the Dream unveiled itself to Dr. Sigmund Freud." Erikson saw every reason to take note of that remark, the fantasy of an exceedingly creative man who had no trouble recognizing that the unconscious not only "contains" memories but lives in history and even makes it. In fact he was writing a paper to suggest that Freud's dream reveals something more than concealed (and of course "infantile") wishes. Freud's dream may "carry the historical burden of being dreamed in order to be analyzed, and analyzed in order to fulfill a very special fate."

For a change, the psychoanalytically trained or "oriented" reader is asked to look "deeply" into a dreamer's present as well as his past, into his wishes for the future as well as his early desires, into his struggle to make *use* of his life as well as his struggle *with* life. To Erikson, the Freud who dreamed the Irma Dream was, of course, a man trying to fulfill wishes awakened by events of the previous day, and, of course, a man whose drives appeared at birth, whose conflicts appeared soon thereafter, whose mind again and again had to go backward to its first and unforgettable experiences. *But Freud was also Freud:*

The dreamer of the Irma Dream was a thirty-nine-year-old doctor, a specialist in neurology in the city of Vienna. He was a Jewish citizen of a Catholic monarchy, once the Holy Roman Empire of German Nationality, and now swayed both by liberalism and increasing anti-Semitism. His family had grown rapidly; in fact, his wife at the time was again pregnant. The dreamer just then wished to fortify his position and, in fact, his income by gaining academic status. This wish had become problematic, not only because he was a Jew but also because in a recent joint publication with an older colleague, Dr. Breuer, he had committed himself to theories so unpopular and, in fact, so universally disturbing that the senior co-author himself had disengaged himself from the junior one. The book in question (*Studies in Hysteria*) had emphasized the role of sexuality in the etiology of the "defense neuropsychoses," i.e., nervous disorders caused by the necessity of defending consciousness against repugnant and repressed ideas, primarily of a sexual nature. The junior worker felt increasingly committed to these ideas; he had begun to feel, with a pride often overshadowed by despair, that he was destined to make a revolutionary discovery by (I shall let this stand) undreamed-of means.[11]

In other words he was a particular man who faced a particular set of circumstances at a particular moment in his life — and ultimately, in the life of an entire civilization.

This, then, is the situation: within an academic milieu which seemed to restrict his opportunities because he was a Jew; at an age when he seemed to notice with alarm the first signs of aging, and, in fact, of disease; burdened with the responsibility for a fast-growing family — a medical scientist is faced with the decision of whether to employ his brilliance, as he had shown he could, in the service of conventional practice and research, or to accept the task of substantiating in himself and of communicating to the world a new insight, namely, that man is unconscious of the best and of the worst in himself. Soon after the Irma Dream, Freud was to write to his friend Fliess with undisguised horror that in trying to explain defense he had found himself explaining something "out of the core of nature." At the time of this dream, then, he knew that he would have to bear a great discovery.[12]

Freud's dream and his interpretation of it are now a significant part of Western man's past. He distinguished between what his dream obviously had to say and what he found it saying upon analysis. To bridge these two messages, the "manifest dream" and the "latent dream," requires study of the dream "work," the mind's use of imagery, of memory, imagination and fancy, of irony and ambiguity and figurative language — all to express and at the same time conceal desires. He pointed out how revealing the mind's associations can be: one dream can ultimately lead anywhere and everywhere as the person allows himself to go from thought to thought, each connected to the next, in a chain that sometimes seems endless. Freud wanted to make discoveries, and his dream was an exciting opportunity to do so. Even today one can feel the explorer's surprise and sense of victory as he lets his daytime thoughts bring out a kind of truth that his fleeting night-time vision could only hint at.

Yet Freud never intended that dreams be classified and turned into "types": incest dreams, or rape dreams, or dreams "about" murder. He knew that "the dream is fundamentally nothing more than a special *form* of our thinking, which is made possible by the conditions of the sleeping state." As a kind of mental activity the dream can only have meaning when it has a context, which only a person's life can provide. Nor is there some fixed and hidden "kernel," some specific and buried center of "real truth" in every dream. Imagery was important to Freud, and imagery is still important, said Erikson:

The psychoanalyst, in looking at the surface of a mental phenomenon, often has to overcome a certain shyness. So many in his field mistake attention to surface for superficiality, and a concern with form for lack of depth. But the fact that we have followed Freud into depths which our eyes had to become accustomed to does not permit us today to blink when we look at things in broad daylight. Like good surveyors, we must be at home on the geological surface as well as in the descending shafts. . . . We hurry at every confrontation with a dream to crack its manifest appearance as if it were a useless shell and to hasten to discard this shell in favor of what seems to be the more worthwhile core.[13]

Erikson wanted to show how utterly profound an analysis of the so-called surface can become, especially the dream's "manifest content" — that is, what the patient remembers and tells the analyst. He picks up those "shells," those leftovers of interpreted guile or evasion; and in them he finds the dreamer's *particularity*. In other words, a given patient's dream may be short or long; it may be primarily a series of quiet, black and white scenes, or it may be dominated by talk or noise or even color; it may contain one person or many people or indeed no one; it may take place at one time or occur in sequences. The dreamer may have felt any number of sensations — pain, excitement, passion, fright — or he may report a bland almost lifeless experience; he may have seen himself and others as always in action, always moving about — embracing, contending, running — or he may find it hard to recall anything but a "picture" or two, a hushed countryside or a room whose occupants are frozen and still.

Again, dreams vary in style, and Erikson agrees with Henry James that the most apparent and conventional behavior — in a real parlor or in one that is dreamed up — can tell the interested observer all sorts of things about our "inner" selves. Erikson was emphatically *not* disputing the value of "traditional" psychoanalytic dream interpretation. He unequivocally accepts Freud's hypothesis that we have in us urges and strivings that are universal, biological, rooted in human development. From the start of life we crave food, struggle to be heard and cared for and gradually to assert ourselves with others by seeking their attention and affection. Dreams reveal all that as it happens. Our energies find expression. We love and hate, and at night the story is told. But we love and hate in different ways. We are driven, but we also *do something* to our drives. We respond to them and — it comes down to this, finally — we turn them into a "life," a progression of days and nights, achievements and failures, deeds and dreams. A dream is one more part of the mind's effort to make itself work. Yes, in a dream our instincts slip into tentative expression. More happens, though. In a dream we reveal a greater or lesser capacity for arranging the daily business of our emotions. And in every dream the dreamer's world appears — his history as a person whose job is this rather than that, who grew up here, not there, and now rather than then.

For Erikson "the healthy ego, in dreams, quietly retraces its steps; it does not really sacrifice its assets, it merely pretends that, for the moment, they are not needed." Instincts and memories invade the night, but so do obligations and responsibilities, as defined by the various social and cultural institutions that are with us no less constantly than the first childhood memories. As a matter of fact what we freely accept as "unconscious" or hasten to call "conscious" obviously varies from person to person. Many of today's psychoanalyzed liberals cannot see themselves as influenced by "unconscious religious, political or ethnic patterns," but with "a certain clannish and individualistic pride" they almost boast of the "instinctual patterns" that press upon the mind in dreams.

To illustrate his clinical and theoretical emphasis Erikson starts with Freud's own account and exploration of his dream, and then makes a number of amplifications.

Here is Freud's dream narrative:

A great hall — a number of guests, whom we are receiving — among them Irma, whom I immediately take aside, as though to answer her letter, and to reproach her for not yet accepting the "solution." I say to her: "If you (*du*) still have pains, it is really only your own fault." She answers: "If you (*du*) only know what pains I have now in the throat, stomach, and abdomen — I am choked by them." I am startled, and look at her.

She looks pale and puffy. I think that after all I must be overlooking some organic infection. I take her to the window and look into her throat. She offers some resistance to this, like a woman who has a set of false teeth. I think, surely she doesn't need them (*sie hat es doch nicht nötig*). The mouth then opens wide, and I find a large white spot on the right, and elsewhere I see extensive grayish-white scabs adhering to curiously curled formations which are evidently shaped like the turbinal bones of the nose. I quickly call Dr. M., who repeats the examination and confirms it. Dr. M. looks quite unlike his usual self; he is very pale, he limps, and his chin is clean-shaven (*bartlos*). . . . Now my friend, Otto, too, is standing beside her, and my friend Leopold percusses her covered chests and says: "She has a dullness below, on the left," and also calls attention to an infiltrated portion of skin on the left shoulder (which I can feel in spite of the dress). M. says, "There's no doubt that it's an infection, but it doesn't matter; dysentery will follow and the poison will be eliminated." . . . We know, too, precisely (*unmittelbar*) how the infection originated. My friend, Otto, not long ago, gave her, when she was feeling unwell, an injection of a preparation of propyl . . . propyls . . . propionic acid . . . trimethylamin (the formula of which I see before me, printed in heavy type). . . . One doesn't give such injections so rashly. . . . Probably, too, the syringe (*Spritze*) was not clean.[14]

All of which made the following sense to Freud:

The dream fulfills several wishes which were awakened within me by the events of the previous evening (Otto's news, and the writing of the clinical history). For the result of the dream is that it is not I who am to blame for the pain which Irma is still suffering, but that Otto is to blame for it. Now Otto has annoyed me by his remark about Irma's imperfect cure; the dream avenges me upon him, in that it turns the reproach upon himself. The dream acquits me of responsibility for Irma's condition, as it refers this condition to other causes (which do, indeed, furnish quite a number of explanations). The dream represents a certain state of affairs, such as I might wish to exist; *the content of the dream is thus the fulfillment of a wish; its motive is a wish.*

This much is apparent at first sight. But many other details of the dream become intelligible when regarded from the standpoint of wish fulfillment. I take my revenge on Otto. . . . Nor do I pass over Dr. M.'s contradiction; for I express in an obvious allusion my opinion of him: namely, that his attitude in this case is that of an ignoramus ("Dysentery will develop, etc."). Indeed, it seems as though I were appealing from him to someone better informed (my friend, who told me about trimethylamin) just as I have turned from Irma to her friend, and from Otto to Leopold. It is as though I were to say: Rid me of these three persons, replace them by three others of my own choice, and I shall be rid of the reproaches which I am not willing to admit that I deserve! In my dream the unreasonableness of these reproaches is demonstrated for me in the most elaborate manner. Irma's pains are not attributable to me, since she herself is to blame for them in that she refuses to accept my solution. They do not concern me, for being as they are of an organic nature, they cannot possibly be cured by psychic treatment. Irma's sufferings are satisfactorily explained by her widowhood (trimethylamin!); a state which I cannot alter. Irma's illness has been caused by an incautious injection administered by Otto, an injection of an unsuitable drug, such as I should never have administered. Irma's complaint is the result of an injection made with an unclean syringe, like the phlebitis of my old lady patient, whereas my injections have never caused any ill effects. I am aware that these explanations of Irma's illness, which unite in acquitting me, do not agree with one another; that they even exclude one another. The whole plea — for this dream is nothing else — recalls vividly the defense offered by a man who was accused by his neighbor of having returned a kettle in a damaged condition. In the first place, he said, he had returned the kettle undamaged; in the second place, it already had holes in it when he borrowed it; and in the third place, he had never borrowed it at all. A complicated defense, but so much the better; if only one of these three lines of defense is recognized as valid, the man must be acquitted.

Still other themes play a part in the dream, and their relation to my non-responsibility for Irma's illness is not so apparent. . . . But if I keep all these things in view they combine into a single train of thought which might be labeled: concern for the health of myself and others; professional conscientiousness. I recall a vaguely disagreeable feeling when Otto gave me the news of Irma's condition. Lastly, I am inclined, after the event, to find an expression of this fleeting sensation in the train of thoughts which forms part of the dream. It is as though Otto had said to me: "You do not take your medical duties seriously enough; you are not conscientious; you do not perform what you promise." Thereupon this train of thought placed itself at my service, in order that I might give proof of my extreme conscientiousness, of my intimate concern about the health of my relatives, friends and patients. Curiously enough, there are also some painful memories in this material, which confirm the blame attached to Otto rather than my own exculpation. The material is apparently impartial, but the connection between this broader material, on which the dream is based, and the more limited theme from which emerges the wish to be innocent of Irma's illness, is, nevertheless, unmistakable.

I do not wish to assert that I have entirely revealed the meaning of the dream, or that my interpretation is flawless. . . .

For the present I am content with the one fresh discovery which has just been made: If the method of dream interpretation here indicated is followed, it will be found that dreams do really possess a meaning, and are by no means the expression of a disintegrated cerebral activity, as the writers on the subject would have us believe. *When the work of interpretation has been completed the dream can be recognized as a wishfulfillment.*[15]

To which Erikson would add:

The dreamer, at first is a *part of a twosome*, his wife and himself, or maybe a family group, vis-à-vis a number of guests. "We receive," under festive circumstances in an opulent spatial setting. Immediately upon Irma's appearance, however, this twosomeness, this acting in concert, abruptly vanishes. The wife, or the family, is not mentioned again. The dreamer is suddenly *alone* with his worries, vis-à-vis a complaining patient. The visual field shrinks rapidly from the large hall to the vicinity of a window and finally to Irma's oral aperture; the festive present is replaced by a concern over past mistakes. The dreamer becomes active in a breathless way: he looks at the patient and thinks, he looks into her throat and thinks, and he finds what he sees ominous. He is startled, worried, and impatient, but behaves in a punitive fashion. *Irma*, in all this, remains complaining and resistive, and finally seems to become a mere part of herself: "*the mouth* opens." From then on, even when discussed and percussed, she does neither act nor speak — a good patient (for, unlike the proverbial Indian, a good patient is a half-dead patient, just alive enough to make his organs and complexes accessible to isolation and probing inspection). Seeing that something *is* wrong, the dreamer calls *Dr. M.* urgently. He thus establishes a *new twosome:* he and the "authority" who graciously (if foolishly) confirms him. This twosome is immediately expanded to include a professional group of younger colleagues, Dr. Otto and Dr. Leopold. Altogether they now form a small community: "*We know . . .*"

At this point something happens which is lost in the double meaning of the manifest words, in the German original as well as in translation. When the dreamer says that he can "*feel*" the infiltrated portion of skin on the (patient's) left shoulder, he means to convey (as Freud states in his associations) that he can *feel this on his own body:* one of those fusions of a dreamer with a member of his dream population which is always of central importance, if not the very center and nodal point of a dream. The dreamer, while becoming again a doctor in the consenting community of doctors, thus at the same time turns into his and their *patient.* Dr. M. then says some foolish, nonsensical phrases, in the course of which it becomes clear that it had not been the dreamer who had harmed Irma, not at all. It is clear with the immediacy of a conviction that it was

Dr. Otto who had infiltrated her. The dream ends, then, with Otto's professional and moral isolation. The dreamer (first a lonely investigator, then a patient, now a *joiner*) seems quite righteous in his indignation. The syringe was not clean: who would do such a thing? "Immediate" conviction, in harmony with authority, has clarified the past and unburdened the present.

The study of dreams and of culture patterns and ritualizations reveals parallels between interpersonal dream configurations and religious rites of conversion or confirmation. Let me repeat and underscore the points which suggest such an analogy. As the isolated and "guilty" dreamer quickly calls Dr. M., he obviously *appeals for help from higher authority*. This call for help is answered not only by Dr. M., but also by Dr. Leopold and Dr. Otto, who now, together with the dreamer, form a group with a *common conviction* ("we know"). As this happens, and the examination proceeds, the dreamer suddenly feels as if he were the sufferer and the examined, i.e., he, the doctor and man, fuses with the image of the *patient* and *woman*. This, of course, amounts to a surrender analogous to a spiritual conversion and a concomitant sacrifice of the male role. By implication, it is now *his* mouth that is open for inspection (passivity, inspiration, communion). But there is a *reward* for this. Dr. M. (symbolically castrated like a priest) recites with great assurance something that makes *no logical sense* (Latin, Hebrew?) but seems to be magically effective in that it awakes in the dreamer the *immediate conviction* (faith) that the causality in the case is now understood (magic, divine will). This common conviction restores in the dream a *"We-ness"* (congregation) which had been lost (in its worldly, heterosexual form) at the very beginning when the dreamer's wife and the festive guests had disappeared. At the same time it restores to the dreamer a *belongingness* (brotherhood) to a hierarchic group *dominated by an authority* in whom *he believes implicitly*. He immediately benefits from his newly won *state of grace:* he now has sanction for *driving the devil* into Dr. O. With the *righteous indignation* which is the believer's reward and weapon, he can now make "an unclean one" (a disbeliever) out of his erstwhile accuser.[16]

Though the correspondence between Freud and his friend Wilhelm Fliess had not been translated into English when Erikson wrote "The Dream Specimen of Psychoanalysis," in 1950 the letters had been published in German and Erikson had read them. Only once in all the published correspondence does Freud address Fliess with the word *Liebster* ("Dearest"): in the first letter following the Irma Dream (August 8, 1895). It was in Erikson's words "a singular appeal to an intellectual friend, and a German one at that"; and it showed how very much Fliess meant to Freud at the particular time he dreamed so obviously about other (and less sympathetic) doctors. A lonely and eminently creative man, filled to the brim with original and very controversial ideas, Freud looked both inward and outward for support and justification. He looked to his dreams — which for him were like the "promised land," a source of milk and honey — and he looked to the one doctor he felt able to trust. In other words, the man who was analyzing himself more thoroughly and more unnervingly than he himself realized needed Fliess, and also needed the support of a strongly remembered dream.

Erikson made no great discovery when he emphasized Freud's genius; but he did manage a psychoanalytic *tour de force* by giving that genius a social and historical perspective — of all ways, through dream analysis. Rather than take Freud's ideas as "given," he wanted to ask: given by what and whom, psychologically? While Freud's dream helped him to understand why Irma and her troublesome affliction plagued his sleep, even Freud could not fully comprehend his own turbulent creativity. The ideas that *came* of that creative struggle continue to preoccupy psychoanalysts. Erikson urged them to look at the struggle itself, and keep in mind not only Freud's childhood and his wishes and fears — very much like anyone else's — but his particular determination to study himself, be the observer and the observed, and be the professional iconoclast whose daytime courage makes him nervous at night.

Years after he dreamed the Irma Dream, Freud talked about what it means to be a Jew. He was talking to the members of a Jewish lodge, and he used the word "identity" — the one and only time he did so:

But plenty of other things remained to make the attraction of Jewry and Jews irresistible — many obscure emotional forces, which were the more powerful the less they could be expressed in words, as well as a clear consciousness of inner identity, the safe privacy of a common mental construction. And beyond this there was a perception that it was to my Jewish nature alone that I owed two characteristics that had become indispensable to me in the course of my life. Because I was a Jew I found myself free from many prejudices which restricted others in the use of their intellect; and as a Jew I was prepared to join the Opposition and do without the agreement of the "compact majority."[17]

For Erikson that is the neglected and important point of the Irma Dream: a man is prompted to use his intellect in a new and upsetting manner; in so doing he risks exile from the "compact majority." He wants to go ahead and assert his mind's independence, but he is also frightened, made guilty at the prospect of asserting himself and denying the "accepted" ideas that others hold dear. In the dream he equivocates, and perhaps readies himself for the isolation and scorn he will inevitably experience at the hands of all sorts of respectable and knowing people — like the ones he dreamed about.

Freud was trying to be himself. To do so he had to come to terms with himself, and fall back upon others — many of whom he would have to bid good-bye. Jews learn to do that. They learn to take everything and nothing for granted, to rely upon themselves and fate (God-given) with a certain studied casualness, and to worry endlessly about the unfriendly neighbors, the *goyim*. In the Irma Dream an investigator was trying to claim his right, his duty to persist. Courage was calling upon whatever support it could find — personal, religious, cultural. A man was girding himself for and dreaming his way through a crisis: "Dreams, then, not only fulfill naked wishes of sexual license, of unlimited dominance and of un-restricted destructiveness; where they work, they also lift the dream-er's isolation, appease his conscience, and preserve his identity, each in specific and instructive ways."[18]

Friends can also do what dreams do. They can be *there*, available to the floundering, fighting mind. Through dreams we achieve sleep — and sometimes in the morning a new and vivid kind of awareness. Through friends, too, we find our waking hours more "real," more reliable. We are not alone. We know someone. We feel the offer of trust and we feel the desire to trust. When Freud was boldly and fearfully taking on his own unconscious, and particu-larly his dreams, he was also involved in an extraordinary friendship with Fliess — a "relationship" that for years escaped the interest or even the knowledge of his most devoted followers. In 1954 the quality of the friendship came to light with the publication of *The Origins of Psychoanalysis*.[19] The volume contained Freud's side of a long correspondence between the two men. In addition to letters, there were "drafts" and "notes," in sum a whole range of ideas, observations and feelings that were written between 1887 and 1902. Erikson was asked to review the new book for the *International Journal of Psychoanalysis*, and the result appeared in 1955 — a long essay called "Freud's 'The Origins of Psychoanalysis.' "

Erikson found the friendship between Freud and Fliess far more significant than any particular idea or piece of biographical information contained in the letters. Once again — as in the Irma Dream — Freud emerges as a lonely fighter alternately sure of himself and doubtful, convincing and petulant. Once again — as he did in his analysis of the Irma Dream — Erikson wants to know how as well as why Freud did what he did. How did this gifted man persevere, manage to endure banishment from his fellow physicians, succeed in arranging and rearranging his life, his thoughts, his purposes — all in the interests of a psychological theory that seemed to him, let alone to others, elusive and insubstantial? Is it a matter of brilliance unfolding itself, perhaps in alliance with (or indispensably "energized" by) certain persisting childhood conflicts? Or does Freud's life, like anyone else's, reveal how *contingent* human existence is? Do small accidents and large historical trends make or break even the most gifted, driven and self-centered geniuses?

In his later years Freud destroyed the letters he received from Fliess, and asked Marie Bonaparte to do the same with his letters, which she had secured from Fliess' family after he died and they fled Nazi Germany. Erikson immediately declines the temptation to follow the psychoanalyst's "occupational habit of reading and treating such a one-sided record as if it were a kind of free association" — even though the letters and drafts do indeed show "great freedom in the description of moods and in improvisations of thought." Characteristically, he emphasizes the formal or public aspects of even the most private kind of written correspondence: "much of the passion of intellectual intimacy, and much of the mutual aggrandizement notable in these letters are familiar features of intellectual correspondence of the past century."

The two men also had their "congresses." They carefully and somewhat breathlessly chose a city or town where they could meet, talk, and walk, walk, walk (*Spazier-Gange*). They obviously were close, even devoted to one another; but they transcended the "normal" bounds of manly friendship in a particular, stylized manner that, finally, put on them the mark of the extraordinary rather than the abnormal. In a sense, then, they discovered and took advantage of what societies have always permitted and even celebrated: the inspiration that one man's mind can find in another's willing and eager company.

We are asked to take note of the "almost deliberate moodiness, indulgent dependence and radical self-doubt" that comes across in the letters, though clearly they were not *all* the emotions Freud possessed in the decade from 1890 to 1900. In point of fact how significant *were* those particular emotions? The answer will tell a lot about a person's assumptions. Freud can be declared a genius, with his moods and doubts either irrelevant to or part of the inevitable neurosis each of us has to experience. Freud can be declared an exceedingly troubled and "sick" man, who nevertheless — even, to some extent, consequently — had the ability to make the best of his difficulties by looking into them and recording them for the rest of us. Or Freud can be declared the "founder" of psychoanalysis, the man whose theories others must now accept and study; and as for Fliess, or Irma, or even Jung and Adler, they were not very much more than people who happened to appear and figure in his life — and so, whatever went on between him and them is strictly anecdotal.

To Erikson, however, the Freud who sought out Fliess and became so unashamedly attached to him was a man in mid-life going through a severe and illuminating psychological crisis, not the kind that can be called a "repetition" of earlier ones. At age thirty he had exchanged the "academic monastery" for the "medical parsonage." He was a handsome, sturdy man, an original thinker; and he seemed destined for a quietly outstanding career as a scientist. Yet rather dramatically he began to withdraw from the laboratory and take up instead the medical specialty that concerned itself with so-called nervous diseases. A man who had been studying the pharmacological properties of cocaine now gravitated toward patients afflicted with "hysteria," that strange and enigmatic "disease" whose sufferers can be lifeless or excited, unable to walk and move their arms, or driven to agitated movement of all four extremities. The thoughts of "hysterics" are as "bizarre" as the dysfunction of their bodies; but in 1890 doctors had not made much of that fact. It was Freud who would do so, and thereby resume in his thirties the role of investigator.

How did Freud happen to abandon one line of work and take up another? More generally, what (if any) generalizations can a psychoanalyst make about the lives of gifted men — political or religious leaders, writers, scientists — who often enough "go off on their own," and only later command a following? How does one look at a man's work, his day-to-day effort, say, as a doctor? If Freud had all sorts of unconscious reasons prompting him relentlessly to look into his own mind or the minds of his various patients, what enabled him to do the job so consistently, effectively and boldly? His intellectual ability or his high intelligence? His implacable will, driven on by a turbulent neurosis that could never be satisfied? His luck — as a man who stumbled on something at the right time and in the right place?

Those are the questions that keep coming up; they haunt anyone who does not see genius as God-given. In our time, as a result of Freud's work, it is hard not to look backward and offer a person's early life, with all its conflicts, as an "explanation" for any interest, any achievement. Freud himself traced things back, and did so as a neurophysiologist long before he became a psychiatrist. In the laboratory one distills, reduces, tracks down, and deduces. Things only appear to be what they are. Always there is the hidden truth, the substance that can be boiled down or extracted. So the man who wrote strong, grateful and admiring letters to Fliess was to teach us how "deep-rooted" their "real" inspiration was; and some of us have learned our lesson so well that we have stopped asking any more questions. After all, given Freud's "needs" for Fliess, his unconscious "drives" toward him, why should we ask about the immediate and more "obvious" value that such a friendship might have had for a man who was about to publish a long and controversial psychiatric book, and in so doing, eventually establish himself as a genius, rather than a madman or a "neurotic"?

As a doctor Freud could never shake himself free of sick people; and besides, their problems fascinated him. As a biographer he sought in the artist, and particularly in his various productions — statues, pictures, stories, plays — evidence of those same problems, however disguised or "sublimated." When he pushed himself hard, and asked what makes for the difference — between the sick and the well, between the commonplace and the gifted, and, in fact, between himself and hundreds of other Viennese doctors — he had to answer as the democratic realist and fatalist he was. Life is unfair. We are differently endowed at birth. We grow up under favorable or discouraging circumstances. Some have good minds to begin with, and then go through a kind of rearing that favors the intellect. Others are ordinary or less than ordinary; and nothing that happens to them can or does work to redress their grievances, if that is the word to describe their all too common and unavoidable fate. But one thing is certain: all people meet up with difficulties, labor under them, and only more or less solve them. All people lose their way and find it again. We are both relatively and distinctly separated, one from the other, by the quantity of intelligence we have, the amount of good luck we have encountered, the intensity and complexity of our early experiences.

In 1955 and now, Erikson could only agree with all that. He would, however, ask whether normal or gifted people have been given the kind of careful, respectful attention that psychoanalytic patients receive. Have we looked at life histories (in contrast to case histories) with the same unlimited, unencumbered curiosity Freud once directed at the puzzling, "hysterical" visitors who came to his office? For that matter, have we looked at Freud himself as instructively as we might? Or are we so dazzled and overawed by the answers he found to *his* questions that we dare not even ask our own — about him and others like him?

The Freud-Fliess letters stirred Erikson, and what they revealed strengthened his earlier formulations on "identity" and the nature of the "life cycle." In his early middle age Freud struggled with an almost overwhelming burden of psychological awareness, and his letters to Fliess show how redemptive a friendship can be. Any "analysis" of what went on between them or prompted their intense "relationship" would therefore have to take into account the "use" they made of one another, the search they jointly and unwittingly made. "In the first place," said Freud, "I hope you will explain the physiological mechanism of my clinical finding from your point of view; secondly, I want to maintain the right to come to you with all my theories and findings in the field of neurosis; and thirdly, I still look to you as the Messiah who will solve the problem I have indicated by an improvement in technique."

Remarks like that prompted Ernest Jones to declare that Freud wanted and needed "sanction" from Fliess, and Freud himself thanked Fliess for "the powerful impulse" that allowed him to take his work so seriously. Erikson speaks this way of their closeness, their caring and sharing:

That in the ensuing correspondence unrestrained terms of mutual lioniza-tion should appear; that Fliess should be made an Apollonian tower of calm strength while the writer becomes a driven Dionysian (and "shabby Israelite"); that figures of speech should occur which picture the writer as a feminine womb for the intellectual sireing of the other — all of this is, to a considerable extent, sanctioned by a tradition of intellectual and poetic friendship, not to be confused with "transference." Men in development often appreciate in one another their early and innermost aspirations rather than what they are or are going to be.[20]

Many ideas Erikson had developed in the thirties and forties were anticipated in a way he could never know, because the letters between Freud and Fliess had not then come to light. Freud even used diagrammatic sketches very much like the ones that appear in *Childhood and Society*. He also speaks of particular ages, when this or that happens; and he refers to periods of special vulnerability and relative calm. Like Erikson, he saw life — all life — as epochal, that is, made up of distinct or recognizable crises which follow one another right up to the end.

The letters show a Freud not only time-conscious but restless and fearful. He worried that he would die young, before he had completed his self-prescribed task of discovery. He told Fliess of his wanderlust, of his urge to see Rome, of his visions of glory and his sense of failure, and of his loneliness. ("We are terribly ahead of our time.") In sum, he told Fliess that he was living a certain kind of life and asks Fliess to share in it. Years later Erikson would describe the many dimensions to that life:

To summarize a summary, the letters and drafts contained in this volume show the reflection in a correspondence of the fabric that creative thought is made of. We see mirrored in a correspondence-personality the inner relationship of a man's thoughts to the main currents of his time, and that of a man's gifts to his inner motivations. This correspondence does much to dispel that nebulous uncertainty which surrounded the origin of psychoanalysis and easily led to the impression that our science had issued from Freud's head as did Athene from Zeus. Since from such an image we have derived some reflected omnipotence, this book is somewhat of a trauma, albeit beneficial if slowly absorbed. To neutralize its immediate impact we may feel tempted to highlight the neurotic in it or the creative, the infantile or the great, the emotional or the intellectual, the medical or the psychological. To this Freud, if he cared, could say with (Prof. Francis Cornford's) Pythagoras: "What is your warrant for valuing one part of my experience and rejecting the rest? . . . If I had done so, you would never have heard my name."[21]

What Erikson said to his American colleagues he repeated in an elegant and literally momentous lecture before a German audience on May 6, 1956. That day marked the hundredth anniversary of Freud's birth, and a ceremony to celebrate the event was held jointly by the universities of Heidelberg and Frankfurt. An entire generation of German students had heard practically nothing about Freud, and Erikson was invited to address them and their teachers. He was to give the *Festrede*, the principal lecture, and deliver it in the *Aula* at the University of Frankfurt. People were dressed quite formally, flowers were everywhere, and Mendelssohn's music was performed once again in Germany. President Heuss of the West German Republic had been asked to introduce Erikson and honor Freud. The president was a very old, white-haired man, and had some reservations about Freud's ideas. Before the festive exercises began, he told Erikson in his most charming Swabian that he would feel strange introducing him, since "frankly, if I look into myself I can notice absolutely nothing daimonic. And you know, I don't think I ever had any infantile sexuality." To which Erikson replied, "Presidents don't need that kind of thing." Heuss gratefully said, "Thank you, thank you," and together they walked toward the academic procession. A little while later President Heuss introduced Erikson and then promptly fell asleep.

The lecture turned out to be exceptionally lucid and affecting. (Later that year it was published in the *Yale Review* under the title "The First Psychoanalyst," and since then it has appeared in both English and German anthologies.) Erikson wanted his audience to share intimately the doubt and agony Freud had experienced for so long — as if then they would really remember him and seek out his books. The "principles" of psychoanalysis he discussed could perhaps be taken in stride as "more facts"; but it would be harder to forget a lecture that tried to do justice to "the dimensions of lonely discovery" — and began in the following way:

It is not easy (unless it be all too easy) for a "Freudian" to speak of the man who *was* Freud, of a man who grew to be a myth before our eyes. I knew Freud when he was very old, and I was young. Employed as a tutor in a family friendly to him I had the opportunity of seeing him on quiet occasions, with children and with dogs, and at outings in the mountains. I do not know whether I would have noticed Freud in a crowd. His notable features were not spectacular: the finely domed forehead, the dark, unfathomable eyes, and certain small indomitable gestures — they all had become part of that inner containment which crowns the old age of good fighters.

I was an artist then, which can be a European euphemism for a young man with some talent, but nowhere to go. What probably impressed me most was the fact that this doctor of the mind, this expert of warped biography, had surrounded himself in his study with a small host of little statues: those distilled variations of the human form which were created by the anonymous artists of the archaic Mediterranean. Certainly, of Freud's field, of conflict and complaint and confession, there was no trace in their art. This respect for form, so surprising in a man who had unearthed mankind's daimonic inner world, was also obvious in his love for proud dogs and for gaily bright children. I vaguely felt that I had met a man of rare dimensions, rare contradictions.[22]

Erikson then left Freud briefly to discuss Darwin, another lonely explorer who dared challenge the conventional. Like Freud he couldn't seem to settle down into a profession and simply work at it. Like Freud he seemed to hesitate, to stumble about from idea to idea, to wander — to come almost by accident upon the Galápagos Islands, which virtually became his laboratory. And like Freud, when he finally did hit upon something important he became anxious, fearful and plagued by all sorts of aches and pains. *The Origin of Species* took years of apprehensive work, as did *The Interpretation of Dreams;* and the two men we now know as geniuses were judged quite otherwise by their contemporaries. But perhaps a creative man has no choice in the matter:

He may come across his supreme task almost accidentally. But once the issue is joined, his task proves to be at the same time intimately related to his most personal conflicts, to his superior selective perception, and to the stubbornness of his one-way will: he must court sickness, failure or insanity in order to test the alternative whether the established world will crush him, or whether he will disestablish a sector of this world's outworn fundamentals and make place for a new one.[23]

From Darwin, Erikson moved to Freud, to *his* Galápagos, the doctor's office. Step by step he retraced with his audience of young Germans what a somewhat troubled and fiercely proud Jewish doctor had done in nearby Vienna a half-century ago:

Freud had investigated the nature of brain lesions by slicing the brains of young animals and foetuses. He now investigated memories as representative cross-sections of a patient's emotional condition. In successive memories he traced trends which led, like pathways, to the traumatic past. There, experiences of a disruptive nature loomed like lesions interfering with growth.[24]

The emphasis was on the continuity in a man's life, on the way men struggle to use what they have learned in order to learn new and different things — not without paying a psychological price. Freud discovered a new kind of treatment, a new view of what goes on between the doctor and the patient. He also went through a prolonged personal crisis — which Erikson did not shirk discussing in a university any more than he did in a psychoanalytic journal. German youth who had been told how "sickly" and "weak" the Jew is — and how important "strength through joy" was — would now hear what could be done by a small, dark, bearded man who had his share of phobias and anxieties.

The American psychoanalyst did more than let his European audience in on Freud's achievement as an innovator. He set forth the essence of psychoanalysis: it is at once a therapeutic contract, a conceptual design and a means of systematic self-analysis. He also showed how an Austrian doctor working in the beginning with middle-aged, "neurotic" (and often childless) women had managed to provide the world with "a fundamentally new ethical orientation" toward children and childhood, and toward women, too — as the ones who bring up children, and (so it turns out) make and fashion the adult in ways we often refuse to acknowledge.

In the middle of the lecture mention was made of a more familiar man, Martin Luther. Freud's difficult effort to relinquish the nineteenth-century doctor's godlike position in favor of the listener's role was not unlike "young Martin Luther's religious crisis," out of which a new view of man also emerged: "Whoever has suffered under and identified with a stern father must become a stern father himself or else find an entirely different quality of moral strength, an equal measure of strength." The young audience had no way of knowing that the speaker also knew quite a lot about Luther.

VIII

Luther and History

HOW should a psychoanalyst go about studying the youth of a man like Martin Luther? The most common approach is to subject the words and deeds of the historical figure to "analysis." A man like Luther becomes a patient whose thoughts and feelings may admittedly be remote, fragmentary or inaccessible — but still revealing in the sense that anyone's actions, anyone's statements tell something about his "mind." After all — so it is argued — a psychoanalytically sensitive reader or critic can notice the consistent symbolic concerns and struggles of a writer, an artist or a leader. Often they themselves have written of their own childhood, and often they themselves make casual but repeated mention of their parents, wives or friends. What is more, literary productions were scrutinized for their thematic content long before Freud's time, and the lives of great men have been gone over — from what might be called a psychological viewpoint — ever since biographies first appeared. Psychoanalytic theory merely offers those who study lives a new "frame of reference"; and though psychoanalysts work with patients, and scrutinize their fantasies and dreams, which are *not* the same as a poem, a novel or a political act, psychoanalytic theory insists that anything said by anybody at any time and in any place has at least potential interest or significance.

In contrast, Erikson's transition from clinical work to historical research is made the subject of a strong introductory statement in *Young Man Luther:*

Here I will say only that any comparison made between young man Luther and our patients, is, for their sake as well as his, not restricted to psychiatric diagnosis and the analysis of pathological dynamics, but is oriented toward those moments when young patients, like young beings anywhere, prove resourceful and insightful beyond all professional and personal expectation. We will concentrate on the powers of recovery inherent in the young ego.[1]

He goes on to indicate that Freud and Luther both freed themselves: Freud from his personal blind spots, then from those in his profession; and Luther from the authority of the medieval Church. As for Erikson, if *Young Man Luther* is not a work of *his* emancipation, it is at the very least an important intellectual breakthrough — on the part of a loyal follower of Freud's who at the same time stubbornly sought after his own way of looking at things. Not only was Luther's achievement going to be seen as far more than neurotic self-deception. The clinician who had allowed patients to surprise him with their adaptive and recuperative powers dared take on even more difficult subjects, such as the nature of ideology, the religious leader and the nation-state: "My choice of subject forces me to deal with problems of faith and problems of Germany, two enigmas which I could have avoided by writing about some other great man. But it seems that I did not wish to avoid them." So writes an analyst who found patients surprisingly "resourceful and insightful," and who declared "exceeding good fate" to be as critical in some lives as "special help" is in others.

Faith can mystify and even cheat the believer; it can also heal and nourish him. What is more, faith can drive men on, or separate them; it can bind the young and inspire the young, and in our flat, unrevealing terms be "psychologically supportive." As for Germany, or any nation, Erikson long ago learned what effect a mere country can have on the privacy of the "unconscious." His own life had gone through one profound change after another because of events that could in sum be called part of "the German problem." He knew how a "religious" issue or a "political" one can touch every fiber of one man's being, and in *Young Man Luther* he wanted to make that knowledge — so easily and arrogantly dismissed as "common-sense" by some "pure" clinicians — illuminate the way individuals grow and particular men become historical figures. And so immediately before taking up young Luther, a middle-aged author sets the tone of his second book:

When speaking about Freud to the students at Frankfurt and at Heidelberg, I remembered an event in my own early years, a memory which had been utterly covered by the rubble of the cities and by the bleached bones of men of my kind in Europe. In my youth, as a wandering artist I stayed one night with a friend in a small village by the Upper Rhine. His father was a Protestant pastor; and in the morning, as the family sat down to breakfast, the old man said the Lord's Prayer in Luther's German. Never having "knowingly" heard it, I had the experience, as seldom before or after, of a wholeness captured in a few simple words, of poetry fusing the esthetic and the moral: those who have once suddenly "heard" the Gettysburg Address will know what I mean.

On occasion we should acknowledge emotional debts other than traumatic ones. Perhaps, then, this study is a tribute to a spring morning in that corner of Europe from which Schweitzer came; and an attempt to grasp something essential in that reformation which stands at the beginning of our era, something which we have neither completely lived down nor successfully outlived.[2]

Luther, then, would be Erikson's "patient" only in the very broadest sense of the word — a sense that Erikson's fellow Dane, Søren Kierkegaard, had sanctioned when he called the great German Protestant "a patient of exceeding import for Christianity." In fact Erikson took Kierkegaard's remark as a "motto" for his book. He wanted to speak as a clinician, but he also wanted to speak about "a life style of patienthood as a sense of imposed suffering, of an intense need for cure, and (as Kierkegaard adds) a 'passion for expressing and describing one's suffering.' " A cure can be a cause, and the passionate articulation of one's suffering can actually do away with it and make a victor out of a victim.

In *Young Man Luther* all of Erikson's earlier struggles with the mind's ambiguity are put squarely before the reader. Concepts like *identity*, *identity crisis*, and *moratorium* were formulated by a man who could be called historically minded, who knew that time is fickle, and that one moment's "illness" can be followed by another's considerable accomplishment. Psychiatrists are doctors, and thus "case historians." Yet again and again they dwell on the "still point" as if it were not in a million ways connected to a "turning world." Erikson calls the first chapter of *Young Man Luther* "Case and Event." Young Martin battled for some "working unity" that would enable him to find a significant day-to-day purpose for his particular interests (as they began to develop through his childhood). Presumably there was a time in his life — as in all lives — when he could be justifiably called a "case" by those whose job it is to do so. Certainly he had his scruples, his paroxysmal outbursts, his severely rebellious and insistently wayward moments. He was a "problem" to his Church. In Kierkegaard's eyes he ultimately failed to find "a doctor's commanding view," and no doubt in his last years he could be cranky, mean, bilious and vengeful. As a young monk he was reported to have suffered a fit and raved like a madman, or as his contemporaries would put it, a man seized or possessed by demons or their chief, the Devil. On the other hand, young Martin became Luther. Erikson studies precisely that "becoming," in which a "case" became an "event," so that a half a thousand years later the "troubled man's" words and ideas persist not only in songs memorized by rote or sermons automatically believed, but yes, in the unconscious minds of twentieth-century men.

Erikson goes back and forth between history and psychoanalysis so constantly and adroitly that it is hard to know what to call his book on Luther. Certainly it is not the usual exercise in "applied psychoanalysis"; nor is it a traditional biography. Erikson means every word of the subtitle, "A Study in Psychoanalysis and History." He is not "using" one theoretical "model" to "explain" the mysteries that continue to plague another discipline. In a way he is splitting his own identity, by trying to survey the terrain of two kingdoms he believes to be neighbors. He wants to look at territorial borders but also at a landscape that ignores man-made distinctions.

If he is to be a psychoanalyst and a historian, he cannot very easily be a theologian. Yet at the beginning of the book he discusses that tired cliché of the twentieth century — "psychology and religion," which is something "interdisciplinary." Luther was, of course, a monk, a heretic, and ultimately, a great religious statesman. Erikson is very definitely not going to take such a man's religious faith and make its vicissitudes an appendix to Freud's *The Future of an Illusion*. Before a book like *Young Man Luther* could be written the following had to be made immediately clear:

Psychology endeavors to establish what is demonstrably true in human behavior, including such behavior as expresses what to human beings seems true and feels true. . . . Religion, on the other hand, elaborates on what feels profoundly true even though it is not demonstrable: it translates into significant words, images, and codes the exceeding darkness which surrounds man's existence, and the light which pervades it beyond all desert or comprehension.[3]

How does he join the life of one man's mind to the history of mankind? How does he get away with the division of labor staked out above, between psychology and religion? Luther, after all, fought hard for *his* Christ — and now a psychoanalyst comes along to say that the *validity* of young Martin's beliefs is not the issue. Yet sometimes an overwhelming, either/or question can be a deadweight and lead only to rhetoric and polemics. Rather than analyze religion as a psychological "need," Erikson wants to show how a particular youth could take a prevailing religious viewpoint and *use* it, use it shrewdly to cement together in himself a growing and eventually confident sense of manhood. Today's Martins do not need ministers and philosophers as passionately and devotedly as they once did. Now it is political men — or indeed, psychoanalytic theorists — who receive youth's attention and faith. Nevertheless, for all their modernity, our leaders and our young followers have demonstrated the same mixture of enthusiasm, zealotry and ideological fanaticism that their medieval precursors so "ignorantly" displayed as Christian crusaders, pilgrims or monks-in-training.

The key word for Erikson is once again "ideology"; it is the concept that helped him turn the clinical question of "identity-formation" into a universal and historical issue: "In this book *ideology* will mean an unconscious tendency underlying religious and scientific as well as political thought: the tendency at a given time to make facts amenable to ideas, and ideas to facts, in order to create a world image convincing enough to support the collective and the individual sense of identity." Because young people are desperately uncertain, they often become desperately hungry for a leader to say what must be believed, accepted, or scorned. The banal psychological truth that every generation chooses its own heroes (or fails in the attempt) becomes something important to think about when a new kind of spiritual man suddenly emerges, peculiarly the "product" of his time, and specially able to speak for it. The Luther we now find a rather familiar figure in our "Western tradition" was once a fiery and controversial heresiarch. But in the very beginning he was a young man, a youth of thirty-three who nailed ninety-five theses on the door of a church in Wittenberg, Germany. His words and his deeds caught fire, and he led his generation into a new era. His "identity crisis" kindled a moment of sweeping ideological change. Millions of men and women rallied round the personal conflicts of one strange burgher, whom we today might call "atypical" or "alienated." And in the end, of course, Luther's anguished outcries, so personal and never intended by him to be coherent and of a piece, became yet another body of accepted simplifications for his countrymen and others all over Europe. "This is a book on identity and ideology," says Erikson as he prepares to discuss Martin's "fit in the choir." The conceptual bridge is done; the land between two "disciplines" — between a man and the masses — is vaulted. We will indeed learn about a troubled Martin, but we will also learn how a troubled Martin moved and inspired an entire continent.

Luther had his problems, everyone agrees. Loyal Protestant theologians, stout defenders of the Catholic Church, and more recently a few interested doctors and psychologists have all tried to come to terms with his tempestuous spirit — or as we know it, his mind. He was born on November 10, 1483, at Eisleben, in the county of Mansfeld. His parents, descendants of German peasants, had moved to Mansfeld from Möhra in Thuringia. Martin's father, Hans Luther, had been for many years a miner. Mansfeld was the center of an iron-ore mining and smelting industry, a sort of industrialized "new world" to which "backward" and poor farmers came in search of a better life.

There is every reason to believe that Martin was born into a conventionally pious yet superstitious home. His parents were strict and ambitious for their children. In our terms, the family was "on the rise." The discipline exerted on Martin at home was matched by the strict teachers of the Latin school he attended from the age of seven on. Martin's father was going to be a prosperous burgher, and Martin was going to be educated, like it or not. At fourteen the boy went to Magdeburg for futher schooling. He reportedly was an able and willing student, even though much later in life schools like those he attended and teachers like those who taught him would suffer merciless condemnation in his written and spoken sermons. At Magdeburg he was taught by members of the Brotherhood of the Common Life, who essentially were educational enthusiasts and reformers. Like many other children, Martin earned money by singing in the streets.

Luck intervened, however, in the form of Kuntz Cotta and his wife. They were a well-to-do couple who lived in Eisenach, where Martin was sent after a year at Magdeburg. They took the lad into their home and made it unnecessary for him to beg the favors of strangers. Martin also came into contact with the Rector Trebonius and his assistant Wigand, who spotted a bright student and taught him Latin grammar, composition and poetry for three years. They vouched for his outstanding qualities, and encouraged him to go on — something of course that his father also wished.

In the spring of 1501, at seventeen, Martin entered the University of Erfurt, certainly one of the leading German centers of learning. He studied what students of his day studied — grammar, logic, rhetoric, physics and philosophy. Two of his teachers were Trutvetter and Ulsingen, who were so-called nominalists, philosophic followers of William of Occam, an English monk and teacher of the fourteenth century whose writings supported the various emperors against the Pope, and in fact gave enormous intellectual support to the developing idea of a nation-state. Though Occam challenged the Pope, he never did so in a personal and unyielding way. He did, however, differ theologically with Thomas Aquinas and Duns Scotus; for instance, he denied that the existence of God could be proved by strict syllogism, and he fought for the individual person, the individual soul — which he considered to be a victim of man's psychological desire and philosophical determination to make abstractions about "people" in general.

Luther called Occam "my master," but not because he was then planning to build a revolution on the words of an earlier skeptic or rebel. There was ferment in the Church and in the various European universities, and one danger — mentioned again and again by Erikson — that faces *us* is the temptation to extract both Occam and Luther from their respective times and make of them two conveniently "related" figures, psychological and intellectual kinsmen, as it were. Occam was one of many thinkers who periodically gave Rome trouble, but the real threat to the Church was not his ideas but the concrete reality that made those ideas so persistently significant, namely, the rising power and authority of any number of kings, princes and dukes. As for Martin Luther the college student at Erfurt, his eagerness for and affinity to the Occamist or "modern" school of thought was certainly not unusual — a historical point that a psychoanalyst obviously has to take the trouble to learn.

By the autumn of 1502 Luther had secured his bachelor's degree, and in two years he was ready for the next one, a master's. He placed second in a list of seventeen candidates. The year was 1505. Luther was twenty-one. In May of the same year he embarked upon the study of law, at his father's behest. Two months later, on July 17, he made an abrupt turnabout. The law was not for him; the

Church was. He left the world for the monastery of the Augustinian Eremites at Erfurt. His family was shocked. His father became very angry. The decision seemed unexplainable to everyone, probably including Martin. Though the matter is argued by Luther's many biographers, the crisis and decision appear to have been sudden and unpremeditated. Luther himself merely said that he was quietly returning to Erfurt from his parents' home in Mansfeld, only to find himself in the midst of a severe thunderstorm. He was knocked down by a bolt of lightning, and took the event as a sign from heaven, meant directly for him. He vowed on the spot to become a monk, and abruptly took the actual steps in that direction as soon as he returned to the university. A successful and much-admired law student voluntarily immersed himself in a monastery very near the University of Erfurt — and pursued the priesthood as zealously as his previous "goals."

The Erfurt Augustinians were a severe and scrupulous order, in contrast to the Conventuals, who were far more easygoing. Luther first had a year's novitiate to complete, a time of testing in which the strict, even harsh regimen confronts the candidate every day with the temptation to leave or the need to gird himself and stay — no matter what. It is perhaps hard even for devout Christians today to realize the faith that was both assumed and tested by certain medieval orders. Nor did the trials end when the young novitiate took his vows of poverty, chastity and obedience, as Martin did at age twenty-two. He was assigned a preceptor, in Martin's case a man named Nathan, who taught him theology. He was asked to live a humble, penitent and grinding life, full of tasks and challenges calculated to bring out — and bring down — the pride and arrogance that reside in anyone. Today we want our young men to feel "self-esteem," to go out and "*find* themselves," find what is so often called "maturity." Martin had to *lose* himself, again and again lose himself, and hope thereby to apprehend — the verb has to be vague and only suggestive — God's gracious Presence.

In 1507 Martin Luther was ordained a priest of the Holy Catholic Church. He was twenty-three, and considered promising indeed by his superiors. Ordination of course is the beginning, a mere and literal falling into line. There was much more theology to study: the Bible, the writings of Augustine, St. Bernard, D'Ailly and Biel. A man who had become a bachelor and master at one institution had to work for the same degrees from another. Ultimately, in October

1512, at the age of twenty-eight, Martin Luther obtained a doctorate of theology.

Erikson is interested in what happened before Luther became controversial and famous. At twenty-one he was a good student who unexpectedly decided to become a priest. At thirty-three he nailed his ninety-five theses on the church door in Wittenberg. In those twelve years young Martin established the foundation of what may be called the historical Luther. Obviously he had no such "goal" in mind; yet just as obviously he was no "ordinary" man. Luther was not the first one to notice and abhor the corruption that had become a daily fact of life in Rome; but where others were saddened he was outraged, and where others kept silent he spoke out. Much more, he spoke out forcefully, brilliantly, cleverly — and persistently. Nor did he knuckle under when the inevitable resistance and counter-attack came.

What sort of youth could become the great religious leader Luther? Is it possible to find anything *particular* in young Martin that seems to point him toward the later destiny we all know so well? These are the kinds of questions Erikson asked himself when he studied the existing biographical data on Luther's life. He was interested in looking at any available evidence that would make Luther's later and familiar life seem a reasonable or understandable continuation of his youth. The point was not to "interpret" what Luther "did," but search for some trends in a given life, to find coherence in that life.

Erikson begins his study of Luther with a discussion of an event that allegedly took place sometime during Martin's early or middle twenties. Three of his contemporaries report that he fell to the ground in the choir of the monastery at Erfurt and appeared wild and possessed. He is said to have shouted, "Ich bin's nit, ich bin's nit!" or possibly in Latin, "Non sum, non sum!" The German literally translated would be, "It isn't me!"; in Latin, "I am not!"

It isn't known which language Martin used, but the reporters agree that his reaction followed an upsetting occasion — the reading of a section from Mark (9:17) that describes Christ's cure of a man possessed by a dumb spirit. ("And one of the multitude answered and said, Master, I have brought unto thee my son, which hath a dumb spirit.") To those who saw Luther's fit, or heard of it, the explanation was fairly clear: he had been seized by demons of some kind, and indeed felled by them. He fought back, though; and in so doing either denied them their victory or protested whatever implication their assault on him might have. Presumably the demons were struggling with him, or accusing him of something — and he was saying that he was *not* theirs, *not* under their sovereignty, and *not* all the things they wanted him to be or asserted that he was — perhaps dumb or mute, like the man brought by his father to Christ for healing.

In any event, the youth who went through a time of panic during a thunderstorm — and thereafter shifted conclusively the direction of his life — apparently continued to experience swift and painful "moments," which seemed to come from nowhere, or indeed everywhere — that is, heaven or hell itself. Sometimes Martin was sad, doubtful and self-accusing; and on at least one occasion — the fit in the choir — more drastically "troubled." Erikson holds off "analyzing" all this; instead he presents and discusses the interpretations of others; and there have been enough critics and theories to make up several "schools" of opinion. Some Protestant theologians or philosophers, for instance, knew all too well that Luther had his brooding and even violent moods, when the whole world had to suffer the condemnation of a man who would not keep his misgivings and his complaints to himself. Yet Lutheran scholars and ministers often see their great hero's outbursts as spiritual rather than psychological crises. Certainly Luther was sick, but from *Seelenleiden* or *Geistreskrankheit*, suffering of the soul or sickness of the spirit.

From the other side, the Catholic side, came a somewhat less lofty view of Luther's trouble. He did indeed have trouble, and it could even be called spiritual — in the sense that the anti-Christ in any form is a spiritual problem. Erikson quotes one of Luther's detractors, a sub-archivar of the Holy See, who talks of the "self-delusion" in the future Protestant's mind when at twenty-one he claimed to feel the inspiration of the Holy Ghost during a thunderstorm, and decided to give his life to the Church. To one set of believers Martin was struggling with the perilous challenge of God's word; to another set he was a fool, a knave, or an instrument of the Devil.

Then there is an additional breed of experts, and here is how Erikson introduces one of them, in fact a countryman of his:

An extremely diligent student of Luther, the Danish psychiatrist, Dr. Paul J. Reiter, decides unequivocally that the fit in the choir is a matter of severest psychopathology. At most, he is willing to consider the event as a relatively benign hysterical episode; even so, he evaluates it as a symptom of a steady, pitiless, "endogenous" process which, in Luther's middle forties, was climaxed by a frank psychosis.[4]

To Dr. Reiter the years of Luther's life that interest Erikson in *Young Man Luther* — twenty-two to thirty — were part of one long *Krankheitsphase*, an unyielding and growing nervous disease which persisted in different forms throughout an entire life. Up to the age of thirty-six, Luther was depressed on and off; thereafter he went into a brief "manic" period, accompanied by a high level of "productivity"; and finally in the forties his depression returned, worse than ever. That is that.

There even is a psychoanalytic, in contrast to a traditionally psychiatric, expert for Erikson to mention, a man interestingly named Preserved Smith, who once was a professor at Amherst College. Preserved Smith wrote a biography of Luther, edited his letters, and in 1915 published a paper called "Luther's Early Development in the Light of Psychoanalysis." Smith saw Luther as a "thoroughly typical example of the neurotic quasi-hysterical sequence of an infantile sex-complex." There is talk about Luther's troubles with his father and his rather obsessive or extreme scrupulosity as a youth. The Yankee scholar also directs his attention to the fit in the choir, in a way that Erikson dutifully records, "Professor Smith, incidentally, translates the reported outcry in the choir as 'It is not I' — words which I doubt even a New Englander would utter in a convulsive attack."

If Luther at some point in his twenties had to decry something, say no to someone, Erikson may also have had to clear the decks, so to speak, before taking up in his special way a portion of Luther's life. He is very frank and very personal in describing his purpose:

Why did I introduce my discussion of Luther with this particular event in the choir, whose interpretation is subject to so many large and small discrepancies?

As I tried to orient myself in regard to Luther's identity crisis by studying those works which promised to render the greatest number of facts and references for independent study, I heard him, ever again, roar in rage, and yet also in laughter: *Ich bin's nit!*[5]

A little later he states that he is not going to "present a new Luther or to remodel an old one." He wants to know how a young man became a great man. He feels that his particular concepts help cast light on that "process," and he says so:

It must have occurred to the reader that the story of the fit in the choir attracted me originally because I suspected that the words "I am *not*" revealed the fit to be part of a most severe identity crisis — a crisis in which the young monk felt obliged to protest what he was *not* (possessed, sick, sinful) perhaps in order to break through to what he was or was to be.[6]

Martin in his mid-twenties was defying a father's desire that his son take up the profession of law and become a success in *this* world. Accordingly, he was a source of great disappointment to the aging Hans Luther — who lacked faith in his son, even as the father of the child with a "dumb spirit" lacked faith in Christ. When Martin first decided to enter the monastery his father saw him as possessed rather than inspired, seized by some form of the Devil rather than summoned by God. Fit or no fit, Martin had a painful time of it in the monastery. He could not rest easy with his calling, and even though a certain amount of tense self-examination was generally present in candidates for the priesthood, Martin's religious scruples were by common knowledge severe and outstanding. To Erikson a certain sense can be made of it all. The son who defies his father's wishes cannot quite rest easy for doing so. In the monastery he lives with his act of rebellion, even as he tries harder and harder, day after day, to obey his new (religious) superiors. In the fit and in the words spoken at the time of the fit, Hans Luther is both rebuked and affirmed. The very occurrence of a fit proves the father's point — the youth *is* possessed. But the fit also paves the way for an act of defiance against the father. And later on, the unusual quality of Martin's priestly devotion — its intensity, its extreme yet wavering force — shows the struggle he continued to face with himself and his God. In a spectacular fit, and in everyday fits of anguish and fear, the youth tried to have it both ways, and settle it one way or another. He could not quite accommodate himself to the Church, but he certainly could not fall back on the life his father intended for him: "We find the young monk, then, at the crossroads of obedience to his father — an obedience of extraordinary tenacity and deviousness — and to the monastic vows which at the time he was straining to obey almost to the point of absurdity."[7]

From what he read of Luther's own words and the many accounts of his life, Erikson sensed in Martin the struggle he saw again and again in his young patients. Perhaps some of them were at Austen Riggs seeing Erik Erikson for the same reason that Martin Luther had taken himself to a monastery. In 1955 they needed to mark time, as Luther did, say, from 1507 to 1517. In the sixteenth century men could enter or leave a monastery without evoking scandal or even surprise. They could come, seek haven and a chance to take stock, and stay on or depart. For reasons somewhat similar, Freud spent years in the dark corner of a physiology laboratory; and St. Augustine gave himself over for a long time to Manichaeism before he came upon his "real" or "true" faith. Erikson sees Luther's struggle as similar to theirs, the struggle of a great man before he is great. Obviously such men do not *know* they are headed for greatness, or even want it or seek it. They do not even know that the delay, the "moratorium," is anything of the sort. On the other hand, Erikson is trying to find out whether there is any common thread that runs through "greatness," through the lives of many, if not all, leaders. In Luther's youth he found the same kind of ironic delay and confusion that he noticed in the lives of Darwin, Shaw, Freud — and indeed, Hitler. Not all men become for a significant number of years almost the opposite of everything they later seem to advocate or demonstrate. And naturally, thousands of men who are not "great" have their "identity crises" — such as young Luther or young Freud faced. Erikson is both sure of himself and wary. He doesn't want to foist yet another set of special "labels" on Luther, or anyone else. Nor does he want to sum up in a word or two the complexities of the individual's relationship to history. Yet he has become increasingly aware of certain similar themes in the lives he has studied, both in his office and in history books. And he does want to show how the general, even the universal in psychology takes a particular form in lives that make history or strongly shape it.

He was working on the borderland not only of psychology and history, but also of neurosis and creativity — perhaps the two most overused words in our time. Ordinary and gifted men in many ways are similar. We all have our oedipus complexes, our fights with this or that authority. Some few, though, seem to take their struggles very seriously, and take their time in solving them. I suppose we call them "gifted" or "great" when they find a way to offer the rest of us what they have, what is "wrong" with them as well as valuable and rare in them; and that "way" will be a craft or a message or a style which turns secret preoccupations into an open, lively message or vision felt to be irresistible by others. So the psychologist and sociologist need not totally withdraw from the vexed issue of "creativity." It seems plausible to assume that there are enough first-rate genes around to make a strictly biological explanation of leadership or genius hard to justify. We have to fall back on "old-fashioned" psychological qualities like will and determination, like lonely and perverse stubbornness. Or we must remember that the "worst" of times can again bring out the "best" in people, that accidents and incidents can "resonate" — the word has to be vague — in a person so persistently that he becomes almost wedded to them, and thus "more" than he might otherwise have been, and more than analysis of him can ever comprehend. It is all a bit elusive, a bit sticky, a bit dangerous — trying to figure out how the potentially prosaic becomes the strikingly exceptional. Always the temptation is to find a neat, clear-cut formula, any formula; and if some people catch on quickly and find the formula too categorical or facile, others can always be counted on to cheer, not the least among them the formulator himself.

Young Man Luther offers no formulas whatsoever. If Martin wanted his freedom, Erikson is inclined to give him just that. No effort is made to saddle Luther's youth with diseases and complexes. He is not confined and pinioned by psychiatric terminology, and if he does come off with an "identity crisis" it is described very concretely and vividly as a recognizable expression of his, of any man's, evolving effort to be a particular person.

Luther described his own torments, his own ailments. So did others who knew him. To say he was a great man is to say the obvious. And today it is equally obvious that in his childhood at least the seeds of his greatness were planted. But what in Luther, what in his childhood, significantly preceded and even led up to his greatness? Erikson takes Luther to be, preeminently, a spokesman, a man who said at the Diet of Worms, "My conscience is bound by God's words. Retract anything whatsoever I neither can nor will. For to act against one's conscience is neither safe nor honorable." Luther was a teacher, an orator, a writer, a preacher. Above all, though, he possessed a voice; and above all he knew how to be heard. Presumably he had once learned that very well, how to make others listen.

If Luther did anything for Western man he helped him examine once again the priorities of his various allegiances. Whom do we obey, and with what degree of commitment and order? Luther first challenged, then disobeyed the authority of authorities, the Pope;

then he proclaimed again and again, to all who heard him and read him, God's direct, unmediated interest in each of us. To our way of seeing things, Luther had a "problem"; he was rebellious, out-spokenly so, and he questioned customs that others took for granted. What is more, he acted on his beliefs — and in the process eventually changed the beliefs of others. Clearly, Erikson will have to "deal" with Luther's struggle to obey; with his disobedience; with his per-sistent and extraordinary defiance in the face of the Pope's censure; with his urge to speak that defiance, shout it again and again; and finally, with his ability to command the attention of others.

First Erikson speaks as a social historian. He discusses the German peasantry of the fifteenth and sixteenth centuries, and in particular the Luther family as an example of former peasants become — in Martin's time — city folk. He discusses migration and its psychologi-cal consequences: the search on the part of a migrant or immigrant for new standards of behavior and new ideals. Martin Luther called his father and his grandfather *rechte Bauern*, real peasants. Martin actually grew up in a town, but his father was an émigré, a man who left a Thuringian farm, and with it a whole way of life, for Mans-feld's copper and silver mining industry. All of Erikson's previous work in linking up childhood with society now served him in good stead. He was able to ask what kind of boyhood Martin would have as the child of a disinherited peasant who wanted desperately to be a burgher, and a mother who herself was of urban origin, so pre-sumably in favor of her husband's effort to "rise up." Peasants do not act like industrial workers or shopkeepers. Peasants and mem-bers of the *petite bourgeoisie* expect different things from their chil-dren. Interestingly enough, those who have written about Luther have known that kind of thing all along, and Erikson is quick to show what they have said:

In one place a reference to his peasant nature is made to underline his sturdiness; in another, to explain his vulgarity and blockheadedness; and Nietzsche, for example, calls him a *Bergmannssohn*, a miner's son (literally, the son of a man of the mountain) when he wants to do him honor.[8]

A good deal of space in *Young Man Luther* is given over to a description of the social and cultural atmosphere in young Martin's home: the purposes, strengths, and vulnerabilities of his parents as they worked hard and above all aimed high — among other ways, through the achievements they asked of their children. The reader is also made to consider the specific historical questions that once plagued the Holy Roman Empire and the medieval papacy, and now bother our century's "big powers." The world was getting smaller, because men were sailing all around it, even as today we fly all over it in planes and spaceships. Men were in touch with one another more intimately, because printing was developed, even as today television brings pictures and words to the most inaccessible regions. Ideological struggles were being waged, "Holy Wars" between Rome and Islam, even as we are still divided between the West and the East, with religious conflict replaced by the economic kind. Technological changes were becoming unusually significant. Feudalism was giving way to an international banking and business class very much associated with the Church, even as we watch the nation-state struggling for its life in the face of technological developments that bind together continents and indeed the entire earth. Finally, chivalrous knights were of no avail when guns appeared, just as today atomic bombs and missiles have made obsolete all sorts of weapons and "styles" of warfare.

How did these changes affect Hans and his son Martin? For that matter, how do "external" events — wars, revolutions, economic and social upheavals — "register" in our minds? In periods of severe change, existing institutions fight hard to keep themselves intact, even as new institutions and the men who "speak" for them seem to rise out of nowhere. In a few sentences Erikson can bring "history" into one child's experience:

What Hans Luder realized of all this, we do not know; but I think it is fair to assume that he employed his personal idiosyncrasies in the service of certain overwhelming apprehensions and hopes fed by the world situation. He wanted his son to be a lawyer, that is, one who would understand and profit by the new secular laws which were replacing those of the Roman commonwealth. He wanted his son to serve princes and cities, merchants and guilds, and not priests and bishoprics and papal finance — an economic attitude which at that time did not preclude a devout Christian sentiment. Most of all he wanted, as did millions of other ex-peasants and miners, to see his son employ his mind in higher matters, instead of dulling it with miners' superstitions, and to enjoy the wealth unearthed by others instead of dirtying his hands in shafts sunk into the earth. This, then, was what the history books call the "peasant" father of a "peasant" son.[9]

Yes, Luther's parents were fearful, worried and superstitious. What miner doesn't have good cause to live in some dread of the earth's arbitrary capacity suddenly to kill those who want to take away its treasures? As for the superstitions that Luther's parents had, that in one form or another we all have, Erikson treats them as he does religious beliefs: they are not "primitive obsessions," entertained by pitiable or "neurotic" people, but efforts to make sense of the world, and indeed master it. Martin's father and mother wanted him to go beyond their own "condition," and in a curious way he fell back upon their superstitious qualities at the most critical moments in his upward career — when thunderstorms and "fits" and "revelations" had to accompany the decisions he made.

Luther himself made two oft-quoted statements about his parents. In each instance he recalled the whipping, the caning he received from both his father and his mother: "My father once whipped me so that I ran away and felt ugly toward him until he was at pains to win me back"; and "My mother caned me for stealing a nut until the blood came. Such strict discipline drove me to a monastery although she meant it well." Those are familiar translations — which Erikson finds not quite adequate. He translates the German that Roland Bainton put into "I ran away . . . I felt ugly" rather literally, with different results: "I fled him and I became sadly resentful toward him, until he gradually got me accustomed to him again."

That translation reveals the subtleties of a particular "father-son relationship," as the current phrase goes. Martin was angry at his father, but unable to express that anger, except by becoming sad, or angry at himself. And the father could stay unhappy with his son only so long; eventually there had to be a reconciliation. Throughout Luther's writings one can note his search for the correct way to please and placate the Father of us all, and throughout the writings one can also find the strong and at times vulgarly expressed hate he felt toward particular persons or groups.

Like everyone, Martin Luther had a childhood dilemma to solve. He had to learn to be the kind of person his father and mother wanted, or fail in the attempt. He was the oldest son of a father desperately anxious for more money, more prestige. He was a boy who every day had to face the force his father was willing to exert. He was a boy who could not quite admire or revere his father — for the very reason that the father thought very little of himself. The father's hope was that the son would do him one better; and the sons of such fathers have a hard time accepting the wisdom and advice of admittedly bigger and stronger men — who nevertheless get the message of their own sense of worthlessness across to their "innocent" children. Moreover, Luther was a boy whose father really meant what he said, and would not let his sons forget it — or indeed forget him, be done with him, or be free of him.

When Erikson has described what happened between Hans and the father and Martin the son he pauses a moment for the following paragraph:

Millions of boys face these problems and solve them in some way or another — they live, as Captain Ahab says, with half of their heart and with only one of their lungs, and the world is the worse for it. Now and again, however, an individual is called upon (called by *whom*, only the theologians claim to know, and by *what*, only bad psychologists) to lift his individual patienthood to the level of a universal one and to try to solve for all what he could not solve for himself alone.[10]

Then there was the mother, whose caning also supposedly caused Luther to seek out a monastery. Certainly the gentle, loving, affectionate side of Christianity — its maternal quality — does not come through in his theology. In Erikson's words, "the Madonna was more or less gently pushed out of the way." I suppose we would call Luther's family "patriarchal." Hans was a strong, controlling figure; and his wife heeded his commands faithfully. Yet Martin gives his mother credit — and blames her — for "driving" him to a monastery.

Once again Erikson looks carefully at the origin of a statement and its translation. The German does not say "into the monastery" but "in the monkery" (*in die Moencherei*). Monkery refers to a sort of monk-business, or monkishness, a caricature of the devotedly religious man who retires from the world. Perhaps Luther was saying that his mother taught him how to be overly watchful and scrupulous. Later on he was to say this: "From childhood on, I knew I had to turn pale and be terror-stricken when I heard the name of Christ; for I was taught only to perceive him as a strict and wrathful judge."

Whether he chafed mainly at his father's wrath or at his mother's canings, he was a son to each of them. In later years he became as suspicious and stern and punitive as his father; in fact he turned on the very peasants he first championed. He also could be as superstitious and fearful as his mother. Yet, like his mother, he could speak soothing words and sing gentle songs. Erikson warns the reader not to take Luther's relative disregard for his mother as the whole truth. Of course Martin trembled before his sturdy, angry father — and never stopped doing so even when a man himself. On the other hand, we know some things so well that we never have to remind ourselves of their presence; and often they are the "better" experiences, the happy ones that continue to influence us year after year. The child psychoanalyst in Erikson insists that Luther's words — often strong, sometimes tender, usually very touching to the reader, as they must have been to the listener — must also tell us about the quality of his childhood. A boy who was neglected or *only* punished by his mother could hardly know how to *care* so much, to lead others, sing with them, talk to them, and worry about their welfare.

Were Luther's personal "problems" and experiences in any way representative? If it is true that his own resentments and suffering ultimately made him challenge the Pope's arbitrary domination, what caused others by the many thousands to respond so quickly and enthusiastically — so that an unknown priest in his lifetime became a historical figure? The historian in Erikson had studied the Middle Ages intensively, and could quote at length from Huizinga's *The Waning of the Middle Ages:*

At the close of the Middle Ages, a sombre melancholy weighs on people's souls. Whether we read a chronicle, a poem, a sermon, a legal document even, the same impression of immense sadness is produced by them all. It would sometimes seem as if this period had been particularly unhappy, as if it had left behind only the memory of violence, of covetousness and mortal hatred, as if it had known no other enjoyment but that of intemperance, of pride and of cruelty.

In the records of all periods misfortune has left more traces than happiness. Great evils form the ground-work of history. We are perhaps inclined to assume without much evidence that, roughly speaking, and notwithstanding all calamities, the sum of happiness can have hardly changed from one period to another. But in the fifteenth century, as in the epoch of romanticism, it was, so to say, bad form to praise the world and life openly. It was fashionable to see only its suffering and misery, to discover everywhere signs of decadence and of the near end — in short, to condemn the times or to despise them. . . . No other epoch has laid so much stress as the expiring Middle Ages on the thought of death. An everlasting call of *memento mori* resounds through life.[11]

Then, as if one historian is speaking to another, Huizinga is asked to remember that even in the worst of times there are many people who persist in living full and useful lives, "lusty and decent lives" Erikson calls them. There are people who can be called "as moral as they must be, as free as they may be, and as masterly as they can be." In other words: "If we only knew it, this elusive arrangement *is* happiness" — all of which is not to deny the brittle and dangerous moments in history, when it seems almost anything can happen. I find it interesting and characteristic that Erikson the historian is like Erikson the clinician: given any pathology, he will look for the hopeful or the still active and redemptive side of the story.

Obviously Luther's message fell on fertile and waiting ground; things were not so bad that no one's ideas could make a difference. It is probably accurate to say that things were getting better — and needed only the articulate words of a Luther to reveal how *much* better. In fact, the northern Renaissance was on its way: "These upper classes no more wanted to be the emperor's then growing economic proletariat than they wished to end on the day of judgment as God's proletariat who (as they could see in the paintings which they commissioned) were to be herded into oblivion by fiery angels, mostly of Italian extraction." German burghers were becoming their own masters, taking all sorts of initiative into their own hands, and preparing in many areas to shed an entire world view. The young man who left Hans Luther for college could not fail to sense the ferment around him, even if *his* instructions were to take orders, study hard, and get ahead. So, like many a college student, Martin had to face a conflict between home and school, between his origins and his contemporary environment — at a time when the larger society itself was in similar conflict, in similar crisis:

But it undoubtedly took a father and a son of tenacious sincerity and almost criminal egotism to make the most of this crisis, and to initiate a struggle in which were combined elements of the drama of King Oedipus and the passion of Golgotha, with an admixture of cussedness made in Saxony.[12]

We are asked to go back and forth between the particular and the general. Yes, Luther had such and such a life, but so did others. Yes, the world of the Middle Ages was in serious and general decline by the year 1500, and most German students must have sensed that fact — but it was, after all, Luther who hastened the process incalculably. No effort is made to single Martin out as a particularly fortunate or gifted or lucky child. Indeed for long stretches what we have is good social history: vivid, carefully documented descriptions of the homes, schools, streets and marketplaces of fifteenth- and sixteenth-century Germany. The book reads like *Centuries of Childhood*, whose author, Philippe Ariès, has provided a notable account of what it was like to be six and seven, or ten and twelve, in the various periods of Western history.

As a youth Luther did not live a "different" or "unusual" life, but eventually he did fail to achieve the destiny that for a long time he seemed quite happy and anxious to pursue — by singing and playing the lute and studying hard in school. His many friends at school even singled him out with the nickname Philosophus; because he was an able rhetorician, his scholarly biographers assume, and because he was a brooding, seriously depressed person, one of his psychiatrically inclined interpreters has claimed. Erikson is content to call him a "deep down sad youth," and wonders whether the nickname Philosophus did not in some fashion attest to Martin's seriousness, his almost fierce pride and willfulness. In any event, no one will ever talk to the youth who was Martin Luther, and ask him the questions all his students, defenders, opponents and biographers have asked these four centuries since his death. In an interesting paragraph Erikson does only what he can do, speculate about what Martin was like. The description — uncannily firm yet tentative — contains Erikson's view of many great men besides Luther:

With only this information, anybody can sketch his own Martin, and I already indicated some of the sketches which have been made. Here is my version. I could not conceive of a young great man in the years before he becomes a great young man without assuming that inwardly he harbors a quite inarticulate stubbornness, a secret furious inviolacy, a gathering of impressions for eventual use within some as yet dormant new configuration of thought — that he is tenaciously waiting it out for a day of vengeance when the semideliberate straggler will suddenly be found at the helm, and he who took so much will reveal the whole extent of his potential mastery. The counterpart of this waiting, however, is often a fear of an early death which would keep the vengeance from ripening into leadership; yet the young man often shows signs of precocious aging, of a melancholy wish for an early end, as if the anticipation of prospective deeds tired him. Premonitions of death occur throughout Luther's career, but I think it would be too simple to ascribe them to a mere fear of death. A young genius has an implicit life plan to complete; caught by death before his time, he would be only a pathetic human fragment.[13]

Luther himself described in Latin the feelings he had when he actually did come near death: *terrore et agonis mortis subitae circumvallatus*, as if completely walled in by the painful fear of a sudden death. The occasion was the famous thunderstorm, during which he was struck down by a bolt of lightning, and after which he entered a monastery. When he fell on the wet ground — summoned to die, he believed — the following words came from him, quite without thought or intent: "Help me, St. Anne. I want to become a monk." Later he described the words almost as if they were not his, as if they were imposed on him — *drungen und gezwungen, coactum et necessarium*. He had been called, even against his own will, or so he told his friends.

We are asked to imagine how torn and divided Martin's state of mind must have been at that time. He had invoked St. Anne, his father's patron saint; but now that he had survived the bolt from heaven, he decided to defy his father in the most decisive of ways. He called on the saint who prevents sudden death; but he promised to enter the profession that prepares people for death. And he called on the saint who grants prosperity to supplicants (some of them) only to vow a life of poverty for himself.

How *is* one to look at that thunderstorm, and its effect upon Martin Luther? Was it God's voice, calling the conflicted youth to higher things? Was it the Devil using one man's career to undermine, in whatever degree possible, the Holy Catholic Church? Was it nothing but one of nature's ordinary events — significant only to Martin because he was anxious and depressed anyway? This third possibility did not tempt Erikson. He sees Martin as sensitive and vulnerable, prey to any number of doubts and fears, but by no means "sick."

Certainly few men have so dramatically changed their minds about a career. It can be said that Luther went through a "conversion" — like St. Paul, after a kind of "fit." Paul's conversion was far more clear-cut and public. He had been interested in the "law," and in fact was a prosecutor of sorts, an assistant to a high priest. For a while he and his superior hunted down "enemies," like those who followed Jesus of Nazareth and believed him to be the Christ. Martin was also headed for a career in law, or so he and his father believed for a time. Erikson points out what Martin and Paul shared as men and religious leaders: for both of them there suddenly came the realization that there was a higher law, higher than high priests and ambitious fathers, higher than anyone alive. Together they now are still remembered for their antiliteralism. Let the pharisees quibble over this and that phrase, and let Rome's high priests weigh out this or that papal indulgence or decree. Between God and man there is some ineffable but transcendant communion that no law, no earthly authority can comprehend, let alone define or dispense.

Luther himself later described his conversion in these words:

> When I was a young magister in Erfurt, verily, I used to go around in sadness, oppressed by the *tentatio tristitiae*. But God acted in a miraculous way, and drove me on, innocent as I was; and He alone, then, can be said to have come a long way [in bringing it all about] that there can be no dealing between the Pope and me.[14]

This brief assertion conveys a number of themes: Luther's anguished state of mind, his relative innocence in the face of God's willfulness, and indeed the existence of some plan on the part of God to separate the Pope from one of his priests — in such a way that all Christendom would take notice and never again be the same. Yet this is later knowledge, spoken by a much older Luther who could look back and say: yes, it happened like that, and it came to this. The cynic, the doubter, the reasonably curious man, and the psychologist (who can be any of the former, too) will want to know what Luther had in mind at the moment of conversion, and during the immediate months that followed. After all, in anyone's life do retrospective formulations — autobiographical or psychoanalytic — account for the actual "motives" or "desires" that prompted decisions or choices made long, long ago?

Erikson puts his concept of *identity* to a crucial test by using it to help make young Martin's "conversion" somewhat understandable. Whatever "problems" with his father the youth had, he made his life far different when he entered a monastery. True, he was hard put to obey his father and his mother; but now he had to obey priests, bishops and Popes — and in that sense his obedience or lack of it suddenly became a public or social matter, and ultimately a historical one. Not everyone can or will do that — give his specific fears and desires a chance to be of almost universal significance. Luther's theological development did rather consistently reflect his psychological makeup. His father refused him permission to enter the monastery, so he defied him. The father became "almost mad" (*wollte toll werden*) and the mother backed her husband up. Then pestilence struck. Two of Martin's brothers fell sick and died. The elder Luther became frightened, and was persuaded to relent. Martin now had his father's approval; but he would simply not let the matter drop there. He doubted the old man's sincerity, and would never stop doubting it. Once again, though, his psychological doubts turned into religious qualms. It was Luther who again and again would ask man to examine his faith and make sure he "really" meant what he said, meant what he professed. To Luther, man and God — with no one's mediation — can sometimes face one another in purest candor; yet often they don't, as Martin didn't with his own father, and as Luther said even the Church's fathers often don't with one another. Put a bit differently, Luther was not one to let go of an issue, even when it seemed to be working itself out. Perhaps great men don't have "different" problems, merely stronger and more persisting versions of the ones we all have.

To Erikson, Luther's youthful religious struggles come to something like this:

All these experiences are at least convincing in their total psychological involvement — whether one calls it inspiration or temporarily abnormal behavior — in that they give a decisive inner push to a young person's search for an identity within a given cultural system, which provides a strong ideological pull in the same direction.[15]

Martin took to a monastery and said good-bye to his childhood; while there he suffered in mind and soul, and became a man who eventually would exhort, direct, lead, and assault other men. His life amounted to something, as we all know. In contrast, others all over the world and in all ages have less successfully faced some of the awful and ordinary struggles that he faced with himself, his family, his fellow monks, his faith. Here is young Martin's biographer reaching out for those others — in Erfurt, or Rome, or in any clinic of any American city:

It is probable that in all historical periods some — and by no means the least gifted — young people do not survive their moratorium; they seek death or oblivion, or die in spirit. Martin must have seen such death of mind and spirit in some of his brethren, and came to feel close to it more than once. Those who face the abyss only to disappear we will, of course, never know; and once in a while we should shed a tear for those who took some unborn protest, some unformed idea, and sometimes just one lonely soul, with them. They chose to face nothingness rather than to submit to a faith that, to them, had become a cant of pious words; a collective will that cloaked only collective impotence;

a conscience which expended itself in a stickling for empty forms; a reason that was a chatter of commonplaces; and a kind of work that was meaningless busy-work. I am speaking of those "outsiders" who go their lone way, not those who come back to poison the world further with a mystical literature which exhorts man to shun reality and stay outside, like Onan.[16]

Erikson goes further and manages to describe many youths from many centuries at one or another moment in their lives: "strange young creatures of pride and despair, of sick minds and good values, of good minds and fractured perspectives." He discusses what he has discussed before in technical papers: young men and women often experience serious fluctuations of mood, in which moments of near grandiosity alternate with periods of almost total hopelessness. He reminds those who have already read him how desperately alone a certain kind of youth can be, and indeed needs to be. He tells those who are reading him for the first time what he means by "identity" — positive and negative. Then he points out how determined Martin's father was that his son marry early and go directly after a career. Martin eventually found a career and marriage that would in and of themselves startle and divide the world. It is not every youth who can make history out of one of life's conventional hurdles. Martin found a job, and he married, and in so doing he managed to change the world.

For a while, though, he hesitated, his very life in balance. He feared death and he feared a million forms of vengeance. He fought the war that strong-minded and passionate men have to wage. Sometimes he was so angry he lost himself in fits or paroxysms. Sometimes he was so earnest and well-meaning that his superiors wondered why he worried himself so much, why he took even the Christian religion so seriously. When an urge to build and an urge to destroy exist side by side in us, and the urges seem equally strong and unyielding, how is the impasse to be settled? Erikson sees youths like Luther struggling with an "eerie balance between destructiveness and constructiveness, between suicidal Nothingness and dictatorial Allness." To some extent the outcome depends upon what can be called "inner" developments, such as the severe and strict nature of a youth's conscience, which can finally cause him to devote his life to a cause. Once that commitment is made, the world can become as evenly divided as the mind once was: there are good people and bad people, friends and enemies. When Luther was famous he was known as a man who could be gentle with some, and utterly abusive toward others. We don't know how Luther behaved as a child, but we do know that all children walk, then fall down, build towers, then knock them down, and in general live constantly and openly with contrary emotions. Slowly a given child becomes more one thing than another — and perhaps children "destined" to be great (for the good or the bad) experience sharper, more ironic struggles that indeed last and last: "Leonardo, the creator of the immortal da Vincian smile, was also an inveterate tinkerer with war machines: on occasion he caught himself, and relegated a design to the bottom of a deep drawer."[17]

In his time Martin was one of many brilliant and honestly critical young monks who felt horror and shame at the spectacle of the Church's daily scandal, its betrayal of Christ for Mammon — and a collection of petty Caesars. Rather than dub Luther with a psychological name or attribute that begs the question, Erikson declares the critical importance of *circumstance*, *coincidence* and *fate*. Driven men come upon opportune moments. Terribly hurt men find others who feel hurt, who need to hurt, who want their hurt recognized, spoken, and avenged. Foolish men become the heirs of an absurd past, and crafty men sense that the indifference most of us feel toward any number of "conditions" can immeasurably help a boss, a spokesman, a leader. In Erikson's troubled and honestly puzzled words, "Now and again, history does seem to permit a man the joint fulfillment of national hopes and of his own provincial and personal strivings."

And what of the followers, those who by the million rush to a Luther and show that radically new ideas and goals can swiftly take command of countries and even continents? When do we learn to follow others, and when do we most need to do so? Children, of course, are full-time followers. Every day they look up to someone for food, for advice, for direction. When we stop being children we do not stop needing and wanting direction. The most rebellious youth takes his parents or teachers seriously enough to oppose them. And many youths do indeed have a hard time finding "others" — parents, friends or lovers whom they can respect and approach and follow. A few remain forever lonely. A few make their eventual success an answer to their earlier failure: they become sought-after and thus less lonely, but they never find real companions. Luther eventually succeeded in becoming a much-admired and followed man, but whether he ever enjoyed or accepted the very people who applauded him is another matter — and a historical as well as a psychological one, in view of the venom he poured on his devoted German peasants when they took his message so seriously.

The devotion he obtained from peasants could not quite satisfy Luther. He still felt alone and his hunger for God, for faith, became more rather than less intense. Erikson knows that Martin's disappointment in his father and mother didn't "cause" his specially intense search for God, but it is still important to say that "of all the ideological systems . . . only religion restores the earliest sense of appeal to a Provider, a Providence," and it is still important to make clear the reassurance and affirmation that a religious life can offer a youth like Martin, and indeed other youths in every era. St. Paul said, "For now we see as through a glass darkly, but then face to face; now I know in part, but then shall I know even as also I am known." Many young men and women today prefer doctors to priests, but need what St. Paul describes — not the "neutral" facelessness of a scrutinizing analyst, but his willingness to be seen as well as see, and to see a life in the making as well as a life stalled, jeopardized or flawed.

Martin Luther's particular search took him to a monastery; and Erikson's eye for opposites, for the tensions that come from contrary psychological forces, appears once again in his analysis of the life in those monasteries. He goes into the history of monkhood, from the beginning, when monks were hermits, "deliberately seeking a state of radical readiness for that lonesome valley which must be crossed alone, sooner or later," to later centuries, when all sorts of houses, centers and domiciles existed to guarantee any monk the regular company of others. He notes a series of polarities. The two styles of life that together could be called "eremitical-conventual" have analogues in the two practices of contemplation and manual labor, both of which monks engage in. Moreover, monks will alternate between serious self-scrutiny and the most selfless kind of involvement with others. They will spend hours in prayer, and examine themselves with a kind of pitiless tenacity that makes the process of psychoanalysis seem less severe if no less profound. Then they will stop thinking altogether and work the land, care for the sick, teach the young, and indeed labor so hard and so long that their ability to follow such toil with later introspection, such "activity" with later "passivity," can only be called remarkable — especially today when consistency is considered such an important psychological virtue.

Monks also struggle with the twin traditions of mysticism and intellectuality. They give themselves over to the utterly mysterious, utterly unknowable, and then they spend hours trying to learn what they can and impart what they have discovered to others. To a youth like Martin, himself in conflict, there was obviously plenty to do, and enough contradiction and ambiguity to make his own troubles seem rather natural. Actually he was not an ordinary monk. In the sly manner of certain rebels he was very loyal to the father he found so impossibly demanding: "Quite in his father's spirit he chose the best school within his horizon," a monastery that was respected and well known. What is more, in becoming a monk he was emphatically not linking himself up with odd or eccentric people, or indeed uncommonly preoccupied ones. He was joining what Erikson calls the "clerical upper-middle-class" in — be it remembered — a thoroughly Catholic world. He was joining men who did quite "ordinary" things — diplomacy, social work and spiritual work that took the form of a hundred or more programs. When Martin took upon himself "the latent sadness of his age and the spiritual problems of its theology," he left behind thousands of colleagues — monks who planted and harvested crops, who did what teachers, doctors and bureaucrats always do.

The Church had become a power, a principality, a part of the world's scheme of things; but it was also tied to its spiritual mission, and in no century has Catholicism lacked truly spiritual workers. The point is that Martin rather quickly became "a strange, noteworthy and sometimes questionable monk," who took the Church quite a bit more seriously than many others within it did. The Church wanted and encouraged men like him to become passionate and even literal-minded believers, but it also had long ago become an institution, and a very strong one at that, with a capital city and a leader. That inner tension — between the spiritual and the "practical" — would of course eventually seize Martin's attention and give to his mind a large issue that somehow stood for and summarized many smaller or more personal ones.

Erikson analyzes not only the position of monks in medieval society, but their interesting routines and customs. He describes Martin's cell, "a little more than three metres long, three wide," with its table, chair, lamp and cot. He describes the austerity, the discipline, the careful, watchful, secluded life in which Martin found himself utterly immersed. He describes the concentrated moments of high drama — the prayers, the confessions, the recital of psalms, the singing:

For the first of the liturgies, the monks are awakened by a bell at about 2 A.M. — except in high summer, when this liturgy is sung at the end of the long day. The liturgy begins (as the last one ends) with prayers to Mary, *sanctae dei genetrici*, the mother of God, who will intercede with her sternly judging son: "For you are the sinner's only hope."

Food is not taken until noon, and on fast days not until early afternoon — that is, not before four liturgies have been completed; between them, there is domestic work, study, and instruction from the master of novices.[18]

In sum, Martin had found his sanctuary. Whatever temptations he faced were now forced aside by a total commitment of time and energy to his Augustinian superiors. He lived a life of long silences and utterly significant rituals. He lived in a world where good and evil were fought, but also accepted as inevitable. If he as a young man had any doubts or fears, so did all mankind, for whom Christ had suffered and died. Perhaps nothing can be more reassuring to a deeply troubled youth than evidence that he does not stand alone. Martin found not only "time" (to think, to grow, to become someone and something) but a place to do it all, and company to keep.

He could forget himself and pay heed to religious and philosophical problems. He could hold his rebelliousness in check because obedience was in constant demand. The scrupulous, thorny, literalminded person is easy game for us today; we know how angry he must be — "inside." But Erikson does not deny that same knowledge to Martin's superiors. They had an extraordinary seminarian on their hands and knew it. When Martin said his first Mass one of them is said to have restrained him from flight.

Exactly what happened at that first Mass is not known. Both Luther and his listeners eventually gave the event a mythical quality, as if the world's great Protestant had his destiny carved out from the very start. In his later years Luther said he "almost died" from nervousness, because in the midst of celebrating the Mass he felt no faith (*weil kein Glaube da war*). He remembered trying to leave the altar, to flee; and he connected the impulse to a particular moment in the Mass, when he read the words *Te igitur clementissime Pater*, "Thou most merciful Father." Even then — or so he claimed when he was much older — the idea of speaking to God directly, with no papal mediation, came to his mind.

What really happened, though? How can one interpret Luther's "reaction"? Is it possible to disentangle an old man's memory of an event from what actually took place? Of course the lives of all great men fall prey to the distortions that followers and antagonists construct. Nor does anyone, no matter how "normal," fail to emphasize or forget various events in his past. Erikson mentions the "folksy exaggeration" of an older Martin Luther's "table-talk vocabulary," and the "literalism" of his listeners, who obviously craved drama for the spreading Reformation. Yet he explicitly refuses to use psychiatric terms like "projection" to account for the mixture of fact and fancy that is, in fact, history:

As is so often the case with Luther, exaggerations and conjectures can neither enhance nor destroy the simple dramatic constellations which characterized his moments of fate. In this moment he had the presence of the Eucharist in front of him — and the presence of the father behind him. . . . In front of him was the Eucharist's uncertain grace; behind him his father's potential wrath.[19]

Erikson's discussion of the Eucharist is impressive. He demonstrates an obvious grasp of history and of religious history in particular. His sensitivity as a writer and an analyst is evident — and, at such a point, utterly refreshing. What some analysts and those thousands who ape them can do with the Eucharist needs no spelling out; the words, I fear, have become part of our everyday life — orality, incorporation, introjection, whatever. In contrast we are asked in this instance to imagine the original *experience* that was the Eucharist, the devotional meal that over the years Christ's followers again and again took together in memory of *the* meal, the one at Passover we know as the "last supper." The Eucharist enabled believers to give thanks, to eat and drink in a way that commemorated Christ and His sacrificial death. To Erikson:

When those early Christian folk heard it said: "For we being many are one bread, and one body: for we are all partakers of that one bread," and when they heard it said: "Take, eat; this is my body, which is broken for you: this do in remembrance of me," they participated in magic formulations of the kind which can only be created by a merger of the imagery of the unconscious with the poetry of the people.[20]

What happened, though, to that natural, warm, intimate rite, in which men of like mind huddled together and reaffirmed their common and passionate trust — their belief in trust, their faith in Him who *was* trust? St. Paul's worst fears become facts; in Erikson's words, "Dogma, given total power, reinstates what once was to be warded off, and brings back ancient barbaric ambiguities as cold and overdefined legalisms so unconvincing that, where once faith reigned, the law must take over and be enforced by spiritual and political terror." Martin's struggle with terror, with his tormenting and powerful need to know God wholeheartedly, had a counterpart in the history of Christianity. In time, parents, ministers and priests simply pushed doctrine upon willing children. Christ's words became tools in the hands of a million big and petty tyrants. In fact, the roots of the idolatrous, fake, pretentious "worship" that exercised Martin Luther — and persists today — can be traced way back. The *Eucharistia*, an act of thanksgiving, became the *Missa*, a means of ridding oneself of the unworthy. A poignant and honest occasion became a perfunctory and legalistic one. In the Eucharist men "tasted" their "inner condition"; now we enter church, recite our lessons, and leave. So in *Young Man Luther* the Eucharist is not declared an "illusion" or an example of the "primitive" coming to the fore but one more betrayed moment of truth.

Martin took Mass too emotionally, as did his father. The son hesitated, and the father had an outburst. Martin did not know how worthy he was before God, and Hans Luther "carried on, in front of all the doctors, magistrates and other gentlemen," or so Martin Luther remembered when much older. "You scholars, have you not read in the scriptures that one should honor father and mother?" To which, among other paternal remarks, the son eventually replied, but only when a famous man: "You again hit me so cleverly and fittingly that in my whole life I have hardly heard a word that resounded in me more forcefully and stuck in me more firmly. But I, secure in my justice, listened to you as a human being and felt deep contempt for you; yet belittle your word in my soul, I could not."

The father had not really "meant" it, had not really approved of the youth's decision. After his son's first Mass he is said to have cried that "God give that it wasn't a devil's spook" — the thunderstorm that so deeply affected Martin and prompted his entry into a monastery. What else could the thoughtful, sensitive and loyal son of such a father do but struggle to find out an answer, any answer, *the* answer? The father was not sincere. The son in time felt driven to find out what religious sincerity was all about. Alone, unworthy by his own estimate before God, afraid and resentful of his father, yet unable to forget him and his wishes — "belittle your word in my soul, I could not" — he became deeply troubled and forever marked by those troubles. Erikson puts it this way: *"To be justified* became his stumbling block as a believer, his obsession as a neurotic sufferer, and his preoccupation as a theologian."

When he was much older and already one of Rome's established antagonists, Luther looked back at his years in the monastery as an awful time, full of wounding and insulting experiences. Here it is helpful to be both a historian and a psychoanalyst. How is one to square Luther's remarks about his ordeal with the actual facts? In his middle age he charged that his superiors drove him to sickness by demanding that he pray, pray, pray — and read, read almost endlessly. To which Erikson in a way "replies" with the following observation — offered almost as a doctor would when faced with an apparent contradiction: "Yet he reported himself that in 1510 he was able to walk from Erfurt to Rome, which was exceptionally rainy that year, and back over the wintry Alps, without any sign of weakness worse than a fleeting cold." Again, an aging Luther claimed that as a monk he had to fight for the right to read the Bible, when in fact the Bible was then a constant possession of his. Was he senile? Did he lie? Is it a legend that he and his followers deliberately set out to create? Were they all confused or deluded?

Of equal interest is the change in the *Church's* evaluation of Martin. In his monastery days he was tolerated, even highly respected. Later on, of course, he became a formidable opponent of the Pope's, and then others added to his own distortions: the monk who had in fact been considered gifted and promising was considered an agent of the Devil all along — a demon who had somehow penetrated the walls of Erfurt's monastery to do his insidious work. At the very least, the man lacked a genuine vocation.

Erikson neither defends nor attacks Martin and his followers or the Church and its spokesmen. When W. H. Auden read *Young Man Luther* he found it "full of wise observations not only about Luther but also about human life." The discussion of Luther's eventual break with the monastery provides one of those wide-ranging "observations":

This spiritually unsuccessful ordination ended Martin's honeymoon with monasticism and doomed their marriage to an eventual divorce which confused all the retrospective information about Luther's next phase.

While he was still in the cloister nothing much was found worth recording about this excitable and yet impressive monk. Only after his dramatic separation from monasticism did he and the other monks begin to appraise his years of monkhood in bitter earnest. Whatever ends in divorce, however, loses all retrospective clarity because a divorce breaks the *Gestalt* of one love into the *Gestalten* of two hates. After divorce the vow "until death us do part" must be explained as a commitment made on wrong premises. Every item which once spelled love must now be pronounced hate. It is impossible to say how good or how bad either partner really was; one can only say that they were bad for each other. And then the lawyers take over and railroad the whole matter into controversies neither of the partners had ever thought of.[21]

Erikson's use of the analogy of a marriage that ends in divorce was all the more relevant in view of the Church's own use of that analogy in describing the vows taken by a priest or a nun. Luther and the Church resorted to the mutual recriminations that only one-time intimates can feel. When Luther was older he was clearly a leader, and in the midst of a severe and sticky fight with a powerful institution. Around him other institutions were also beginning to rise — new churches, principalities, whatever. Under such circumstances almost forgotten events become newly important: they are pieces of a budding ideology, elements in a growing myth, a developing historical "picture." The leader and the led, the rebel and the tyrant, the old authorities and the young challengers — they all take their stands accordingly, and once they have done so their memories have to fall in line and do the right (ideological) thing.

Martin's monastic years also provoked Erikson's mind in a number of other directions. In a longer digression than the one on marriage and divorce he discusses the psychoanalyst's training, "which demands a total and central personal involvement, and which takes greater chances with the individual's relation to himself and to those who up to then have shared his life, than any other professional training except monkhood." Psychoanalytic institutes can go the way of the medieval Church:

Because the reward for psychoanalytic training, at least in some countries, is a good income; because, for decades, the psychoanalyst seemed primarily preoccupied with the study of sexuality; and because psychoanalytic power under certain historical conditions can corrupt as much as any other power, an aura of licentiousness is often assumed to characterize this training.[22]

In point of fact, the greatest corruption that analysts, like priests, face may be much less dramatic or tantalizing. They both go through a long, austere, closely supervised apprenticeship, not unlike the one that Martin did hundreds of years ago. The monk gives up the world, and the young, would-be analyst has to give himself over to a systematic relentless scrutiny that surely matches anything the monks of Erfurt experienced. The result may be a prosaic but awful kind of human failure:

There is, first of all, what I would like to call the asceticism of the "expendable face." The analysand reclines on a couch at the head of which the analyst sits; both of them put, as it were, their faces aside, and give the most minute attention to the patient's verbal productions which are interrupted by the analyst only when his technical sense demands that an interpretation be given. He, of course, can see, not the analysand's face, but his gestures and postural changes; while the analysand sees the ceiling, maybe the top of a bookcase, or one and the same picture for hundreds of hours. (I wish to acknowledge a small fragment of an original Greek sculpture in faintly glowing marble.) The restriction of the visual field, the injunction on muscular or locomotor movement, the supine position, the absence of facial communication, the deliberate exposure to emerging thought and imagery — all these tend not only to facilitate ordinary memory and meditation; they produce (as they are supposed to do) a "transference neurosis," that is a transfer to the analyst and the analytic situation of the irrational and often unconscious thought contents and affects which characterize the analysand's symptoms or blindspots.

The analyst patiently continues to explain the patterns of unconscious thought, whether the material strikes him as boring or lurid, appealing or nauseating, thought-provoking or infuriating. It stands to reason, however, that when a devotional denial of the face, and a systematic mistrust of all surface are used as tools in a man's worklife, they can lead to an almost obsessional preoccupation with "the unconscious," a dogmatic emphasis on inner processes as the only true essence of things human, and an overestimation of verbal meanings in human life.[23]

Some men cannot take either the Church's regimen for would-be priests or the "requirements" that a "candidate" must fulfill if he or she is to be designated a psychoanalyst. In a monastery and in a psychoanalytic institute the weak, the wild and the errant have to be sorted out; but every once in a while another kind of "problem" appears, a young man who is not so much "unsuitable" as he is a radical challenge. He startles his superiors and supervisors with unconventional questions and interesting but unsettling answers. He is called "original" at first, though soon there is something "wrong" or devilish about him. He is special, true, but ultimately he is a troublemaker or an eccentric, and he has to leave. For that matter, how did he get accepted at all? ask the nervous and frightened officials, whose job becomes in consequence one of "tightening up things," to make sure there is no chance of a repetition. Institutions must protect themselves, in the name of Christ or Freud, in the name of words like "freedom," "equality," "property" and "proletariat."

So Martin struggled to be a good and fitting monk, and his superiors watched him solicitously and then nervously. Erikson draws on Luther's own descriptions of his experiences in Erfurt to show how torn he must have been, anxious to obey but constantly impelled to defy. No wonder Martin Luther is known in history as a man who told other men how impossible it is to appease, placate, and win over God Almighty. One of the most clarifying moments in *Young Man Luther* comes at this point. The reader gets a real "feel" for the antecedents, both ordinary and powerful, of Lutheran theology. A desperately scrupulous but desperately troubled young man tried everything to gain peace for himself, to earn God's grace — and failed. Eventually he would tell others what he did succeed in finding out, what he dared to believe was his fate and theirs: faith somehow precedes "works"; and no act of prayer or atonement, no papal indulgences, no recitations or gestures of contrition and allegiance can by themselves earn God's favor. What matters is the *spirit* — in Luther's words the faith, love, joy and will (*Glaub, Lieb, Lust und Willen*) in which the act is done.

Of course, to some extent Martin's struggles have been shared by youths in every century and in many societies. The clinician can call in evidence, for example, James Joyce's *Portrait of the Artist as a Young Man:*

This idea of surrender had a perilous attraction for his mind now that he felt his soul beset once again by the insistent voices of the flesh which began to murmur to him again during his prayers and meditations. It gave him an intense sense of power to know that he could by a single act of consent, in a moment of thought, undo all that he had done. He seemed to feel a flood slowly advancing towards his naked feet and to be waiting for the first faint timid noiseless wavelet to touch his fevered skin. Then, almost at the instant of that touch, almost at the verge of sinful consent, he found himself standing far away from the flood upon a dry shore, saved by a sudden act of the will or a sudden ejaculation: and . . . a new thrill of power and satisfaction shook his soul to know that he had not yielded nor undone all.[24]

Luther talked quite frankly about the power of sexual drives; no matter how sincerely the priest vows his chastity, he can never take his sworn intentions for granted. The body has its own rhythm; the mind inevitably will fight that rhythm and from time to time lose out; and always, in one way or another, the mind will pay the respect that an adversary does to an opponent. Erikson sees Luther as very much a predecessor to both Schopenhauer and Freud. Luther bluntly, almost brusquely, acknowledged sex as an insistent force in human life, a force that affected in various ways the "whole person" a good part of the time. The reaction to him was one of severe outrage, not really any worse, though, than the kind this century gave to Sigmund Freud:

It has been pointed out derisively by churchmen that in all of this rethinking Luther anticipates the pessimism of Schopenhauer's will and the pansexualism of Freud's libido. And it is true that, like them, he gradually came to consider it mandatory that one acknowledge the total power of drives. One can call this attitude defeatism, and Martin's initial insight certainly is based on what he experienced as personal defeat; but one may also view it as his refusal to make his honesty in such things a matter of optimistic denial, or of small victories which serve nothing but self-deception.[25]

As a monk Martin was not alone. There were others like him, including a host of older teachers and superiors who could easily sympathize with his difficulties. One of them, John Staupitz, became his "fatherly sponsor" and advisor. It is quite possible that more than anything else that friendship helped Martin Luther settle his doubts — as much as they ever could be settled — and put his energies to the kind of work we all know about.

Martin was twenty-five when he was transferred to Wittenberg. Dr. Staupitz was a professor of theology there and vicar-general of the Augustinian monastery. (Erfurt and Wittenberg were sister monasteries.) At Wittenberg Martin met up with all sorts of "liberal" and "humanist" philosophers and theologians. He also came under the protection of Frederic the Wise, a prince who in later years would stand by him. Most important of all, he found in Staupitz — at long last — an older man he could genuinely trust and admire. He and his father had been anything but close, and as a monk Martin found himself predominantly fearful and anxious before God the Father, and for that matter, the priestly "fathers" who shared the monastery with him. In Staupitz he found a man who evoked not terror and guilt, but self-confidence and a desire to please through achievement. I suppose we could call Staupitz a good teacher, a wise leader, a shrewd psychologist — or simply someone who was "there" when a man destined for "greatness" needed "help," or reassurance or whatever.

So Staupitz did more than the history books credit to him. We are told that he pushed Martin along academically, gave him a boost up the Church's hierarchy, groomed him for his own professional chair, and in a way encouraged his wayward and ultimately Protestant ways. He also gave him what Erikson calls "sanction," the same kind of sanction Fliess gave to Freud. Staupitz was the "right" listener any number of gifted men desperately need at a certain moment in life. It was not that he said or did anything very special, very stimulating. Who can "analyze" the "things" that go on between such people? Sometimes a chance remark from a man like Staupitz is all that a "counterplayer" like Martin Luther wants or needs to hear. Staupitz, for example, told Martin "to take a good look at the man who bears the name Christus." Erikson is fully aware that it was "nothing terribly original to say, as theologians have reiterated, pointing to Staupitz's on the whole mediocre stature." The point is that the remark was offered to a man who hungered for just those words, a man who needed a shove toward what he himself scarcely dared recognize as his own ideas. Staupitz's remark, then, "meant to Martin that he should stop doubting and start looking, use his senses and his judgment, grasp Christ as a male person like himself, and identify with the man in God's son instead of being terrorized by a name, an image, a halo."

Erikson is even willing to wonder whether in fact Staupitz ever actually spoke some of the words Luther attributed to him much later on: "maybe he was merely that right person of whom one likes to believe or to remember that he said the right thing." Men like Staupitz and Fliess usually get no recognition, even though they give, for whatever reason of their own, exactly that: recognition, a kindly, approving face to the Luthers and Freuds of this world.

Interestingly enough, a papal bull gave John Staupitz, as provincial general of all Saxony, sweeping new powers; and in 1510 Martin was ordered to accompany an older monk to Rome on an errand of protest. The Erfurt monastery — to which Martin had returned in 1509 after a year with Dr. Staupitz at Wittenberg — was one of seven (out of twenty-nine) that objected to the Pope's administrative reforms. Martin was ordered to take part in a routine complaint from within the bureaucracy, directed not at Staupitz personally but at his overriding authority.

The two monks crossed southern Germany and northern Italy, mostly on foot. They traveled through the forests and mountains and valleys that Erikson himself knew so well as a youth, and they spent time in Florence, where Erikson had lived for a number of months. Eventually they came upon Rome, The City; in a few days they took care of their business and set out on their way back. In all they were on the road seventy days.

Young Man Luther reaches its climax in the section that deals with the young monk's trip southward and his "behavior" in the immediately following years — "The Meaning of 'Meaning It.'" The writing and thinking at this point becomes exceptionally luminous — whether because the author himself loves both travel and Italy, with all its artistic treasures, or because the emergence, finally, of an enormous and powerful talent in a great man could only demand of the biographer a fitting and comparable effort of his own.

At times in his life as a scholar and writer Erikson has had to fight his dramatic inclinations. This was no time to do so. Luther's arrival in Rome, his unobtrusive stay there, his quick departure, surely qualify as some of the great moments of irony in history. Nothing at all seemed to happen. A monk from the hinterland came, saw, and left. Yes, he was made nervous and uneasy by the sight of this or that bit of pomp or idolatry; but so have others in every generation, including most recently Pope John XXIII. Troubled or not, disedified or not, he persisted in looking, sightseeing, praying. Only upon his return, many months later, would he let all hell loose on Rome — and reveal how much he had noticed, how anguished and horrified he had actually been made by the Holy Church's various lapses, sins, and so far as Christ the Son goes, betrayals. I suppose the historical and dramatic lesson is clear: no power, however secure and universally acknowledged, can quite take itself for granted, or effectively spot and screen out the man or men who will one day somehow help to usher in its relative or absolute decline.

"He passed through Florence," says Erikson in describing Luther's visit, "where, as yet a public novelty of a few years, Michelangelo's gigantic David stood on the porch of the Signoria, a sculptural declaration of the emancipation of youth from dark giants."

Then the historian takes over from the artist:

Little more than a decade before, Savonarola had been burned in Florence: a man of fiery sincerity; a man who, like Martin, had tried academic life, and had found it ideologically wanting; who also had left home to become a monk, and, at the age of twenty-nine, after a long latency as an orator, had burst out preaching against the papal Antichrist. He also became the leader not only of a local political movement, but of an international movement of rebellious northerners. Luther later called him a saint; but there is every reason to believe that at the time of this journey both the visual splendor and the passionate heroism of the Renaissance were to him primarily Italian, and foreign; the social leadership of Savonarola, with its Christian utopianism, must have seemed far removed from whatever Protestant yearning Martin may have felt. What he did notice in Florence was the devoted and quiet *Riformazione* which went along with the noisy and resplendent *Risorgimento:* he admired the personal service rendered to the poor by anonymous aristocrats; he noted the hygienic and democratic administration of hospitals and orphanages.[26]

When he describes Luther's time in Rome, Erikson writes as if he had just spoken with Kafka about the whole, ironic business — the young, lowly, provincial monk and papal Rome, with its "ministries, legations, financial houses, hotels and inns." Martin's view of the city is described, as are his various tasks and visits:

Once established, Martin seems to have gone about his errand like a representative of some firm or union who accompanies an official to the federal capital to see the secretary of a department about an issue already decided against them. He spent much time commuting from his hotel to the department, and more time there in waiting rooms; never saw the secretary himself, and left without knowing the disposition of their appeal. In the meantime, he saw the sights which one must see and attempted to be properly impressed; also he heard a lot of gossip which, when he returned home, he undoubtedly distributed as inside information. All in all, however, the inner workings of the capital have remained mysterious to him.[27]

He did wrap himself up in prayer and ceremony. He visited churches, fasted, took communion at St. Peter's. Everywhere he was surrounded by the inspiring and the corrupting. It was the Rome that Martin Luther would shake to its foundations; and the innocent, innocuous monk, one among thousands, was taking his measure there, speedily but with deadly accuracy. We read of the city's bureaucrats, lobbyists, shyster lawyers, and the "political agents attached to the various office-holders; and the prostitutes of both sexes who beset them all." We are reminded that the Normans had burned the city in 1084, and that in 1510 it had not yet been restored. It was, in essence, a medieval city, with twice as many people as Erfurt, situated on the flatlands of the Tiber. When Martin was there the Pope was away, leading his army in a thoroughly secular war.

Much of the Rome we now know did not exist at the time of Martin's stay. Avenues and palaces were largely being planned rather than built. Michelangelo was at work on the ceilings of the Sistine Chapel. Raphael was "adorning the walls of the Pope's chambers." St. Peter's was being laboriously rebuilt. "What in style was a renaissance of Caesarian antiquity, no doubt seemed primarily Italian to the busy German monk." There was, however, a "flourishing relic business," which Erikson must describe in all its awful detail, because Luther eventually would do just that, tell the world what men can do in the name of God. There were the arms of St. Anne, Martin's beloved St. Anne, "displayed in a church separately from the rest of her bones." There were the halves of the bodies of St. Peter and of St. Paul — "which had been weighed to prevent injustice to the church harboring the other halves." There were other "saintly slices." Upon their deaths the bodies of saints — or likely saints — were "carefully boiled to prepare their bones for immediate shipment to worthy bidders." It was all, in Erikson's words, a sort of "permanent fair," where for a fee one could see a footprint made by Jesus or a silver coin once owned by Judas — and in so doing win years and years of time. A look at one of Judas' coins could save the viewer fourteen hundred years in purgatory. For that matter, "the wanderer along the holy road from the Lateran Church to St. Peter's had done his afterlife as much good as by a pilgrimage to the holy sepulchre in Jerusalem. And so much cheaper."

What did Luther make of it all — that is, *then* and not later, when of course he raged and raged at such idolatry? In his mid-twenties he was one more ordinary man, as susceptible as millions have been and still are to the "forces" that control any society. Erikson can sum up more than young Luther, the Roman visitor:

It is easy to say that the relics were just for the people and that the Church's intellectuals worked hard to reconcile faith and reason. Luther was, and always remained, one of the people; and like highly intelligent men of any age who do not challenge the propaganda of their government or the advertisements of the dominant economic system, Martin had become accustomed to the worst kind of commercialism.[28]

So Martin tried, tried desperately to do as he should. Years afterward he remembered just how hard he tried, but at the time he could only go from place to place, bent at every moment on securing deliverance for himself and his family:

He had desired above all to say Mass on a Saturday in front of the entrance to the chapel *Sancta Sanctorium;* for this act would contribute materially to his mother's salvation. But alas, the rush was too great; some mothers, Martin's included, never had a chance. So he went and ate a salted herring.[29]

Though he was destined to be a man of the Renaissance, Luther ignored its most explicit artistic manifestations, which grew out of a rising humanism and an increasing dissatisfaction with the Church's pagan characteristics. In every century those who do most to "change things" are not necessarily aware of what is *about* to happen; they may be much too obsessed with what *is,* and what *ought* to be. They leave the future to take care of itself, and their shortsightedness is rewarded by immortality. And so today visitors "will find in the Uffizi in Florence, among the grandiose works of Renaissance painting, Cranach's small, exquisite, and sober portrait of Martin Luther."

The question still has to be asked, even if it can never be satisfactorily answered: What *did* go through Martin's mind in Rome? In a few years he would be thundering at the city and its churches, cardinals and Pope. While there did he fume and seethe and prepare in his thoughts the sermons he would one day deliver? Or was he blind and deaf to everything — the good and the bad — and merely an obedient monk on a hurried trip? And if so, what happened to make him a reformer who singled out the very Roman excesses he seemed to ignore while a witness to them?

To deal with such issues Erikson again draws on his clinical work. In his patients, some of them gifted youths, he had seen years put into the service of "storing up." For a while the person unselfconsciously and indeed unconsciously "takes things in" without seeming to do so, or for that matter wanting to do anything else. He asks questions and answers them in the back of his mind, and seems all the while not only "average" or "unconcerned," but even a little slow or naive. Take Freud and Darwin; they seemed to wander about, undecided and in apparent conflict. Suddenly they emerged, and almost with a vengeance told the world what they thought — which must have been "brewing" in them for years, without anyone's knowledge, including their own. Such men go through a characteristic and complicated "moratorium." Now the concept of *moratorium* is not meant to unlock the secret of genius or creativity, but give a certain coherence to what does appear rather often and even somewhat predictably in a significant number of lives. The best that can be said is that a "configuration" of personal "problems" and social or political developments led a man like Luther eventually to say and do things that even he would have found surprising, were he told about them in his youth. How those "things" (that are said and done) become *historically* significant is "another problem." Perhaps the Luthers and Darwins and Freuds of history do on a smaller scale what Erikson says Christ tried to do for all time: "A few simple words had once more penetrated the disguises of this world, words which at one and the same time were part of the language of the child, the language of the unconscious, and the language of the uncorrupted core of all spiritual tradition."

Yet, alas, the sense of immediacy that Christ gave his followers could last only so long. Organizations and the careerism they inevitably produce had to take over. Eventually the Father, the Son, the Holy Ghost became not only "objects" of devotion but possessions. Soon "monopolists of salvation" emerged, and men were left with only one thing they could definitely take for granted, the "identity of a potential sinner." And so it finally comes to this:

As in the case of all terror, the central agency can always claim not to be responsible for the excessive fervor of its operatives; in fact, it may claim it has dissuaded its terrorists by making periodic energetic pronouncements. These, however, never reach the lowly places where life in the raw drives people into being each others' persecutors, beginning with the indoctrination of children.[30]

The corruptions of the medieval Church do not require a man writing much later to overlook its achievements. For pages Erikson discusses Plato and Aristotle, St. Paul, St. Augustine and St. Thomas.

He shows how in its best moments the Catholic Church blended "Antiquity and Christianity, Reason and Faith." The result was a "dignified piety, an immaculate thought and an integrated cosmology." Everywhere there was a real and profound sense of *style* — in the cathedrals, in various ceremonies, even in wide stretches of ecclesiastical bureaucracy. Anticipating a paper he would write ten years later ("The Ontogeny of Ritualization"), Erikson pays his respects to the Church's "genius for hierarchic formulation [which] spread from the Eucharist to the courts, the market places, and the universities, giving the identity of medieval man an anchor of colors, shapes, and sounds." Man — at least some men — found "symbolic and allegoric order," and a "static eternity of estates and classes." Or static and eternal it seemed, until guns appeared, and the printing press, and such "increasing dangers [as] the plague and syphilis, the Turks, and the discord of popes and princes."

Eventually the Church began to feel the threatening presence of man in general rather than a particular king or duke. Pico della Mirandola wrote *On the Dignity of Man*, and the Renaissance came to exalt "the organs and functions of the human body, especially insofar as the body serves (or is) the mind." Once men were ascetic (and on occasion indulgent) in a human, all too human, effort to please and find God. Now men like Leonardo and Ficino struggled "to make the body an intuitive and disciplined tool of reality." Subservient man was straining to push aside a stern, moralistic and essentially fatalistic ethic, but it would take more than the words and deeds of a Leonardo or a Lorenzo the Magnificent to do the job. Luther may not have taken to the "disciplined sensuality" of the Renaissance — in Rome or later in Germany — but Erikson argues he did something more for the cause:

One could make a case that Martin, even as he hiked back to Erfurt, was preparing himself to do the dirty work of the Renaissance, by applying some of the individualistic principles immanent in the Renaissance to the Church's still highly fortified homeground — the conscience of ordinary man.[31]

Artists and writers, men whose vision and words *were* the Renaissance, wanted to be rid of the Church's arid, categorical strictures. Christ came to save men, among other things from the brutally punitive force of powerful, self-centered institutions, including religious ones. "The letter killeth," said St. Paul — though to what avail a few really devout men were doubtless wondering in the very Rome Martin Luther so loyally visited in 1510. Yet Renaissance men were Christians, and of course members of the Holy Catholic Church. How "free" could they become — in the arts and budding sciences — if deep inside their minds were all the outworn, harsh prohibitions of the Middle Ages? If the Renaissance was to become something more than a rarefied, special and transient phenomenon, its implicit and explicit values would have to achieve a force of their own in hundreds and hundreds of communities all over Europe. People by the thousands — plain people and unusual people, poor people and influential people — would have to "think" differently, have a new "feeling" about the world and their place in it, and view things from a new "perspective." Luther became a leader of those thousands. He reached them with words, not paintings or sculptures, and words directed at the "heart and soul" rather than the rational and curious mind.

Erikson is naturally fascinated with Luther the preacher and teacher, not only because his sermons and lectures made such a difference in history, but because they in a sense enabled young, troubled and indecisive Martin to become the grown and extraordinarily effective Luther:

Forced to speak his mind in public, he realized the rich spectrum of his verbal expression, and gained the courage of his conflicted personality. He learned to preach to the heart and lecture to the mind in two distinct styles. . . . His posture was manly and erect, his speech slow and distinct. This early Luther was by no means the typical pyknic, obese and round-faced, that he became in his later years. He was bony, with furrows in his cheeks, and a stubborn, protruding chin. His eyes were brown and small, and must have been utterly fascinating, judging by the variety of impressions they left on others. They could appear large and prominent or small and hidden; deep and unfathomable at one time, twinkling like stars at another, sharp as a hawk's, terrible as lightning, or possessed as though he were insane. There was an intensity of conflict about his face, which might well impress a clinician as revealing the obsessive character of a very gifted, cunning, and harsh man who possibly might be subject to states of uncontrolled fear or rage. Just because of this conflicted countenance, Luther's warmth, wit, and childlike candor must have been utterly disarming; and there was a total discipline about his personality which broke down only on rare occasions.[32]

In his late twenties, then, Martin Luther became a man of the Word. Upon his return from home he moved to Wittenberg, and delivered sermon after sermon, lecture after lecture, to students and monks. He poured out his soul when he talked. He knew how to reach people and deeply affect them. (In his words, "You must preach as a mother suckles her child.") At last he "found himself" — by finding a "way," a means of putting to use both his gifts and his troubles. At last he knew exactly what he could do and would do. At last he was in the midst of a busy, active and extraordinarily productive life. The shy, retiring monk who was nobody in particular became a very definite somebody, and in fact was on his way to becoming *the* somebody of his age.

It is not known exactly when and how Luther went through his intellectual, emotional and religious "conversion" or, as it is called, "revelation." We do know that he was tired, depressed and afraid of an imminent death just before he became convinced that God's righteousness was forever shown to man by Christ, whose moment of faith in God was decisively illuminating for all men in all centuries. Erikson picks themes from Luther's first lectures and discusses them "side by side with psychoanalytic insights" in order to show all that can be shown, and correlate what can be correlated — the progressive development of a man's ideas and his mood:

Theological readers will wonder whether Luther saved theology from philosophy only to have it exploited by psychology; while psychoanalysts may suspect me of trying to make space for a Lutheran God in the structure of the psyche. My purposes, however, are more modest: I intend to demonstrate that Luther's redefinition of man's condition — while part and parcel of his theology — has striking configurational parallels with inner dynamic shifts like those which clinicians recognize in the recovery of individuals from psychic distress. In brief, I will try to indicate that Luther, in laying the foundation for a "religiosity for the adult man," displayed the attributes of his own hard-won adulthood; his renaissance of faith portrays a vigorous recovery of his own ego-initiative.[33]

Luther found his own voice, and went on to insist that every man's voice is sacred. He became independent enough to find his father's disapproval no longer important, even as at the same time he saw in the Son's passion evidence of the Father's "face," that is, His continuous and gracious presence among us. All men can find direct and personal access to God. All men can find through Him the precious justification and acceptance that is in the end a life's most important achievement. In Luther's theology God's compassion is utterly beyond guile, calculation or earthly riches. In a sense, then, His compassion is affirmed, made more significant, more majestic, more affirmative. Christ is the Son who did indeed doubt, and whose faith was indeed jeopardized. But Christ persisted in a divine way, even if for a moment (on the cross) he was human and therefore very much alone and apprehensive. Christ's Sonhood eventually was redeemed, though; and all men ought not forget that fact if they desire salvation. Therefore, nothing a man does, or a church does for a man, can remove the haunting example of Christ about to die, of Christ addressing His Father, of Christ asking about His fate and God's justice. A Father and a Son found one another, became mutually confirmed and united as One, and Luther wanted that example to become mankind's chief hope. Again, Erikson does not want to "interpret" religious history, in this case the so-called myth of Christ as the Son of God. Nor does he consider it sacrilegious to look for the earthly analogues to divine moments. Luther made the world think again about what has to happen before a person can really rest secure, eternally secure. If he himself had been terribly insecure, and in a way as fatherless as the Devil is godless, then his "recovery" was both a religious and a psychological event. At last he could say what he emphatically meant and had learned out of the very depths of his own life — out of his own experience as a son, a youth, and finally, a grown man.

And so it came about that Martin Luther — troubled, peculiar, rebellious, literal-minded Martin Luther — could not quite relax and behave like everyone else:

Luther, instead, made a virtue out of what his superiors had considered a vice in him (and we, a symptom), namely, the determined search for the rock bottom of his sinfulness: only thus, he says, can man judge himself as God would: *conformis deo est et verax et justus.* One could consider such conformity utter passivity in the face of God's judgment; but note that it really is an active self-observation, which scans the frontier of conscience for the genuine sense of guilt. Instead of accepting some impersonal and mechanical absolution, it insists on dealing with sincere guilt, perceiving as "God's judgment" what in fact is the individual's own truly meant self-judgment.[34]

Then the heart of *Young Man Luther* comes forth:

Is all this an aspect of personal adjustment to be interpreted as a set of unconscious tricks? Martin the son, who on a personal level had suffered deeply because he could not coerce his father into approving his religiosity as genuine, and who had borne with him the words of this father with an unduly prolonged filial obedience, assumes now on a religious level a volitional role toward filial suffering, perhaps making out of his protracted sonhood the victory of his Christlikeness. . . . Christ now becomes the core of the Christian's identity: *quotidianus Christi adventus*, Christ is today here, in me. The affirmed passivity of suffering becomes the daily Passion and the Passion is the substitution of the primitive sacrifice of others with a most active, most masterly, affirmation of man's nothingness — which by his own masterly choice, becomes his existential identity.[35]

Luther called on Christ with all possible passion, and Erikson realizes how mixed a blessing Christ's presence can be for any man, any leader:

The men revered by mankind as saviors face and describe in lasting words insights which the ordinary man must avoid with all possible self-deception and exploitation of others. These men prove their point by the magic of their voices which radiate to the farthest corner of their world and out into the millennia. Their passion contains elements of choice, mastery, and victory, and sooner or later earns them the name of King of Kings; their crown of thorns later becomes their successor's tiara. For a little while Luther, this first revolutionary individualist, saved the Saviour from the tiaras and the ceremonies, the hierarchies and the thought-police, and put him back where he arose: in each man's soul.[36]

On October 31, 1517, Luther nailed his ninety-five theses against indulgences on the door of the Castle Church in Wittenberg, not so defiant and unusual a gesture as we now may think. He was then thirty-three and well on his way to a place in history. Only seven years earlier he had gone to Rome, a young and unknown monk. Only a few years later he would be one of the most admired and hated men in Europe. It all seemed to take place so quickly. Luther himself must have wondered what possessed him. In Rome he had been forlorn and confused. Back at home he suddenly began to talk and talk. His ideas virtually poured out. His message became pointed and decisive. He seemed controlled yet forceful, respectful yet an unsparing critic of what he believed wrong. And it did not take long for him to be heard all over. A lot must have happened — to him and to Europe.

Perhaps the success of *Young Man Luther* can be measured this way: the sudden and surprising confrontation that Luther — in his thirties — had with history becomes more comprehensible after a reading of Erikson's book. Europe's particular vulnerability in the late medieval period appears to have been almost "made" for a certain kind of stubborn, unflinching and moody leader, who would have to come from the continent's geographic and religious "heart" — and want to save and purify, rather than destroy, what was in fact a very powerful and stable as well as (in certain respects) shaky order of things. Martin knew both love and hate particularly well. He knew how to build and destroy, or rather, destroy and build. For every bit of convincing anger, he had a matching amount of love and self-doubt. He was, in sum, the man who could make a believable and inspiring protest. As his father and his superiors knew, he could be perversely loyal, disarmingly mutinous, unnervingly compliant and refreshingly defiant. If history was waiting for him, he was waiting for history — all of which *Young Man Luther* shows, not by flashy, boastful, twentieth-century formulations that explain, everything and nothing, but by a systematic (and by no means exclusively psychological) analysis of countless documents, letters, sermons, discourses, texts, records and books. (The book's footnotes would suggest that the author is either a historian or a theologian.)

One more thing: Erikson indicates not only how Martin became Luther, but how Luther became what he eventually did — a turnabout, a man who in the end surprised the German peasants, took after them, and even today confuses anyone interested in understanding his dramatic, puzzling and apparently inconsistent reactions of those later years. The fact is that we seldom really put ourselves back into an earlier time, let alone into a great man's life. We think of Luther in his late thirties at the Diet of Worms, facing the Pope's emissaries and ultimately telling them no, he would not budge. We think of him as the man who *did* something, *started* something, and helped shape *our* world. Take, for instance, William James' estimate, which Erikson quotes: "When Luther, in his immense manly way, swept off by a stroke of his hand the very notion of a debit and credit account kept with individuals by the Almighty, he stretched the soul's imagination and saved theology from puerility."

Well, what about that "immense manly way"? Its origins are described in *Young Man Luther*, and neither derogated nor overestimated. But Luther did not fight only the Pope. He fought himself;

and at his strongest he was far more hesitant and fearful than we can reasonably be expected to know at this time, when centuries of words and deeds have buried him in glory and infamy. It could just be that the Luther who protested papal indulgences had no idea what his particular and seemingly innocuous complaint would set loose. Luther, that is, nailed his ninety-five theses upon a church door because he wanted to talk, to discuss things, to get an answer:

But the answer came from elsewhere, from everywhere. The German translation of the theses evoked an immediate, wide, and emphatic echo: from the general public, who were anti-Italian and patriotic; from the dispossessed, who were anticapitalist and equalitarian; from the petty plutocrats, who were antimonopolistic; from the princes, who were particularist and territorial; from the educated, who were anticlerical and secularist; and from the knights, who were Teutonic and anarchistic. From all of these groups came encouragement so personal and folksy that it can be rendered in American only as "Atta boy, Monk!"[37]

Obviously Luther never intended to take on the whole Church and indeed history itself. Political events that seem retrospectively inevitable may once have been easily avoidable. History is littered with accidents that became so-called inevitabilities:

The explosiveness of the popular response immediately warned both Luther and the Church that many kinds of rebellious desires had been ignited by this one issue of alien taxation. There were moments in the following months when Luther seemed ready to recant, and when the Pope made amazing concessions by publicly "clarifying" some of the excessive claims for the papal power of divine intercession which had been made, implied, or not denied by his operatives. But Luther and the Pope acted mostly like animals who withdraw when they hear the echoes of their own growls, then are emboldened by the other's withdrawal, and soon find themselves irrevocably engaged. There is no retreat once blood is drawn.[38]

Almost in spite of himself Luther became a prophet, an ideological leader. At Worms it no longer mattered what his personal conflicts were, even though they had "caused" his appearance before the papal "commission," or "board of inquiry," as we might call the Diet today. The point is that *he* could not be as settled and decided in his mind as his supporters became in *theirs*. A man says something, does so with urgency, but also hesitation; then others hear and make his words their creed; and then the man finds a thousand things happening that he never dreamed possible or desirable. At that point he will either submit or fight back, either go along with the tide of history, or ironically fight the very developments his troubled and gifted mind helped bring about. Luther chose to do the latter:

Luther's letters from the Wartburg indicate the psychological setting for his future actions: having openly challenged Pope and Emperor and the universal world order for which they both stood, and having overcome his own inhibitions in order to express this challenge effectively, he now fully realized not only how ravenous his appetites were, and how rebellious his righteousness, but also how revolutionary were the forces which he had evoked in others.[39]

From then on drama and irony take over:

The development of Luther's personal and provincial life, on the one hand, and of the general social dislocation, rebellion, and evolution, on the other, now took on a combination of naive eagerness, unconscious irony, and righteous frightfulness fit for a drama of Shavian dimensions. The Augustinian monastery in Wittenberg, abandoned by the friars, was turned over by the Elector to Luther's personal use. After his marriage it was shared by his wife, a former nun, and their children — certainly an ironic architectural setting for the first Lutheran parsonage. Then, just as he was about to settle down, his revolutionary poetry came home to roost. The peasants rose up all over Germany.[40]

The peasants quoted Martin Luther as they rose up, but he advised caution, restraint, compromise. They ignored him, disobeyed him — and enraged him. He shouted at them like a man who knows how to shout because he has borne the brunt of countless tirades. Erikson asks: "Do we hear Hans, beating the residue of a stubborn peasant out of his son?" Luther was then a middle-aged man, but the demons of his youth would not leave. At thirty, he had fought them to a standstill; at forty they were again powerful. Sons become fathers. Children remind a parent of his forgotten childhood.

In 1526 Luther's son was born. He was named Hans. The boy would grow up in the shadow of a great father, though in many respects one not unlike the old grandfather, Hans. If, as Erikson suggests, the mind has a dialectical quality to its "action," if we never forget, and are never free of our past, if "negatives" and "positives" inevitably live side by side in us, if certain themes appear, disappear, and reappear in every life, if consistency means nothing to the unconscious, and indeed if contradiction is the inevitable result of the necessary and continual struggle that each mind wages for that elusive "condition" or state of armistice called "sanity" — then, of course, the son of Hans, who became the father of a Hans, would find stability and obedience and respectability terribly important, and inexcusably threatened by the German peasantry. So the old loyalties and memories reasserted themselves, even if for a while Luther had kept their influence in check. He who fought his father became very much like him in later years, to the confusion of his contemporaries and many others later on. Historically, though, everything worked out rather appropriately. Luther may have had a psychological reversal, or regression, or whatever, but the effect of his actions was always in one direction. As a youth, and for all the troubles and disagreements he had with his father, Luther did the old man proud. He was a good student; he rose steadily in every school; he won steadily, no matter what the odds. In the long run he paved the way for a later union (in Max Weber's well-known phrase) of "the Protestant ethic and the spirit of capitalism," which his father would no doubt have found congenial — and familiar: "In spite of having reacted more violently than anyone else against indulgences and against usury, Luther helped prepare the metaphysical misalliance between economic self-interest and church affiliation so prominent in the Western world. Martin had become the metaphysical jurist of his father's class."[41]

In fact, Martin became everything his father might ever have wished: well-to-do, respected, powerful, world-famous, and the father of a son named Hans. Of course, Luther himself became depressed at just such a turn of events; and in his various discussions of the "life cycle" Erikson has mentioned why. In middle life and beyond we begin to see not so much what we wanted to do, but what we actually have done — given birth to, generated, inspired by word or deed. A divided self by then has to sense if not see its failures — and they may exist in the face of the most triumphant successes imaginable. At some "level" one realizes how little *healing* has occurred, how unnervingly the old curses reassert themselves, whether in the guise of breakdowns or impressive achievements. No wonder some of us in our forties and fifties feel "in a rut" and full of despair. Perhaps the despair is not only "existential" or even related to immediate circumstances, but long-lived and tied to the mind's ability to look back and recognize its own particular losses and defeats.

In a sense, then, Luther in his final years was resigned. Like a number of other great men he found his achievements to be futile: they did not solve the conflicts that prompted them, and much worse, they created new, surprising or frightening conflicts, in others if not in himself. In his last years Freud also was resigned. He saw psychoanalysis used as an excuse for all sorts of foolish, bizarre and stupid things. And there are other similarities between Luther and Freud. Both men tried hard "to increase the margin of man's inner freedom by introspective means applied to the very center of his conflicts." Through prayer, through psychoanalysis, men were asked to find out what they "really" believed, and to mean what they say. More significant perhaps is another (and I think remarkable) comparison:

In this book I have described how Luther, once a sorely frightened child, recovered through the study of Christ's Passion the central meaning of the Nativity; and I have indicated in what way Freud's method of introspection brought human conflict under a potentially more secure control by revealing the boundness of man in the loves and rages of his childhood. Thus both Luther and Freud came to acknowledge that "the child is in the midst."[42]

A little while later Erikson ends his book; and perhaps none of his writing reveals so well the quality of his "mind" — its blend of the sensual, factual, visual and analytic — as the last few paragraphs of *Young Man Luther:*

The Reformation is continuing in many lands, in the form of manifold revolutions, and in the personalities of protestants of varied vocations.

I wrote this book in Mexico, on a mirador overlooking a fishing village on Lake Chapala. What remains of this village's primeval inner order goes back to pre-Christian times. But at odd times, urgent church bells call the populace to remembrance. The church is now secular property, only lent to the Cura; and the priest's garb is legally now a uniform to be worn only in church or when engaged in such business as bringing the host to the dying. Yet, at night, with defensive affront, the cross on the church tower is the only neon light in town. The vast majority of the priest's customers are women, indulging themselves fervently in the veneration of the diminutive local madonna statue, which, like those in other communities, is a small idol representing little-girlishness and pure motherhood, rather than the tragic parent of the Savior, who, in fact, is little seen. The men for the most part look on, willing to let the women have their religion as part of women's world, but themselves bound on secular activity. The young ones tend toward the not too distant city of Guadalajara, where the churches and cathedrals are increasingly matched in height and quiet splendor by apartment houses and business buildings.

Guadalajara is rapidly turning into a modern city, the industrial life of which is dominated by the products and techniques of the industrial empire in the North; yet, the emphasis is on Mexican names, Mexican management. A postrevolutionary type of businessman is much in evidence: in his appearance and bearing he protests Mexican maleness and managerial initiative. His modern home can only be called puritan; frills and comforts are avoided, the lines are clean and severe, the rooms light and barren.

The repudiation of the old is most violently expressed in some of the paintings of the revolution. In Orozco's house in Guadalajara one can see beside lithographs depicting civil war scenes with a stark simplicity, sketches of vituperative defamation of the class he obviously sprang from: his sketches swear and blaspheme as loudly as any of the worst pamphlets of Martin Luther. In fact, some of the most treasured murals of the revolution vie with Cranach's woodcuts in their pamphleteering aimed at an as yet illiterate populace. But will revolutions against exploiters settle the issue of exploitation, or must man also learn to raise truly less exploitable men — men who are first of all masters of the human life cycle and of the cycle of generations in man's own lifespace?

On an occasional trip to the capital, I visit ancient Guanajuato where the university, a formidable fortress, has been topped by fantastic ornamental erections in order to overtower the adjoining cathedral which once dominated education. The cathedral wall bears this announcement about death, judgment, inferno, and eternal glory:

> *La Muerta que es puerta de la Eternidad*
> *El Judicio que deciderá la Eternidad*
> *El Infierno que es la habitación de la desgraciada Eternidad*
> *La Gloria que es la mansión de la feliz Eternidad*

The area of nearby Lake Pátzcuaro is dominated by an enormous statue erected on a fisherman's island. The statue depicts the revolutionary hero Morelos, an erstwhile monk, his right arm raised in a gesture much like Luther's when he spoke at Worms. In its clean linear stockiness and stubborn puritanism the statue could be somewhere in a Nordic land; and if, in its other hand, it held a mighty book instead of the handle of a stony sword, it could, for all the world, be Luther.[43]

IX

From Clinician to Professor

THE Eriksons lived in Stockbridge, Massachusetts, and worked at the Austen Riggs Center for a decade, from 1950 until 1960, when he was appointed a professor at Harvard, one of the last appointments made while McGeorge Bundy was dean. (The Harvard faculty offered no objection to a man without a college degree. Actually, Harvard provides an honorary M.A. to all permanent faculty members, perhaps so that every professor, whatever the attainments he brings to the university from elsewhere, starts out in Cambridge on an equal footing.) *Young Man Luther* had established its author as a scholar whose interests ranged considerably beyond psychoanalytic theory and whose work was in fact broadening the concerns of that theory. It is fair to say that in the middle and late fifties he became something more than a leading psychoanalyst; historians, theologians, philosophers and biologists took an increasing interest in his work and so did students of all kinds — in colleges, in graduate schools, in medical schools, in the postgraduate programs that train interns and residents. He was invited to dozens upon dozens of meetings, and was asked to lecture in colleges and universities all over the country, indeed the world. He had to learn to say no, to attend and speak at only a limited number of scientific sessions here and abroad. All the while his bibliography grew longer and longer. Two of his last three books are collections of essays: *Insight and Responsibility* (1964) and *Identity: Youth and Crisis* (1968); and their contents reflect the diversity and depth of his intellectual life during the decade at Riggs and of course in the subsequent years at Harvard. In *Young Man Luther* and in the papers that go to make up the monograph *Identity and the Life Cycle* he had completed the real structure of his thought. In essays he has written since 1958, he could "roamingly explore" the implications of his ideas — and their bearing on a substantial number of issues or problems: the ways young people think and act; the relationship between psychoanalysis and contemporary events; the position of women in our society, and the nature of psychological development in girls or, later on, mothers; the matter of race, particularly as it plagues America's black and white people; and repeatedly, the ethical principles which form the foundation of all clinical, psychoanalytic work. At the same time he let the exacting methodological conscience of his colleague the late David Rapaport induce him to review his own concepts and fit them into the changing psychoanalytic theory of the fifties.

At Riggs he was rounding out more than his intellectual life. As a husband and a father he began to see the rewards that only middle age can bring. His wife has always been part of his work, especially since she edits every word he writes. At Riggs she also contributed generously to the work of other analysts. That is, she began to play a role of her own as "director of activities." She was convinced that the capacities and potentialities of patients, particularly young ones, could be developed through the pursuit of daily activities which brought immediate, tangible and significant rewards. One day she heard the doctors talking about the more "prosaic" needs of the institution, for things like new curtains. "Why not let the patients make new curtains for you?" she asked, somewhat to their surprise. In the mid-fifties psychiatrists were resolutely looking into the unconscious terrain of their patients, but not at their day-to-day lives as *people*. Joan Erikson believed that a psychiatric patient, like anyone else, needs to *do* something, involve himself or herself in something, feel useful as well as psychologically understood. Eventually she started an extraordinary program at Riggs. The curtains were made by the patients. Then the patients started doing all sorts of other things. They organized a film series that demonstrated the history of cinematography, and invited the town's residents to attend. They started a newspaper. They put on plays — coached by William Gibson, whose wife, Margaret Brenman, is an analyst at Riggs — to which they invited the general public. They held exhibits of their painting and sculpture. They began a nursery school, first for the staff's children, later for anyone in Stockbridge —

and they really had earned the concrete respect and trust of the town's people when parents agreed to give over *their* children to "the mentally ill." A greenhouse was soon flourishing and flowers and vegetables were sold to the public. A shop opened, the outlet for jewelry, leather goods and furniture — all made by "patients."

Mrs. Erikson did more than encourage new programs; she inspired them with the example of her own work. She is a professional craftswoman, and her abilities soon became known far outside Riggs and Stockbridge. She makes necklaces, rings, earrings and pins. Her jewelry has been widely exhibited, and she has won regional and national recognition at exhibits. She took a leading role in the formation of the Berkshire Arts Association. She searched for something the young people at Riggs could do during the long winters, when Stockbridge becomes a very small, very snowbound town, with the activities of Tanglewood and Jacob's Pillow a distant memory. Eventually the association decided to give itself over to a special theme each winter — say, Japan. There would be Japanese dinners and movies, and needless to say, Japanese products of all kinds were on display. I suppose that such efforts could be called "occupational therapy" or "art therapy" or "rehabilitation"; but perhaps the people who took part in all of them would want to use other descriptive words to convey the spirit that moves people to work, to give, to design, to build, to entertain.

In the fifties Erik and Joan Erikson saw their children grow up. The boys became two tall, sturdy men; the girl, a light-haired, attractive woman of grace and poise. The older son Kai went to Reed College, and later to the University of Chicago, where he did graduate work in sociology. He became interested in deviance, in the wayward, irregular, contrary or disobedient people who make up society. In 1957 an issue of the *Chicago Review* carried an article titled "Confirmation of the Delinquent," written by Erik and Kai Erikson. In it that amorphous and puzzling "phenomenon" called "juvenile delinquency" is not merely analyzed once more, with a series of prescriptions recommended. Instead, a modest but significant point is made: often a "troubled" youth's future very much depends on the way his actions are viewed — by judges or teachers, and obviously, by parents. The delinquent may seem and be provocative, yet crave some kind of intelligent, sensible control. He may be perversely, outrageously looking for a conventional, settled life — a "normal" one, if you will. Of course we need to protect ourselves, and maintain certain standards. But whose standards, and at what cost, not only to law-breakers and "troublemakers" but in the long run to the very society we seek to preserve? It may be easy to herd youths into jails (or into hospitals, where their heads are examined); but the two Eriksons point out how ineffective and futile punishment can be — when, in fact, a certain kind of youth is actually looking for punishment because he dares not seek anything else, anything "better."

The paper is an interesting one because Erikson's concept of *identity* (both negative and positive) is brought to bear on a social problem. The paper also shows the younger Erikson's influence: youths at odds with themselves meet up with social institutions such as schools and courts of law, which are equally torn and conflicted. A young man may turn to delinquency because he distrusts himself, because he has been brought up to expect the worst of him. Then he meets up with a judge who tells him he is hopeless, and deserves to be so labeled for the rest of his life — and that does it, a man's fate is sealed. Of course neither of the authors is attempting to provide "answers" for what is a very complicated problem with dozens of twists and turns to it. They know and say that all sorts of deeds are lumped together (by psychiatrists as well as lawyers and policemen) under catch-all terms like "juvenile delinquency." They simply want to suggest that each person's life, his particular habits and inclinations, be considered when one or another fateful judgment is made. The psychoanalyst's concern for the individual is obvious in the paper; equally significant is the strong suggestion that societies have a way of defeating their own purposes at the very moment they seem to be defending themselves most resolutely.

While Kai Erikson was working along these lines, his brother Jon was majoring in economics at the University of California in Berkeley. As a student there, and in subsequent years, he gradually shifted his interests toward the humanities, the theater and particularly photography. One son began to take up his parents' study of society, and the other son became more involved in the arts and in travel. Like his father, Jon Erikson has been all over the world, and become familiar with all kinds of people. Like his father as a young man, Jon Erikson has wanted to look long and hard and make what he sees apparent to others. Some of his photographs, like some of his father's drawings, evoke a mood in the observer by emphasizing one particular aspect in the subject — his eyes, his way of holding his head. Obviously photographs differ in the importance they attach to the individual's "inner" life. Jon Erikson's photographic portraits, including several he has done of his father, bring out what I suppose can be called the *person* — so intangible, so real, so hard to pin down in language, however precise, however scientific or even imaginative. Perhaps in a glance, a gesture, a posture, we do something active, something that gives expression to a dozen things. Certainly we invest static psychological categories or "qualities" with movement and style and form. We can spot this or that "trait" or "neurosis" in a person; but what he *does* with it, does with the things that we describe as "parts" of a "personality," makes for *him*, and often enough him alone.

In one photograph of Erik Erikson his son has caught the eyes — blue, wide and open, prominent. I haven't the slightest idea how a man's psychological characteristics occasionally come to be reflected in his physical appearance; but Erikson's eyes seem both commanding and vulnerable. It is as if he demands to see everything possible, and in so doing protects his eyes less than others do. They are not piercing or penetrating or brooding eyes; "childlike" may be the best approximation. Children often haven't quite learned to seal off what is theirs from what goes on "outside." They see more, but risk more too.

The quality of Erikson's eyes is balanced by other things about him: his ample white hair, not flowing, but very much present to indicate his years; and most of all a certain stillness in him that one does not associate with children, unless they are infants or are with grown-ups, unless they are rather old. He can stand at rest and seem to be taking the whole world in, sorting it out, sensing it, coming to terms with it almost physically rather than theoretically or intellectually. It can happen in a few seconds, in the time of a brief pause that precedes whatever remark or reply he may be making. It is not that he is always staring, and certainly he is not a hesitant or withdrawn person — or, as I may seem to be suggesting, a noticeably "serious" one. On the contrary, those who work with him or who are his friends find him warm, spirited, humorous.

The Eriksons' daughter was away from home by the late fifties, at Oberlin, where she majored in philosophy. Later she would go into social anthropology as a graduate student at Berkeley. She is a very bright and able scholar, yet in mind as well as manner she is very much a certain kind of woman: quietly wise and intellectually giving rather than argumentative and self-assertive. In Berkeley she met her husband, Harley Bloland. He is of Norwegian stock and an educator who in his doctoral thesis began to explore the relationship between higher-education associations and the federal government. The Blolands were married in a small French village near Nice — Erikson had gone there to do some writing — by the town's mayor in a quiet civil ceremony. In recent years Harley Bloland has continued and developed his interest in what might be called the politics of education. Like psychoanalysis, and indeed all the professions, the field of education has a number of organizations that grapple both with issues and for power; and then, there is always the rich federal government to approach and influence and try to win over as a friend, then hold on to as a generous companion.

In the fifties and early sixties Erikson traveled to Europe several times, and at the invitation of continental scholars presented his work in lectures and papers, now published both abroad and here. While much of what he wrote and discussed in Europe had already been thought out and written out for Americans, trips to England, Germany and Austria took on great personal and professional significance. For example, because he was born in Frankfurt, it was a particular honor for Erikson to be asked to speak about Freud at Frankfurt University. And then, there was the meeting of the World Health Organization in 1953. A dozen leading scientists came together in Geneva to consider "the influences of biological, psychological and cultural factors in the development through childhood of the adult personality." Konrad Lorenz was there, and so were Margaret Mead, Jean Piaget, John Bowlby and Julian Huxley. Erikson presented to them the heart of *Childhood and Society* and *Identity and the Life Cycle* — and they found his ideas hard to put aside. Under the title *Discussions on Child Development*, four volumes were published, in essence providing an edited transcript of all that went on during four such meetings: presentations, criticisms, general conversation. Erikson's work figures prominently in two of the four volumes, and perhaps never before had he been pressed so hard by such a diverse and weighty group of scholars.

A comment by Julian Huxley shows how one man's ideas can stimulate another man's mind:

I was very much interested in Erikson's chart. We may disagree with this or that detail, but we now have a comprehensive statement of the method of psychobiological development and the possibility of its continuity: It is not uniform but epigenetic, as you rightly said, in that novelty arises during the process. Novelty arises through two methods — first of all through the development of new mechanisms of change, and secondly through the effects of the environment becoming incorporated into the process. To take a parallel from biology, new mechanisms arise during the development of the sea urchin or the frog, or indeed, almost any organism. . . . Another interesting analogy is this: in psychological as in biological development, as Erikson stressed, the structuring which arises in each of his phases persists in some measure into the later ones. So in a sense the first state is the most important; in psychiatry it is useful to go back to the past, though you can often detect it by looking at the present state of affairs. . . .

Then another point: I have just been reading Bronowski's very interesting book on William Blake, in which many things seem to me to be highly relevant to what various people have been saying and especially, perhaps, Erikson.

For instance, Blake began one of his books with a statement that "without contraries is no progression. Attraction and repulsion, reason and energy, love and hate, are necessary to human existence. From the contraries spring what the religious call Good and Evil." (Here we have Blake hitting on the idea of the dialectic long before Hegel expressed it in formal terms.)[1]

Of course, Blake was anticipating not only Hegel, but Freud as well. Blake saw the child's innocence constantly meeting up with the world's hypocrisy. He also saw that there is a limit to how much hypocrisy, how much evil, any mind or any group of minds can take — before madness and revolution take over. Like Freud, Blake saw the inevitable conflict that human beings, even the best-off, face; like Erikson, Blake saw just how intimately we live with the "world," and strenuously fight to survive its "influence." What Huxley has done, with Blake's help, is point out the exact spirit of Erikson's mind — its dialectic and programmatic quality, and its diverse concerns for the biological, the social, the aesthetic, and finally the ethical problems human beings face. Huxley the biologist quotes Blake the writer to comprehend Erikson the artist who became a psychoanalytic observer.

At one European conference Erikson had his first chance in a long time to see Frankfurt. The war over, Germany was rapidly rebuilding its cities. He was put up in a new hotel, and from it saw the city he once knew so well either in total ruins or (in some sections) on the rise again. The next morning he found himself almost

speechless as he began to address a group of German psychiatrists.
He could not banish his old memories: he could not forget what
Germany had done to Europe, to itself, to millions of innocent men,
women and children. His eyes filled up in grief. How could it all
have come about? And the German psychiatrists? They saw
their guest lecturer visibly shaken, and hastened to help him out.
They reassured him. There was no need for tears, for sadness.
Yes, they (the German doctors!) had suffered. But things were
really much better now. As if he had cried for their condition!

I suppose a generalization or two can be made about the several
"periods" of Erikson's life in America. In the mid-thirties and
forties he was the father of young American children, and a psychoanalyst who devoted his time to treating and observing young
American children. *Childhood and Society* in a sense marked the
end of a phase of its author's life; it was published in 1950, the year
his youngest child became a teen-ager. That same year Erikson
moved east across the country to Austen Riggs. There he worked
with young men and women, even as his own children were becoming young men and women. He again lived nearer Europe, the
scene of his own youth — and with the end of the war and the immediate postwar period he could return there for the first time in a
very long time.

The titles of his books tell in bare outline what happened; from
an interest in childhood he moved to an interest in youth. In addition he began to rely more heavily on the methods of the social
historian, in contrast to those of the social or cultural anthropologist. The issue is not abandonment, but progression; in his life —
as in all lives — involvements and preoccupations appear, change,
take on different forms, but do not "disappear." (If the mind has an
unconscious, and is "driven" by the power that the past constantly
exerts, how can anything we once find important or significant
really disappear?) Perhaps someone bent on "correlating" things
in Erikson's life, on pulling together threads and showing the pattern they form, could say that his "roles" as father, healer, teacher
and writer "supported" one another, or were "related" to one another.

The demands upon him became increasingly impossible over the
years. Hundreds and hundreds of letters came to him — from medical schools, colleges and professional organizations of all sorts. Perhaps one day we will know how many meetings go on every day

in America — and what happens to people who become well known. Obviously they either take to the road and try to oblige every demand they can, or they learn how to protect themselves. Even when they *do* succeed in securing some privacy they have to watch for other more insidious dangers. A public hungry for various kinds of heroes and leaders will not let them off very easily, once found. In America a man's words may be quickly embraced, systematically cheapened, and finally discarded for "new" ones. To some extent, though, a confrontation takes place: a person's ideas may be eagerly and glibly accepted, advocated, and misrepresented (all at the same time); but then he himself either has to go along with what happens or offer resistance. That is, he eagerly or energetically or meekly submits to the various blandishments that come his way — from editors, commentators and interviewers of various kinds — or he persists in doing exactly what his moral, intellectual and professional obligations require. He cannot prevent anyone from finding anything in his writing, but he *can* make sure that he writes when and what and where and how he wishes.

Certainly Erikson and his concept of *identity* have become widely known in America. Week after week the term is invoked, so that the man who developed its meaning could only stand back and say what he did at a workshop on identity held at the San Francisco Psychoanalytic Institute in January 1966:

To come back to San Francisco in order to open a workshop on the concept of identity is, for me and the concept, a homecoming from something like an Odyssey. If we can not claim any heroic exploits, we can at least say that we have gone in many previously unexplored directions, have been tossed around quite a bit, and bring back the experience of successes and failures, never quite sure which successes were failures and which failures triumphs. At any rate, we now return to behold, once more, the roots of it all. For it was twenty years ago and in this city that this concept was first discussed in the particular sense and in the particular context which will be discussed today. Since then, the usage of the word has been so varied and its context so expanded that we may well feel the need for a better definition and a final delimitation. And yet, by its very nature, what bears such a definitive name, as yet eludes definition. It often seems to belong to those mythical conceptions — character, personality, ego — which are used to circumscribe processes felt to be of great relevance in observation and even in conduct and which yet continue to be of questionable definability and measurability.

"Identity" and "Identity Crisis" have come to be used in a great variety of fields. But more often than not they circumscribe something so large and seemingly also so self-evident that to demand a definition would be petty. At other times, they designate something made so small for purposes of measurement that the overall meaning is lost and the thing could just as well be called something else. If, to pick a few items from the top of my desk, the papers discuss the "Identity Crisis of Africa," or of the Pittsburgh Glass Industry; if the American Psychoanalytic Association is addressed by her president on the "Identity Crisis of Psychoanalysis," or if, finally the Catholic Students at Harvard announce that they will hold an "Identity Crisis" on Thursday night at 8 sharp, the quotation marks are as important as the term they bracket: everybody has heard of it, it arouses enough of a mixture of mirth, irony, and discomfort to attract attention, and it promises, by the very play with the word "crisis," not to turn out to be something quite as bad as it sounds. In other words, it has become the ritualized usage of a suggestive term.

Social scientists, too, sometimes attempt to make it more concrete, by making such words as "identity crisis," "self-identity," or "sexual identity" fit whatever they are investigating. For the sake of logical or experimental maneuverability (and in order to keep in good academic company) they try to treat these terms as matters of social roles, personal traits, or conscious self-images, shunning the less manageable and the less obscure (and often more sinister) implications of the concept. But if they try to come closer to the essence of the conception by quantifying the responses to the question "Who am I?" then one sees no reason to be profusely thankful for the thing having been made accessible to scientific inquiry at last. Such usages have, in fact, become so indiscriminate that the other day a German reviewer of a new edition of my first book (in which I first used the term in the context of psychoanalytic ego theory) called the concept the pet subject of the *amerikanische Popularpsychologie*.[2]

It turns out that from the beginning of his stay here Erikson was a very good student of American popular psychology. He never could dismiss his patients' social and cultural heritage as a "background" to their "problems," and maybe for that reason he knew that ideas do not exist in a vacuum once they are expressed, that a society has a particular way of dealing with both the ideas and the man who propounds them. He went on, year after year, expanding and clarifying concepts such as *identity* in journals and books one might consider immune from the "general public"; and yet all the while he knew (and said) that under certain historical conditions a certain idea becomes needed and then discovered by all sorts of different people.

His first articles on identity appeared in psychoanalytic journals. In 1956, a paper on "Ego Identity and the Psychological Moratorium" appeared in a book called *New Perspectives for Research on Juvenile Delinquency*, published by the Children's Bureau of the U.S. Department of Health, Education and Welfare. In 1958, an address to the World Federation for Mental Health (meeting in Vienna) was titled "Identity and Uprootedness in Our Time." In 1959, he wrote "Late Adolescence" for *The Student and Mental Health*, issued by the World Federation for Mental Health and the International Association of Universities. In 1960 *Children*, a journal of the U.S. Department of Health, Education and Welfare, offered its readers "Youth and the Life Cycle," an interview with Erikson. In 1961, Erikson's introduction set the stage for Graham Blaine's and Charles McArthur's *Emotional Problems of the Student*. And in 1962, a *Daedalus* issue on youth contained his article "Youth: Fidelity and Diversity," in which he tried to show what the search for "identity" actually means to young people — who seek from one another and from significant grown-ups a real and sturdy sense of concern or devotion, and who also seek the freedom to look around and try out things casually and feverishly and with no strings attached. In essence he was writing for what could be called a "select" or "professional" group, but the essays and the ideas in them spread out, and, along with *Young Man Luther* and *Identity and the Life Cycle*, became the property not only of those who work with and study youth, but of youth itself.

At Harvard Erikson quickly became a charismatic and renowned teacher whose influence has been rather like that of Paul Tillich when he was a professor there. He called his course "The Human Life Cycle"; it is an upper-level course in the social sciences, open to juniors and seniors and given under the auspices of the college's General Education Program. Each year an attempt is made to keep the membership manageable — so as to encourage student participation and enable intimate teaching. And each year hundreds and hundreds of students have tried to enroll. He also leads a small seminar, whose general purpose is to study the lives of "great" or historical figures. The seminar attracts students and professors of literature, history and political science, as well as others like theologians or doctors who have a particular biographical project under way. In a given year Erikson hears about a dozen participants discuss the lives of, say, St. Augustine or Charles de Gaulle, Jonathan Edwards or William James, Simone Weil or Malcolm X. He shares with others his continuing effort to comprehend the precise points at which an individual's life history intersects with history itself. The emphasis is both historical and psychological. In sum, the emphasis is on life history, case history and history.

As a Harvard professor he is now very much a member of an intellectual community rather than a strictly psychoanalytic or psychiatric one. He is active in the American Academy of Arts and Sciences, and constantly called upon to participate in meetings sponsored by historians, political scientists or theologians. Harvard students want from him what they have wanted from Santayana and William James and Whitehead and I. A. Richards and Tillich, a kind of ethical or spiritual leadership that they can accept — even as they scorn and reject all sorts of advice and counsel from other "older" people. For one thing he looks the part of the sage — tall, of ruddy complexion, with ample white hair; for another, he is a humanist who is also a psychoanalyst, a man who writes as well about Shaw and Gorky and Luther as about the unconscious, and does so in a way that illuminates lives rather than fits them into a series of stock complexes.

In the *Question of Lay Analysis* Freud argued passionately that his beloved discipline be kept out of the reigning hands of physicians, many of whom he considered rigid, narrow-minded, unimaginative, and thus poor candidates for psychoanalytic work. In America Freud's fears materialized. "We need *doctors*," some analysts have said again and again. They have them; but it is another question whether they have men at ease with ideas, men able to work with anthropologists, historians, artists and philosophers. Freud may have been a doctor in the beginning, but he became a new kind of worker, a psychoanalyst, and he also developed into an avid and wide-ranging social critic. His followers have frequently chosen sides (against each other) by emphasizing a particular aspect of his lifework; but not many analysts have demonstrated even a semblance of his ability — an ability Erikson shares — to mix careful observation with literate speculation.

X

Ethics and the Preparation for Gandhi

BETWEEN 1957 and 1962 Erikson wrote five essays which (with the earlier essay on Freud, "The First Psychoanalyst") eventually became a book called *Insight and Responsibility*. The titles of the essays reveal their author's loyalty to both his clinical and intellectual interests. "The Nature of Clinical Evidence" was first given as a contribution to a scientific symposium (on "Evidence and Inference") at the Massachusetts Institute of Technology in 1957. "Identity and Uprootedness in Our Time," as mentioned, initially took the form of an address before a plenary session of the World Federation for Mental Health, held at the University of Vienna in 1958. "Human Strength and the Cycle of Generations" is an enlarged version of a lecture given at the Mt. Zion Medical Center in San Francisco and sponsored by the San Francisco Psychoanalytic Institute. "Psychological Reality and Historical Actuality" was presented to the American Psychoanalytic Association in a plenary session of the midwinter meetings, held in December 1961. And, finally "The Golden Rule in the Light of New Insight" was Erikson's response to a request that he deliver the George W. Gay Lecture on Medical Ethics at the Harvard Medical School. That lecture was expanded into another one given at the India International Centre in New Delhi in January 1963.

On each occasion he spoke as a psychoanalyst first — but one who also insisted on being an ethically concerned citizen, and a professional man very much involved with contemporary and historical *events* as well as clinical *problems*. In a field whose partisans have taken on the various names of their leaders, Erikson can be called a strict Freudian because he is loyal to the essential principles that Freud declared to be the core of psychoanalytic work, and because he is very much like Freud — a writer, a man at home in history and philosophy, a clinician who won't let go of the world outside the office. As a matter of fact he wants to bring today's clinicians closer to the traditions of their own profession, to the history of medicine as an art and a science. "The Nature of Clinical Evidence" begins with a reminder that the word "clinical" is an old one, and can refer "to the priest's ministrations at the death bed as well as to medical ministrations to the sick. In our time and in the Western world the scope of the clinical is expanding rapidly." And that expansion is taking place elsewhere, too:

In the Far East, the word "clinical" is again assuming an entirely different historical connotation, in so far as it concerns mind at all: in Communist China the "thought analyst" faces individuals considered to be in need of reform. He encourages sincere confessions and self-analysis in order to realign thoughts with "the people's will." There is much, infinitely much to learn about the ideological implications of concepts of mental sickness, of social deviancy, and of psychological cure.[1]

All over the world, however, people need help for themselves, for bodily pain or mental anguish. And all over the world there are acknowledged helpers. I doubt the needy and the helpers have ever heard their encounter made so explicit:

Their *contract* is a therapeutic one: in exchange for a fee, and for information revealed in confidence, the therapist promises to act for the benefit of the individual patient, within the ethos of the profession. There usually is a *complaint*, consisting of the description of more or less circumscribed pain or dysfunction, and there are *symptoms*, visible or otherwise localizable. There follows an attempt at an *anamnesis*, an etiological reconstruction of the disturbance, and an *examination*, carried out by means of the physician's naked senses or supported by instruments, which may include laboratory methods. In evaluating the evidence and in arriving at diagnostic and prognostic inferences (which are really the clinical form of a *prediction*), the physician *thinks clinically* — that is, he scans in his mind different *models* in which different modes of knowledge have found condensation: the *anatomical* structure of the body, the *physiological* functioning of body parts, or the *pathological* processes underlying classified disease entities. A clinical prediction takes its clues from the complaint, the symptoms, and the anamnesis, and makes inferences based on a rapid and mostly preconscious cross-checking against each other of anatomical, physiological and pathological models. On this basis, a *preferred method of treatment* is selected. This is the simplest clinical encounter. In it the patient lends parts of himself to an examination and as far as he possibly can, ceases to be a person, i.e., a creature who is more than the sum of its organs.

Any good doctor knows, however, that the patient's complaint is more extensive than his symptom, and the state of sickness more comprehensive than localized pain or dysfunction. As an old Jew put it (and old Jews have a way of speaking for the victims of all nations): "Doctor, my bowels are sluggish, my feet hurt, my heart jumps — and you know, Doctor, I myself don't feel so well either." The treatment is thus not limited to local adjustments; it must, and in the case of a "good" doctor automatically does, include a wider view of the complaint, and entail corresponding *interpretations* of the symptom to the patient, often making the "patient himself" an associate observer and assistant doctor. This is especially important, as subsequent appointments serve a *developing treatment-history*, which step by step verifies or contradicts whatever predictions had been made and put to test earlier.[2]

Then, as if still not satisfied, Erikson gives yet another interpretation of what happens:

Let me restate the psychotherapeutic encounter, then, as an historical one. A person has declared an emergency and has surrendered his self-regulation to a treatment procedure. Besides having become a subjective *patient*, he has accepted the role of a formal *client*. To some degree, he has had to interrupt his autonomous life-history as lived in the unselfconscious balances of his private and his public life in order, for a while, to "favor" a part-aspect of himself and to observe it with the diagnostic help of a curative method. "Under observation," he becomes self-observant. As a patient he is inclined, and as a client often encouraged, to historicize his own position by thinking back to the onset of the disturbance, and to ponder what world order (magic, scientific, ethical) was violated and must be restored before his self-regulation can be reassumed. He participates in becoming a *case*, a fact which he may live down socially, but which, nevertheless, may forever change his view of himself.

The clinician, in turn, appointed to judge the bit of interrupted life put before him, and to introduce himself and his method into it, finds himself part of another man's most intimate life history. Luckily he also remains the functionary of a healing profession with a systematic orientation, based on a coherent world image — be it the theory that a sick man is beset by evil spirits or under the temptation of the devil, the victim of chemical poisons or of faulty heritage, racked by inner conflicts, or blinded by a dangerous ideology. In inviting his client to look at himself with the help of professional theories and techniques, the clinician makes himself part of the client's life history, even as the client becomes a case in the history of healing.[3]

Erikson is of course known as a psychoanalytic theorist, a social observer, a particular kind of biographer; but he was first a clinician, and his particular way of being a clinician, and seeing the clinician's work, continues to inform everything he does. The paragraphs just quoted, like a few others scattered through his various writings, reveal particularly well what I suppose can be called his "cast of mind," his sensibilities — and again, they are at once clinical, historical, analytic, narrative and literary.

The rest of the paper on clinical evidence contains a moving report of one of his patient's dreams, with an equally moving, frank and self-critical report of his own (analytic) response. In the course of the presentation some marvelous comments and asides appear — which can be strung together to read like sections of Pascal's *Pensées:*

I know only too well that many of our interpretations seem to be of the variety of that given by one Jew to another in a Polish railroad station. "Where are you going?" asked the first. "To Minsk," said the other. "To Minsk!" exclaimed the first, "you say you go to Minsk so that I should believe you go to Pinsk! You are going to Minsk anyway — so why do you lie?" There is a widespread prejudice that the psychotherapist, point for point, uncovers what he claims the patient "really," and often unconsciously, had in mind, and that he has sufficient Pinsk-Minsk reversals in his technical arsenal to come out with the flat assertion that the evidence is on the side of his claim.[4]

As to the rest of the hour of the dream-report I listened to the patient, who faced me in an easy chair, with only occasional interruptions for the clarification of facts or feelings. Only at the conclusion of the appointment did I give him a résumé of what sense his dream had made to me. It so happened that this interpretation proved convincing to us both and, in the long run, strategic for the whole treatment. (These are the hours we like to report.)[5]

The first "prediction" to be made is whether this dream is the sign of an impending collapse, or, on the contrary, a potentially beneficial clinical crisis. The first would mean that the patient is slipping away from me and that I must think, as it were, of the emergency net; the second, that he is reaching out for me with an important message which I must try to understand and answer. I decided on the latter alternative. Although the patient acted as if he were close to a breakdown, I had the impression that, in fact, there was a challenge in all this, and a rather angry one. This impression was, to some extent, based on a comparison of the present hour and the previous one when the patient had seemed so markedly improved. Could it be that his unconscious had not been able to tolerate this very improvement? The paradox resolves itself if we consider that cure means the loss of the right to rely on therapy; for the cured patient, to speak with Saint Francis, would not so much seek to be loved as to love, and not so much to be consoled as to console, to the limit of his capacity. Does the dream-report communicate, protesting somewhat too loudly, that the patient is still sick? Is his dream sicker than the patient is?[6]

Clinical work is always research in progress, and I would not be giving a full account of the clinician's pitfalls if I did not discuss in passing the fact that this patient's dream happened to fit especially well into my research at the time. This can be a mixed blessing for the therapeutic contract. A research-minded clinician — and one with literary ambitions, at that — must always take care lest his patients become footnotes to his favorite thesis or topic. I was studying in Pittsburgh and in Stockbridge the "identity crises" of a number of young people, college as well as seminary students, workmen and artists.[7]

Therapists of different temperament and of various persuasions differ as to what constitutes an interpretation: an impersonal and authoritative explanation, a warm and fatherly suggestion, an expansive sermon or a sparse encouragement to go on and see what comes up next.[8]

You will note, then, that in naming the rock-bottom concepts of repression and regression, transference and libido, I have tried to keep each linked with the observation and experience of the clinical encounter as a new event in the patient's life history.[9]

More and more Erikson the clinician was asking himself and others why people *don't* become patients; how people not only survive, but persist and grow strong; what makes psychoanalysis "work" or fail; and indeed when does the "reality" that analysts use as a treasured yardstick lose its practical and conceptual significance. In his paper "Identity and Uprootedness in Our Time" he was speaking to psychiatrists gathered together from all over the world to consider the problems of refugees. Rather than point out the obvious tensions and anxieties faced by such people — the millions displaced in the wake of this century's terrible wars — he tried to indicate the challenges and opportunities that uprootedness can bring out in even the most desperate refugees, among whom would have to be counted the pioneers who first settled America a long time ago. He emphasized that "transmigrations, like all catastrophes and collective crises, produce new and traumatic world images, and seem to demand the sudden assumption of new and often transitory identities" — out of which, of course, whole new lives can be made. Those who have suffered, who have become terribly brutalized or victimized, can find fresh initiatives in new countries, and turn a state of passive suffering into the active conquest of inner sadness and outer uncertainty. Moreover, it is no great leap from refugees to more "ordinary" sufferers:

Patienthood, then, is a condition of inactivation. *Agens* is the opposite of *patiens* and we will use this opposition here in order to give additional meaning to such terms as "passive" and "active," and to free them from such connotations as aggressive and submissive, male and female. *Patiens*, then, would denote a state of being exposed from within or from without to superior forces which cannot be overcome without prolonged patience or energetic and redeeming help; while *agens* connotes an inner state of being unbroken in initiative and of acting in the service of a cause which sanctions this initiative. You will see immediately that the state of *agens* is what all clients, or patients, in groups or alone are groping for and need our help to achieve. But it is also clear that we are not speaking of a condition of overt activity, but of an inner state which we conceptualize as active tension in the ego.[10]

The mind can ail but it can also heal itself, despite the gloomy predictions of determined psychopathologists. It is the world that forces parents to uproot children from every honorable possibility, and it is the world that forces upon "advanced," technological man a terrible sense of loneliness and uprootedness. Refugees can flee one world and try to make do all over again someplace else. In contrast, proud and ingenious men can manipulate the whole world and have no refuge whatsoever — for themselves and from their own triumphs of gadgetry. So on this planet there may be more desperate "patients" than "sick" refugees or even analysands who both complain and boast about their neuroses: "Our professional struggle is with the magic thinking, the social exploitation, and the thoughtless destructiveness which always have a hand in man's mastery of tools and weapons. We challenge *man-made patienthoods*, regardless of the exalted theories or ideologies which mask them as inevitabilities."[11]

Freud wanted psychoanalysis to become a *general* psychology, a view of man capable of tracing and comprehending human strengths as well as weaknesses. If some of his followers won't allow themselves to do that — see what a person *can* do as well as what he *fears* to do — then their very orthodoxy is an ironic form of continuing disobedience. In the paper "Human Strength and the Cycle of Generations" Erikson cast a look around for the critics he knew lurked somewhere and took the plunge:

The psychoanalyst has good reason to show restraint in speaking about human virtue. For in doing so lightly he could be suspected of ignoring the evidential burden of his daily observations which acquaints him with the "much furrowed ground from which our virtues proudly spring." And he may be accused of abandoning the direction of Freudian thought in which conscious values can find a responsible re-evaluation only when the appreciation of the unconscious and of the irrational forces in man is firmly established.[12]

He went on to speak, as he had before, of the child's developing ability to feel *hope*, to exert his *will*, to find *purpose* and achieve *competence*. He noted how earnestly so-called adolescents struggle to find someone and something they feel to be their very own. He described the *love*, the *care*, the *wisdom* that men and women sometimes and in varying degrees come to possess or experience. He explicitly and in detail affirmed what could be called the existential and philosophical aspects of psychoanalytic theory. That is, each of the "stages" he described in *Childhood and Society* results in something, leads somewhere. The struggles that inevitably characterize all growth can generate utterly reliable talents as well as intractable "problems"; and the time has come to spell out both sides, both directions with equal diligence. There is, in the beginning, *hope*, "the enduring belief in the attainability of fervent wishes, in spite of the dark urges and rages which mark the beginning of existence." Hope is more broadly "the ontogenetic basis of faith, and is nourished by the adult faith which pervades patterns of care." The look of the Madonna with her child in a Renaissance painting is thus prototypical — the necessary prelude to everything else that is valuable. (It is nice to be reminded that determinism can work two ways! We can be somewhat destined to live reasonably untroubled lives.)

Next comes the beginning of the Fall, the beginning of free will, the first moments of willfulness: "*Will*, therefore, is the unbroken determination to exercise free choice as well as self-restraint, in spite of the unavoidable experience of shame and doubt in infancy."

Nor does (or at least should) "free choice" or "self-restraint" exist in a vacuum. The child learns to do things, to attain objectives, to share words and join in activities: *"Purpose,* then, is the courage to envisage and pursue valued goals uninhibited by the defeat of infantile fantasies, by guilt and by the foiling fear of punishment." The child also learns to keep on doing things, particular things. He learns (hopefully) that he *can* learn, and enjoy learning, and accomplish something by learning. (Or, like millions of children in ghettos and elsewhere, he learns quite otherwise.) If he is lucky he learns to possess a certain kind of *competence* (depending upon where and when he lives) which can be called "the free exercise of dexterity and intelligence in the completion of tasks, unimpaired by infantile inferiority."

When children become youths they search for the inspiration that "confirming ideologies and affirming companions" can offer. A young man or woman often sees the world's hypocrisies more clearly than he ever did or in a few years ever will. He or she is in the midst of *choosing* — sides, friends, co-workers, a career, a wife or husband. If he comes through well he will have in him a quality of *fidelity,* an "ability to sustain loyalties freely pledged in spite of the inevitable contradictions of value systems."

At some point we begin to become rather conscious of time. We are grown up and getting older. There are new youths behind us and the time before us no longer seems infinite. Presumably we now know and feel what love is. When Erikson talks about love he has in mind love in the "evolutionary and generational sense." Of course in one form or another love pervades all ages — from an infant's adoration of his mother to a grandfather's warm and affectionate embrace of a grandchild. Among grown men and women love is sensual and by biological definition complementary. Lovers have their cultural and personal styles, too. They choose, actively choose one another, and they learn to give to one another, so that together they are what alone each of them can never be. And as every analyst and every husband and wife know, living side by side is no easy matter for two people, however "suited" to one another: *"Love* then, is mutuality of devotion forever subduing the antagonisms inherent in divided function." Needless to say, we can love work and ideas as well as one another, and pass on to the future not only our children but the years of passion we devote to our labor. Eventually the real test of all love comes down to this: Do we *care* enough to offer anything to others? *Care* is "the widening concern for what has been generated by love, necessity or accident; it overcomes the ambivalence adhering to irreversible obligation."

And what of the end, the last few years of life? Is it only "old age" or "senility" or "impotence" that awaits us? As he comes to the last stage Erikson asks his listeners (and later his readers) to leave America, where all too many have a "world-image [that] is a one-way street to never-ending progress interrupted only by small and big catastrophes." He draws on the Asian: "In office a Confucian, in retirement a Taoist." And he draws on Tillich's "ultimate concern":

Individuality here finds its ultimate test, namely, man's existence at the entrance to that valley which he must cross alone. I am not ready to discuss the psychology of "ultimate concern." But in concluding my outline, I cannot help feeling that the order depicted suggests an existential complementarity of the great Nothingness and the actuality of the cycle of generations. For if there is any responsibility in the cycle of life it must be that one generation owes to the next that strength by which it can come to face ultimate concerns in its own way — unmarred by debilitating poverty or by the neurotic concerns caused by emotional exploitation.[13]

Before we die we may manage that long look sometimes called *wisdom* — a "detached concern with life itself, in the face of death itself." By then we know how far we have evolved, gone through something in our life very similar to what Darwin described as man's "rise." At the end there is in us more than a bit of the child, even as at the beginning there were moments when we were noticeably serious or grave or reflective. Erikson is repeating himself and saying the obvious, but like a poet, in a way that crystallizes what is intuitively known by some, yet goes undeclared and gets overlooked by others.

Above all he wants us to see how intimate we are with our own lives: the years spread their net wider and wider, and a life is just that, an intricately connected net, rather than an accumulation of years or achievements. A childish adult is not a child, and a precocious or "adult" adolescent is not a tired but wry and sage old man. The whole thing is hard to write about, because words, even the best of them, the strongest of them, can be so confining:

It is not easy to admit, while speaking with some conviction of an evolving ground plan, that one does not yet know how to observe or to formulate its components. In this first attempt to name basic properties of the "strong" person (matters so far left to moralists and theologians), I have given these properties their everyday names: this is what they look like when observed in others; this is what they feel like when possessed; and this, above all, seems absent when "virtue goes out" of a person. Now, the negative of this kind of virtue cannot be vice; rather, it is a weakness, and its symptoms are disorder, dysfunction, disintegration, anomie. But "weakness" fails to convey the complexity of disturbance and to account for the particular rage which accumulates whenever man is hindered in the activation and perfection of the virtues outlined here. Only when active tension is restored, do things fall into place, strongly and simply. I, for one, remember with pleasure the exclamation of a patient: "You sure know how to de-complicate things!" Such flattery, however, is only as good as the surprise behind it: one cannot pre-decomplicate things. In this sense, the list of virtues only points to an order which, I believe, will be found to be violated in every new form of perplexing disorder and restored in its (always surprising) resolution. To consider such order, then, is a matter of long-range study and contemplation: for the virtues seem to me to point to principles of cohesion as well as to defects in the "fiber" of generations and institutions.[14]

Erikson himself was attempting the very "long-range" kind of contemplation he declared necessary. He keeps coming back to ethical, political and historical issues. He also keeps on reminding doctors and psychoanalysts that they see human strengths every day — yes, in the very sick patients they treat. He asks them to look at man the doer, the fighter, the winner, the leader, the maker, the artist. Can they "conceptualize man only if he is fragmented in acute inner conflict"? In their emphasis on "adjustment" to "reality" do they make a "half-hearted and ambiguous conceptualization of reality [that results in] a failure to account for important features of adaptive and productive action"? And the concept of libido, just what or how much can it explain?

During a recent discussion in a small circle, Anna Freud made the observation that children who came to feel loved became more beautiful. Does libido, then, so the discussants wondered half-humorously, "jump" from one person to another? At any rate our theory of inner psychic economy does not tell us what energy transforms the whole appearance of a person and heightens, as it were, his tonus of living.[15]

To Erikson *phenomenal reality* — that is, the ability to see without distortion what Heinz Hartmann called the "real features of an object or a situation" — has to be distinguished from *actuality*, which is "the world of participation, shared with other participants with a minimum of defensive maneuvering and a maximum of mutual activation." He was trying to say that not all "life" is a matter of impulses warded off or successfully "defended"; in fact, people cannot only be "driven" (to do things or to "invest libido" in one another) but can find themselves sharing circumstances, responding to historical, political or social events, and more generally, inspiring one another to deeds, actions, moves, achievements or accomplishments — both "ordinary" and heroic. We share interests, opportunities, a citizenship, a church, a faith, a number of experiences and loyalties; or we share hunger, the scorn of others, and a whole web of impossibilities that others call our "social condition." And what we share makes a difference to *us*, as people who not only "act-out" (express our yearnings) but act on one another — in the sense of prompting, persuading, encouraging, setting in motion, causing to do.

Strictly psychopathological terms (and the imagery they invoke) begin to lose their value when we think of a man's resiliency, his competence, his resourcefulness, his real-life, down-to-earth qualities that make him a person who *does* this and *has done* that. In Erikson's words, such psychiatric terms as "absence of conflict" and "neutral energy" do indeed "seem somewhat miserly ways of characterizing our tie to actuality and to the world of deeds." Even when we psychiatrists talk about sleep, about the dreamer and his dreams, we are apt to impose upon people our preoccupations with illness, with weakness and deficits and flaws. Again and again, for example, one hears about the sleeper's "vulnerable" or "weak" ego. He is not awake, alert, able to use his "defenses" — and so he becomes flooded by instinctual demands, which in turn force their way into his dreams. Indeed they do, but here is another way of looking at it all:

To conclude: Good sleep, by contract with the community, permits us to relax the safeguards of wakefulness and to recapitulate some past events. Dream life weaves the most recent dangers to the ego's sense of mastery into the tapestry of previous and distant ones, using personal delusion and private cunning to make one meaningfully patterned past of them all and to bring this past into line with anticipated actuality. As long as the sleeper can thus relax, dream well, and wake ready for action, do we really have a right to say that his ego in the state of sleep was "weak"?[16]

Nor is psychoanalysis only a means of *understanding* things — dreams and other events. "What a good dreamer can do for himself, psychoanalysis must restore to the patient: a productive interplay between psychological reality and historical actuality." There are reasons why that outcome does not always happen. Psychoanalysis is *itself* an actuality, one "of fearfully restrained locomotion and minimal conventional interaction. Such an actuality, however, by arresting time as well as motion in the study *à deux* of unconscious processes and inner dynamic changes, imparts a sense of historic process which can be in sharp contrast to the tempo of contemporary events."

He was speaking to his colleagues about a touchy subject. How do they look at the world, and how does their work affect both them and their patients — who are also citizens, living in a century that has seen revolutions, wars and attempted genocide take place virtually next door to psychoanalytic consultation rooms? What the Hitlers of this world have done cannot be explained as madness, even madness on a grand scale. Nor can psychoanalysts, any more than others, fall back on the privacy of their work and shirk their responsibilities as citizens and professional men:

History is as yet a relatively neglected field in psychoanalysis, although psychoanalysts have turned to past history to test their tools of reconstruction. But we can no longer abide by the one-way proposition which explains the behavior of leaders and of masses on the basis of the childhoods they had or had shared. In *Young Man Luther* I used Luther's childhood and youth to show that a reformer and his childhood and the to-be-reformed and their childhoods, as well as the political actuality which brings them together in one decisive historical deed, are all aspects of an epoch's style of adaptation and readaptation.

There is a big step, then, from the clinic to history, a step not diminished in size and complexity by considering history a gigantic psychiatric hospital. In saying this, I paraphrase the statement of a drama critic in London who not long ago took a look around the London stage and exclaimed that history had become the dramatist's mental ward. He referred to plays which put such historical figures as T. E. Lawrence and Martin Luther on the stage, depicting both as almost too plausible mental patients and neither as the inspiring and effective man of action which he was in historical actuality, each, to be sure, for a limited period, bounded by neurotic suffering and historical tragedy.

.   .   .   .   .

Theories do not become truer by being made to fit emergencies, and there are dangers of a magnitude which forbids their being drawn into hasty theoretical controversy. But neither is it possible to ignore a shift in historical conditions which gives us a chilling sense of conceptual un-preparedness. At the end of the First World War, Freud could express the hope that after the carnage Eros would reassert its healing and recon-ciling power. Today it would be a fatally poisoned Eros trailing catastrophe.

Knowing this, some of us become strong partisans, as is anybody's birthright and duty when he feels his moment of participation in con-certed action has arrived. We are concerned here only with the use of psychoanalytic concepts in dealing with political actuality. Here, most of us feel inhibited not only by the apathy we may share with other professions, but also by our special insights into human nature. For the conditions under which inner dynamics can be analyzed seem almost diametrically opposed to those under which political decisions can be made or influenced — opposed, that is, in the relative ratios of observa-tion and action, and of introspection and resolution. To see this may be the first step in finding access to *ongoing history*.

We are often told that practitioners listening to life-histories for countless hours should be able to form an opinion about the influence of historical change on individuals. We wonder about this ourselves when, shaken by ominous turns in world events, we listen to our reclining customers associating "freely" and facing psychic reality staunchly, as they circumnavigate the concerns of the world community. Nor are we blind to the fact that only a limited number of patients or students after years of habituation to the psychoanalytic situation return to their actuality with a reinforced sense of familiarity. Not a few appear to be rather burdened and promptly undertake to burden home and work, profession and citizenship with the compulsion to superimpose psychic reality on shared actuality. In dealing with political change they insist on spreading this sense of reality over the social scene, un-masking disguises, exposing defenses and combating denial, and this with little consideration for the structure of public affairs. This tendency originates, of course, in the ethos of enlightenment which in psycho-analysis has found a new tool — and a new weapon. And since the psy-choanalyst's professional identity is by its tradition and nature allied with the doctrines of rational enlightenment and personal freedom, he re-inforces (as he finds himself reinforced by) those methods and weapons of liberalism which share a relative overestimation of the value of mere awareness of "reality" and a neglect of the nature of political leverage.

· · · · ·

But I think that there is a more "actual" reason for the fact that man's ruthless striving for competence, mastery, and power has come under psychoanalytic scrutiny only gradually: I mean the understandable reluctance to recognize it in one's professional actuality. Activities of curing, understanding, and theorizing are viewed with a suspicion of hidden sadism only if knives are used, living creatures dissected, or weapons refined. Yet, the history of psychoanalysis makes it clear that, like any investigative method, it can serve the drive for power and the need for a sharp if seemingly unbloody weapon. In this time of a tragic confrontation of "selfless" and "objective science" with its murderous results, however, it may well be up to psychoanalysis to initiate a self-scrutiny of the scientific mind.[17]

Erikson has scrutinized his own psychoanalytic, scientific mind in the hope of securing for himself an ethical dimension to that value of values among his colleagues, awareness. In his essay on the Golden Rule he reiterated the distinction between a *reality* that is "perceived and judged by others" and an *actuality* within which one must commit oneself to "ceaseless interaction." He pointed out how many ways the ancient and famous Rule can be interpreted. It can be a bit of prudent advice or it can be used to urge altruistic sacrifice. If the psychoanalyst knows how moralistically and even vindictively that Rule or any rule can be promulgated, certainly he can indicate that what is legal and even moral may not be ethical. As children we learn about the law, and we learn all sorts of "rights" and "wrongs" that later go to make up our "moral code." Yet the ethical man is one who has somehow gone beyond what he learned as a child by threat, coercion, bribery or sometimes uncritical, ingratiating love. From his own work as a *partner*, someone who joins other human beings in a disciplined but emotional search for what did happen and is happening in their lives, Erikson arrives at a reformulation of the Golden Rule's terse advice to "do as you would be done by." Characteristically, he stresses a kind of active sharing that makes the original Rule seem perhaps a little self-serving:

I would advocate a general orientation which has its center in whatever activity or activities gives man the feeling, as William James put it, of being "most deeply and intensely active and alive." In this, so James promises, each one will find his "real me"; but, I would now add, he will also acquire the experience that *truly worthwhile acts enhance a mutuality between the doer and the other — a mutuality which strengthens the doer even as it strengthens the other.* Thus, the "doer" and "the other" are partners in one deed. Seen in the light of human development, this means that the doer is activated in whatever strength is *appropriate to his age, stage, and condition,* even as he activates in the other the strength appropriate to *his* age, stage and condition. Understood this way, the Rule would say that it is best to do to another what will strengthen you even as it will strengthen him — that is, what will develop his best potentials even as it develops your own.[18]

He also draws upon St. Francis and Gandhi. In the famous prayer of St. Francis "active choice" is powerfully expressed: "Grant that I may not so much seek to be consoled as to console; to be understood as to understand; to be loved as to love; for it is in giving that we receive." In Gandhi's "principle" Erikson saw the historical or political counterpart to a more personal (or in today's word "psychological") Franciscan parable:

The shadows of defeat, violence and corruption hovered over every one of the "lofty" words which I am about to quote. But to Gandhi, any worthwhile struggle must "transform the inner life of the people." Gandhi spoke to the workers daily under the famous Babul Tree outside the medieval Shahpur Gate. He had studied their desperate condition, yet he urged them to ignore the threats and the promises of the mill-owners who in the obstinate fashion of all "haves" feared the anarchic insolence and violence of the "have nots." He knew that they feared him, too, for they had indicated that they might even accept his terms if only he would promise to leave and to stay away forever. But he settled down to prove that a just man could "secure the good of the workers while safeguarding the good of the employers" — the two opposing sides being represented by a sister and a brother, Anasuyaben and Ambalal Sarabhai. Under the Babul Tree Gandhi announced the principle which somehow corresponds to our amended Rule: *"That line of action is alone justice which does not harm either party to a dispute."* By harm he meant — and his daily announcements leave no doubt of this — an inseparable combination of economic disadvantage, social indignity, loss of self-esteem, and latent vengeance.[19]

Shortly after those words were written, Erikson became very much taken up with Gandhi and with a number of social and historical issues that can be connected to Gandhi's life, and for that matter to the life of St. Francis, whose deeds and philosophy Mrs. Erikson has studied. St. Francis and Gandhi both took the side of the weak, the suffering, the exiled. Each of them did so lovingly. Theirs were not fiercely ideological struggles, but hauntingly individual ones that will live in history. Both men refused to urge one cause by attacking another. They were not interested in "wars to the finish" against "enemies," or indeed in violent upheavals of any sort. They lived in different places, different continents, different centuries; yet they stand together, two men who tried not to hate, two men who wanted to work alongside the poor, share their fate, and help better their lot without attacking and killing people.

The shift in Erikson's concern from Luther to Gandhi was accompanied by a more or less definitive statement on (and, perhaps, farewell to) the subject of "identity." In the winter of 1961–1962, *Daedalus* brought out an issue on youth which later became a book called *Youth: Change and Challenge*, edited by Erik Erikson. His article "Youth, Fidelity and Diversity" again emphasized his belief that there is "a certain strength inherent in the age of youth . . . a sense of and the capacity for Fidelity." While he had talked about young people many times, about their need to believe, to find other human beings reliable and trustworthy, he had never before spelled out so pointedly the paradoxical essence of the young person: he can be so awake that he feels overwhelmed by the diversity of his tastes, inclinations and interests; at the same time, he feels himself gradually required to narrow his commitments, to become faithful to the choices that are made, in order that soon, all too soon, he will become a particular man, a particular citizen of a country — who works at a particular job, is married or single, a father or childless, a church-goer or a skeptic, and on and on. If diversity and fidelity are opposites, they also serve to "make each other significant and keep each other alive. Fidelity without a sense of diversity can become an obsession and a bore; diversity without a sense of fidelity, an empty relativism." More than anything else, young people feel self-conscious; they make significant and largely irreversible decisions, and as never before they take long and pointed looks, wistfully backward, nervously or ambitiously ahead. They know firsthand what the historian studies: time and the changes it brings. They also can begin to obtain about themselves what the historian seeks: a sense of perspective.

It can even be said that young men and women enter history as well as the world. That is, a given generation begins to test the old moralities and submit to them or assert its right to reform them or rebel from them. And always there are the leaders, the Luthers and Gandhis — sometimes "with an uncommon depth of conflict," sometimes possessed of "uncanny gifts, and often uncanny luck with which they offer to the crises of a generation the solution of their own crisis." Yet, if promising ideologies at some point do indeed spring from private passions, the world now needs something more than another self-assured ideology that speaks to and gives understanding or expression to man's demonic side:

The overriding issue is the creation not of a new ideology but of a universal ethics growing out of a universal technological civilization. This can be advanced only by men and women who are neither ideological youths nor moralistic old men, but who know that from generation to generation the test of what you produce is in the *care* it inspires.[20]

If a youth wants to care it is because he or she has known care, and most particularly the care of a woman. As he shifted his field of study from Luther to Gandhi, Erikson also felt required to reflect on "womanhood," on that half of mankind responsible for giving birth to children, bringing them up, cooking, healing and caring for them, and for their fathers, too. Men — powerful men who conquer space and one another — may need much more from women than their company as "equals" in voting booths, schools, and the marketplace. Again the occasion was a *Daedalus* issue (spring 1964), and again Erikson was talking about *care*, about girls who know even when very little that nature has endowed them with an "inner space," whose purpose is to "bear the offspring of chosen men and, with it, a biological, psychological and ethical commitment to take care of human infancy. Is not the disposition for this commitment (whether it be realized in actual motherhood or not) the core problem of female identity?"

He does not deny the early psychoanalytic preoccupations, the insistence that little girls feel "penis-envy," and that "masochism" and "passivity" go with being a woman, with submitting and yielding to the "aggressive" man. Instead he once more insists that the original psychoanalytic formulations about women and their "mental life" were based on clinical work done — so often by men! — with patients, and a particular kind of patient at that, women born into the nineteenth-century Viennese middle class who for one reason or another had become very hysterical, very dissatisfied with themselves, very frightened and rigid: "However, the cumulative experience of being and becoming a man or a woman cannot, I believe, be entirely dependent upon fearful analogies and phantasies."

Women are not the tangle of shame, envy and resignation that some psychopathologists make them out to be: "One thinks not only of pregnancy and childbirth, but also of lactation, and of all the

richly convex parts of the female anatomy which suggests fullness,
warmth and generosity." If women experience "penis-envy," they
also experience, feel, sense (whatever) something else: "in this total
actuality the existence of a *productive inner bodily space* safely set
in the center of female form and carriage has, I think, a reality superior to that of the missing organ."

Yes, a woman does have very specific difficulties, and here is one
way of looking at them without letting them overshadow everything else:

No doubt also the very importance of the promises and the limitations of the inner productive space exposes women to a sense of specific
loneliness, to a fear of being left empty or deprived of treasures, of
remaining unfulfilled and of drying up. This, no less than the strivings and disappointments of the little "Oedipus" are fateful ingredients
of the human individual and of the whole race. For this reason it seems
decisive not to misinterpret these feelings as totally due to a resentment
of not being a boy or of having been mutilated.[21]

What women go through as a matter of course a number of men
seek:

The inner life which characterizes some artistic and creative men certainly also compensates for their being biologically men by helping
them to specialize in that inwardness and sensitive indwelling (the German *Innigkeit*) usually ascribed to women. They are prone to cyclic
swings of mood while they carry conceived ideas to fruition and toward the act of disciplined creation.[22]

Erikson has no doubt that the entire world — all its people, its
men and women both — now needs at the highest "levels" of political power and "decision-making" some of the qualities that ("inferior") animals and ("inferiority"-ridden) women seem "naturally"
able to summon: a sense of what survival means, a willingness to
stop short of murder, an interest in producing life and maintaining
it. To many self-consciously "aggressive" or assertive men, Gandhi
might be considered, among other things, oddly womanish. He advocated nonviolence and in appearance he could be viewed as fragile
or delicate. He fussed over food. He advocated a return to "primitive" or "rural" ways — spinning and weaving and all that. In contrast, we in the West have to face "reality," the issues of power, *real*
power, atomic power. We know there is no return to the quaint old
ways. Our task is to harness the "advanced" knowledge we possess,

to achieve the complicated kind of political arrangements "advanced" nations require. We know — we are so sure of ourselves! — that Gandhi belongs to another age, another world.

Yet the life of Gandhi reveals magnificent ironies. Almost by himself he made the mighty British Empire tremble. His actions caused infinitely more "powerful" and "practical" men to feel weak, confused and even a bit ashamed of themselves. The only weapon he owned was Satyagraha, the practice of a particular kind of nonviolence, or passive resistance. Erikson knew that a psychoanalytic study of Gandhi's work called for, to begin with, a fresh examination of subjects such as aggression and violence. In his well-known letter to Einstein, Freud had written, "Conflicts between man and man are resolved in principle by the recourse to violence. It is the same in the animal kingdom from which man cannot claim exclusion." And that is the way many knowing, fatalistic people still think. War is awful, but man is the way he is, and naive efforts to make him "better" or more "peaceful" are doomed by the facts — the facts of our deepest, most fundamental "nature," our biological inheritance.

In a paper ("Psychoanalysis and Ongoing History: Problems of Identity, Hatred and Nonviolence") read at a joint meeting of the American Psychiatric Association and the American Psychoanalytic Association in May 1965, Erikson for the first time in public made the connection between the rituals animals use to achieve their mutual survival and Gandhi's use of nonviolent protest. (By that time his study of Gandhi was under way.) The work of Konrad Lorenz enables a willing psychoanalyst to take a fresh look at violence — even as Gandhi forced both his fellow Indians and the British to look at one another in a provocatively new way:

The recent book by Konrad Lorenz, *Das Sogenannte Boese*, summarizes what is known of intraspecies aggression among some of the higher animals and corrects the easy conviction that our "animal nature" explains or justifies human forms of aggression. Lorenz describes, of course, both threatening and murderous behavior on the part of animals who are hungry and go hunting; who must settle competitive questions of territorial occupation or utilization; or who are cornered by a superior enemy. The question is, under what conditions hatred and murder make their appearance among animals, and whether violence of the total kind, that is, of the kind characterized by irrational rage, wild riot or systematic extermination, can be traced to our animal nature.

Within the social species closest to man (wolves, deer and primates), Lorenz describes ritualized threatening behavior which, in fact *prevents* murder, for such mutual threats usually suffice to establish an equal distribution of territory governed, as it were, by instinctive convention. Out in the wild, so he claims, such threatening behavior only rarely escalates into injurious attack; and one may well say — as is, indeed, the case with some human primitives who share the institution of highly ritualized warfare — that some "aggressive behavior" prevents war.[23]

The critical point here is the animal's capacity to make a ritual work. Gandhi discovered that Satyagraha — very much a ritual as he urged it and lived it out — can work well enough under certain circumstances to make man worthy not only of animals but of his earliest childhood: "beginnings, however, are apt to be both dim in contour and lasting in consequences. Ritualization in man seems to be grounded in the pre-verbal experience of infants while reaching its full elaboration in grand public ceremonies."

Gandhi took part in and even arranged a number of those "grand public ceremonies." He had an uncanny sense, and in view of what Lorenz tells us, an "animal-like" sense of what confrontation could safely and usefully do to all the "sides" in a struggle. Among modern leaders he knew best how to balance things, by combining religious principles with political acts, by weighing the possibility of new injuries committed in the name of necessary change against the terrible presence of old injuries. In essence, he was artful, sensitive and incredibly determined. The birth of free India was his desire, his dream, the inspiration for his daily tasks. Sometimes great men treat their ideas and purposes as mothers do infants.

Can it be that there is a connection between the way mothers behave with their children and the way a man like Gandhi taught his followers to act? In 1966, the *Philosophical Transactions of the Royal Society of London* offered an essay of Erikson's called "Ontogeny of Ritualization in Man," in which a good deal of discussion is devoted to "Infancy and the Numinous."

Let me begin with the "greeting ceremonial" marking the beginning of an infant's day: for ritualization is to be treated here first as a special form of everyday behavior. In such matters it is best not to think at first of our own homes but of those of some neighbours, or of a tribe studied or a faraway country visited, while comparing it all — how could some of us do otherwise — with analogous phenomena among our favourite birds.

The awakening infant conveys to his mother the fact that he is awake and (as if with the signal of an alarm clock) awakens in her a whole repertoire of emotive, verbal, and manipulative behaviour. She approaches him with smiling or worried concern, brightly or anxiously rendering a name, and goes into action: looking, feeling, sniffing, she ascertains possible sources of discomfort and initiates services to be rendered by rearranging the infant's condition, by picking him up, etc. If observed for several days it becomes clear that this daily event is highly ritualized, in that the mother seems to feel obliged, and not a little pleased, to repeat a performance which arouses in the infant predictable responses, encouraging her, in turn, to proceed. Such ritualization, however, is hard to describe. It is at the same time highly *individual* ("typical for the mother" and also tuned to the particular infant) and yet also *stereotyped* along traditional lines. The whole procedure is superimposed on the periodicity of physical needs close to the requirements of survival; but is an *emotional* as well as a *practical* necessity for both mother and infant. And, as we will see, this enhanced routine can be properly evaluated only as a small but tough link in the whole formidable sequence of generations.[24]

We are born with the need for someone to do more than feed us. We need to be held, recognized, and affirmed. We need recognition. We need to gain another person, whose loving intimate presence in turn enables us to become distinct. Throughout life we hunger for "ever new, ever more formalized and more widely shared ritualizations and rituals which repeat such face-to-face 'recognition' of the hoped-for." A child who has known a loving mother's eyes and nose and mouth has experienced a "hallowed presence" — has experienced what Erikson calls the "numinous." In a leader's charisma or a church's atmosphere the numinous reappears, as indeed it does — less exaltedly perhaps — between friends or lovers.

The point is not that later rituals must be relentlessly traced back to infantile ones. Rather, Erikson wants to suggest "an ontogenetic beginning and a reintegration on ever higher levels of development." Emotionally and symbolically we *use* the past — which does not mean at all that we feel compelled merely to recapture and relive its psychological moments. Erikson sees the child's first learning as enduring, but not utterly compelling. We never forget, but we continue to learn, and we don't always repeat ourselves, pure and simple:

I will now try to list those elements of ritualization which we can already recognize in the first, the numinous instance — emphasizing throughout the opposites which appear to be reconciled. Its mutuality is based on the *reciprocal needs* of two quite *unequal* organisms and minds. We have spoken of the *periodicity of developing needs* to which ritualization gives a *symbolic actuality*. We have recognized it as a highly *personal* matter, and yet as *group-bound*, providing a sense both of *oneness* and of *distinctiveness*. It is *playful*, and yet *formalized*, and this in *details* as well as in the *whole* procedure. Becoming *familiar* through repetition, it yet brings the *surprise* of recognition. And while the ethologists will tell us that ritualizations in the animal world must, above all, be *un-ambiguous* as sets of signals, we suspect that in man the *overcoming of ambivalence* as well as of ambiguity is one of the prime functions of ritualization. For as we love our children, we also find them unbearably demanding, even as they will soon find us arbitrary and possessive. What we love or admire is also threatening, awe becomes awfulness, and benevolence seems in danger of being consumed by wrath. Therefore, ritualized affirmation, once instituted, becomes *indispensable* as a periodical experience and must find new forms in the context of new developmental actualities.[25]

In his discussion of ritualization before the Royal Society, he was essentially reformulating his own "schema," the one he first had presented some twenty years earlier in the scientific papers that later went into *Childhood and Society*. Again he resorts to a chart or diagram; but now he wants to indicate a developmental order to what happens *between* people as well as *inside* them. We learn to trust because we learn about another person. Each of us learns to know a mother, to recognize her in a particular way — which is encouraged and sanctioned and given ritual form by a society and its traditions. Similarly, we learn about what is right and wrong, what is and is not ours, what we can and what we dare not initiate — all through the experience of approval and disapproval, through meeting up with the applause or discouragement of other people who, again, offer that applause or discouragement in more or less ritualized ways. And so, rituals vary and "progress," even as do the lives of those who "make" the rituals. We unfold not only as progressively better "defended" — by the ego against the id or the "archaic" superego — but as increasingly initiated into a diversity of profoundly psychological experiences or rituals or styles of behavior and action, which at the same time are social events, involving another person or persons, and indeed the silent presence of a larger (consenting or frowning) "world." The new chart (Figure 3, page 289) dovetails with the earlier one that portrayed the "stages" of man's life cycle.

Infancy	Mutuality of recognition					
Early childhood	↓	Discrimination of good and bad				
Play age	↓	↓	Dramatic elaboration			
School age	↓	↓	↓	Rules of performance		
Adolescence	↓	↓	↓	↓	Solidarity of conviction	
Elements in adult rituals	NUMINOUS	JUDICIAL	DRAMATIC	FORMAL	IDEOLOGICAL	GENERATIONAL SANCTION

FIGURE 3

For example, a youth who is struggling with issues whose resolution will provide a sense of identity and a capacity for fidelity is also a youth who is learning how to take his stand beside certain people in a particular way and for particular (ideological) causes or purposes. Astronauts, healers, money-makers, commissars, peasants, workers, full-time revolutionaries — all have more or less settled within themselves both what they are about and exactly whom they can (and feel able to) rely upon and call upon for support. We all learn how to act in public and what to uphold or espouse — as allies of some and in opposition to others.

It is no accident that Erikson became concerned with ritualization in man when he was trying to look at Gandhi's life, in which both principles and deeds combine into an almost indefinable "philosophy" or "program." Gandhi was a leader who tried to reach and influence each follower's heart and soul. Much more, his leadership was overwhelmingly personal — tied to his life and tastes and habits, to what and whether he ate, where and how and with whom he slept, what he wore. He is known to most of us as the Indian who unnerved the vastly more powerful British without resort to the sword; but in fact he was a teacher who wanted all men, whether his supporters or his enemies, to learn how to live with one another in a radically new way. In that sense he was a stubborn psychologist — determined first to know himself, and then to persuade others that the old encounters and ceremonies were harmful and wrong, that

new ones are needed. The man known for his fasts, for his nonviolent political struggle, was a man who struggled to lead himself and
set an example that aimed to change far more than India's rulers:
the minds of ordinary men and women, who eventually (so Gandhi
at least hoped and certainly dreamed) would look at one another
across the barriers of class, caste, nation and continent with a respect
that emerges not from rhetoric and more rhetoric but from an experience — a meeting, a ritual of the kind Erikson describes, in which
wills challenge one another but don't kill, and eventually give in to
one another, hence come together.

Sometimes a scholarly paper can be an experience. Sometimes in
one paper a gifted scholar or writer who has written many papers or
essays and a few books, too, comes up with a quiet and unselfconscious but pointed summary of his various interests, involvements, and ideas. Not that the author really intends such a summary,
and not that his essay or paper is all that comprehensive; but the
hints and implications and allusions are there, and if they were all
pursued the richness of a particular mind's life would be realized. I
am thinking of Thomas Mann's "Fantasy on Goethe," written late
in life by a novelist who much earlier had written *The Beloved
Returns*. Mann's essay (like his novel) tells a lot about Goethe — but
just as much about the author of *Buddenbrooks* and *Doctor Faustus*
and *The Magic Mountain*.

I believe one of Erikson's papers on Gandhi is this sort of achievement. The paper was written in late 1967 and early 1968 for
the American Academy of Arts and Sciences, and was part of a
series of "studies in leadership," each of which struggled with one of
the central riddles of history: Who becomes the leader and in fact
what is it after all that makes a leader? Many of the other studies
rely heavily on Erikson's work — not only *Young Man Luther*, but
the analysis of Hitler's imagery and Gorky's youth in *Childhood
and Society*, and the brief but brilliant (come to think of it, very
Shavian) analysis of George Bernard Shaw that first appeared in
"Identity and the Life Cycle." At the very beginning, for instance,
we are reminded that "about a decade ago, when I first participated
in a *Daedalus* discussion, I represented one wing of the clinical arts
and sciences in a symposium on 'Evidence and Inference.'" Then,
for several introductory pages the reader is given a quick but careful
and constantly suggestive look at Erikson's professional past — as a
clinician, a psychoanalyst, a man interested not only in case histories

but in life histories, and particularly the life histories of men like Martin Luther, men who make history.

Some powerful and touching things come forth in the first section of the paper, all the more powerful and touching because they are not forced upon the reader, not made part of a lecture or series of dogmatic assertions. Thus, in a part of a sentence the psychoanalyst and the historian are brought precisely and appropriately together in a way that long, heavy essays, even books, could not improve upon: "for he [the historian] like the clinician, must serve the curious process by which selected portions of the past impose themselves on our renewed awareness and claim continued actuality in our contemporary commitments." Then, in an equally strong and evocative way, we are asked to think of the struggle that patients make — and with them their psychoanalysts also make — as something restorative and redemptive, as an achievement that cannot be measured in numbers and percentages, but has to do with "a semblance of wholeness, immediacy, and mutuality."

There he is, a scholar unquestionably, writing in a journal issued by the American Academy of Arts and Sciences, and in addition, a psychoanalyst, able a few paragraphs later to give exact and well-rounded meaning to terms like "resistance" and "transference" and "countertransference" — yet, at the same time, someone rather more, someone willing to use psychology as Kierkegaard once did, as more recently Buber and Tillich did when they insisted that we all have a right to need and want more than a strict and supposedly "value-free" confrontation with our own "psychodynamics." We do indeed need to understand ourselves, become conscious of our mind's deviousness, of the hurt and sorrow and anger that we have known and forgotten, but actually, ironically, never forgotten. But we also need to find ourselves, become intact, feel life fully, and share what we feel and do with others. As Erikson keeps on emphasizing, we have to *do* something with our problems and tensions and anxieties. We have to put the past to use, as well as meet up with it and analyze it. We have to make history as well as "take" histories, if we are doctors, or learn about our own histories, if we are patients.

The rest of the paper goes into Gandhi's "case," and a good deal of the discussion subsequently was included in *Gandhi's Truth*. But there is one concluding section of the essay which does not appear in the book but deserves brief mention now: a few observations on salt; yes, on the psychoanalytic "significance" of salt. Gandhi's

march to the Arabian Sea, his effort to ridicule the British law that
taxed salt, gets a careful but also delightfully humorous treatment
from Erikson. Some analysts have declared that salt symbolizes
semen, and that Gandhi's protest, including his refusal to use the
condiment at all, had something to do with "sexuality" and "orality"
and "regression." Neither Ernest Jones (who wrote about such
psychoanalytic things) nor Victor Wolfenstein (who as a political
scientist interested in Gandhi gives Jones' ideas a good deal of
credence) are denied their right to be taken seriously. Yet Gandhi
was a shrewd politician waging a very real struggle against very real
injustices, including an outrageous and concrete and unfair tax on
salt, which millions of poor people needed and couldn't afford.
Therefore, "before we ask how salt may come to mean semen, it is
only fair to state that through the ages it has had a powerful significance as itself." And anyway:

The one way symbolization suggested in psychoanalysis, by which the
nonsexual always symbolizes the sexual, is grounded in the assumption
that the erotic is more central to infantile and primitive experiences
than are the cognitive and the nutritional. . . . But in the immediate
context of the chronic semistarvation that has undermined the vitality
of the Indian masses and considering the periodic threat of widespread
death by famine, it would seem appropriate to assume, first of all, that
salt means salt.[27]

Moreover, when Gandhi decided to lead the Salt March, "he was
obviously in command of his political and economic as well as his
psychological wits." Indeed, "in any context except that of irrationality clearly attributable to sexual repression, one should take any
interpretation that explains a human act by recourse to sexual symbolism with a grain of salt."

Perhaps the point is a little overworked, but if so there is every
cause. There comes a time when ideas become dogmas, and dogmas
mercilessly and foolishly pronounced upon everyone and everything. Like others in our part of the world who have struggled to
fashion new thoughts, new values, new ethical principles, Gandhi
tried hard to take what was valuable and give it all a new life. In the
opening passages of the Gita he saw a summons to Satyagraha, a
summons he wanted others as well as himself to heed. It may well be
that Erikson hoped when he wrote his paper for *Daedalus* not only
to bring alive Gandhi's truth, but Freud's truth — for so long the
claimed property of any great man's worst (if most seductive)
enemy, the tireless sycophants who, alas, are part of history's story.

XI

The Mahatma

GANDHI'S TRUTH is an account of a search for "the historical presence of Mahatma Gandhi and for the meaning of what he called Truth"; a search by a Western man for the enduring side of a great Indian leader's character; a search by a psychoanalyst for a particular person's ethical spirit — a spirit that has moved many people to change at least some of their ways, a spirit that has failed to move many others, and a spirit that we all desperately need, whatever its practical limitations, its inadequacies as a source of inspiration for political and economic change. A search, of course, can have an immediate beginning, a place where the journey starts, and then older origins and antecedents which are less distinct, harder to spell out, but thoroughly consequential, as a psychoanalyst certainly must know. So the preface to *Gandhi's Truth* tells us that Erikson first went to India in 1962 because he had been invited to lead a seminar on the human life cycle. The seminar took place in Ahmedabad, an industrial city not usually frequented by Western tourists, perhaps because it does indeed remind Americans and Europeans of what they have left behind — hardly what they have traveled so very far in order to see yet again. The leader of the seminar and his wife were given accommodations on the estate of Ambalal Sarabhai, a mill owner and one of Ahmedabad's leading citizens, a kind and generous host, but also a man with a very significant past, as the Eriksons would find out.

In 1918 Sarabhai, as Ahmedabad's largest mill owner, had been Gandhi's chief opponent. The men who labored long hours in the mills were pitifully underpaid, and Gandhi had assumed the leadership of their struggle to obtain higher wages from men like Sarabhai

— whose sister Anasuyaben was close to Gandhi and much devoted to the workers' cause rather than her brother's. Forty-four years later, and fourteen years after Gandhi's death by assassination, Ambalal was still alive, and as cordial to the visiting American professor as he had been to Gandhi, whatever the differences between them in 1918 and later. And the professor, a psychoanalyst, felt himself drawn to the past but also moved to connect the past with the present:

I experienced that sense of *déjà vu* which can come to a visitor in a foreign city that he has been able neither to visualize nor to pronounce properly before. When I was young, I had known that Gandhi lived in or near the city of Ahmedabad or, at any rate, by the Sabarmati River. My generation of alienated youth in Europe had, in fact, read of Gandhi's first trial between the World Wars and had compared it with that of Socrates: this trial had taken place in the "Circuit House" which in Ahmedabad we passed daily on our early morning walks. And I had read in Gandhi's autobiography of a strike in 1918 which he had led in Ahmedabad.[1]

In the preface to *Gandhi's Truth* other memories are also recalled, ones that have to do with European history. We are reminded that 1918 marked the end of an awful war — four years of killing and more killing, of lies and deceptions and betrayals, all in the name of "civilization," as it was variously interpreted by those great European colonial powers who were, in fact, fighting to keep or gain property, to gain or stop others from gaining power. That year Gandhi's leadership at Ahmedabad was barely noticed even in India; the world's eyes were on Wilson and Lenin, on Lloyd George and Clemenceau.

Yet, because of something that happened in Ahmedabad (among other places) and in 1918 (among other years), India was destined to feel far more sure of itself. By the same token Mr. M. K. Gandhi, because of the spiritual and political leadership he continued to demonstrate in one Ahmedabad-like situation after another, became a very special person — not a president or a premier or a dictator, but indeed a man of power, for Gandhi could mobilize Satyagraha, "truth force." There in Ahmedabad in 1962 the American professor couldn't stop wondering what had happened a few decades before. Erikson was coming to know a little bit about a vast and puzzling subcontinent, was coming to know various Indian citizens, friends of Gandhi, old but still alive, and perhaps was also coming to realize that not only did a seminar on the life cycle have to be conducted, but a particular life cycle, his own, had to be allowed further development. Both quietly and restlessly he was going through one more of those "periods" that all of us have — which years later we can abstract with descriptions like "time of work on Gandhi's life, and most especially on Gandhi's use of militant nonviolence."

From the beginning, the author of *Gandhi's Truth* wants to make it clear how he came to write such a book. He is not interested in a lot of public soul-searching, which can become a caricature of the systematic introspection a psychoanalyst has to put himself through all the time in connection with his work. He does, however, want the reader to stop and think: here is a particular person, from a certain part of the world and from a certain professional background; he came to India for a purpose; he has now written a book about a period in a great leader's life, about that leader's cause, his deeds and the philosophy he tied so closely to deeds; the book is about Gandhi, not about the authors' reason for writing about Gandhi — but certain things ought to be spelled out when history books (not to mention biographies) are written, such as who, under what set of circumstances and with what hope in mind, is studying whom. In other words, a historian makes history by selecting certain things to think about and put on record; and those who have been part of history, who have had this "role" or that position, also make history when their words become public — whether of their own accord or at the prompting of an interviewer, which is what Erikson became with Gandhi's friends and antagonists. If all this seems unsurprising, one need only pick up one biography after another, even one history book after another, and note how often personal judgments are given the authority of unequivocal facts, and strong opinions of one sort or another are called, rather casually, biographical "data" or parts of something "objective" like a "record."

In contrast, *Gandhi's Truth* starts "as subjectively as seems proper" with the author's effort to describe how it was to come near that truth, near it geographically, near those who helped make it, near the scene of its unfolding — the city, the streets, the buildings, the river, the people. The book has been written by a man who has a highly personal way of working and is not afraid to say, at the start, what he does and how:

This very method, however, decrees that I should begin by letting subjectivity and even circumstantiality reign. I will, therefore, start with a brief travelogue. This consists of excerpts from letters such as those I like to send to family and friends when traveling, perhaps because I like to address my diary to those I wish were with me to share my impressions. And impressionistic it will be, this beginning, for I am the kind of worker who must find his way from personal observation to what seems relevant enough to be recorded; and this means also that I must find my way from strong esthetic impressions to what survives as ethically urgent.[2]

Those impressions are offered us in a long prologue called "Echoes of an Event." The prologue is no mere introduction, the description of a task, the setting of a stage for what follows, though that is accomplished, too. The prologue actually contains three chapters, which collectively are meant to help the reader get a sense of what India is like to a stranger from the West, and what it was like for Erikson to give a seminar in Ahmedabad, a seminar on the life cycle attended by Hindus, who have a clear, traditionally sanctioned view on the subject, and finally what happened to bring about "a growing interest in this confrontation of Gandhi and Ahmedabad."

India: Gandhi walked all over India, loved India passionately, fought for India's freedom, died trying to keep the new nation of India undivided: "As the plane sets down at the Delhi airport before dawn, the newcomer is enveloped in a new world of sights, sounds, and smells which darkly command him to reset all his senses before asking any questions."[3] The newcomer goes on to tell about those sights and sounds and smells; about faces, beckoning and gentle ones, fearfully desperate ones; about the ironies and paradoxes that nearly scare the visitor away for good, but at the same time utterly captivate him: the mass of people, the lovely fragility of a particular person or building, the richness of things, and of course the terrible poverty, the warmth, be it of weather or of a whole culture, the chilling presence of death at work, always at work. In India death has allies that never leave — hunger and malnutrition — and as a result diseases; dozens of diseases afflict people who see no doctors, who often enough have no homes, who are a sea of thoroughly apparent human beings within a giant peninsula, a great subcontinent of almost two million square miles and a half billion men, women and children.

It is especially appropriate in connection with Gandhi, but altogether in keeping with the thrust of books like *Childhood and Society* and *Identity: Youth and Crisis,* that an effort to understand the Mahatma starts with an effort to say something suggestive about

India. This is not to say that Erikson goes into a long analysis of the nation's history, its social traditions, its various cultures and "subcultures." On the contrary, we are to meet not India but Gandhi; we get to know him, and him we will live with as readers and later on, too, as readers who have been touched, affected, made a little different because of an experience with a book. Gandhi was rarely alone; people were constantly around him, near him, feeling his presence and causing him to respond to theirs. We are asked to realize (perhaps hopelessly if we have never been there) how literally full of life India is, and how lively a man Gandhi was, not a distant and austere and self-important man who lived away from others and handed down programs for them and edicts to them, but rather a man who gave himself generously to those many, many people who sought him out and whom he actively tried to meet by moving, from village to village, province to province, all over his beloved country's land.

Gandhi became for millions of Indians an embodiment of what they felt important and valuable about themselves. If we are to understand Gandhi we have to understand whom he spoke with and to and eventually for; and maybe Erikson did indeed go about achieving this understanding in the best way: by taking the strenuous walks he mentions in the first section of his book, by going here and there, by meeting a lot of different people, from all walks of life, of all ages and classes and castes, by gaining a person-to-person sense of Gandhi's countrymen (not to mention some of his friends and sometime opponents) rather than by reading books and more books about India and its various problems.

The Eriksons saw, felt, and experienced many things in India. On their first visit they came from Israel, and at the very beginning of *Gandhi's Truth* a comparison is made, a sign of the author's spirit as he wrote:

Only a day or so before, we had swum in the Lake of Galilee and had walked at night on the shores where, even among militant and pragmatic Israelis, one can never forget Him who had the gift to speak of fishermen in a manner remembered through the ages. Now I sensed again what I had known as a youth, namely, the affinity of that Galilean and the skinny Indian leader enshrined in Delhi. There is a word for what they seem to have had in common: presence — as pervasive a presence as only silence has when you listen.[4]

In Delhi there was Birla House to visit, the scene of Gandhi's assassination, the setting for a huge mural that covers three walls and depicts episodes in the Mahatma's life. Then, there was the monument being built at the site of Gandhi's cremation, and nearby, the Gandhi Museum with its photographs and quotations, one of which Erikson chooses to quote: "I am told that religion and politics are different spheres of life. But I would say without a moment's hesitation and yet in all modesty that those who claim this do not know what religion is."[5]

In the beginning the Eriksons spent most of their time in Ahmedabad, which reminded them of the Pittsburgh they knew so well. The Banias, an ancient merchant caste, dominate Ahmedabad and give it a business-like atmosphere: life is hard and tough; work is all-important; one must do the best one can, have few illusions, be careful, and expect very little in the way of favorable surprises. Gandhi was a Bania; his name means "grocer." If Gandhi lived any place in India after his return from South Africa at the age of forty-five, he lived in Ahmedabad, in his ashram by the Sabarmati River. To the outsider, and to many Indians as well, the cities to be visited and known are Calcutta, Delhi, Bombay and Madras; but Gandhi came to those cities, and to all India, from Ahmedabad and its nearby towns. (He was born in Porbandar, a town on the Arabian Sea, slightly to the south and west of Ahmedabad.) Ahmedabad was not only where Gandhi lived, where he and those who worked with him settled down, but also where he worked, where he wrote, and more significantly, where he began to live out what he wrote about — that is, take various public positions that would change many lives, including the life of an entire empire. Ahmedabad was also where the Sarabhai family lived and where Erikson met Shankerlal Banker, a man close to Gandhi, once his co-defendant, for a year his fellow inmate in a British prison. Shankerlal, as Erikson calls him, was in fact the man who seemed to help crystallize something in the Western psychoanalyst's mind, something out of the past: "I told Shankerlal how much Romain Rolland's book [*Mahatma Gandhi*] had meant to me when I was young, and the next day he brought me a copy.[6] Subsequently, a lovely description of Gandhi by Rolland would appear in *Gandhi's Truth*, at the end of a chapter called "India: First Encounters."

The next chapter is called "A Seminar in Ahmedabad" and appropriately enough begins, "But I had work to do; and work is a welcome counterbalance when impressions become too varied and too crowded." The rich, colorful, alternately joyful and sad descriptions give way to the tasks a seminar had before it, a seminar whose participants included physicists and industrialists, physicians and teachers, all interested in sharing with Erikson thoughts about "life," about the stages Hindus believe we go through, about Tagore's childhood, about tribes and castes and how they affect an Indian youth's sense of himself — in short, about new and characteristically Indian matters and yet, at the same time, matters that we all struggle with as human beings. *Gandhi's Truth* pays only brief attention to Erikson's "life cycle," as it compares with the Hindu view of man's various experiences — which are believed to stretch over centuries and take the form of births and rebirths. Still, we do get a hint of what the seminar in Ahmedabad offered: the meeting of ideas, the similarities noted, the differences accepted. Erikson gradually saw how his ideas fitted in with Hindu ideas; he also began to find in Hindu theology particular affirmations of what others — we in America — also go through and upon occasion think about and want characterized.

We learn, for instance, that Hindus do not pay the attention we do to early childhood. Until he becomes eight years old, a boy is considered, in essence, newly born, the product only of his caste, rather than of a whole range of psychological experiences, such as we in middle-class America know about and explicitly spell out to one another when the subject of "children" comes up. Ceremonies of sorts are conducted, held "over" the child, but he is thought not to understand them or take part in them. The ceremonies do, however, stress just the things we all do as parents; that is, subjects like hope come up, and on the negative side, grief and sadness. If the themes are universal, they are handled variously and fitted into distinct world views, each with its own chronological sense: "where we would view hope as the fundamental human strength emerging from the first years of life, the Hindu world view would (fairly enough) allocate it to the beginning of all time."

It is easy enough to skip over the parenthetical "fairly enough," except that once again, as he did among the Sioux and Yurok Indians, Erikson wants to understand how "others" feel, and to do so on their terms, rather than by submitting them and all their beliefs to a particular system of thought (the psychiatric, the psychoanalytic) which a number of people in metropolitan areas of certain

Western countries happen to find convincing. We learn about the Hindu view of birth and rebirth, about *desha,* which has to do with where a child is reborn, and *kala,* when, and *gunas,* the child's constitutional inheritance (of sorts), and *shrama,* what is to be expected of a particular boy or girl who this time around, so to speak, belongs to a particular caste. The child may be born to a family of cultivated Brahmans or be among the Kshatrias, who are fighters and rulers, or the Vaisyas, who deal in goods and own land, or the Sudras, who are workers, or finally, the Untouchables. Yet to Hindus what one is, whether very high or very low, cannot be taken for granted; the next life may well be quite different. There is no way of knowing exactly what form the various lives, one after another, will take, but each member of each caste, if he is a believing Hindu, feels that a lot has happened to him before his present existence and that a lot will happen to him in the future. Such a view of things, so radically different from ours, prompts Erikson to say:

We in the West are proudly overcoming all ideas of predestination. But we would still insist that child training can do no more than underscore what is given — that is, in an epigenetic development fixed by evolution. And we can certainly sense in any seminar — clinical or historical — how we continue to project ideas of doom and predetermination either on hereditary or constitutional givens, on early experience and irreversible trauma, or on cultural and economic deprivation — that is, on a past, as dim as it is fateful. And let us face it: "deep down" nobody in his right mind *can* visualize his own existence without assuming that he has always lived and will live hereafter; and the religious worldviews of old only endowed this psychological given with images and ideas which could be shared, transmitted, and ritualized.[7]

Hindus have ideas about what is needed and what is to be done at which time in a person's life that do bear a certain strong resemblance to Erikson's stages in the life cycle. Although, in traditional theory, early childhood is relatively ignored, or is taken for granted as something given, namely, a link to a previous phase of existence, the Hindus very definitely have a concept of youth. *Antevasin,* they call it, a time of learning, a time when youths become apprenticed and get (from a guru, a teacher) a sense of what their work will be like, what they will be trying to accomplish — weave, forge, harvest, carve, build. Erikson sees in *Antevasin* what he calls the child's growing sense of competence as well as the youth's "fidelity," received and reciprocated by teachers — two developments that are essential for a person's emerging identity. Still, "what we treat as a matter of maturational stages for the Hindu is *dharma*," which takes a life to achieve, and is moved along by previous lives as well as by the way we manage our affairs in this particular life.. *Dharma* means realization, actualization — a lifetime of it, worked at long and hard by a person, but always, be it remembered, in conjunction with others. In India a man's thinking, however obscure or "private," is thought to be influenced by his relatives, friends and neighbors, by his caste, by a whole world of values, prescriptions, rituals, beliefs. Obviously Erikson would and did find in *dharma* a congenial way of seeing man's efforts, struggles and achievements.

He examined as well many other Indian words, and the thoroughly complicated psychological reality it is their purpose to describe, words such as *Grhastha*, which means householder, *Artha* which has as its province the family, the community and a person's overall effectiveness and productivity, *Vanaprastha* and *Moksha*, which suggest that after a while, after one has learned and loved and built a family and fitted into and helped strengthen a neighborhood or a community, there comes a time to begin saying good-bye to a given life — a given self, a given body, a given series of involvements with other human beings — so that what existed and soon will disappear can be actively affirmed one more time, by a firm leave-taking.

Yet *Gandhi's Truth* is not taken up with drawn-out comparisons between essentially different ways of looking at life. That there are differences is to be expected — the lives of Indians are not, after all, the lives of Americans — and that there is something we all share by virtue of our common humanity is also to be expected. "It would be fruitless as well as impossible to compare these schemes, point for point," says an author who does not want to dwell upon his own efforts to deal with the life cycle as a whole by showing that Indians, too, whatever *they* think of as their philosophical and psychological assumptions, are "really" thinking this or that. Instead, the foreigner became a relaxed admirer, even if his skeptical, scientific mind was not quite convinced — but perhaps skeptical, scientific minds have never really proved themselves to be more than a mixed blessing:

For what an ingenious scheme this is: all caste, subcaste, and not-yet-caste having been predetermined, one comes into life with a curse that can be lived down if one lives up to minutely prescribed ways; and by living and dying well, one becomes deserving of ever better lives until, having exhausted the available life cycles, one is ready for release from the whole big cycle.[8]

One other thing Erikson did in India had to do with his past rather than Gandhi's, and appropriately enough took place in a combined school and clinic operated under the patronage of the Sarabhais. There he heard case histories discussed, and there he saw children laugh and run about and play games. There he was able to ask of those Indian children what he had once asked of American children (and described in *Childhood and Society*): would they, one child at a time, look at some toys (the "cast") placed on an empty table (the "stage") and then go ahead and do as each of them wished (build a "scene")? In America the investigator had asked the children to take those "scenes" from an imaginary movie; in India a "folk play" was to be, in part at least, made up. In America it had been easy to have each child work alone, apart from other children or parents or teachers; in India the children often were inseparable from various relatives, not because they were neurotically dependent "but because they naturally and all the time moved about as part of a family." In America the children would build a clearly circumscribed scene; in India the children were less precise and specific. That is, one could not easily distinguish between the outside and the inside of their constructions, between a house built and a garden or street also built, between a city and a nearby jungle, between several scenes that somehow managed to blend into one another. To Erikson it all added up to the word *fusion* — a need to keep everything together, even on the part of children whose parents often crave solitude in order to meditate.

Not for the first time did Erikson have to make sense of such a contradiction. In view of Gandhi's many contradictions, it was probably for the best that a man who would later study him and his writings and his ambiguities first study the way Indian children and their parents manage to feel so very much part of large families, yet also feel themselves, and no one else. However near people, however almost buried in wave after wave of fellow citizens, Indians know how to achieve their own kind of privacy. They can alternate between open, proud sensuality and a noticeable personal tidiness and restraint — just as they can live fiercely or casually apart from everyone and everything, but at other moments establish for themselves detailed obligations and routines, which in sum bind people together. Indian children do not grow up in the small, discrete homes most of our children come to find familiar — a mother, a father, two or more children. Indian children know all sorts of aunts and uncles and cousins, not to mention a good number of brothers and sisters. Affections are more widely given and resentments less narrowly aimed than in American families. Nevertheless, as elsewhere, an Indian child has only one mother, who is, of course, wanted but only sometimes available; she must be shared, and the child soon learns this. Too, there is only one father, who also must be shared with many others, though there are usually uncles who can be paternal without being coercive, helpful in a quiet and unexacting way. If it all sounds pleasant and not so tense as our homes were or are, it can also be sad and difficult, because children in such large families can want what children in smaller families may get in abundance and sometimes in surfeit, namely, individual attention, the more of it the better — or so the American child feels for a while, until he wishes to be done with the whole "business," be completely on his own, a notion an Indian youth might find utterly inconceivable.

Indian children are used to leaning upon many people for help and support, but perhaps never give up the dream that one day they will have that delicious moment when their mother will *really* be there, and for good; whereas our children, having had all that constantly, begin to wonder what it must be like to be off by themselves, thoroughly and distinctly by themselves. Erikson points out that Indians see "purpose" as "to move on augmented, rather than (as is likely to be the case with us) to complete and leave behind." Perhaps children who never quite get exactly what they want for the length of time they want it, but do get a lot else for long periods of time, grow up different from children who get everything and then are told that (however impossible the achievement) ideally a man tries to be free and independent and his own person.

Erikson the clinician struggled with such matters, struggled to make sense of the observations he heard spoken by Indian scholars in his seminar, struggled to see "life" in India as it is lived by children and experienced by Indian youth. He continued to feel his past coming back to him: the news reports he had read about Gandhi, the book he had once read on Gandhi by Rolland, who, like Hermann Hesse, had conveyed to a generation of European youths what it is like in the East, where one lives in a sea of humanity, and maybe in a sea of time, too. To think about the past meant more and more to think about not only what Gandhi meant to Rolland and his readers back in the twenties (*Mahatma Gandhi* was published in 1924), but about how such a man made influential both at home and abroad a special, demanding, challenging philosophy tied to deeds as well as to ideas, to an uncanny mixture of thoughtfulness and the stubborn, active exertion of the will — a mixture which would naturally interest the author of *Insight and Responsibility*, and particularly the author of the essay in the book titled "Psychological Reality and Historical Actuality."

Neither Gandhi nor his various biographers have made much of an event in Ahmedabad which, interestingly enough, marked Gandhi's first public fast. Erikson's host, Ambalal Sarabhai, was in 1918 one of several mill owners who resisted the demands of their workers for higher wages, and Gandhi (his friend), along with Ambalal's sister Anasuyaben, had become an advocate of the workers, but a most extraordinary kind of advocate, as *Gandhi's Truth* gradually shows. The drama was obvious: brother against sister, friends against one another, a public fast entered into by a man already famous for his achievements as a leader of his people in South Africa. Yet in his autobiography Gandhi mentions the event rather briefly and casually — almost as if he didn't care to write about it at all, and Erikson's diligent search of the press found no reference to Gandhi's first fast in any public document or in the news sections of any major Indian newspaper. Actually, in March 1918, Gandhi had indeed made mention of the fast, as Erikson discovered by becoming a rather persistent investigator. In a "crumbling number of the *Bombay Chronicle*" he finally found a long letter signed by M. K. Gandhi and apparently written right after his fast. The letter begins:

Perhaps I owe an explanation to the public with regard to my recent fast. Some friends consider the action to have been silly, others cowardly and some others still worse. In my opinion, I would have been untrue to my Maker and to the cause I was espousing if I had acted otherwise.

The letter ends with:

I felt that it was a sacred moment for me, my faith was on the anvil, and I had no hesitation to rising and declaring to the men that a breach of their vow so solemnly taken was unendurable by me and that I would not take any food until they had the 35 per cent increase given or until they had fallen. A meeting that was up to now unlike the former meetings, totally unresponsive, woke up as if by magic.[9]

It can be said that the man who had with such patience and determination found these words was in the midst of a "sacred moment" of his own. Erikson had come to suspect that the fast Gandhi had taken up "represented a demonstrable crisis in the middle age of a great man and was worthy of study as such." He had in the past been asked about Gandhi and his "identity crisis." Well before Gandhi worked on behalf of Ahmedabad's textile workers he had gone through that crisis: in the railroad station of South Africa's Maritzburg he had refused to travel as a "coolie," as a "coloured," and had been put off a train. From then on he would not practice the law he had learned so well in England, not in South Africa or India. From then on he would give his high intelligence and considerable energy to the cause of India's millions, subjugated on the continent of Africa and of course on their own subcontinent. But in 1918 Gandhi was no young man making a stand against the injustice practiced by the British-run South African railroads. He was almost fifty, and for a long time had settled upon his life's priorities, upon his identity as a spokesman — one of many leaders his people had and certainly needed. In 1918 Gandhi was sort of "in-between" things, or so Erikson began to view the matter: "The South African Gandhi already had become historical and had earned himself the renown due to *a* Mahatma, while the history of Gandhiji, *the* Mahatma of all India, had not yet begun."

The men and women who in 1962 were alive and remembered what had happened in 1918, who even had taken part in the events, had then been young, in their twenties and thirties, and so going through in Ahmedabad what Gandhi had experienced in South Africa. Erikson could ask them what they recalled, and could ask them to go back and try to make sense of what they as youths had tried to do, and had seen a middle-aged leader trying to do — as he struggled for justice and reconciliation and as he, by his own later descriptions, also struggled with himself. Such a "growing interest" in Gandhi and the confrontation he had with Ahmedabad's industrialists in some measure reflected the obvious curiosity a mind can feel in the presence of an absorbing country, a courtly and intriguing host, and a legend (Gandhi has, alas, become one). In addition, Erikson had come to India in 1962 fresh from a conference on disarmament held by the American Academy of Arts and Sciences, a conference full of talk about man's ability to destroy all life on earth. Gandhi's methods and beliefs seemed a striking alternative to such an awful possibility. But something else was at work, and was to be stated both humorously and directly:

I should admit that I must have been looking for a historical figure to write about. What could be more fitting than (as my students put it) letting "Young Man Luther" be followed by "Middle-Aged Mahatma"? And here I had witnesses: the survivors of a generation of then-young men and women who had joined or met Gandhi in 1918, and whose lives had not been the same since, as if one knew what they might have been. They included, besides the mill owner and his sister, individuals now retired or still in the forefront of national activity in industry, in the Union Cabinet, or in Parliament. These I set out to meet and to interview on my subsequent visits to India.[10]

Characteristically, he did not plunge into those interviews during his first stay. He went home and thought out his "inquiry"; he tried to figure out what he would eventually ask of whom. One by one the witnesses would have to be called upon: in the first place, Gandhi himself, through his autobiography, then the others, beginning with Ambalal and Anasuyaben — and all this testimony would hopefully shed light on how men make history.

Gandhi's autobiography, to be drawn from again and again, has to be understood as something written in a very definite style and during a particular period in a man's life. Each living witness will be similarly understood: When and how did he become involved with Gandhi, that is, at what age and under what set of circumstances? *An Autobiography: The Story of My Experiments with Truth* was begun in 1925, when Gandhi was an acknowledged leader of his people, yet sad and frustrated. Erikson quotes several passages to indicate how openly unhappy and worried the Mahatma was — torn between his genuine humility and his honest recognition that he did indeed have a lot to offer a people badly in need of guile as well as innocence, a combination that Christ insisted was necessary and not at all "wrong" or incompatible. The activist, the animated, vigorous and forceful organizer, the exceedingly canny political leader was, at least in the twenties, rather afraid that his increasing prominence was to no avail. He was running the personal risk of becoming prideful, and his achievements were questionable, or so he then thought. Clearly, a man rather burdened with self-doubt, very definitely in the doldrums, not quite sure what to do, what anyone can possibly do, will not be the most impartial and generous self-observer, especially when he is writing about relatively recent deeds, which are part of the very struggle whose merits in the first place caused so much apprehension. The autobiography was written in spells, in brief installments; it was originally not even meant to be a book, nor was it meant to apologize for a life, to explain a life, to heighten the significance of a life, or to ask for the reader's mercy and kindness.

Gandhi constantly wrote messages, to himself and for others. He talked to himself, and at himself. He had a light, cheerful touch, as Erikson shows as he gets closer to the man and his childhood. But *Moksha* was Gandhi's serious purpose. How, then, could an autobiography help him and his readers feel less tied to the world's bothersome details, to the pettiness and meanness of everyday life? To write is to call attention to oneself, especially when the subject *is* oneself; yet writers like St. Augustine and Gandhi meet the contradictions head on and say to themselves, "I will dwell on myself, even if pride is thereby augmented, even if *Moksha* or renunciation itself is thereby renounced — because maybe another contradiction can also happen, maybe the boldest, most explicit kind of self-centeredness can, like a dangerously high fever, mark a turn in things, the beginning of pride's end, the start of a certain acquiescence, whereby the world can at last be let go a little bit, taken for granted a little more, because all the temptations to do otherwise, to hold on and grab for more, have been thoroughly, ruthlessly even, brought to light and examined."

So Gandhi wrote and wrote, and clearly suffered, but also smiled; he wrote in his native language Gujarati, and in an open, warm way that the English translation does not convey — which Erikson emphasizes, even as he has noted the distortions (both of fact and spirit) many translations of Freud's writings contain. The point is not that distortions or misrepresentations are deliberately rendered; the point is that the "tone" of a man's mind can get lost, as can his cumulative purpose, which defies particular words and facts or incidents, but does indeed reveal itself in a succession of words and phrases, whose temper and character may not come across. Erikson finds Gandhi's autobiography in English formal, a little stilted and awkward, and prim, even moralistic. From other sources, from what the man did, from what others report him doing and saying, and from what those who speak Gujarati report reading in *An Autobiography*, a different view of the man comes across, a view which makes him fuller and more complicated, and a view which helps us understand what he must have gone through in Ahmedabad in 1918.

The "others" who spoke to Erikson about Gandhi (and themselves) were by the early sixties, when Erikson met them, survivors
of sorts: survivors of long lives, of Gandhi's struggle, of India's many
tragedies. Who were they? Who are they? How did they come to
Gandhi? What did Gandhi mean to them — and ask of them, and do
with their energy and devotion, or as the case may have been, their
opposition? In 1918, Ambalal Sarabhai was twenty-five; his sister
Anasuyaben, twenty-seven. Shankerlal Banker was twenty-eight
when he first met Gandhi, and Ambalal's rich and powerful industrialist friend Kasturbhai Lalbhai was twenty-four in 1918. All of them
were youths; as Erikson points out, all were the age he has tried for
years and years to understand, through young patients, young soldiers returned from a war, young Sioux and young Yurok, even
through the young Luther. Now he could talk with men and women
in their seventies, ask them to look back upon their youth, and ask
them how they had managed with a man old enough to be their
father, who it turns out was going through a crisis, if not an identity
crisis.

Before he takes some of his informants up, Erikson describes the
general problems he faced interviewing old people about a time long
since gone, one-time followers about a leader, and those who helped
make history about an event in history. Today the "interview" is
quite familiar to thousands of people, who have been asked questions and more questions: What man will they vote for; what do
they think about this or that; which product do they use and why;
what are their attitudes, their expectations, their values, their beliefs?
There are "carefully researched" interviews and "balanced" interviews and interviews conducted with a "selected population" and
"statistically valid" interviews and interviews "designed to elicit a
broad range of data." Social scientists "do" interviews, or "conduct"
them; they use questionnaires or "interview protocols" or "forms,"
and they have people say yes or no or maybe. Sometimes interviews
are tape-recorded and then edited, or they are offered verbatim or,
as it is also put, "raw." Sometimes interviews are "fed" into a com-
puter. The contrast of all this with Erikson's approach to his "witnesses" is, to say the least, both distinct and instructive. He wanted
information from certain people, even as the U.S. Census Bureau
does. But he kept on asking himself why: Why do I hear what I do,
and hear it now, from men and women who have their own questions
to ask, their own answers to find, who have to defend and make sense

of and come to terms with their lives? And he kept on thinking of the life cycle: "for it is in the logic of the life cycle that they should try to end their lives with *their* integrity and not only with a reflection of the Mahatma's."

We, each of us, of course, have our own ways of maintaining a certain integrity, which means that what we offer as an opinion may not be all we have to say about a given subject. With respect to Gandhi, Erikson began to see that some of the people he talked with could only be comfortable as worshipful admirers of the Mahatma, others as kindly or severe critics. There were those for whom Gandhi was a virtual god; nothing ill could be spoken of him, and in fact his memory had to be coated with sweet sentiment. There were those who claimed to know exactly what Gandhi said and did, indeed what he would say and would do were he alive today. Inevitably, they reminded Erikson of Freud's fate, to become the claimed property of ardent followers and zealous disciples, each certain that never would this be allowed, never would that be encouraged, always it must be the way he put it — in book X, in article Y, in a letter written to Z.

In India, there were those who wanted to talk as honestly and openly as they knew how, but feared the motives of a psychoanalytic investigator. Would he call Gandhi "neurotic"? Would he take a complicated, dedicated, sensitive and restless man and make him one more patient, one more bit of evidence that we are not at all what we seem? As a matter of fact, a few of the Indians he met were familiar with psychiatry and psychoanalysis: Erikson knew when he was in India, and candidly admits in *Gandhi's Truth*, that the "apprehensions" some of his informants felt about the uses and abuses to which certain psychoanalytic terms and theoretical constructs can be put are not "altogether unfounded." As in *Young Man Luther*, *Gandhi's Truth* contains the most explicit warnings possible against the glib transfer of psychoanalytic terminology from the clinic (where it helps explain things, but can even there be exploited, be used to judge and condemn) to the world of politics and social struggle, in which the real issue is a man's deeds, his commitment to one or another program. *Gandhi's Truth* is not to be a book about Gandhi's "problems" or "nonviolence as a form of therapy" or "the charismatic personality." *Gandhi's Truth* is about the answers that the following two questions prompted — in many Indians, and so far as the second question goes, in the man who asked it in this manner:

"I asked them all these questions: where and when did you first meet Gandhiji? And what would you say was to you the essence of his presence?"

The *essence* of his *presence* — how can one ever talk "scientifically" about an "essence" of a "presence"? And then there are the answers, the impossibly subjective answers, not to mention the way they are offered to us: "Mostly the answers would be preceded by a quick smile which was like a dawn breaking through fog, while each reply was highly personal. 'Gandhi?' Ambalal sitting behind his big desk, said without a moment's hesitation. 'Oh, he was like a good night's sleep.' " Anasuyaben said he was her mother! Most said that in the Mahatma's presence one could not lie. Zakir Husein, then the Vice-President of India, was utterly respectful, though not always in agreement with Gandhi's ideas. In short, the man was universally revered in very personal ways — or else some "had learned only too well how to respond politely and vaguely to inquisitive foreigners." What Erikson saw was that answers lead to more questions, that Gandhi was many things to many people — only some of which they were prepared to talk about, only some of which they may have known or thought about or cared to think about. Like the rest of us, Gandhi himself was many things. By making all that clear at the outset, any investigator sets himself a very difficult task: What *will* he do if he will not deny ambiguities and complexities, but rather emphasizes them; if he will not settle for a particular (psychoanalytic or historical or political) "line," which has Gandhi at the very least *almost* sick, or has him an inspired but mixed-up prophet, or a canny politician, or a simple-minded idealist, or a willful apologist for a backward society, or an interesting but "irrelevant" person, the product of an age long gone?

A question like that is rhetorical, and the only answer it can have is the entire book *Gandhi's Truth;* but obviously Erikson must have wondered what to make of all the responses he was getting, particularly since he was not simplifying matters for either himself or his informants. He was doing just the opposite; by using words like "essence" and "presence" he was asking for a whole range of replies, for anything one felt and wanted to say. And of course the more he heard the more he had before him the thoughts and passions of individuals. What a man does with all these various responses we can learn when we have finished his book; but we are reminded in the beginning of the book that the inquiry was aimed at understanding inescapable contradictions, discrepancies, variations, puzzles of sorts, rather than at formulating a position and then massing information and interpretations to defend it.

And, indeed, the first witness called upon (the "counterplayer," Ambalal Sarabhai) is described as causing the author "a strangely upsetting experience" and "difficulties" which must be reported because they show what goes on between an interviewer and his informants as well as between a man like Gandhi and one of his friends and (at the same time) opponents. Ambalal was Erikson's host, even as he was Gandhi's. During the Eriksons' first stay all had gone well between them and him; he was a fine man, generous and gracious and in fact full of talk about the past, full of stories about Gandhi. During Erikson's second stay Ambalal saw Erikson as a psychoanalyst, a man who would pry and come up with God knows what. He was on his guard. The psychoanalyst was told to come to Ambalal's office at the mill rather than talk with him at home. The psychoanalyst began to see his witness as cool, silent, unwilling to be quoted very much, if at all. Nor was Ambalal simply acting as he was out of ignorance, or even lack of experience with analysts. Before he met Erikson he had heard some gratuitous interpretations from an analyst who was visiting India. Even more interesting, many years earlier, Ambalal had wanted to know more about himself and had wanted advice about a troubled relative; consequently, he had visited Sigmund Freud in Vienna, but had requested anonymity from that psychoanalyst even as with Erikson he wanted to say little for attribution.

Ambalal had been a tough but courteous opponent of Gandhi's. Gandhi's job was to protest, Ambalal's to run his mills profitably. Ambalal was a giving man, a thoughtful and kind one; on the other hand, he was a shrewd businessman. When Erikson was getting ready to leave after what could be considered a good bargaining session as well as an interview, the tough though old and slightly paralyzed Ambalal asked, "So what have you learned now?" The response was at once diplomatic and right to the point: "I answered truthfully that I had learned to understand a bit of what Gandhi had been up against with him — and he with Gandhi."

Erikson was up against an exceedingly unusual man, a person of many sides and faces. Ambalal was a man who could give Gandhi money and protection, a home virtually, because there was every reason to do so, out of kindness and affection and out of personal conviction, too. He was also a man who could fight to protect what he believed to be the interests of his business — fight against Gandhi and the workers, and for that matter, fight by yielding at the right moment to Gandhi and those same workers. Like Gandhi himself (Erikson began to realize) Ambalal was both behind and ahead of his time. There was Ambalal the feudal man, of iron will, rich and powerful and not easily approached or seduced into anything he had not already decided to accept. There was Ambalal the man of charity, the man who wanted his workers to be healthy and live well and possess the very dignity Gandhi felt every human being ought to have. There was Ambalal the man who eventually did talk freely with Erikson, not in a whisper, not with instructions that secrecy be the order of the day. There was Ambalal the eminently clear-sighted man who might come to trust his Western guest but continued to worry because "he had sense and resisted the radical determinism with which psychoanalytic determination reduces matters to a core of infantile and neurotic motivation." There was, finally, that peculiar blend of autocratic benevolence and individual compassion that enabled this industrialist to take in Gandhi, and in a sense all his workers, to offer them gifts of many kinds, but do so slyly or gruffly and at times with apparent reluctance. All this Gandhi sensed and in his own manner used — in conversations and discussions, in formal meetings, in the bargaining that went on in Ahmedabad before and during the first fast.

Gandhi had his own reasons to grow attached (within limits) to such a man. Gandhi had lost his father when young and under circumstances he could never forget, never forgive himself for: he had left the dying man's bedside to be with Kasturba, his young wife, and so had not been there at the end. Gandhi had left India, left his father's home and province, in a way his father's caste (he was, of course, excommunicated), for England and the education a barrister requires. Then he had become a prophet of sorts, an advocate of causes, a meditative man — some would say a revolutionary — rather than a Bania businessman, an associate (with his brother) in a law firm. In Ahmedabad he had even taken an Untouchable family into his ashram — with the support of Ambalal. All in all, he was an exile, a man who had left his country, abandoned to some extent his family's traditions; but he must have felt very sad indeed for having done so, because he was no unfeeling renegade, no thoughtless, prodigal son. Ambalal was to some extent a brother to Gandhi, a generous and kind one who offered help and more help, yet of course had to be resisted by a man whose loyalties really transcended the limits of any particular family. It was, as Erikson points out, "a complex matter," not easily settled once and for all by one or two words from a psychiatric textbook.

Gandhi was essentially reticent about the event in Ahmedabad, which Erikson feels marked an extremely important point in the development of his methods, the consolidation of his purposes even, as a Mahatma. The event is mentioned only briefly in the autobiography, and as Erikson slowly came to see, was not easily discussed by certain men and women who had witnessed it or had taken part in it. Why? one wonders. Did Gandhi for some reason find that struggle especially difficult, both to wage and, later on, to mention? He "won," after all. The mill workers achieved a substantial increase in earnings. Against intelligent, supple, and resourceful opposition Gandhi managed to prevail — and his leadership, as always, was tested by his so-called followers as much as by his supposed enemies. He prevailed significantly in the sense that an atmosphere of nonviolence by and large was maintained; and he also prevailed in a very interesting and prophetic way — by fasting until his personal restraint, both utterly concrete and enormously symbolic, became a force of its own, an unforgettable and decisive presence, to use the word Erikson always used in asking Indians about Gandhi. Yet, in spite of all that (maybe because of it), Gandhi was diffident indeed about his work in Ahmedabad during 1918, a strong contrast with his willingness to talk about other challenges he had faced.

In the first section of *Gandhi's Truth* we are not told why Gandhi and his friends were so reticent about the strike. Erikson wants the reader to go along with him, to feel the questions rise up, to feel the puzzle he himself noticed only over time. He does mention the "complex matter," and suggests we at least note, as we meet Ambalal and others, that they too match Gandhi's discretion and in fact demonstrate how shy, wary, cautious, reserved, and upon occasion thoroughly suspicious it is possible for men and women to be about an event one would now think does them all proud, whatever their position in the past. The workers did get more money. To a certain extent an organized labor movement was securely begun. Gandhi's leadership became evident, and its quality was established — deliberate, considerate, even-handed, self-critical but thoroughly persistent, and at a given point, uncompromising and sacrificial. Again, why the stillness, the reticence, or the evasive wordiness?

Erik and Joan Erikson both talked at length with Ambalal's sister

Anasuyaben, so close to Gandhi for so long, so devoted to the poor, to sick children, to hungry and underpaid workers. She answered questions, but suddenly turned and gently but firmly had two of her own to pose: "Why all these old details? Why not let the ripe fruit fall?" Nor were the Eriksons unsympathetic. It was perhaps easier to hear those questions than to listen to extravagant, pietistic worship of Gandhi, a lot of self-serving nostalgia, and a lot of clever propaganda meant to bury an already obscure event in words and more words that prove over and over again Gandhi's faultless brilliance.

It was probably harder for Erikson to interview three of the "four old Indians": the old friend of Gandhi's, Shankerlal Banker; Gulzarilal Nanda, India's Home Minister; Indulal Yagnik, an outspoken and passionate member of the opposition in Parliament; and Pyarelal Nayar, Gandhi's biographer and for three decades his secretary. As with the Sarabhais, brother and sister, Erikson doesn't introduce only "theories" about the "material" he secured from these distinguished Indian leaders. Rather, we are encouraged as readers to appreciate "the varieties of styles" each of the aging but thoroughly aware and sensitive men displayed toward an American analyst who wanted to get from them, one suspects, less a series of facts than a *sense* of them — as participants, as associates, as friends, as survivors of Gandhi. Certainly each of them could tell about this situation, that episode; but an analyst is interested in feelings, in what facts and more facts mean to the men and women who recount them. If Gandhi is to be seen clearly, one way will be through the oblique vision his still-living friends can provide; their views of him (which inevitably will contradict as well as amplify one another) tell what kind of persons they were and are, and also what kind of individuals Gandhi chose to be near and to work with (or against), and therefore, to some extent, what kind of man he was.

Shankerlal Banker was twenty-nine in 1918, and in his late seventies when Erikson met him. Erikson saw in him a number of qualities that others have described in Gandhi, and that Gandhi's own words seem to confirm as present: a certain childlike charm and gaiety of manner, a sense of humor. Shankerlal was also "entrepreneurial," twice in so many pages Erikson calls him that; and he does not condemn him with the word. No, Gandhi too was defiantly entrepreneurial, even as he was insistently political. He knew he was in a tough fight, and he knew how to fight, how to calculate things, weigh them, and mull over them, and how to look for approaches, strategies, tactics, whatever. He knew, in other words, that energy has to be used at just the right time, that justice has to do with power, that nowhere do the weak automatically win anything, however worthy their cause. So, like Shankerlal, he had guile, was tough, and above all, was full of energy.

The two of them, Shankerlal Banker and Gandhi, must have come to know one another rather well during the year they spent together in prison. Gandhi apparently was warm, concerned, open, giving; he liked to amuse and sometimes tease not only friends but strangers and even enemies. One feels that Shankerlal teased Erikson a bit, came up with a fair share of murky, slippery remarks, pretended more directness than he was prepared to offer; but he was a man of decency and above all humor — and he was the one who confirmed in detail Gandhi's "Franciscan gaiety." He did not take himself too seriously. He laughed when interrupted in order to be asked something bluntly, and "nothing would please him more than to catch somebody (and especially himself and me) in the trickery of some double talk." For a while he quoted endlessly "the Gandhian scriptures," but once he stopped he really stopped, and in fact did his best to steer the Eriksons toward new people to interview. And he had about him something — an air, a manner — that Erikson saw as a mixture of "pragmatic efficiency and meditative passivity," not a very easy mixture to live with, but one congenial to many Indians, and one Gandhi apparently was quick to notice and put to use.

In Delhi Erikson met Gulzarilal Nanda, the Home Minister. Although their interviews were circumscribed by the press of historical circumstance, a lot of both him and Erikson comes across in the description of their meetings. For the first one Nanda told his aides to give him ten minutes absolutely alone with his visitor. Erikson has this to say about that rather brief period: "Under such turbulent conditions I felt that ten quiet minutes could be a significant span of time: after all, one can sleep, dream, and awake refreshed in ten minutes." In any event, Nanda wanted to know what Erikson wished to ask; and Erikson said that he had just come from Ahmedabad, and had seen where Nanda once lived and began his work in behalf of India's workers; now that he was able to speak to Nanda, he wondered "how far *was* it from the Textile Labor Association in Ahmedabad to the Home Ministry in New Delhi?" The minister felt the lightness of touch, its inviting, ironic simplicity. "Not very far at that!" he answered. More seriously, Gulzarilal Nanda described Gandhi's ability to elicit devotion from others, to ask of them and receive from them, to inspire.

During the second interview, a year after the first, Nanda again talked about the almost miraculous effect that Gandhi's confidence could have upon its recipients, but he went on to say something more general, something not easily forgotten: "Non-violence will be the weapon of choice wherever democracy itself has made issues so opaque and complex that a return to an utter simplicity of approach becomes mandatory — as is the case now in your country." He ended the interview by telling Erikson that for him the event at Ahmedabad had become a spiritual one, an example of reconciliation achieved, almost by ritual rather than moves and countermoves and stratagems and postures, though admittedly Gandhi did not shun the hard work of bargaining almost incessantly with his adversaries. "By then, he had given me twenty minutes," Erikson says, and that was that.

Erikson calls Indulal Yagnik, a member of India's Parliament and a political opponent of Nanda's, both "fiery" and a "firebrand." Nanda is quiet and pensive; Yagnik wants to change India drastically, the India Nanda has recently helped rule. To Indulal Yagnik, Gandhi was "a consummate politician," a man who was not at all a saint; or if he was, the source of his saintliness was in an ability to appraise a given social and economic situation, then get the most out of it — politically as well as spiritually. Gandhi knew the Indian masses. He also knew the British. He planned his every move, calculated, even plotted the positions he took — which for Indulal Yagnik would be no bad thing at all. Indulal, as Erikson calls him, admired Gandhi's energy, his willingness to spend it, every ounce of it, for his cause, but he refused to worship Gandhi or describe him with the familiar adulatory phrases. He could admire a man for being in the best sense of the word calculating, and yes, in a clinch, uncompromising. He could admire a man for selecting just the right time to say something, to do something. He could admire a man for taking advantage of an accident, for waiting until another "right moment" or accident comes along. He could insist that no man becomes the leader of millions, a world-renowned figure who takes on a powerful empire, without being ambitious, adroit, both politic and politically minded, without having a sense of timing, an ability to manipulate as well as stand up and state a particular set of beliefs. Nothing would Indulal consider more insulting or demeaning to the memory of great men like Gandhi than the "treatment" they get from succeeding generations; tributes and more tributes; unqualified praise; and worst of all, no mention of the tough, hard battles they waged against great odds, and most important, waged by being just a little something else than prayerful or wiser than all other men.

Gandhi was wise not only in a spiritual sense, as his admirers have no trouble emphasizing, but wise about the world, wise about men and their weaknesses and vulnerabilities and strengths, wise about how things go when combatants face one another in the undeclared and less dramatic wars that take place when classes and castes and colonies struggle for freedom, not necessarily across traditional battle-fields, but battlefields nonetheless, places of confrontation and fear and alarm, however camouflaged or disguised. Indulal emphasized more than anything else Gandhi's ability to wage these struggles, his complete commitment to them, his thorough preparation for them, his self-possessed readiness to die, to surrender voluntarily his life in the interests of a cause he had studied well, honestly believed in, and felt himself upholding as justly as he knew how. Indulal still tries to be a fighter; a position in one of India's bureaucracies is not for him, and perhaps for that reason he more than the others who knew Gandhi emphasized the long, long hours Gandhi gave over to defining (for himself first, for others later) exactly how he intended to do something and why and for which purposes and where and at what risk — but with the anticipation of a given gain, too. Gandhi was more spiritual than Indulal could perhaps see, even as he was probably more calculating, more of a bargainer, than some of his other friends and associates now care to see. This is doubtless why Erikson went after all of them, and saw in each response a partial truth, and in all of their remarks a helpfully cumulative outline of the man. Still, there remained the task of filling things in, choosing what to emphasize, constructing a plausible and suggestive picture of the man, one that, importantly, evokes him as he actually was rather than as others remember him.

To do that, to sketch Gandhi himself, having heard others do so out of their experiences, or what they retain of them and elect to talk about, Erikson next called upon Gandhi himself, through his letters and autobiography, his other books and essays, and also through pictures of him as well as recordings of his speaking. Just before he does so, perhaps as a self-directed warning, mention is made of Pyarelal Nayar, who for three decades worked with Gandhi as his secretary and has written a several-volume biography of the Mahatma.[11] During one of their stays in India the Eriksons lived across the street from the Navajivan Trust, which owns Gandhi's works. There Pyarelal had an office. A good deal of communication developed between the two men who shared a common biographical interest. Erikson learned a lot from Pyarelal, and yet, as a man sensitive to language not only aesthetically but because he has spent a lifetime analyzing it, he felt obliged to come up with some comments, at once humorous and sad, about the man's way of putting things:

An erudite Indian's attempt to express himself in the best of the King's English often leads him to write in the Queen's — Victoria's, that is. It is painful, for example, to see Pyarelal, this devoted old friend of Gandhi, quoting *Kipling,* of all people, in order to find the right words for the kind of man *Gandhi* was ("If you can dream — and not make dreams your master"), or using such chapter headings as: "A Whiff of the Romantic Past" for historic Kathiawar and "A Tale of Two Cities" for Porbandar and Rajkot.[12]

So it is that Europe affects Africa and Asia; the colonial country colonizes, but it also becomes for the colonized people, particularly the educated, a powerfully attractive source of ideas, values, and images. Thus, a Muslim boy is quoted by Pyarelal as saying to young Gandhi, "Observe my physical prowess and daredevilry." Erikson points out that Tagore wanted to avoid all that, wanted to make Indians more aware of their traditions and less responsive to England's; and of course, Gandhi himself wrote in and spoke Gujarati. Yet Gandhi could not protect himself after he died:

But alas, even Gandhi's *Collected Works* painstakingly and soberly effected under the auspices of the government he helped create, must offer the writings of the Mahatma in a language made on foggy North Sea islands. I know how unfair this critique must sound, coming as it does from one who is a stranger in India and an immigrant in his own country. Maybe for this very reason one searches for authenticity.[13]

In part two of *Gandhi's Truth* Erikson takes up the search he speaks of, and does so on his own, informed about what others saw and felt and cannot forget, and also freshly aware of what he has always known, namely, that there is no one truth, so far as a person's life goes, but dozens and dozens of truths. And if it takes a sharp scientist to find them, trace them back, and figure them out so that the mysterious and baffling becomes suddenly all too obvious, the artist is the one who puts them all together, gives believable coherence to rays of light which come from various directions, bounce, and collide, and often enough cause glitter and glare more than anything else. The search is for Gandhi, but also for more: How did a boy and a young man become a mahatma and then *the* Mahatma? And how did that man, that Indian leader, come to advocate militant nonviolence, live it, preach it, use it, show its power, believe in it enough to risk his life for it again and again — and in the end, die struggling for its triumph in India? Erikson, in a sense, resumes with Gandhi's life what he left off doing in *Young Man Luther*, and as he was in that book, so he is in this one — worried indeed that his effort to understand will be misunderstood, and worst of all, taken as an excuse by others with purposes different from his in mind:

In applying my traumatological métier to Luther, I tried to understand his conflicts and his failures, attempting, however, not to underestimate the fabulous restorative energy of youth which gave his native genius the vitality to renew and restate Christian faith reaffirmingly. For that youthful energy, in fact, I called the book *Young Man Luther*. Since then, the application of traumatology to life histories has become standard practice. And because on occasion it is applied with more or less explicit reference to my work, I must try to be circumspect in this matter; for I consider any attempt to reduce a leader of Gandhi's stature to earlier as well as bigger and better childhood traumata both wrong in method and evil in influence.[14]

Gandhi himself once speculated about life's events this way: "How all this happens — how far a man is free and how far a creature of circumstances — how far free will comes into play and where fate enters on the scene — all this is a mystery and will remain a mystery."[15]

Erikson would perhaps say "not quite a mystery," and indeed a man like Gandhi doesn't write about himself at such length and subject himself to such close and intense scrutiny if he doesn't believe that a few lessons can be gleaned about "how all this happens." Nevertheless, it is instructive and refreshing to be reminded by a psychoanalyst that "what a man adds up to must develop in stages, but no stage explains the man." It is no less important that those stages are at the very outset called "Moniya's friskiness" and "Mohan's gloom" and the "unsure student days in England" and "young man Gandhi's firm householdership in South Africa." We are not going to get a psychiatric diagnosis — which may disappoint more than a few readers.

Before he takes up Gandhi's childhood and youth, Erikson refers briefly to his own past writings, and especially to *Young Man Luther*. Without certain assumptions Mohandas "makes little sense" to him, "certainly not as the predecessor of Gandhi." He wants to state those assumptions, ones he has already spelled out at length, but which bear repeating. Gandhi in ways resembles St. Augustine, St. Francis and Kierkegaard. Gandhi's struggles as a child and a youth are not unlike some of Luther's major conflicts. It seems that certain men come to believe in themselves, but not in the conventional sense of feeling destined for leadership. Instead, they are racked with self-doubt and confusion, but still they are doggedly set upon gaining mastery over themselves, upon knowing what it is to have self-command, and once that is won, upon living out the victory by achieving with and for others what was privately gained for themselves.

Erikson notes that Luther and Gandhi, and others like them, seemed to have as children (and later, too) a sense of their own toughness, "a certain inviolacy of spirit," which no psychological test can ever record and quantify but which such men often themselves quite humbly remark upon and indeed in their memoirs look upon with detached awe. There is, too, the "precocious self-awareness" that Gandhi's autobiography certainly demonstrates in abundance, and his sense of being special, of having a "special mission" — which does *not* mean that a great man "knows" he will be great, but rather that in a number of great men their sense of themselves, their self-involvement, their obstinate, often enough unspoken belief in the wider significance of the particular struggles they go through all are evident. If "great men" are the rest of us writ large, they have exerted themselves consistently to achieve that size, or have been ready when a fortuitous moment comes — and obviously a state of preparedness can require all sorts of prior exertions. Faith prompts exertion — faith that there is a point to writing or doing or saying or whatever; faith in oneself and in the notion of a destiny; faith in the point of acting, of summoning energy to make oneself distinct, distinguishable, maybe even distinguished.

The Gandhis of this world have not been alike, and it is unlikely that anyone will ever satisfactorily account for their energy and passion and intelligence — qualities that are an inheritance and a gift, and perhaps that is all we will ever be able to say with certainty. But Gandhi would be the last man to deny that he was driven hard and long by certain growing, unsettling experiences he tried to forget yet succeeded in making unforgettable – in the sense that what once was his sadness or resentment or remorse became everyone's, or at any rate, England's and India's. What is more, implicitly and sometimes quite explicitly, men like Gandhi make for themselves the connections between certain private and continuing experiences, often begun in childhood, and the public events in their lives that the rest of us know about and wonder about and sometimes try to explain or fathom or interpret. Maybe it is impossible to put into words the way some men learn to want certain things, learn to win certain battles with themselves and others around them, and then never forsake what they have learned, but instead feel called upon to keep on wanting and doing and learning and trying to win – and then out of luck or a given chain of circumstances get a rare chance to do on the stage of history what they have mastered in their lives.

Such riddles, the great riddles of history, will not let go of the man who wrote *Young Man Luther* and *Gandhi's Truth;* certainly he will not brush them aside with an improbably lucid, cut-and-dried formula. He knows, for instance, that Gandhi was a tease – as a child, with his father, and as a man, with the British Viceroy. Was then teasing – or some other psychological characteristic – the "key" to the Mahatma's greatness? Thousands and thousands of Indian children, among others, are teasers – and get away with it at home, and perhaps later in life, too. What separates them all from Gandhi? Erikson dares lead us to that kind of question. He does so aware that the answers are hard to provide. Of course Gandhi's later teasing can be traced back to his childhood. But if we are to comprehend Gandhi's ability to get to the Viceroy's palace, *there* to be a tease, a whole life has to be considered, a life which repeatedly (one sees) brought the man living it closer and closer to that palace – with assists from the Viceroy himself, because the Gandhi who learned how to waltz in London seemed forever looking for partners with whom he would dance on the stage of history.

What are we to learn about Gandhi the child? Moniya, we are told by Pyarelal, "had a cheerful, sweet face and lovely eyes." Erikson (who begins the section on Moniya and his mother with: "The earliest available photograph of Moniya makes it plausible that . . .") immediately emphasizes something else, though; the boy also had large ears, and while they helped round out his face, they robbed "the Mahatma's countenance of its proportions, especially when he laughed in his toothless way." Gandhi first is *seen*, then.

And the child Gandhi's pleasant face is linked to his later appearance: he could always console his mother by making her laugh, and as a man and a leader he was constantly seen laughing and causing others to laugh with him and sometimes at him — though for doing the latter they would soon enough feel mistaken or sorry.

Erikson promptly moves from the child in an early photograph, the child whose disposition somehow persisted all through eight decades of life, to the child's family and to the setting, the atmosphere, the concrete surroundings that Moniya would day by day absorb and feel to be his. Here Erikson again shows his ability to bring alive a scene, be it the life of a medieval miner or the Rome of Luther's time or Porbandar on India's Arabian Sea coast, where on October 2, 1869, Mohandas Karamchand Gandhi was born, the youngest son of a father who then was forty-seven and chief minister of a Gujarat state, and the last son of a mother of twenty-five. Porbandar faces west, toward Arabia and Africa. It is near Cambay, which Marco Polo considered one of India's two finest ports. It is, in Erikson's words "a fisherman's and sea trader's world, renowned for its toughness and shrewdness." It is a town of narrow streets and bazaars and crowds everywhere and buildings made of white soft-stone and temples and most of all a town by the sea, with docks and ships and an atmosphere of commerce, an atmosphere that stresses the existence of other nations, such as South Africa and England, to which ships from Porbandar constantly went.

Moniya grew up in a large, three-story home, situated near temples, near the sea and its openness. The home was spacious, but it was also crowded, shared as it was by six brothers and their families. For six generations Gandhis had been home ministers or prime ministers (*dewans*), which is what Karamchand Gandhi was. His child Moniya soon learned that relatives were everywhere, cousins and aunts and uncles, members of a "joint family" as it is called. Gandhi's mother is said to have been kind, hardworking, intensely religious and available to all who needed her. She looked after not only her own children but many others — as did her husband, who constantly helped her out, busy as he was with his work. Erikson draws on Pyarelal's biography and his own observations to suggest the close parallel between Gandhi's style as a leader and his experience growing up in a large, rather comfortable, but no doubt difficult home where people had to learn to live at very close quarters, where no one could be quite sure where he or she stood with others, where tact and self-control were all-important to a child, who simply had to learn how to live among a crowd of people. Later Gandhi would take to the sea, board one of the ships he must have seen often as a boy, have his own kind of commerce with England and South Africa. Later Gandhi also would live among crowds, speak to them and in his own ashram have all sorts of people around him, sharing him, struggling for him, contending with one another. Later, too, Gandhi would not be far removed from prime ministers and temples; he would be dealing with officials for decades, and he would be a religious man, who always tried to find out what he actually did believe, and always in his mind wanted to refine and sharpen his various allegiances.

What of his mother and his father? How did Moniya get along with them? Apparently Moniya did have a rather special meaning to both of them. As "the last child of a young mother and an aging patriarch," he made the best of it. Moniya was to some extent "spoiled." He could be playful with his parents, and at times more than playful; he teased them — and apparently they didn't jump all over him for doing so. Erikson is the child analyst when he describes Moniya's teasing and his parents' restraint: "For a child is easily overcome by the fear of his own initiative and curiosity, while the native strength of his personality cannot as yet match the precocity of either his brashness or his sensitive conscience."

Moniya was also restless, curious, hard to hold down and keep in tow. As a child he walked and walked, wandered all over; as a man he would spend the last decades of his life walking all over India; indeed he would die walking. Moniya also was "inclined to usurp strange rights." He would remove the image of the ruling prince from its position in the house, and sit there himself. Erikson is half-serious and half-ironic when he says that such an act was "a habit of pretending to be his father's master of which we shall make all we can." Moniya also was wont to scatter things all over the floor, and indeed to write on the floor: "When his mother tried to forbid this, he (in Pyarelal's words) 'stoutly dissented,' in what may have been the ontogenetic origin of the sit-down."

I quote such passages to indicate that amid a very serious discussion of a great man's childhood Erikson does not let himself get carried away with excessively pedantic and unqualified explanations for seventy-nine years of living, being, and doing. There are indeed themes to be found and pointed out, but in a spirit that suggests rather than declares outright or insists. Gandhi himself had a sense of humor, as a child and all through his life. He and his many biographers did not abstain from discussing little Moniya and the older child and youth, Mohan. Yet Gandhi was many things, a man of many sides, a man of exceptional flexibility, in many ways a man who lived several lives in one: the precocious Indian child, the exile, the charming English-educated barrister, the South African attorney, the political leader and religious thinker, the man who bargained with viceroys, the man who went to prison, the world figure whom many believed to be the most important moral and social philosopher alive. How can any formulation about such a man's childhood lack a certain flexibility of its own? If in addition to relaxed though suggestive hypotheses, we also get in *Gandhi's Truth* a touch of facetiousness and dry wit, then perhaps we *are* getting to the first, though not the only Gandhi, the child who cared about a lot of things and took seriously many people and issues, so that he must have learned quite early how funny human beings are, even in their seriousness, and how much they need to know just that, what it means to be able to laugh at oneself, to be kidded, to be brought up short, to be made aware of the ridiculous, the inconsistent and farcical and incongruous part of life, all of which a growing boy or girl can see with devastating clarity, as parents both know and try to forget.

Moniya's parents took him rather more seriously than some, which may have helped him later in life, when he most definitely had to take himself seriously in order to speak for and lead so many people. His parents also allowed him to care for them, maybe even encouraged him to do so. Gandhi said this to Pyarelal, which Erikson quotes:

I was my mother's pet child, first because I was the smallest of her children but also because there was nothing dearer to my heart than her service. My brothers were fond of play and frolic. I found not much in common with them. I had no close bond with my sister either. Play had absolutely no fascination for me in preference to my mother's service. Whenever she wanted me for anything, I ran to her.[16]

Moniya's mother also had other things going on between her and her children. She liked to spin yarn. She loved coarse cloth. She belonged to an ascetic Hindu sect which emphasized a direct and intimate meeting of God and man. She fasted. She was a religious woman, a woman who tried hard to keep things clean, to purify herself. She knew what it was to confess, to take vows. She also knew what it was to work. Dedicated, inclined toward austerities, conscientious, yet warm and giving — she must have set quite an example for her son, her last son. And a child picks all those things up, notices what his mother does, how she reacts under various circumstances, what her values and sentiments are. Naturally, the child doesn't think of "values" or "sentiments," but he sees, he hears, he notices and learns that his mother is not a Hindu, not a Jain and not a Muslim, but something of each, and that she seeks after the spirit rather than the letter. A child also can sense any sadness around, or become sad himself because he cannot quite get all he wants, because his conscience is too sensitive, because illness strikes a parent. Gandhi knew sadness. At thirteen he was married to the child-bride Kasturba at his father's insistence. The wedding picture shows him scared. His father was almost killed on the way to the wedding when the carriage taking him there overturned. Indeed, there is evidence that the marriage was hastily arranged because his father feared he would not live much longer.

Mohan was devoted to his father, and somehow never quite separated in his mind his marriage with Kasturba and the loyalty he owed to his father. Particularly, he could never forgive himself for being with Kasturba when his father died. In this regard, Erikson takes up Mohan's "oedipus complex," the whole business of how a child and later a youth comes to terms with his mother and his father — in Gandhi's case with his father most especially. We know the father was aging and strong-minded, a man short in stature but stocky and impressive to look at, diplomatic but firm, quiet but capable of saying something right to the point — in brief, a man who commanded from everyone, within and without his family, deference and respect, which he earned by being thoughtful and considerate. We also know (from the Mahatma's descriptions) that Mohan was at times a frightened, timid youth, unsure of what he could "do with" that father of his, and maybe everyone else, including himself. Perhaps Gandhi went through a serious "emotional crisis," which he could never quite shake off. Perhaps in his later life we see the delicate, impressionable and susceptible youth still there in the charismatic leader, still there in the serious but teasing man, the man at times almost desperately aroused and alarmed, at other times peaceful in a virtually reproachful way. *Gandhi's Truth* has a lot to tell the reader who wants to know about the "adolescence" of that man; but there is something else the book offers; in another age that something might have been called edifying. I have in mind the manner of approach that comes across in the following passage, a manner respectful both to Gandhi and to Sigmund Freud, respectful enough to take considered issue with both of them when the need is felt to do so:

Yet Mohan seems so much stauncher, so much more exquisitely put together than one would gather from the sum of the stories told about him by the Mahatma. Who can describe, who "analyze" such a young man? Straight and yet not stiff; shy and yet not withdrawn; intelligent and yet not bookish; willful and yet not stubborn; sensual and yet not soft: all of which suggests that integrity which is, in essence, unexplainable — and without which no explanation is valid. We must try to reflect on the relation of such a youth to his father, because the Mahatma places service to the father and the crushing guilt of failing in such service in the center of his adolescent turbulence. Some historians and political scientists seem to find it easy to interpret this account in psychoanalytic terms; I do not. For the question is not how a particular version of the Oedipal Complex "causes" a man to be both great and neurotic in a particular way, but rather how such a young person, upon perceiving that he may, indeed, have the originality and the gifts necessary to make some infantile fantasies come true in actuality, manages the complexes which constrict other men. This one cannot learn from Freud because he primarily described the conscience which inactivates ordinary people, and neglected to ask aloud (except, maybe, in a cryptic identification with Moses) what permits great men to step out of line. He was content to demonstrate the unconscious restoration of mastery over our inner complexes by nightly dreaming, but he neglected to dwell on the question of what additional mastery made it possible for him to understand his own dreams. This, like morality, he took for granted.[17]

In any event, Mohan's youth was not an easy one. He found himself married too young, and his wife not amenable to his troubled, intense efforts at making her over: she was to become literate, a "cultivated" person, conversant with books and the knowledge they have to offer. In that attempt Gandhi failed. Kasturba never stopped being herself: strong-willed, a simple, forthright woman, unimpressed by all sorts of pretentious people who called themselves "civilized" or "educated." She had a direct, proud, earthy quality, and no doubt strengthened that direction in her husband. For years they were mere children unexpectedly and a bit arbitrarily married, drawn to one another, parents themselves rather soon, but frightened and for some time not able to feel grown, confident, at ease with one another. All of this meant that there was in Mohan and no doubt his wife, too, a certain desperation which Erikson tactfully approaches:

At any rate, a true account of Mohan's youth (and here good fiction would be truer than any composite of the tendentious "facts" available) would have to show him from day to day in the overlapping and yet also deeply conflicting duties of attending father, wife, and school and (the reader will be almost glad to hear of it) experimenting with a bit of juvenile delinquency as well.[18]

Gandhi, to his own mind, did more than merely experiment with a bit of delinquency. He was in later life a stern self-critic — that is, when he was not smiling at life's various ironies. He recalls his youth as a time of temptation, disorder, miscalculations, errors and God knows what. Marvelously, Erikson becomes a little sarcastic in order to point up vividly what a man like Gandhi could do with his own life — make a caricature of himself, render himself far more awkward and even grotesque than he ever was: "And from the Mahatma we have only unalleviated Augustinianisms. 'If with this devouring passion there had not been in me a burning attachment to duty, I should either have fallen a prey to disease and premature death or have sunk into a burdensome existence.' "[19] Alas, the passion Gandhi refers to never could be simply enjoyed; he deeply loved his wife, yet could not really delight in her physically, sensually. In his thirties he stopped all sexual activity — and perhaps found satisfaction in what Erikson calls a "detached physical closeness to both men and women." He loved people, that is; he loved to be close, to hold on to friends, to offer his heart, to receive another's deepest affection. To love with his body, though, was another matter. As a young man he never could relax and enjoy his natural urges, and there is no doubt that as an older man he could upon occasion speak of sex almost brutally — as if it were wrong, wasteful, debilitating, spiritually subversive. Erikson at several points in his book has to take up this matter, and at considerable length. When he describes Gandhi's youth and his sexual life he does so discreetly, courteously, but without refraining from what has to be said:

Clinically speaking, one can only conclude that Gandhi *had* to save his kind of playfulness, intimacy, and creativity from a sexuality which had offended him in the biblical sense and that he was fortunate in his capacity to derive eventually a sense of gaiety from plucking it out. But we shall see that some vindictiveness, especially toward woman as the temptress, survived in him and made him insist on absolute chastity as a necessary condition for leaders in nonviolence.[20]

We are, again, asked only to think about a few hypotheses, mostly based upon Gandhi's own writings, and see where we are led. Thus, young Gandhi dearly loved his father, wanted to be of service to him as much as possible, and spent as much time as possible doing just that. He loved his mother, too. He loved to obey both of them, respond to their values. He wanted to be as fair and decent and lofty as he considered his parents to be. But he also was tempted. He was tempted by his wife, or so he viewed it; tempted of course by his own, natural instincts, and by his Muslim friend Sheik Mehtab, who advocated meat-eating and promiscuity and an abandon Gandhi apparently wished for, even as he said an emphatic no to himself. It is a rather dramatic and engrossing story: the young Mohan wants to defy his parents, but is close to them and respects them; he wants to be an honorable person, but he covets — women, possessions, food other than vegetables and more vegetables; he moves toward his father, toward his mother, toward delinquency, toward his wife, whom he loves, but feels he should shun; and through it all, he struggles to reconcile his various affections and values and impulses, struggles to do so very hard, very long, very tempestuously. This is the young man, we are reminded, who will one day demonstrate "a style of leadership which can defeat a superior adversary only nonviolently and with the express intent of saving him as well as those whom he oppressed."

Gandhi was not alone with such worries and struggles, but he was, again, a singularly determined person, in his family a special person, and he was most especially hurt and shaken when he failed "to preside mercifully over his father's death." Sanction was thereby lost — his father's. And the dark power of grief and self-laceration was added to an already strong brew — the youth's vast energy, his ambitiousness, his eagerness to help, to attend the needs of others. Britain was not his father, his mother, or some other psychological symbol; but in his youth Gandhi *did* writhe and squirm and flounder with his conscience, his ever so meticulous and watchful conscience, and for decades later he would continue to do what as a youth he wanted to do, and sometimes did do: court those he might also somehow disappoint; heal those he looked up to as powerful; conciliate as well as challenge and perhaps most of all, coax — through gentle persuasion and unflinching advocacy. Thus was Britain dared and defied — yet when in danger supported by an ambulance corps Gandhi helped mobilize; likewise the Hindus and Muslims, indeed all those who turned on one another and by their attitudes and deeds prevented India from being a free, intact nation, in command of its own destiny. Gandhi could fight, but always he wanted not to win, but to win over.

Gandhi calls his autobiography "experiments with truth," as if from the beginning of his life and increasingly over the years he was trying to get someplace, figure something out, solve a predicament and puzzle whose psychological presence, in various forms, simply could not be ignored. Certainly the "experiments" had their origin in a boy's efforts to placate and appease an old, dignified father, to have for his very own a young and dearly beloved but only occasionally available mother, and to do so without setting one of them against the other, and perhaps both against a demanding, provocative child. The child grew up to become a skillful organizer and conciliator who unswervingly but patiently kept to his purposes — in such a way, though, that gains rather than losses were emphasized, peace rather than war was held up as an aim. No doubt the "oedipus complex" was tied up with all of this. Yet Erikson calls that "complex" a "human crisis" and goes on to spell out its existential quality as "obviously shared by all men [so that] to highlight it retrospectively in this case of an uncommon man would seem to be a rather minor triumph of ingenuity, if one cannot clarify what makes the man and his complex uncommon."

And anyway, "not all uncommon men are chosen." Again the dilemma is faced, and if not conclusively answered (Can it ever be?), at least we read that the question before us is not only how such men come to experience a particular and rather inescapable conflict, "but how it comes about that they have the pertinacity and the giftedness to reenact it in a medium communicable to their fellow men and meaningful in their stage of history." The emphasis is on *re-enactment* — something we are pointedly reminded "goes far beyond the dictates of that 'repetition compulsion' which characterizes symptoms and irrational acts." The emphasis is on the capacity a particular person can have to use every bit of his ingenuity, intelligence and imagination, his moral and intellectual resourcefulness, to solve various psychological "problems," and at the same time do so in a way that progressively becomes more "public," more tied to daily events. Thereby others become involved in the given man's personal struggle, and he in the struggles of those others. Thereby a drama begins to unfold, in which there is a spokesman or main character, and a cast of millions, in which frustrations and oppressions are fought, sorrows expressed, desires sought after — yes, the way children do all that, but also the way adults do in everyday life, as citizens of a country, as subjects of an emperor, as men and women who only reluctantly work for so-and-so, who wish it were possible to live someplace else, indeed live another kind of life. Enactment is not "neurotic acting-out." Enactment is not "obsessive symptomatology." Enactment has to do with the needs millions of men and women have — needs a particular man or woman, thank God and at last, manages to express. Enactment has to do with control and mastery, with a leader's ability to recognize the desires and fears the rest of us have, and give voice to those emotions, but not allow them to reign devastatingly.

Erikson emphasizes throughout his book Gandhi's "seasoned playfulness," through which he reached millions of his countrymen and with which he took on the world's greatest empire. And no doubt about it, Gandhi knew how to play a fine game of sorts, a serious, demanding game, eventually entered into by a whole subcontinent and its "rulers" thousands of miles away, and for rather high stakes. That is to say, he showed millions how they could work, sit, stand, and thereby confront Buckingham Palace and No. 10 Downing Street as well as the Viceroy's palace in Delhi; and by the same token the men who lived and worked in those places were also caught up in something the likes of which they may not fully have appreciated, though its challenging momentum, its power, even its humor must have soon become obvious. And so when Gandhi left London in 1931 after conferring with the King, among others, he was asked whether he felt a little awkward or out of place, dressed as he was in the simple cloth of an Indian villager. No, not at all, he said: "The King wore enough clothes for the both of us."

There is the kind of playfulness Erikson wants his readers to comprehend: not a "regression," a retreat to earlier ways, and not a failure to "grow up" or "mature," a sort of political "childishness," but a carefully thought out and intricately enacted series of assertions, which reach more and more people, and get from them, even command from them, replies or new assertions. I suppose much of

Gandhi's activity can be described as a series of dance-filled dramas, with declarations and marches and conferences, always those, against a background of increasing public turmoil, which of course reflected the dead seriousness of Gandhi's political and spiritual "playfulness."

The man tested himself constantly. He tried the patience of others. He never stopped being a little uncertain, a little worried, a little fearful — even as he could be a forceful moralist whose words no doubt were meant to shame himself as much as others. The experiments of "experiments with truth" suggest play, an advanced kind of play. Experiments also suggest, literally, trying things out and experiencing them and thereby knowing what to keep and what to discard. Gandhi knew about trial and error. Erikson shows how the child Moniya learned to judge himself, try out and experiment with his parents' restraint and generosity, and test but keep their respect and affection; and how the youth Mohan allowed himself to be tempted, to face in himself the greed and lust every man has, however covered over with self-righteousness and abusively moralistic sanctimony. There was in Gandhi, as Erikson does not fail to acknowledge and try to understand, more than a touch of the latter; in fact, Gandhi could be a stern, unforgiving moralist — but that among other things, and only in passing. He wanted too much the trust of others, whom he liked rather more than he wanted to reprimand, let alone condemn. Perhaps most of all he knew the men and women he led, even as he knew himself. He had, again, experimented. As a youth he had a friend who was tough and carefree and not adverse to breaking a few laws, religious ones and others, too; and later on he had known what it is like to be a London dandy of sorts, all dressed up in formal clothes, a waltzer, a barrister-to-be. He not only knew what he opposed, but he had experienced what only over a period of time he came to be against, which means that his moralistic inclinations fortunately became tempered by personal memories, even as his genuinely moral concerns had to them a touch of charity and generosity which do not come easily, which have to be earned.

Before he can finally discuss what he calls "the Event" in Ahmedabad, Erikson has to give over yet additional chapters to "the past," to Gandhi's years in England and South Africa, to the experiments he entered into, the vows he took, the efforts he increasingly began to make on behalf of others. The first vow (and experiment and struggle) concerned meat; Gandhi sailed for England in 1888, having sworn to his mother and a Jain priest that he would not succumb to temptation and eat meat either aboard the ship or in England. But he was tempted. He was tempted because he was lonely and hungry. He was tempted because he had a lusty appetite. He was tempted because he was very sensitive to the habits of those around him, and wanted to look and act like them, even as he refused to do so.

He did get to know the English — their style, their substance, their susceptibilities and conceits. He also got to know the strength of his own desires. He was no natural-born ascetic, or wayward masochist. He loved music and people and good clothes and a comfortable kind of living. He was a neat man, and he worried over his appearance. In England, a nation whose values and policies would one day be uppermost in his mind, he really came to understand some things about himself. In England he bought Bond Street clothes, learned to dance, took violin lessons and lessons in French and elocution. In England he remained loyal to his beloved mother; he abstained from meat, found a vegetarian restaurant, and read deeply in a literature which championed more than celery and carrots — antivivisection and all manner of progressive social measures. In England he discovered how ingenious and sturdy he could be. He was able to stick with potatoes and no roast beef. He was lonely but defiantly alone, helped — by people who quickly took to him, a pleasant and respectful man — but by no means intimately reached and touched. Erikson notes that Gandhi refers to "my choice" when talking about his battle over meat in England. The choice was perhaps a wider one also: "By facing the whole meat-eating issue in all its tragicomic irrelevancies and exaggerations, the future Satyagrahi had to learn to *choose actively and affirmatively what not to do* — an ethical capacity not to be confused with the moralistic inability to break a prohibition."[21]

In the course of such uncertainty the young Indian learned to be what Erikson describes as a householder, which is exactly to the point of Gandhi's later concern with the village, with each man's right to work for his family's food and clothing. In London Gandhi discovered that he had to fend for himself, ignore customs, resist temptations, discover friends and allies, but above all discover his own agility and competence. In India he would one day tell the masses, the millions upon millions of Indian "householders," that they must learn how to grow their food and clothe themselves and keep themselves busy. Others might call him a "reactionary," a man oblivious of the possibilities technology can offer; but he knew that in thousands of villages men needed not only the necessities of life but a sense of personal achievement. They needed work, work done in a place they knew, a place that was their home, that was familiar and loved and not left in desperation for strange and forbidding cities. Whether Gandhi was right, whether he was a first-rate economist well ahead of his time — we now have come to realize how important "community development" is in the growth of the "underdeveloped nations" — the fact remains that Gandhi learned for himself the difficult kind of self-reliance he later urged upon others, and did so by resisting any number of easy, attractive or merely convenient alternatives.

He did not only resist things, however; he realized what he very much believed. He read for the first time the Bhagavad Gita, but he also read Tolstoy and Pushkin and the Old Testament and New Testament, and particularly was moved by the Sermon on the Mount. He learned, with his own reservations, to be an English gentleman, and to the end of his life he would be respectful of a crown whose authority he did not hesitate to question. Erikson sees him departing Britain a much larger, richer person: "Having learned much that he could rely on later in adapting to the best in the British; but above all . . . an augmented Indian, and that means a stronger man as well as his mother's son."

When he came home his family expected him to become a prominent and successful professional man. He now spoke cultivated English. He dressed formally, even a touch elegantly. Frantz Fanon has recently told us about the so-called native bourgeoisie in the various European colonies of Africa and Asia — the imitation of the master by such men and women, their affected manners and snobbishness, their sense of shame at not being altogether English or French or whatever, and their willingness to lord it over the poor, to take advantage of them, to ignore their needs, and in general to exploit, exploit with the best of them from London and Paris and The Hague and Lisbon and Rome and Madrid and Brussels. Maybe the Gandhi who on June 12, 1891, said good-bye to England and sailed for India would have impressed Fanon as just such a man, and maybe correctly so, to some extent. And there it is, the mystery of life: we are never only what we seem, and consequently we never have to end up being only what we seemed most headed for — as Fanon the doctor (in contrast to the social observer) knew, because he was quick to point out the mixed feelings in those same native clerks and professional men, and the surprising capacities some have to turn their backs on their privileges once "the wretched of the earth" begin to stir. As for Gandhi, he rather quickly turned his back on those privileges, really before he ever took advantage of them; instead, he chose to lead the "wretched," but in a very special way that makes the word "lead" seem inappropriate. Gandhi wanted to share, to spur on, then calculatingly to shrink back, to be part of, to be himself "as naked as possible," as he once wired Winston Churchill. In any event, Erikson speaks candidly of the Gandhi who came home from England — and of the Gandhi who emerged in the years that followed:

There was, and there would be, much vanity in his poverty, much conceit in his humility, and much stubborn persistence in his helplessness, until he would find a leverage to make — for himself and for the destitute Indians — out of poverty, humility, and helplessness a new strength and a new instrument.[22]

Before Gandhi would realize such a personal and public achievement there would be for him a time of disappointment, grief and not a little bewilderment. Upon his return to India he found that his mother had died. He stayed home for two years, and no doubt made his brothers wonder why they ever had hoped for so much from him, English schools or no English schools. In 1893 he left for South Africa, where some Indian lawyers found his credentials promising. There of course he would not be a great lawyer, but would emerge as something else, a whole people's talented and adept advocate. The quiet years, the years of obscurity and worse, outright failure it seemed, are by no means ignored or found inconvenient or puzzling by Erikson; his writings on "identity" had all along stressed the low periods, the "rock-bottom" time in the lives of great men, and for that matter, in many a gifted but ever so troubled youthful patient, who knows more what he is not, what is wrong with himself and the world, than what he wants to risk working at and for.

Unquestionably Gandhi was a saddened man; he did not accuse himself as he had at the time of his father's death, but again he had been away when a beloved parent had left him once and for all, and he seemed for two years after his mother's death at genuine loose ends. Gandhi has been called "maternal" by many who are not psychoanalysts, and Erikson is wary as he takes up the subject: "I am not preparing the reader for an interpretation that Gandhi's identification with his mother was any more 'important' than that with his father — as has been claimed."[23]

Nevertheless, in London Mohan's mother had lived in him, inspired him, it can be said — inspired him not to do things, and more positively, to live a certain kind of life. Now he was back in India again. And now, ironically, he would have to live in India as he had in London, with his mother a memory, a living presence in him rather than in the world. A man whom later millions of Indians would call "Bapu," or the father, was a man uncommonly at ease with the tenderness and gentleness he must have absorbed (can there really be a more precise word to describe how it is done psychologically?) from his mother. At the same time he had his father's sense of dignity, his father's tough, pragmatic qualities. Such a mixture is really a work of art; it is not contrived or planned, not easily come by either, but is the result of forces and circumstances that are at once utterly natural and a little extraordinary. Indeed, again and again in Erikson's essays and books one is quietly asked to consider whether a great man's greatest achievement (and certainly his first one) does not take place out of everyone's sight, inside the mind — where battles are fought and abandoned, and reconciliations brought to a conclusion in a way that makes what comes later, so wondrous and admirable to the world, seem not inevitable, a mere afterthought of sorts, but deserved, the harvest of hard psychological labor.

From 1891 to 1893, before he left India for South Africa, Gandhi labored as a lawyer, but also as a person. He was unsure of himself. He missed London's sophistication. He kept on trying to make his wife more cultivated. He felt she absolutely had to know how to read and write. He lived for a while in Rajkot, not far from his birthplace in Porbandar. He went to Bombay, hopeful that something good would come up there. He was not succeeding as a lawyer. He was anxious and afraid. He thought of being a teacher but didn't have the necessary degree. He was drifting — except for one thing, which he highlights in his autobiography: he had met Rajchandra immediately upon his return from England and had come to admire him enormously. He may have been having trouble with his marriage and his career, but he was very much at work settling for himself what he believed, whom he wanted to heed (and ignore), and what not only his but life's purposes are. Rajchandra was a rich and well-educated Jain, a jeweler by profession. He was also a philosopher and a rather well-known poet. He was brilliant, versatile, and possessed of a remarkable memory. Gandhi describes himself as desperately wanting a guru at the time he met Rajchandra and in him he found one, of special religious and philosophical earnestness. Here was a man who had a universal spirit. He saw all religions as essentially the same, efforts by men on every continent to ask what *really* matters and by God (literally) to find out.

Rajchandra became "the anchor of young Gandhi's religious imagination." By "anchor" Erikson means a person whose ideals mean something to another and, beyond that, a person who for a while can be admired uncritically, even passionately. Freud had Fliess, and Erikson has written about their friendship with the same clarifying spirit he brings to Gandhi and his guru. Sensitive men, stirred by dozens of dreams and doubts, are often lonely indeed; for a few years another man who listens and comes up with his own ideas can be welcomed as a gift from heaven — hence Freud's passionate overestimation of Fliess and Gandhi's willingness for a while to overlook some of Rajchandra's limitations: his loyalty to the caste system, his personal untidiness, his ruinous neglect of his own health — a lack of respect, as it were, for the body's dignity.

Rajchandra helped Gandhi become an Indian once again. The two of them talked and talked, and among the things they kept discussing was the essential wisdom of India's religious traditions, far older ones than the West's. A man just back from England, all taken up with forks and knives and formal clothes (down to the use of socks in a tropical climate!), needed to be reminded not only where he was, but how impressive his own culture could be. What is more, Rajchandra was alive and of Gandhi's generation, unlike Tolstoy and Ruskin, the other two men Gandhi claimed as spiritual counsellors. It is one thing to read Tolstoy's *The Kingdom of God Is Within You* or Ruskin's *Unto This Last*, reflections written far from India, and quite another to deal with immediate and all too concrete issues.

In 1893 Gandhi again left India for another continent, not Europe this time, but Africa. He had been getting nowhere in

Bombay, and had received an offer to work for an Indian law firm in Durban. It is true, Gandhi chose to wear in Durban a frock coat, shiny boots and a turban; and clearly he went to South Africa in order to find good work, to become a well-paid barrister. Still, rather quickly, he seemed more than ready to change the direction of his life, to become not a well-to-do lawyer but a man with a cause, and more than that, a man of vast energy ready to uphold that cause, at whatever cost and for whatever length of time necessary.

Within days of his arrival in Durban Gandhi confronted South Africa's racial laws and customs, at once tragic and comic. He appeared in court wearing a turban, and was told to take it off. He had been unwittingly classified by the judge: he was not an Indian Muslim, and so not an Arab but an Asiatic, and therefore ineligible for the turban. Indians, all of them, were called "coolies," and therefore in Erikson's ironic words, whose implication young Gandhi would have fully appreciated, "Mr. M. K. Gandhi, erstwhile member of the 'Inner Temple,' was a 'coolie barrister.'" Then a question is asked: "But how is it possible that Gandhi had never heard of his countrymen's condition in Africa?" Gandhi seems at first to have been incredulous, confused even — as if utterly unable to understand how people could be so mean, so arbitrary, so insulting. He asked his colleagues why he hadn't heard about the awful things going on, the terrible poverty among thousands of Indians — "indentured laborers" they were called, shipped like cattle to Africa so that they could work in the fields and the mines for five years, then be sent home or allowed to stay as so-called freed Indians — freed but virtual slaves. And Gandhi's lawyer and businessmen friends, how could they put up with the daily humiliations that were their lot? Gandhi was curious, but not in a distant, intellectual way. He was getting annoyed, alarmed — curious in an indignant way. He was becoming socially and politically aware; and as a result he would have to stop and close his eyes again or lose any hope of becoming a well-paid, unbothered, respectable "coolie lawyer." Indeed, the more openly troubled he was by the judge's refusal to let him wear a turban, by the spectacle of his countrymen's fate as virtual peons, the more he was told this: "Only we can live in a land like this because for making money we do not mind pocketing insults. . . . *This country is not for men like you.*"

Erikson chooses to italicize those last words because he sees in them Gandhi's emerging sense of what he was not, what he would not become, what he had to fight against in himself as well as in others. He had come to Africa seeking success, not the leadership of any revolution, not even the work of milder social protest. He came at the invitation of a class, a small and relatively comfortable class, and bluntly he found himself amid "the web of pretenses" which were supposed to offer peace and contentment — "at least in 'adjusted' and moneyed circles."

Erikson does not shrink from pointing out the parallels with the history of the United States, some of whose severely exploited people could also become pretentious and sadly fool themselves. For years a relative handful of middle-class blacks put up with the kind of daily insults Gandhi saw middle-class Indians suffer in silence. For years, too, the efforts of middle-class youth, black youth, to take action against such a state of affairs were dismissed as rash, dangerous, destined to be futile. As recently as 1960 few people in the South, of either race, believed that sit-ins or "freedom rides" could do anything but provoke violence, outrage and further repression from cities and states completely unwilling to alter firm social and economic arrangements, which in turn found expression in corresponding political arrangements. But the "adjusted and moneyed circles" Erikson mentions can be anywhere and everywhere, and as blindly self-serving and self-deceiving as Gandhi saw was the case in South Africa. In the South in the early sixties black youths who insisted upon leaving school and waging non-violent demonstrations in city after city were considered psychologically troubled not only by segregationist judges, who sent some of them away for "observation," but by parents, relatives and teachers, too — who have learned bitterly over the decades how to "cope," how to face "reality," how to curb their "antisocial" instincts and "adjust" and do what they can, which does not exclude making money.

The issue is an important one, particularly for a psychoanalyst: At what point do ethical sensibilities defy psychological categorizations, especially because they so unashamedly respond to the predominant forces at work in a given society? The plain fact is that any number of psychiatric and psychoanalytic terms can be hauled out and fired away at Gandhi, at the nonviolent Southern youth of the sixties, at any citizen anywhere who takes a dangerous and self-sacrificing stand against the authority of his town, his province, his nation. In the Soviet Union, and here also, men have been sent away to hospitals because they impress judges as mad, as beyond comprehension, as dangerous to themselves and others. Some men are willing to take risks that cause others discomfort and outrage. No doubt they are indeed beyond the understanding many of us can manage, intent as we are on managing in general, on making do as best we can, on living those "lives of quiet desperation" to which Thoreau, another of Gandhi's heroes, once made reference. The quietly desperate are, of course, entitled to call the noisily indignant and horrified any names that come to mind, among them "mad" — though this becomes something else when those who call themselves doctors and scientists fall into the same kind of self-protective indulgence and mask what is at best a human frailty (the resort to polemics) by making continued mention of "professional judgments" or "diagnoses."

In any event, some youths are ready to take on any number of judges, South African ones and American ones, and even a few who call themselves experts on psychopathology. These youths make us see; they make us ask why for so long we didn't see — didn't care to, didn't think to, didn't want to. They make us see by putting themselves on the line, placing their bodies where the rest of us will have to notice because of inconvenience and surprise and annoyance and shame and fear. How do these youths come to be so daring, to take on an enemy that is in fact the force of "law and order," as their society defines the phrase and puts it into practice? How did Gandhi get sidetracked, so to speak, into political "agitation"? The answer is that he didn't knowingly and calculatingly do so, even as many youths in the sit-in movement of the sixties kept on remarking upon the series of accidents and unexpected incidents that preceded their involvement, their commitment to change the South, by securing the vote (among other things) for millions of disenfranchised American citizens. In this life we prepare for things, for moments and events and situations, that we never actually know about until they are upon us. We worry about wrongs, think about injustices, read what Tolstoy or Ruskin or Thoreau has to say, speak with a Rajchandra about man's inhumanity to man or God's will. Then, all of a sudden, the issue is not whether we agree with what we have heard and read and studied and talked about with friends; rather, the issue is *us*, and what we have become, which only comes to light over time, and in response to specific, concrete circumstances — and they can be as utterly significant and compelling and "basic" as any "drive" ever is. For circumstances reveal what has been there and waiting in us, or is simply not there — as anyone knows when he suddenly is brought up short by a particular event, cannot shake off its implications, and finds himself "mysteriously" changed, different, moved to this or that commitment.

In June 1893, only a few weeks after he had come to South Africa, Mohandas Gandhi, traveling first class, left Durban by train for Pretoria in the Transvaal. In Maritzburg a white man entered Gandhi's compartment, saw him, refused to stay until he left, and eventually got him to leave, against his will, by calling the police, who unceremoniously deposited him and his bags on the station platform. The bags were seized by the stationmaster, and Gandhi was left alone to spend the night without an overcoat in a dark, cold waiting room. That did it — that experience, that cold night, those long hours spent alone outside. Later Gandhi wrote that "the hardship to which I was subjected was superficial — only a symptom of the deepest disease of color prejudice. I should try, if possible, to root out the disease and suffer hardships in the process."

Once Gandhi had made up his mind he suddenly became taken, completely taken with a new life. He continued the legal work that originally brought him to South Africa, but he also started doing what today would no doubt be called "organizing." He wrote to a prominent Indian merchant and announced that he wished "to get in touch with every Indian in Pretoria." In Erikson's terse sentence, "That was Gandhi." Such "investigative determination" would soon make its mark in South Africa and later in India, "for no matter what he found, decided to do, and managed to accomplish, the situation would most likely be reformed."

In today's language Gandhi would be called a careful grass-roots worker, an organizer who knew his tactics and strategy, knew the rules of the "community action" game, knew that he must get to know, really know, his people and their problems and wishes and hesitations, get to know what they most likely would do, given one or another crisis or set of alternatives, get to know "the facts, man, the facts," as our youthful organizers are wont to put it. Erikson notes that Gandhi's "professional style was set, and we shall see it at work from Pretoria to Ahmedabad." Gandhi himself describes his way of being a lawyer: "I acquired such a grasp of the facts of the case as perhaps was not possessed even by the parties themselves, in as much as I had with me the papers of both parties." But he went on to note that "facts mean truth, and once we adhere to truth, the law comes to our aid naturally."

One sees in the man's deeds and words alike an almost uncanny mixture of assiduous pragmatism and stubborn spirituality, each probably an antidote to the other; together, though, they are quite a mix, one whose antecedents go back at least as far as Christ's remarks on the need for both serpents and doves, both guile and innocence. If Gandhi had a sense of the importance of facts as a road to some larger political and philosophical truths, he also had a developing sense of himself, of his special concern with and involvement in those "facts" as a means of approaching those "truths." Erikson quotes from a letter Gandhi sent in 1894 to Dadabhai Naoroji, an Indian nationalist:

A word for myself and for what I have done. I am yet inexperienced and young and, therefore, quite liable to make mistakes . . . *I am the only available person who can handle the question.* You will, therefore, oblige me very greatly if you will kindly direct and guide me and make necessary suggestions which shall be received as from a father to his child.[24]

Again in *Gandhi's Truth* Gandhi's words are italicized because they are felt to "express the core of his freshly gained identity, for which he was seeking sanction from the 'grand old man' of the nationalist movement." We are shown just how continuous a theme "the only available person" had become in Gandhi's life: he had been the one to care for his sick father, the only one who could do so methodically and constantly; and he had been the only one who had somehow kept alive the family's distinction and local prominence; he had been the one who went abroad, got that valuable and prestigious English education, and returned home a uniquely qualified man, an exceptional man; and before all that, he had been the last but in a way the first, the spoiled child, the one permitted broad leeway, the one allowed to tease and taunt his parents and test and try their patience, and still be loved, and too, never be succeeded by another child, never given the idea that anyone could ever take his place.

None of this means that Gandhi decades later *had to* become India's Mahatma. Yet, at critical moments in life, a man does or does not have the sense that he can take care of himself and do only and exactly what he wants to do, what he has gradually come to feel he wants to do and what he suddenly has decided — without any warning it seems — he wants to do. Other Indians in South Africa had felt a discriminatory hand upon them; they had experiences all the time like the one Gandhi had in the Maritzburg railway station. Other Indians had been scorned or rebuked, or indeed had moved heaven and earth not to be, which only meant that they were, in less obvious but maybe even more awful ways; silently and ignominiously they yielded, obeyed, explained away, and justified their surrender. Gandhi, however, said no, and not just once and by accident or because he was new to the scene or had a temper or was driven by "self-destructive" impulses or fantasies or whatever. He said no because he meant it, because the entire thrust of his life would not allow him to be pushed aside, treated like a coolie, dismissed as of little worth. In other words he said no because he wanted to say yes; he had pride, a lot of it, and for all his doubts he had self-respect. He had grown up to expect something of himself, to believe himself worthwhile, destined for something. And there, in South Africa, he could feel free to draw upon all he had learned at home. As many another wanderer and exile has done, Gandhi went away to find himself, traveled a great distance in order to feel at home with what for years he had been learning and thinking and dreaming about.

Erikson gives substantial attention to that moment in Gandhi's life, because once more as an analyst he is up against the mystery of a man's decision, one that changed a life and changed history. Once again we want to ask why was it Gandhi and not someone else. How did he succeed in doing what others only hoped and tried to do? Was it luck, chance, an accident of fate? It may be difficult for us — we feel lacking or ashamed or envious — to credit a man like Gandhi with imagination, with a brooding but hopeful spirit, with real agility. Certainly some find it easy to call him driven and tormented and a touch crazy, but they are not at all tempted to see him as dedicated and animated and consummately tactful and compassionate and above all a worker, a man who worked because he enjoyed doing so, enjoyed seeing the aims and purposes he believed in at least begin to be achieved.

At any rate, in 1891 Gandhi made his beginning at trying to achieve certain things, and he would not stop until January 30,

1948, when he was cut down by a Hindu fanatic, who, like others, had good reason to fear the nearly eighty-year-old man — because at the end he was in certain important respects the same man who fought for his people in South Africa; that is, he was idealistic and kind and decent, but also careful and fair-minded and unwilling to exploit vulnerable, half-starving people for rhetorical and ideological purposes. A political man to the bone, he obtained his ideology from philosophers, novelists, poets and religious leaders; but again, he was unlike those men because he wanted to change the things of this world as well as meditate on them. Erikson allows himself to become neither sentimental nor abusively and narrowly categorical when he describes such a man. To take on almost single-handedly South Africa's laws (and incidentally, its fearful and apathetic Indian community) Gandhi had to display "a combination of such good English, clear thinking and ruthless honesty" that he could become "a model as well as a force." He had to consolidate "into one way of life his legal competence, his passion as a reformer, and his religious sense of a universal truth."

In order to clarify how Gandhi did that, Erikson develops a very distinct and suggestive view that is not primarily biographical, psychoanalytic, political, historical or philosophical. Elements of all those postures, however, appear in the section that has to do with Gandhi as a "householder." By calling Gandhi a householder, Erikson frees himself of the need to subject a restless and unusual life, particularly full of ambiguities and complexities, to any one theoretical scheme. But why call Gandhi a householder in South Africa, rather than, say, in India? Why call his difficult and hectic years there (the years that immediately preceded his return to India and his rise as that nation's spiritual and political leader) a period in which he "settled down," in which he achieved a "gradual consolidation of his professional, economic and political capacities in an over-all identity of service"?

One is tempted to say that Gandhi in South Africa was the opposite of a householder; he was a social, political and religious revolutionary who was beginning to take on a world empire, in hopes of frustrating it enormously, so that it would realize that its days of undisputed political and military dominance were numbered, not only because other empires were waiting in the wings, but because victims can find through certain leaders and in certain forms of protest an exceedingly powerful and discomforting and embarrassing means of self-defense and self-assertion and self-affirmation. Yet Gandhi has been called many things besides a revolutionary, and though his lively, complicated nature has been smothered with unqualified approval, his purposes have also been subject to an instructive range of criticism. As Erikson prepared to call the man a householder, a householder who *cared*, he must have had in mind other words and phrases — used by other Westerners.

To many, and not only his British adversaries, Gandhi was a crank, clever but untrustworthy, "a naked fakir," an itinerant who turned up anywhere and everywhere (or so it seemed), always in order to make already difficult matters even more dramatically confused. Some have called him naive, preoccupied with all sorts of "irrelevant" issues, a faddist of sorts and an ascetic who helped arouse backward India but had few ideas a modern industrial state can find valuable. Always the British are called a "special case," both in South Africa and India; were Hitler the enemy, Gandhi's nonviolence would not have been tolerated and Gandhi himself would have been shot very quickly. Anyway, India was and still is "primitive." Gandhi is thought by some to have done nothing to change that state of affairs, indeed to have done a lot to strengthen the worst trends in both his country and his people — the mysticism, the "reactionary" village spirit, the superstitiousness. True, he was well-meaning (the ultimate epithet). He did what he could, but at best what he did was a mere beginning. He was hard to pin down, slippery, evasive. He was obviously mixed-up; just look at his dietary habits and his sexual life: no meat, but much desire to eat it; and after his mid-thirties, no sex either. He knew nothing about modern technology. He never analyzed India's hard economic problems. He never realized how corrupting India's social system is, how enervating its various religions can be. He was quaint; he was quixotic even. He did his best, but what he did was actually very little — because, Gandhi or no Gandhi, India would have become independent in the late forties.

Even in 1970, India and South Africa are still full of the same terrible exploitation, the same unspeakable human misery Gandhi protested. India and South Africa are still dominated by elites, by white men or high-caste Hindus, by a few who give very little to the many. India and South Africa still possess masses of ignorant people, blindly religious, obsessed by dead rituals and by elaborate promises about other worlds and states of being — unredeemable promises all dressed up in mumbo-jumbo talk. None of that did Gandhi do away with, or even try to do away with — or so we are told. He was "limited." He failed to see that the whole "system" is rotten, has to be brought down, rebuilt, "restructured." He took on the British Viceroy, but fitfully and modestly and for questionable purposes. He tried to reconcile the irreconcilable, the classes and castes of a divided, impoverished, overpopulated nation. Indeed, he has been called a force for the bad rather than the good; to a great extent he wanted to strengthen what needs to be assaulted, what he never did assault, what on occasion he only coaxed or like a mosquito annoyed: an essentially feudal society controlled by an Asian version of that old and familiar alliance of princes, priests and merchants.

Criticisms like these must have come to Erikson's attention as he worked in India and then started writing *Gandhi's Truth*. He did not do his work, did not write his book, to affirm or refute these lines of analysis and argument, but neither could he ignore them. He seems to handle the problem by insisting on *his* job: to understand, to understand Gandhi, including the social and economic and religious pressures he felt and generated on his own. Yet Erikson also knows that such a man cannot realize all his hopes, but can only make a noticeable and worthy beginning — in Gandhi's case as a householder, whose "house" became, eventually, all India. And here what appears to be imagery is much more — a means of describing and explaining one unutterably complex life's continuity.

So one wants to repeat and repeat that *Gandhi's Truth* is not "for" Gandhi, not "against" him, not a defensive apologia, and not an arrogant bit of Western criticism, full of itself, full of its own certainties, impossibly self-righteous and dogmatic. Erikson has a particular and limited job to do. He has to deal with certain things — with Gandhi's style as a leader; with the choices he made, that is, what he chose to resist or ignore; and, of course, with his personal preferences and his beliefs, which he repeatedly suggested to others as worthwhile. The man was (the more one reads about him, the longer the enumerations) a lawyer, a philosopher, a religious man, a fighter, a politician, a moralist, a writer, a social critic and a person of great and complicated energies who impressed his presence upon the minds of millions, not only in South Africa and India, but all over the world. To call him a householder, and then to write him a letter (which is what Erikson does in the middle of his book, just before he analyzes the Ahmedabad "event" itself) may at first strike the reader as a surprisingly naive way of going about things — a way perhaps worthy of Gandhi. For the fact is that the formulation of "householder," and its subsequent explication, as well as the "personal word" addressed by the author of *Gandhi's Truth* to Mahatmaji are both likely to confront many readers with just the kind of jolting and gradually intriguing experience that thousands upon thousands of "coolie" South Africans or Indians experienced, not to mention British authorities both at home and abroad.

If Gandhi wanted anything he wanted to make people see one another in a way that took them unawares, as a prelude to the new thoughts and inclinations he hoped to inspire in each of his listeners. His was indeed a politics of confrontation, both literally and symbolically. He hoped that old, tired and ignored values could be given a new lease on life, even as he hoped that his own values had more than a spark or two of originality in them. He wanted, moreover, to command the attention of many people, however different their walks of life, their persuasions, their so-called vested interests. He hoped to offer alternatives, ideas that would draw upon the conventional knowledge of the day, but somehow give to it a new and enlivening and commanding substance that hopefully would not only cause agreement but inspire deeds. The word Satyagraha is translated as "truth force," which has to do with the life an idea ought to have in the world of owners and workers, colonizers and the colonized, men of the cloth and men who pray, governors and the governed. And by the same token, the "actuality" Erikson wrote about in *Insight and Responsibility* refers to the way "inner" things in particular human beings, become part of life's daily circumstances, not blandly or innocuously, but pointedly so, or to call upon Satyagraha again, truthfully and forcefully.

Whatever he intended, though, could Erikson really avoid becoming a partisan of psychoanalytic or Marxist materialism, Hindu mysticism or Western political realism, among other competing "schools" or "systems" of thought and criticism? By the time he was ready to write he must no doubt have known what would be expected of him by all sorts of eager readers both in America and abroad. Would he be respectful of Gandhi, or taken in by him? Would he bear down closely on Gandhi's failures, personal and political, or would he stand back and refrain from looking hard at the man and his philosophy — as some in India have done, along with a good number of Western admirers? What would he find? (Aren't psychoanalysts always supposed to "find" something, a remnant of a memory, a revealing habit or desire or fear?) How would he interpret Gandhi's various habits, and the reasons he gave for them? (Aren't psychoanalysts always somehow able to come up with "interpretations" that other people never thought about or believed possible, and that seem to make almost everything fit into place?) Instead, we get "householder" for a formulation, and then a long letter to a dead man.

Obviously, the way a word like "householder" is used is the test of its worth, even as the content of a letter determines its significance. Erikson is unwilling to discuss at any length the "methodological" value of using a letter as a means of enhancing a narrator's power, an analyst's tact, or for that matter, the value of using so prominently a word like "householder" instead of terms which are already a part of this or that intellectual and polemical tradition. Perhaps he believes that the example is quite enough, is quietly instructive, because he simply tells what he means by a householder, and he gets directly to the business of his letter.

During his fifteen years in South Africa, Gandhi practiced law, struggled in behalf of his own people and against the British and local governments, read widely, wrote, fathered children, moved about constantly, and became known all over the world as a rather idiosyncratic reformer who wanted Indians to have the vote and self-respect and decent wages, but also wanted to understand his seeming opponents (if not enemies), and in a way convert them. In South Africa Gandhi learned to farm, cook, nurse people and teach them. He learned about the woeful lack of sanitation among the poor, and how they might be brought to improve their immediate surroundings. He learned how to go from home to home, and enlist the regard and support of strangers. He learned about *brahmacharya*, self-discipline, so that he could take care of himself and persuade others to do likewise, to be their own masters, even if only in "little" ways at first — rather than blind followers and servants. He learned how to draw people together, literally into crowds, and more broadly into alliances and far-reaching "congresses," all based upon an emotional and spiritual brotherhood that he uncannily, instinctively stimulated. He learned how to resist, go against laws and the police, go to jail, suffer assaults and insults from opponents who would crop up out of nowhere with a mean word, a physical attack.

In South Africa, Gandhi also began to learn about the rituals of nonviolent protest, about marches and boycotts, about refusals, about irony and its political uses — that is, about making a mockery out of what *is* a mockery, a mockery of justice. In South Africa, and on his way back and forth from there to England or India, Gandhi began to broaden his sights even more: India must have Swaraj or self-rule, even as the "coolies" in Natal and the Transvaal must no longer be brutalized and demeaned. Finally, in South Africa Gandhi learned to believe in the utter importance of a certain attitude; he became ever more convinced that without courtesy, restraint and candor neither victim nor oppressor has a chance of becoming a little less bound to, a little more freed of, the conditions which in different respects limit and offend everyone. In sum, he learned to make larger and larger numbers of people mean more and more to him; by experimenting and traveling and reading and taking up a succession of causes he became over time a different person, an enormously versatile, obliging and open man — Erikson's householder. Here is what it means to be such a man, such a householder:

He was a Householder in every sense of the word: in the simple fact of presiding over a prosperous household in South Africa; in the Hindu sense of a defined stage of life, concerned with family and immediate community; and in the literal sense of one who learns to know and to "household" the facts of life. In ancient imagery, the center of his territory is a man's "house," be it a home or a farm, a firm or a family, a dynasty or a church; and his "city" marks the boundary of all the houses associated with his.[25]

Nor is the matter dropped there. Gandhi is shown to have applied "to a wider community the lessons of householding," the small but important things he learned, the things that keep people and households going. In other words, Gandhi discovered how to household both his personal strength and his larger resources, his capacity to lead, his spiritual power. He lived with larger and larger numbers of people: in the Phoenix settlement and Tolstoy farm during his South African years — both of them places where he and his cohorts could endlessly talk and examine the progress of their nonviolent campaigns — and finally, in his ashram by Ahmedabad's Sabarmati River. He transformed his "house" from "a home for his family to a hostel for co-workers and followers, and eventually into an agrarian settlement with many characteristics of a religious order."

Erikson feels strongly that Gandhi had about him a magic spell of a kind parents create for children and children for parents: the very essence of life can seem at stake when a mother and father look at a little boy or girl and in return when the child looks back at them. Gandhi made millions care for him, trust him, almost worship him — but not because he curried their favor with promises, or because he had wealth and power. He cared for those millions, really cared. He wanted desperately to earn their trust. To the last moment of his life he tried to speak with them rather than for them, to stand by them rather than in front of them. Erikson captures some of the Mahatma's range of concern, scope of vision, and describes it so that the reader will perhaps understand the wider transition involved, one that transcends particular centuries, religions, ideologies and psychological theories:

St. Francis' householdership began with God's admonition: "Va, Francesco, ripara la mia casa che, come vedi, va in rovina" ("Go, Francis, and repair my house which, as you can see, is in ruins"), the "house" to be repaired meant a single chapel as well as the church in the City of God. But for Gandhi, "repairing," came to mean curing, teaching, reforming, governing — that is, any context in which one can remain a religious craftsman. Gandhi's widest acceptance of power would wait for the time when he also accepted the Indian masses as his family and nothing less than an independent India as his city. How Gandhi consolidated himself as a lawyer and a family man and *then* began to envisage a more inclusive "house" and a widening "city" — that is the story of his young manhood.[26]

Needless to say, the wider one's "family" is, the harder it can get for one to become narrowly partisan or cocksure or propagandistic or dogmatic. Gandhi wanted changes made, dozens and dozens of them, but he never could allow himself to forget *whom* as well as what he wanted changed. People were his passion; and ideas are meant to serve people, not mold them or compel their obedience. Ideas, he knew, can become altarpieces and the purpose of a struggle forgotten in the course of waging it, so that brutality is done again and again in the name of one or another abstraction. His instincts, like those of many healers, were literally conservative, with even radical surgery viewed as a preservative measure rather than a triumphant moment of excision. In *Gandhi's Truth* Gandhi's struggle with all that — and maybe Erikson's, too — is set down in some sentences that are not easy to pass over:

But the borderlines between consolidation and reformation and between establishment and religiosity are often tragically blurred; and nobody could even begin to play with them, who would not feel or come to feel a humility which Ruskin inadvertently formulated for Gandhi in the phrase: "Unto This Last." It was now clear to him that no dogma could claim to be in the exclusive possession of historical revelation. To him that religion was most meaningful which would help him formulate the revelatory essence of daily experience and action. And here Rajchandra's rewording of old Jain precepts seemed to speak to him directly: "I very much like this doctrine of manyness [*anekantavad*] of reality," he would write many years later. "It saves me from attributing motives to my opponents or critics . . . today I can love them because I am gifted with the eyes to see myself as others see me and vice versa.[27]

The "manyness of reality": a man who has spent years trying to make psychoanalysis responsive to just the striking challenge implicit in such a phrase now has to do justice to an incredibly many-sided man. Gandhi could quite knowingly be a fighter, yet were he going to be lynched, he hoped he would live long enough to forgive his assailants. He battled the English for decades, yet helped organize an Indian Ambulance Corps for them during the Boer War. He was a man who protested and protested, yet urged that protests be not indiscriminately or casually taken up, but with the utmost care, and in such a way that self-righteousness and moral arrogance be constantly feared — as more dangerous, perhaps, than any enemy. He married at thirteen, fathered four sons, was drawn strongly to his wife, yet in his thirties foreswore sex — but not simply because he was a puritan or a celibate, but in the interests of what Erikson calls "a wider communal intimacy." There is no easy way to "capture" such a man, to pinion him with words and phrases and concepts. All that anyone can do is demonstrate how marvelously various such a man is, how only over many decades could he pull together some of the inconsistencies and conflicts he wrote about and tried to live with rather than be overwhelmed by.

As a man Gandhi was both lusty and delicate, energetic and frail, serious and possessed of charm and humor alike. Later in life he was monklike, priestlike; he sought after poverty and celibacy, but did so because he loved the world, and less abstractly, loved hundreds and hundreds of particular individuals. He was an intimate man, a man who wanted and needed people, who craved them, who wrote letters constantly, dozens each day, a man who could never have lived a life of pure contemplation. For him contemplation came out of action, out of events that one by one unfold and demand of us the effort of understanding. Erikson suggests that Gandhi was one of those *homines religiosi* each age fortunately produces. They are not necessarily trained to minister, to preach the tenets of a particular religion. They are men who become "living bridges to an eventual clarity of existence, or at least to a sense of consolation which makes it possible to produce, create and serve without debilitating despair." Gandhi knew, Erikson knows, that the forms and rituals such men honestly and beautifully use, the things they say and do, the coherence they manage to find and spell out, can all come to naught or more precisely, to "rigidity, hypocrisy, and vanity," which in turn have to be protested by the next generation's *homines religiosi*. What has become of Gandhi's truth in India today, among all too many pious worshipers of the Mahatma, serves as a rather good illustration of the problem Gandhi faced as he tried to set forth ethical principles that do not become a new form of tyranny in the hands of the pious, the legalistic, the literal-minded.

How did Gandhi at least attempt to avoid such a fate for himself and his ideas and his many books and articles? His book *Satyagraha in South Africa*, for one thing, is written in a quiet, unaffected way. It is not pontifical, not overly serious. Erikson notes its "folksiness." Gandhi wanted not converts but people who would gradually feel themselves drawn to something he knew was hard to put into words, was ineffable almost, something that comes down to trust. To some extent trust inevitably comes and goes; it is lost and then quickly found. Hopefully, though, we can at crucial moments have that trust. A satyagrahi trusts himself enough to trust his opponent. Gandhi could never quite catch hold of the images he wanted to use for those who use Satyagraha, perhaps because he knew how difficult it was for him to come by the philosophy, and even more to feel genuinely and convincingly, trustingly that is, under its spell. Responsively, Erikson remarks upon "the difficulty of finding the right terminology for a nonviolent 'weapon,' which pervades the whole Gandhian literature." As Gandhi tried to describe what nonviolent but thoroughly determined men and women do, how they can be weak yet in their own manner strong, "almost as if teasing [he] would switch in mid-paragraph from the imagery of 'soldiers' to that of 'pilgrims,' while calling himself a 'general' at one time and a 'scavenger' at another." Then again, "he would alternately call his people's attempts to cross forbidden borders 'pilgrimages' and 'Asiatic Invasions' — the last term, of course, mocking the powerful Europeans who were so ungallantly afraid of an 'invasion' from India, after having themselves imported the Indians as slaves when they needed them."[28]

During his years in South Africa Gandhi learned what Erikson calls a "vocation," a lifelong commitment to make good on a vow. We all swear to do this, fight against that. Gandhi took himself and his vows more seriously: if he promised something, he would deliver it, or suffer accordingly at the hands of a proud and strong conscience. Yet a strict conscience can choke a man to death, deny him the flexibility and resiliency he needs if he is to deal with a wide range of men and involve himself in many, different controversies. Gandhi's supple mind was not, however, the kind that knew how to rationalize away ethical principles in order to be "realistic." He seems to have learned at the beginning of his career as a political agitator (among other things) that one sets firm standards and never forsakes them, but one does wait for the right moment, the most promising and encouraging time — in a way, the most dramatic time — to press one's cause. In a few words Erikson conveys the spirit of the man rather nicely: he allowed "events to coerce him into doing what his grand strategy had long committed him to plan." A man who so acts has a sense of timing, and even more important, a sense of time. He knows that everything isn't done at once, that leaders and the led have to sort things out and determine what is today's work and what tomorrow's; and they also have to know what really matters, what they must change, and what they can let be. This quality in Gandhi Erikson captures adroitly when he notes that "Gandhi seems, again, to have been playing the role of one who professes inability to think ill of his revered elders, but who quietly lets them live out their style of 'elitist leadership,' which he fully intends to replace with what we would call a grassroots campaign."

These descriptions show Gandhi getting older in the way a man does who has at last found himself, staked out his territory, and assumed his responsibilities. Gandhi, of course, never studied Erikson's "life cycle," but he did live a long and eventful life, full of the very tensions and turns, the crises, that Erikson describes — and particularly in his most active and busy years, as a developing activist and then a spokesman for an entire people, he experienced the psychological confrontations that are described in *Childhood and Society* and *Identity: Youth and Crisis*. He had to choose how he would live — close to whom and why. He had to decide what he really wanted, what he could overlook, what he would die for. He had to gain for himself perspective, not only on India and its future but on himself — what his responsibilities were, given a reasonably full and healthy life. In South Africa he achieved that perspective. He became the householder Erikson calls him; he became a man who has thought out his place, thought out whom he would have near him as workers, allies, companions — even as co-conspirators and fellow inmates in prison. He became also the judge of men, the psychologist, the man whom Erikson with yet additional tact describes as always emphasizing "the possible weaknesses in each type of co-worker only to show, of course, that Satyagraha made reliable heroes out of them all."

It can be said that Gandhi became adept at analyzing what Freud called "group psychology," by which he meant something other than the way people get along in today's "sensitivity training groups." For Freud, group psychology had to do with man's responses to social, political and economic institutions, with the way men are influenced by one another in a neighborhood, a town, the marketplace, at work or school. Gandhi was constantly trying to figure out how General Smuts and his cohorts would act in South Africa, or what he might expect from the Viceroy in India or his superiors in London, Britain's Prime Minister and monarch. Gandhi was, then, a sociologist and political scientist as well as a psychologist, if one wants to think in those terms; he knew about the "structure and function of institutions." He knew how to mobilize various segments of a society, first one, then another, until gradually a full-fledged popular movement was brought into being. He would appeal to the intellectuals with one voice, the workers with another, and to women with still another. He was not afraid to be outspoken, but neither did he decline deviousness. He knew how to pry and poke and needle an adversary. He could comment on the South African government's "masterly inactivity," and go on to undermine that very inactivity by pushing harder, encouraging more provocative acts — always testing, in Erikson's words, "through small and improvised confrontations, the extent of the popular readiness to become involved and to endure."

Gandhi's breadth of interests and abilities demonstrate on a somewhat larger-than-life scale what Erikson so often has tried to describe in all human beings: their capacity over time to change and grow; their capacity to harbor within themselves contradictions as well as unequivocal "traits"; their bewildering, surprising ability to become themselves and no one else. No wonder the choices we do finally make are surprising; they emerge, after all, in response to life's flow of events, the people we happen to meet, the reactions of colleagues or authorities, the ups and downs of the business world, the mistakes that nations make — which for millions of individuals can be a matter of life and death.

Both Erikson and Gandhi stress the importance of time and the environment, the growth of things that takes place in the mind over the years as a consequence of trials, errors and efforts, the intricate and compelling stimulation that a particular social and political atmosphere can have on the way people think and find themselves able and willing to act. During the South African years Gandhi came to learn, one suspects, what Erikson learned when he studied children and their parents all over America: people can be both more and less than they appear to be; they can be inspired or humiliated; they can find themselves and come up with abilities they themselves never thought possible, or they can lose themselves and never get to know how or why they have become so inert, so aimless. More than we may care to realize, men and women want purposes, want the commitments Gandhi kept on mentioning, the sense of loyalty to something and somebody, the fidelity that Erikson mentions and goes into so fully. Gandhi's genius surely had to do with his understanding of all this; he saw the objective despair of his countrymen, the squalor they endured, their daily suffering, the contempt visited upon them; but he also saw the subjective despair, and knew its roots, not only in poverty and colonialism but in the emptiness a Viceroy as well as a "coolie" can feel.

Gandhi was one philosopher who knew both abstractly and concretely the questions people ask, questions full of words like "hope" and "trust," full of ideas implicit in words like "fidelity" and "identity" and "intimacy." "Truth" to him was not an abstraction; truth comes about when events happen, when things are done, when values (and those psychological "tendencies") come alive in the one way possible, through efforts become achievements, through deeds become part of Erikson's "actuality." The "truth force" of Gandhi's

Satyagraha is truth exercised, exerted, applied, truth given actuality, or as Erikson puts it in *Gandhi's Truth*, given "leverage."

For decades Gandhi improvised, started, and stopped, planned and unashamedly plotted, waited and struck, and always walked and walked — all with the hope of turning the truths he held important into a force, something which has momentum, attracts people, brings them together, urges them on, impels in them resistance, defiance, compassionate but unremitting self-assertion. And always in his quest, his long, arduous, at times tormented but also exuberant pursuit of both ideals and action, Gandhi never lost sight of the individual — or the masses. "Nobility of soul consists in realizing that you are yourself India. In your emancipation is the emancipation of India. All else is make believe." The author of *Childhood and Society* quotes those dramatic words of Gandhi's, and why not? The whole thrust of *Childhood and Society* is in the same direction the Mahatma urged: we do not live in a vacuum; history in one sense is people, people who do things, who take themselves and others seriously; our minds do not "function" automatically, on their own, in some small and private world frequented only by a mother or father and "siblings"; we are not something fixed, a *this* or a *that*, but rather we are what others prompt in us, and we in them, back and forth, all the time, day and night. (Even in the utter privacy of sleep our dreams make a belated response to the larger world, to others met the day before or to people recalled because of that day's evocative character.)

Yet Erikson could not but have reservations about some of Gandhi's ideas. Gandhi's philosophy of Satyagraha had in it not only social and political objectives but an obvious concern with moral and sexual matters; rights and wrongs are spelled out and attitudes approved or disapproved. A psychoanalyst who is writing about both Gandhi and his "truth" cannot ignore those openly psychological issues that the Mahatma constantly comes back to, even as he must not become so preoccupied with them that one begins to forget that Gandhi was an enormously loved and revered man who in numerous ways came to affect not only India and England but people all over the world. As Erikson finished up the section on Gandhi's "past," the past that preceded the events in Ahmedabad, one feels him as a writer, a psychoanalyst and biographer, becoming somewhat tense. He obviously admires what Gandhi did in South Africa. Indeed, he admires not only what was done but the method

— the charity summoned, the intelligence used, the brilliant and effective leadership demonstrated. He also seems in places to enjoy himself writing — because, after all, he is writing about an amusing, daring, challenging man, a man whose life, if it is to be sensibly comprehended, requires an analysis full of the same kind of imagination and verve and originality that Mahatma Gandhi continuously showed. And in *Gandhi's Truth* the man is indeed brought to life; we are enabled to sense his restless, unpredictable but even-handed and honorable ways, and to visualize his contradictions, his psychological near-failures. In South Africa, for instance, when in fact he was just starting out on his long road of political hurdles and adventures, he "was already then thinking of an early retirement to a rural setting, even while he was learning to make himself at home in jail cells as well as at ministerial conference tables." Thus it goes with all of us perhaps, and maybe more so with a man who risks so much of himself, puts his very life "on the line": we worry over what might be; we dream about what might have been; yet we push along with what must be, what we believe ought to be.

Still, Gandhi was having other, less pastoral, reveries; and they clearly trouble Erikson. The book Gandhi wrote in 1909 advocating "home rule" for India (*Hind Swaraj*) is described pointedly as "a rather incendiary manifesto for a man of peace." In the tradition of Socrates, Gandhi used questions and answers to make his point, and though nonviolence is preached, and men such as Tolstoy, Thoreau and Ruskin once again summoned, as they will be repeatedly in future years, and though various young and not-so-young Indian leaders are also singled out for attention and praise, Erikson has to note that "Gandhi used his 'reader's' questions to set up for himself an opportunity to dispose of India's leaders, one by one." In fact, to be courteous but blunt, it can be said, it has to be said, that Gandhi's *Hind Swaraj* leads to the conclusion that "every Indian leader, himself excepted, wants to make India free by un-Indian methods and for the sake of an un-Indian future." What is more, Gandhi shows himself able to do just the kind of thing he elsewhere condemns. Erikson gives a summary of what takes place in the text: "There follow sweeping denigrations of the British Parliament and of the 'free' press, of civilization in general and the railways in particular, of lawyers and doctors, all of whom are said to prostitute, infect, weaken, and cheapen the Indian people, who enjoyed Home Rule in the ancient past."[29]

Erikson also notes that " 'prostitution' is a word used rather often in this document; and clinical judgment cannot overlook the fact that at the time Gandhi was again returning from the metropolis of temptation — which was, of course, London." (*Hind Swaraj* was literally written on that return, on the boat that carried Gandhi back to South Africa after a stay of several months in England.) Erikson also refers to an "outburst" that takes place at one point in the text, and though he is careful to be properly analytic, professorial almost, with Gandhi's writing, one can sense a certain dismay: a man of genuine compassion, a man soon to be India's Mahatma, a man of loving-kindness such as the Bible mentions, reveals himself as capable of egotism, pardonable enough since universal enough, but also not-so-hidden meanness and pettiness, indeed abusiveness — all rather persistently exhibited, at least in this one small book.

Nor was that book the lone exception to an otherwise perfect record of personal nonviolence. Erikson knew as he went further and further into Gandhi's life that *Hind Swaraj* revealed a bit more graphically what were continuing "tensions" in the Mahatma's mental life. He could be cold and indifferent to the needs of those closest to him, his wife and sons, while for the British and the Muslims, almost breathtaking leaps of trust and affection were achieved. Erikson could have taken note of that irony, that discrepancy, that human failing, not unlike ones we all have. He could have gone further, too — analyzed insofar as he was able the sources of such a thing, a "discontinuity" it could be politely called. But he refused that course. One even feels him for a few pages trying valiantly to put aside the whole matter, and get on with "the event" at Ahmedabad. He is, after all, in the middle of a long book, and only at this point ready to take up the "event" he has set out to write about. And yet he cannot go on, not without first setting down a letter, "a personal word," which must surely in its twenty-five pages rank as a milestone of sorts in the history of biographical, historical and psychoanalytic writing — an event that helps do justice to the Ahmedabad event thereafter described.

The letter starts with a writer's consciousness that, in T. S. Eliot's words, he is in "the middle way," about half done with a given journey — but also undone by certain statements he has come across, and not because he is inclined to be small and legalistic, but because the Mahatma has made quite clear that he very definitely wants to be understood as standing upon those very statements. Erikson acknowledges his reservations: "I put my critique into words which I hope I would have had the courage to address to you were you alive." Then comes a sentence that, as much as any single one can, tells why *Gandhi's Truth* was written and what its central point, full of historical irony, will turn out to be:

My justification for approaching you would have been the conviction that psychoanalytic insights happen to complement your kind of truth by a strange reversal of the traditional roles of East and West: for you are now a model of activism in our culture, while Western thought has provided a new technique of introspection.[30]

After that the writer goes ahead directly with the intention of his letter, to quote passage after passage from Gandhi's writings, in order to take issue with him — gently but firmly, affectionately but also, one can't help sensing, in order to make clear "midway through this book" the provoked feeling Gandhi apparently could stimulate even in those who want very much to be on his side. One quotation from Gandhi's *Autobiography* obviously can be taken personally by the author of books such as *Young Man Luther* and *Gandhi's Truth:*

If some busybody were to cross-examine me on the chapters already written, he could probably shed much more light on them, and if it were a hostile critic's cross-examination, he might even flatter himself for having shown up [make the world laugh by revealing] the hollowness of many of my pretensions.[31]

But Gandhi had his own doubts, apart from any nervousness a hypothetical psychoanalytic observer might have inspired in him:

I, therefore, wonder for a moment whether it might not be proper to stop writing these chapters. But so long as there is no prohibition from the voice within, I must continue the writing. I must follow the sage maxim that nothing once begun should be abandoned unless it is proved to be morally wrong.[32]

He did do that. He wrote and wrote; indeed Erikson points out that he wrote in a way which very much resembles the free associative manner patients learn (not always so easily) in the course of psychoanalysis:

I write just as the Spirit moves me at the time of writing. I do not claim to know definitely that all conscious thought and action on my part is directed by the Spirit. But on an examination of the greatest

steps that I have taken in my life, as also of those that may be regarded as the least, I think it will not be improper to say that all of
them were directed by the Spirit.[33]

All this prompts from Erikson this remarkable comment:

If I did not believe something of this kind, I would not be writing
this book. But I must now confess that a few times in your work (and
often in the literature inspired by you) I have come across passages
which almost brought *me* to the point where I felt unable to continue
writing *this* book because I seemed to sense the presence of a kind of
untruth in the very protestation of truth; of something unclean when
all the words spelled out an unreal purity; and above all, of displaced
violence where nonviolence was the professed issue.[34]

In a way, that is that — except for one thing: *Gandhi's Truth* is
also meant to show the truth a psychoanalyst (*and* a historian *and*
a writer *and*, in his own way, a religious man) comes upon when
inspired by one like the Mahatma. Therefore, two sentences like
those, one brief but itself autobiographical, the other long and
forthright and sharp, require elaboration, elucidation, whatever.
And Erikson supplies that immediately. He speaks of the gaiety
and loneliness that Gandhi as a child experienced. He affirms his
respect for Gandhi, his belief that Gandhi, in essence, wanted to
perfect himself as much as anyone humanly can because he "came
to feel that he was the only one available to reverse India's fate." He
credits Gandhi with hard-won triumphs, ones not every psychoanalyst would consider so affirmatively: "You experimented with
what to you were debilitating temptations and you did gain vigor
and agility from your victories over yourself." He tries to describe,
as he did with young Luther, Gandhi's identity as it had certainly
emerged by 1918, when he took on the mill owners of Ahmedabad:

Your identity could be no less than that of universal man, although
you had to become an Indian — and one close to the masses — first. Your
profession could only be that of solicitor for the masses. Your "house"
could only be a hostel for believers, your family only an improvised
religious order, and your "city" only the whole Empire as long as it
promised to play host to an all-human identity.[35]

If all that amounts to an extraordinary accomplishment, fine —
so long as the reader understands what a heavy price was paid by
Gandhi and by his wife and by his sons, and maybe others we will
never know to name. Not that the point is to settle accounts, or

expose once again the "bad side" that any man, however great
and truly noble, will be found to have — as a fact of his humanity
rather than of his psychopathology. Rather, one is asked to respect
a man for the failures and lapses he himself acknowledged, as Erikson demonstrates by saying what he has in mind, with the help of
Gandhi's own words:

> But there are instances where it would seem to an observer that you
> use the word *love* in order to clothe other propensities. I will, there-
> fore, take issue with you only where I perceive a certain false pedagogic
> tone pervading the very kind of apologetic statement which you are
> apt to use in order to explain, for example, your attempts to impose
> literacy on your child bride: "But I was a cruelly kind husband. I
> regard myself as her teacher and so harassed her out of my blind love
> for her." It is this cruel love which is in need of clarification.[36]

Gandhi could indeed be his own severest critic. Erikson does not
want to take after Gandhi with a long line of "interpretations,"
whose import would be this: My God, the man was troubled, sick
as can be! Instead the problem is made much broader:

> Here, I submit, the future of Satyagraha is at stake, and this not be-
> cause you "pretend" a love which you do not feel, but rather because
> you seem either unaware of — or want to wish or pray away — an ambiv-
> alence, a co-existence of love and hate, which must become conscious
> in those who work for peace.[37]

Unquestionably, then, Gandhi had his cruelty, his self-declared
sadism; it is described explicitly in *Gandhi's Truth*, as it appears in
various utterances in which the man's "revulsion against sensuality
turns, for example, against women as a source of evil, against food
intake as no better than defecation, and against milk as a 'dangerous
substance.'" We learn that Gandhi told a friend of his (and of
Erikson's, too) that "one should steer away from beautiful women
as a driver steers away from the gutter" — the way the advice is
paraphrased by Erikson, who allows for the fact that the "association," as people in his profession would call it, between women and
gutter is indirect. He notes that Gandhi once recommended a co-
worker by praising "the fact that she is beyond child bearing,"
though again every effort is made to understand Gandhi, to make
it clear that he "meant to honor" the woman. In any event, at issue
is not whether Gandhi was "right" or "wrong," or said this and
really meant that, but something else: "For the future it is important to affirm unequivocally that what you call Satyagraha must

not remain restricted to ascetic men and women who believe that they can overcome violence only by sexual self-disarmament."[33]

Erikson is arguing that Satyagraha has to become part of our common lives rather than the property of any elite, however well intentioned, however honorable its aims. He is also trying to point out that if violence is to be made less pervasive, the early lives of children will have to be considered and defended as much as any group's social and political rights. When that is done, when we stop and think about children, we will no doubt recognize what doctors see every day: how a child can be taught by parents to be ashamed of himself, his body, his passions, and thus be violated, feel anger, feel scorned, feel as violent as any Viceroy and his troops. None of us anymore, not after Freud, has the right to be a "watchful moralist," Erikson says, no doubt addressing us in the West as well as the Mahatma. We know enough to understand what self-righteousness under any banner can do, has always done: "moralistic terrorism succeeded only in driving our worst proclivities underground, to remain there until riotous conditions of uncertainty or chaos would permit them to emerge redoubled."

Erikson knew that he was taking a chance by writing such a letter to Gandhi. He knew — and acknowledges — that he ran the danger of seeming moralistic. Was he not criticizing a man no longer able to reply? Was he not going beyond the bounds of biography and certainly *his* kind of psychoanalysis by reproving a man for his rather obvious difficulties, rather than describing them and trying to explain their origins? Was he not intruding on another's life, decades later, with retrospective misgivings? What if we made a habit of taking to task people who lived in the past, who are dead, who had their "problems," even as everyone does — all on the basis of information and insight acquired by succeeding generations and unavailable to the people under scrutiny?

On the other hand, Gandhi himself wrote constantly about his own sense that he had dealt unfairly with his wife and children; and, of course, he repeatedly made it quite clear that if he was moralistic with others, he was little inclined to spare himself. In any case, Erikson has something in mind other than dovetailing his observations with Gandhi's self-observations. He knows that Gandhi had certain faults; he learned about them from the Mahatma's writings, as well as from his "witnesses" among Gandhi's friends and associates. He did not do all that as an intellectual exercise. Erikson wants to add something to Satyagraha — make it more than a partic-

ular man's weapon, a particular group's possession; and he also, one
suspects, wants to make it clear that he enormously admires Gandhi —
enough so that he feels moved to resist him (nonviolently!) by re-
fusing to accept what Gandhi himself struggled valiantly and sometimes vainly against, and what others today need not yield to
unwittingly and hopelessly, given the knowledge Freud and others
have offered us.

Moreover, though Gandhi is dead, he is not long dead, and his
ideas and ideals are no bit of past history, merely and sadly to be
discussed and fretted over by scholars. Militant nonviolence, which
Gandhi's Truth is meant to be about, lives on throughout the world,
is sought after and tried, perhaps "struggled for" is the expression,
by young people and older people — who want desperately to
change things, bring down all sorts of corrupt and brutal powers,
but do so (is it possible? they wonder) in a way that does not
set the stage for new and awful tyrannies. Gandhi was — right now
is — a man of this century, in which revolutions have been betrayed,
and millions sacrificed, knowingly murdered even, in the name of
various "virtues" or promises. Against all that Gandhi's ideas still
stand as an alternative, and Gandhi must be seen as the man who
nourished that alternative and wrote about it so that others could
learn and be warned and take heed. His life, therefore, has to be
looked at closely, especially where it threatens Satyagraha, intrudes
upon it to its clear detriment. To look at a great and compelling
man's life firmly and affectionately, and above all so that the influence of his ideals is augmented, requires, it would seem, just
what the Mahatma himself tried for the same purpose: an experiment in truth, a willingness to go the limit, push the bounds of
ritual and tradition, take risks with one's privacy, one's sense of
propriety and decorum. This is what Erikson's letter does.

Gandhi wanted Satyagraha to be a method of action against the
moral (not to mention political and economic) arrogance of others.
He himself may have possessed what he fought in others, but none
of us is in a position to gloat; each of us has the responsibility to
know how that happens, how men in various ways wage fights
against certain enemies, including always their own private ghosts
and devils — and risk losing what they come so close to winning.
If Gandhi was patriarchal, then others in his time were patriarchs,
too; generations of men all over the world once grew up believing
that they must be thoroughly tough and stern and unforgiving.
Erikson refers to "those of us who have ourselves become fathers

in a patriarchal era which only now is reaching a demise in universal unrest, dissent and violence."

In fact, Erikson sees some of Gandhi's struggles as very similar to those Freud had to face, and indeed others continue to face. Gandhi was wise and humble enough to say that truth "excludes the use of violence because man is not capable of knowing the absolute truth and therefore is not competent to punish." Yet, he punished himself and, despite his painful awareness, Kasturba and their sons. He was, of course, no brute, no madman; but in his own way he could be mean and harsh, and he suffered later for having been so, perhaps thereby being driven yet again to anger and hurt. Always, though, he wanted to look inward — and for that reason Erikson places him in a tradition that includes St. Augustine and Kierkegaard and most certainly Sigmund Freud. All of those men wanted not only knowledge but something else, forgiveness perhaps; and each in a different way found it — and in other words became less at the mercy of his own blind spots, less inclined to be his own judge, his own executioner. Still, they could not wholly succeed. Perhaps each of us, though, can make progress, if not succeed — not the "progress" politicians promise in order to win a few votes, not the kind of progress, either, that needs victims.

Erikson wrote his book not to chronicle Gandhi's middle years or to analyze his personality, but because he felt that Gandhi had something very important for all of us to know, something that adds to the ethical possibilities man can henceforth demonstrate. Over the centuries certain men by thought and deed alike have furnished to succeeding generations examples that are not stunningly idiosyncratic but broadly summoning. Nevertheless, as much as we need the respective visions those men came forth with, the men need one another. Dead they are; but they live on in our consciousness, which means that they do have a certain kind of continuing existence, and do therefore have to meet one another, if they are not to have the pseudolife that goes with our unquestioning veneration. In everyday life we change our minds as we learn new things; and by the same token we owe spiritual and philosophical and intellectual leaders of ours, those Freuds and Gandhis, those Augustines and Kierkegaards, Thoreaus and Tolstoys, enough respect to confront each of them with the others and all of them with any new knowledge later generations are fortunate enough to come upon.

To say this once more, a little differently (for it is hard to say, and was inevitably hard for Erikson also to say), a book like *Gandhi's Truth* aims to wrest Gandhi's essential, important and deservedly unforgettable ethical spirit from the particular psychological qualities which may have helped generate and sustain it (there is the ironic twist that haunts us all!) but which most certainly do not in all their banality deserve to be cherished on the one hand, or allowed to go unnoticed or unchallenged on the other hand, thereby nullifying that very ethical spirit, turning it into a lot of excessively guarded dogma. Erikson is not a complete novice at so rescuing great men. It can be said that he breathed life into Luther, whom many obligingly nod toward on occasional Sundays, and into Freud, too, whose words have become a dogma many heed with empty obedience.

In his letter to Gandhi, Erikson puts both himself and his profession, and in particular his intellectual kinship to Freud, right on the line; if Gandhi is to be rescued, it will not be done pompously or condescendingly, but rather in a lively way that conveys the author's wish for an alliance, his desire to share in something, his hope that different yet strangely similar men and ideas can meet and reinforce one another where that is needed — but also bring one another up short. If for the sake of Satyagraha Gandhi is going to be taken down a peg, then the West's psychoanalysis will be shown as something particular men fought for — against the same psychological odds Gandhi faced. And psychoanalysis, like Satygraha, deserves a respect that does not tie its broader truths to the particular psychological propensities (and personal prejudices) of either its founder or his followers. All of this Erikson says, indirectly but strongly. He does not want to become apologetic, or as some psychiatrists would have it, "defensive." He has decided to point out where he and Gandhi part company; but he does so by showing where Satyagraha and psychoanalysis meet, and how the Mahatma and "the first psychoanalyst," as men of just about the same period in world history, shared a number of problems. And maybe we should let the matter rest with the word "share." Here is some of the sharing in Erikson's letter:

And even then, we must admit that you could not possibly have known of the power of that ambivalence which we have now learned to understand in case histories and life histories — and indeed, through the painful analysis of our own symptomatic behavior as parents, having ourselves resisted such guilty insight as long, as illogically, and as meanly as we could. It is, therefore, not without compassion that I must point out that your lifelong insistence on the "innocence" (meaning sexlessness) of children is matched only by your inability to recognize the Demon King in yourself. And this *must* be pointed out because the demons triumph in all hidden and disguised ambivalences: however and wherever we let our children down, we become their demons. If, then, in order to fathom the truth we must hold on to the potential of love in all hate, so must we become aware of the hate which is in all love. Only if we accept the presence of ambivalence in the most loving human encounters does truth become just what you mean by it, namely, that which supports evolving humanity in the antagonisms of divided function, be it in the context of inequalities of size, age, sex, or power. For all these inequalities call for conscious insight rather than for moralistic repression. And it is here, I feel, that your attempts at enlarging human awareness, and Freud's, complement each other.[39]

That will not be all. The sharing, the expression of companionship must be openly stated and spelled out:

Sigmund Freud was, in fact, the only other man in our time who offered to the reading world such candid descriptions of small events in his life as you revealed of yours, and this not in the now-fashionable form of literary self-exhibiting, but strictly for the sake of a theory and a technique of truthfulness.[40]

From Freud we are asked to turn our attention to his work, his discovery, and to reflect upon its kinship with Gandhi's ideas:

Now I should like to point out in all brevity why I believe that the psychoanalytic method itself, by dint of always being a self-analysis paired with an attempt to understand another man's inner conflicts, is a counterpart to your Satyagraha, because it confronts the *inner* enemy nonviolently. Both you and Freud knew (as did other great confessors who expanded man's awareness) that human insight begins in oneself: and as you in your "Experiments" probed your own motivations, so Freud began by dealing "scientifically" with his own dreams as well as those of his patients.[41]

The comparison is pressed further:

In studying your method of Satyagraha, I have become increasingly convinced that psychoanalysis, not if judged by its physicalistic terminology and theory but if understood as it is practiced and lived according to the rules and the intentions of its originator, amounts to a *truth method*, with all the implications which the word truth has in Satyagraha. This, I submit, is more than a vague analogy; it is a correspondence in method and a convergence in human values which may well be of historical, if not evolutionary, significance.[42]

And finally, the "correspondence" is concretely characterized, with the word "shared" used at the end, not dramatically but with unhesitating candor:

Let me tell you briefly what the Viennese doctor refused to do to his patients and what he chose to do instead. Dr. Freud was approaching middle age when he faced the probability that his hysterical patients, far from being degenerates as his colleagues believed, suffered from an oppressive education and a resulting inner repression: they had developed a mortal prejudice against themselves in order to internalize the edicts of their Victorian parents. Furthermore, he concluded that the very doctors who were to free these patients from their inner repressions added to their unfreedom by imposing on them authoritative suggestions often given under induced conditions of dependence or hypnosis. This, Freud felt, did violence to what alone can free a man from inner compulsion, namely, the conscious acceptance of certain truths about himself and others. And this doctor in his consultation room made a decision analogous to the one you made in your South African proving ground, namely, that the instrument of enlightenment to be forged by him would have to include self-analysis, that is, the acceptance of himself as a person who shared his patients' inner mechanisms: the truth could cure the patient only insofar as the doctor had faced the corresponding truth in himself.[43]

If the point has not been grasped, if those who feel Gandhi has somehow been taken advantage of don't see the universal problem Erikson is struggling with — how to separate any man's important ideas from the problems that all men have, but many followers refuse to acknowledge in their leaders, to the harm of the very cause purportedly being upheld — then perhaps this one sentence will help a little: "Yet there is a disconcerting propensity in even the sickest patients on occasion to see through their doctor with almost vicious poignancy, laying bare what he himself neither had seen before nor can quite deny now."[44]

The issue is one we all face. Any craftsman wants his work to have a life of its own. The theologian or philosopher hopes that his observations will not be impossibly bound to his particular psychological tensions or even to his historical time and setting. The novelist hopes that his novel will speak on its own, apart from the various attitudes and preferences he happens to have. However,

Gandhi could not quite let Satyagraha go; possessively he hugged it, kept it close to his particular life. The psychoanalyst is similarly tempted, perhaps because his "method," like Gandhi's, has to do with so much that is personal. Erikson points out that work has been "a man's usual reserve and escape from his private weaknesses." The psychoanalyst's work is to comprehend those weaknesses, and inevitably, see them in himself. Gandhi saw Satyagraha as the same kind of relentless self-confrontation. But if one is to be tested, one had better be prepared to ask for help. Freud eventually learned that such help would be forthcoming from, of all places, his patients, who can teach as well as learn. Gandhi had less time to ask for such help or to get it; he was busy changing the world in ways Freud never had in mind.

Today, of course, many would admire Gandhi's struggle more than Freud's, something by no means unrecognized by the more discerning psychoanalysts. In an address given at the New York Psychoanalytic Institute on April 16, 1968, Anna Freud noted:

The young of today feel that psychoanalysis is now in the hands of the parent generation and, as such, suspect. For many of them it has lost the aspect of being dangerous, a forbidden matter, accessible only to the courageous, a useful weapon with which to attack society; instead psychoanalysis is looked on and avoided as a procedure devised to deprive them of originality and revolutionary spirit and induce them to adopt and conform to existing conditions, which is the last thing they have in mind.[45]

Yet even if we shift our attention back and forth (with a certain single-minded intensity) from political and economic injustice to the more private wrongs and hurts man is heir to, men like Freud and Gandhi have much to teach each other. Together the ideas of the Viennese doctor and the Indian spiritual and political leader mean much more. Freud's views, in the wrong hands, can be sadly misused to justify or support or ignore any particular injustice and corruption that goes under the name of "reality" (as his daughter implicitly recognizes in her remarks); and Gandhi's views, at times in his own hands as well as in those of his followers, can become fussy, prudish, restrictive and (ironically) haughty. Many men and women who have been thoroughly psychoanalyzed crave what Gandhi has to offer, namely, a genuinely principled and charitable social philosophy, a means of effective and thoughtful political action. Yet some of the passages in Gandhi's writings also cry out for something, perhaps for what Erikson has to offer: Freud's sensible, calm humanism, uncluttered by fears, irrationalities, moralisms and near hysteria. At times Freud never quite knew what the analyzed men should *do*, given the punitive and unjust "external" constraints, which, like our "internal" constraints, *also* cripple us, make us afraid and anxious. At times Gandhi never quite knew how to deal with the viceroy and king and prime minister inside him, the fearfully avenging and overly watchful conscience that could tie him up in knots, and undo the nerves and even the lives of those he dearly loved.

One thing Erikson wants to make clear, emphatically clear: what he asks of Gandhi he believes he has to ask of himself, the capacity for self-observation and self-criticism that an analyst must always call upon. Gandhi, of course, was no stranger to self-observation and self-criticism, and maybe the gist of Erikson's letter goes back, again, to a word like "sharing." We need help to see ourselves, to free ourselves of certain parts of ourselves, to become more than we alone ever can be — by taking in what others see about us, feel toward us. Not that Gandhi was a hermit, a man isolated and removed from others; and not that Gandhi needed what today one fears is recommended in some quarters a little too casually and gratuitously — "treatment." Erikson's repeated position is that we have things to offer one another in this world, patients and doctors do, great and different leaders like Freud and Gandhi do. In a most Gandhian way he talks about "the joint experience of truth," as it is experienced by doctors as well as by patients:

Only the full story of a psychotherapeutic event — as detailed as this psycho-historical study of a historical Event — could convey a sense of how an interpretation emerges as the joint experience of a truth which relieves and restores as it enlightens, and how the truth thus revealed could emerge and can be contained only in a joined effort marked by a new kind of ascetic discipline — ascetic not in the repudiation of the erotic facts of life, but in the insistence on a rigorous truthfulness toward them.[46]

Gandhi knew he was being too hard on himself and too demanding of others; he knew he should let up on his natural, God-given, enjoyable, unharmful desires. Yet he was helpless to some extent. Voices within him cried for vengeance, and it was no easier for him than for the rest of us to see that:

Dogmatism induces the fanatic religionist to split himself into a cruel judge and a hopeless sinner, and to derive from this the license to view and to treat others as if they were no better than the worst in himself — whether these others are his own children or such classes of dependent men and women as he judges to be "no better than children."[47]

Still, Gandhi wanted to rid the world of various kinds of dogmatists and their violence: militant nonviolence was directed at violence, at the violence of "princes and principalities," at the violence of the marketplace, of castes and classes and races and religions toward one another. Erikson writes to him that by the same token violence takes place in families and among friends and lovers as well as among obvious military or political or religious antagonists. We learn to be violent by being violated, unreasonably and punitively curbed or scorned; the resentment from such experiences burns inside us, galls us, and soon enough we strike out at someone, perhaps a person more vulnerable than we are, while at the same time keeping our eye out for more powerful people, who have been keeping *their* eyes on us.

So it goes in the nursery, the backyard, the schoolyard, the factory, the college campus, the office. Someday we may be rid of armies and social systems that allow human beings to go hungry, to become malnourished, to live harsh and mean lives; but the violence implicit in such a worldwide state of affairs feeds on the violence that growing children learn from desperate parents: Get what you can. Get ahead at all costs. Don't let others get in your way. And in general: Get, get, get. Gandhi wanted his people to do their fair share of getting, but he knew, as Freud did, as Erikson particularly does because of his years of work with children, that somehow the cycle of violence begetting violence has to be interrupted. Thus, to Mahatma Gandhi Erik Erikson writes this in explanation, in affirmation of their joint purpose, their shared values:

I have counterpointed your pedagogic examples and our insights, then, because we have learned to see in the encounter of adult and child the terrible challenge to anyone who wants to cure man of any of his irrational violence. For this cure it is essential — in your context and in ours — that the moral adult, so easily given to moral vindictiveness, should learn to educate without violence, that is, with a recognition of the inviolacy of the counterplayer even if, and especially when, that counterplayer is a child.[48]

A little further on, the same message is spoken, this time with reference to a larger family, the family of man:

To kill sinners for a "just cause," to become a hero in taking the chance of being killed in the act of so killing, and to venerate such heroism as absolute in the eyes of God — all this frees us from the common human burden of living guiltily and absurdly. And yet we cannot become one species without assuming, together, that burden.[49]

For a moment the author of those words begins to worry. He does not wish to sound preachy, full of unarguable platitudes. "I know these are high-sounding words," he says, not because he has any doubts about what he is asserting, but because he knows that sometimes words, however sensitively used, simply fail. Still, we have to try; books are written, in hopes that those thousands and thousands of printed words will capture the imagination of readers, live on in them as voices of what Erikson calls "informed persuasion." Certainly there are other voices all over this world: strident voices that command people, denounce them, abuse them. Gandhi wanted to stand up against such voices, and he did — yet at times he did the harm to himself that many an Englishman has done to many an Indian. And optimistic as Gandhi generally was, buoyant even under pain, thoroughly cheerful and almost provocatively assured of himself, he could also be gloomy and forbidding indeed. Sex would be called evil, and his own children seen as cursed. In Erikson's words:

And so you do not hesitate to call "sources" of evil those items which become evil only by man's thoughtless exploitation; nor do you hesitate to claim, with a clear reference to your oldest son, that a child may be doomed by having been conceived in an embrace which did not deliberately intend him.[50]

Yet the man who wrote these words is willing to show how much both those who practice psychoanalysis and those who practice or pursue or follow Satyagraha have to learn, how much they already have in common, alas, in contrast to what they should have in common: "To even the score, let me say that this kind of thinking is so universal that in clinical work, too, we always find ways to blame a curse in early childhood — if not a constitutional 'cause' — for man's neurotic inferiorities."[51]

If Gandhi could virtually doom his children, speak of them as if they were the products of sin, and therefore "had no chance for salvation" except by joining their father in renouncing sin, then psychiatrists and psychoanalysts have "cultivated an analogous curse." What a curse it is, too — and here again no written words can quite convey the way presumably decent men can behave in some of those "clinical conferences," where men, women, and children are discussed and discussed, and often enough reduced to a bundle of labels, to grist for this or that theoretical mill. Erikson notes that if Gandhi could see little hope for his children, some "child specialists" see a child as "nothing but the product of his parents' virtues or vices." A Western scientist can have his "abstract curse," one that emerges as no less insulting, confining, and demeaning than the Indian's sense of unavoidable fatalism or sinfulness.

Moreover, what individuals have done, whole societies have in their own fashion done. Erikson does not conveniently forget the "sexual and hedonistic excesses which have spread over some of the most civilized parts of the Western world, often in the name of Freud." Nor does he overlook the riots that came after the Mahatma's nonviolent campaigns. In the case of the West there is this cycle: unforgiving, thoughtless, essentially violent parents turn the child's mind against his body, against his urges to be close to another human being and derive comfort and pleasure from that closeness; the children grow up in a world that is beginning to question old, legalistic moralities, with their oppressive warnings and threats and prophecies of eternal damnation; and the result is not a sensible sensuality, an intelligent balance of work and play, but a so-called freedom which turns out to be smug, angry, and in its own way as vindictive and absurd as any of the Victorian pieties ever were; and the result, also, is obscenity — which is simply another form of puritanical violence. In the East, another and similar cycle is in evidence: empires are undone in the interests of justice, but they give way to new empires; that is, the revolution succeeds, but tyranny persists — again, because the self-righteous anger of the protester quickly becomes the bureaucrat's impatience with anyone and everything "in the way," the "people's" way, of course, or the nation's or the party's. So it goes all over the world: repression and suppression, psychological and political, followed by "reaction," by violence, be it social or sexual or "artistic" or political or military. All one can do — not a little, actually — is insist and insist:

Here, too, I can only re-state my original point: nonviolence, inward and outward, can become a true force only where ethics replaces moralism. And ethics, to me, is marked by an insightful assent to human values, whereas moralism is blind obedience; and ethics is transmitted with informed persuasion, rather than enforced with absolute interdicts.[52]

Ironically, Hinduism can be wonderfully free of the West's worst kind of Calvinism; there is in Hinduism a quiet charity, a thoughtful, even wry detachment, an acquiescence of sorts, a tolerance of life's continuing, inevitable riddles. Gandhi had these qualities, but he was a man who wanted to lead millions of Hindus from other things sanctioned or tolerated by their religious and philosophical tradition. He fought untouchability. He fought inertia. He fought political and social resignation. So he was caught in the middle, torn by conflicting beliefs and principles; and he was hard pressed, no doubt, to reconcile what millions of Indians found important (such as the caste system) and what he himself believed in. Humble, self-effacing, decent beyond description almost, he had his cantankerous and small side, and he could be a difficult man indeed for his wife and sons. If the man is not always to be admired, his essential purposes and values are something else, and they have to be stated in crystal-clear language, so far as that is possible. Erikson makes one final attempt to express the respect he feels for these values and purposes, a respect that caused him to make the considerable and painful effort of his letter:

But all this, God help me, is not by way of an accusation or even a clinical judgment. I can only view with awe a man who (making himself more transparent than any of the saviors and saints of the mythologized past) improvised every item in the inventory of saintliness — nakedness, poverty, silence, chastity, and charity — without being baptized or ordained in any traditional investiture; and who attempted to apply the power of that position in every waking minute to the Here and Now as lived by the masses of men.[53]

After that the letter ends, and with it, perhaps, a concentrated, determined effort to find and declare the truth, and do so effectively so that it has the kind of force Gandhi had in mind, truth's force, Satyagraha: "Having told you all this, I can now simply narrate, without argument or discussion, the years of your ascendance to the job of a prophet in his own country. And I can conclude this letter more truthfully: with abiding and affectionate respect, yours as ever."[54]

In January 1915, Gandhi returned to India. He was forty-five years old, and firmly set on his course; he had set it for himself while abroad, and he would continue on it at home. In the rest of part three, "The Event," Erikson shows just how it all happened — the encounter between a man and his destiny, a man and India, a man and an empire. There was about Gandhi, from the moment he set foot again on Indian soil, a sense of mission — to which he gave expression immediately. He was no longer the English dandy, the Indian lawyer on the make. At a rather formal and lavish welcome-back reception he wore noticeably simple clothes, and he spoke in his native Gujarati rather than in the King's English. By implication he was already urging his countrymen to throw aside silly pretensions and accept their responsibilities to work with one another, to work for India's future.

And work he did. Erikson does justice to the man and his activities; he writes about Gandhi with strong and suggestive language, and one feels that somehow his letter really did clear the air between the Indian leader and his strong but not unqualified Western admirer. In fact the writing becomes brisk and forceful to an extent that one wonders whether the author hasn't (unconsciously, of course) picked up the psychological qualities Gandhi demonstrated in the years that immediately preceded the Ahmedabad strike and fast. We read of a man really ready to go. We get a sense of the energy and self-possession he had, once he settled his doubts and qualms. Erikson has described in previous books the way "ordinary" men settle down into a particular life, and live it — do things, have and care for children, develop interests and hobbies. He has also described the bursts of creative effort "great men" experience after everything falls into place — when beckoning circumstances make possible the expression and achievement of what has been secretly stirring in a given man's heart and mind. Still, each great man has his own style, and maybe a responsive and fascinated and conscientious observer who looks closely at the lives of those men picks up more than he himself realizes, however dedicated he is to introspection and self-awareness.

In any event, Gandhi's habits upon his return to India are described in great detail in chapters appropriately entitled "Prophet in His Own Country" and "Companions and Counterplayers." The man's energy was incredible, and this comes across in Erikson's account. Gandhi is called a "pilgrim in loincloth" and, importantly, a "pilgrim on wheels, spending every fourth night on the train — third class of course." Then we are asked to imagine, to look and see:

And what a scene, worthy of a modern Giotto: the slight "Kathiawadi peasant," almost falling asleep while standing and swaying all night in a rattling railway compartment, because he was unwilling to wedge himself between the impudent passengers who had spread themselves on the seats and on the floors.[55]

Though he was everywhere, it seemed, Gandhi had enormous powers of concentration. He had more and more people around him over the years, and could be dozens of different things to them. He wrote incessantly, letters and articles and pamphlets and more "serious" pieces. He planned, too; indeed, he did his own kind of research. Before he got involved in anything he asked himself what he was doing and why. He asked others what they thought and believed and wanted and were prepared to do, and why. He took stock of his resources, of his liabilities. He estimated the most he could hope to see done, given the principles he held so dear.

Erikson tries to show his readers how Gandhi went about doing all this. Intense calculation went into the man's seemingly "spontaneous" decisions. He was cautious, diligent, deliberate. He was thoughtful. But he was also charming, lively, and forever responsive to life's comic moments. A man of many sides, he elicits from Erikson writing which is historical, reportorial, narrative, analytic, descriptive, evocative, speculative. For example, the Ahmedabad of 1915–1918 gets extraordinarily broad yet intricate analysis; the city's social, economic and political life, its history and traditions, all are taken up. We are reminded that Gandhi chose his headquarters in an industrial city, where Gujarati is spoken. We are also reminded that he was interested not only in political issues, but in social and commercial ones. Millions of his countrymen lived (and still live) idle, bitterly poor, futile lives. Gandhi wanted them to rule themselves, and, just as important, to have something to do, something useful but also something that helped people feel pride in themselves. He "blamed the disruption of native crafts for the deterioration of Indian identity." In Erikson's crisp, concise but wide-ranging words, "he was soon to elevate the spinning wheel to significance as an economic necessity, a religious ritual, and a rational symbol."

Increasingly, upon his return from South Africa, Gandhi labored over India's history. He tried to figure out what went wrong over the centuries — and not only because of the British occupation. He examined the nation's guilds, its castes and religions. He took note of the military power of the British, and he also saw rather clearly how divided and vulnerable his own people were — some of them quite happy to have foreigners around, indeed to profit from their presence. He speculated where lay his best chances for a beginning of change. It is tempting to forget these various issues and problems as Gandhi saw them in 1917 or 1918. We prefer to stick names on him, to classify him: he was an agrarian organizer or a village orator, a political moderate, a man who didn't push hard enough, didn't bestir the kind of revolution India really needed — so we know, today. Erikson is aware of the need we all have to second-guess others, while overlooking where and when they lived:

Gandhi had a dialectic problem before him which is all too easily belittled by Western ideologists who demand that he be found "consistent." He had to call for a rapid modernization of awareness and aspiration and yet also to acknowledge and even preserve those aspects of the ancient social structure which alone could provide irreplaceable elements of a traditional identity.[56]

We do indeed have no business talking about Gandhi's methods, or India's problems, without knowing the facts Gandhi had to face — and before that, sort out and clarify in his mind. To see what Gandhi was up against, we are brought to Ahmedabad again, not as we were in the beginning, when two American tourists named Erikson first came there, but as we now have to be if we are to understand Gandhi. Nothing is spared: the city's architecture, political and social history over the centuries, industrial history, economic life, geographical relationship to other Indian cities. We are shown in a table what Ahmedabad's population was like in 1918 — how many Hindus, Muslims, Jains, Christians and Zoroastrians. We are told what percentage of each religious group could read and write. The serious medical problems of the city's poor are discussed, and so is India's complicated legal tradition.

Nor is Ahmedabad singled out in such a way that the problems it shared with the rest of India are ignored. Gandhi increasingly saw India as the victim of a "fourfold ruin": its economic, political, cultural and spiritual life had each been badly hurt by years of colonial exploitation. He knew that such a national disaster becomes for each individual a personal one because large events become part of one's daily life by defining it, limiting it, setting its characteristics, its tone. Nehru also knew this, and as a matter of fact summoned Erikson's often used word "identity" to describe what he (Nehru) believed

Gandhi "gave back" to India. He went further by saying Gandhi had achieved for India "a psychological change, almost as if some expert in psychoanalytic methods had probed deep into the patient's past, found out the origins of his complexes, exposed them to his view, and thus rid him of that burden." He meant of course the burden of blindness. The more "objective" burdens remain, but at least they are not tucked away in the distant but profitable recesses of the British Empire.

Erikson once described identity as "a process 'located' in the core of the individual and yet also in the core of his communal culture, a process which establishes, in fact, the identity of those two identities." In a book about Gandhi, this definition takes on particular importance because, as Nehru knew, the Mahatma wanted just such an "identity" for his countrymen. He wanted each Indian to be India; and he saw India's problems as not only "technical," but also deeply spiritual and psychological. He knew the nation was torn by fiercely subjective loyalties and antagonisms that were historically grounded, culturally and religiously sanctioned, economically and politically exploited, and with a continuing life that only new passions and enthusiasms and devotions could counteract and eventually help do away with.

Before the Ahmedabad strike and fast, before he became all India's leader, Gandhi went everywhere, teaching all the time. He wanted to reach as many people as one man possibly could, and to each of his audiences he essentially said the same thing: India has been gravely wounded, and we must become healers, each of us, and try to end her pain, restore her health. Erikson's account of those many speeches is as touching as it is historically suggestive:

His wide-ranging addresses can well be compared to St. Paul's Epistles and to Luther's early pamphlets. St. Paul and Luther, of course, were greater writers and orators. St. Paul's message had to navigate from shore to shore and had to be sustained over the years by the promise of the next visit or the remembrance of the last one. Luther's pamphlets, in all their formidable formality, could count on the fast multiplication and distribution of printed matter — hot off the press. But Gandhi entrusted himself to the railroads, and while loudly complaining against the miserable conditions of third-class travel, he made the very most of joining the masses in motion, in stations, and especially in the compartments, where they were thrown together most indiscriminately, often far away from home, and yet sure to return there or to arrive in new places with such news as spreads from rail centers to villages via oxcarts and camelback. And then Gandhi stopped and stayed and talked, a quiet, almost tender orator, but a man of the most intense and convincing presence, and a speaker who could make intimate contact with each particular audience.[57]

We are offered sections from the various addresses, and they are arranged in chronological sequence, so that one can watch unfold the Mahatma's rising effectiveness and anger against the injustice his people had to endure. Gandhi just about seized an audience; he appealed to their reason, but he also offered them affection and sympathy. He could thoroughly unsettle his listeners, and thereby make sure they would not soon forget him and his ideas. He was a minister, a lecturer, an ironist, a speaker intent on social and political change. But he was not given to simplicities, however much he tried to reach a mass audience — an effort that required lean, direct language. He wanted an upheaval; at the same time, though, he did not want chaos, nor did he want to appear an impossible visionary, whose ideals are fine but utterly impractical, even laughable when considered in the light of existing political circumstances. And once again the reader is warned against judging Gandhi from our vantage point, as Westerners alive in the seventies. The years were 1915 to 1918, and if the man dreamed of an end to the evils of the caste system, he knew this aim had to be worked at steadily and concretely rather than shouted and shouted — at a time when the words would fast become hollow, because, in Erikson's words, perhaps of importance to some of us today, there were "no immediate revolutionary alternatives."

Gandhi was always probing. He explored, tested, verified, sifted things out, speculated, then explored once again. He was not cautious because he was afraid, or in someone's debt, or because he believed in slow approaches to terribly urgent problems. He was cautious because he respected individuals, of whatever belief or color or background. He was cautious because he did not want to become a shrill orator, an incessant propagandist, a wily rhetorician, full of heady ideas, and messianic political pronouncements, but without an ounce of specific suggestions about what can be done and where and how. The essence of the man's style comes across in a few of Erikson's sentences:

Gandhi knew that as a nation's reformer he had to engage in experiments which involved him and the nation in action on an ever-larger scale. As he staked out the area for such action, the center remained in the daily life of the ashram, while the periphery was to be tested in the systematic study of such acute grievances as would permit him to involve well circumscribed segments of India's vast population – one at a time – in discrete Satyagraha campaigns for limited but representative goals.[58]

Amid all that travel, all those probes made here and there, Ahmedabad was home: "an almost geometrically ideal point of origin and return for a charismatic traveler." Ahmedabad would also be the scene of a major struggle, a campaign of sorts – though just before the Ahmedabad "event" took place Gandhi (in April 1917) became concerned with the serious difficulties that the indigo workers of Bihar province were up against. The peasants there were exploited grievously. Whether they worked the land or rented it from wealthy landlords and tried to make an independent go of it, they were discriminated against by all sorts of taxes, regulations and laws. Almost by accident Gandhi got into the struggle, but once on the scene, once in a place like Champaran, he would not leave ("For me Champaran is my domicile").

Erikson briefly described that project, the first Gandhi took up in India, because not only was it directly followed by the Ahmedabad "event," but it showed how carefully thought-out Gandhi's deeds were. He studied ever so carefully the facts: how much it cost to raise indigo, the profits the planters made, the taxes and levies the peasants had to pay. He decided upon a course of action, and was not deterred by dozens and dozens of threats, insults and warnings. He shrewdly estimated his opponents' weaknesses, their probable course of action, their needs and fears. He earned the unqualified support and admiration of the local population, the peasants and small farmers whose struggle he had joined, whose problems he gave expression to, for whom he would suffer if need be. He also shamed the landlords, the planters, the government's officials – and earned their collective respect, because he knew whereof he spoke. Since his appeal was to justice and to reason, and since he was also a tireless organizer, a brilliant dramatist, an effective diplomat, he could in turn puzzle, astound, anger, and impress his supposed enemies, to the point that they started out resisting him but gradually fell prey to his increasing power, which was a function of his popular support, which in turn was a function of the work he did among the people, the attentive listening, the ardent speaking.

And could he disarm people with his earnest, innocent manner! He merely wanted to do what is right. He merely wanted to find out what was going on. He merely wanted to be of help — to everyone, to administrators as well as to the common man. He was harmless. If declared disobedient, if called a lawbreaker, he would suffer the penalty; he would, that is, protest but he would certainly understand if the powers-that-be decided to lock him up — and with him the dreams and aspirations of thousands upon thousands, whose vague stirrings and precise thoughts he first had spoken of and would act upon in Champaran and then in Ahmedabad.

In Champaran, Gandhi succeeded. He helped to destroy *tinkathia* — a system which forced farmers to plant indigo in a certain portion of their best land and deliver it over to the landlords at fixed prices. Some money illegally acquired by the landlords was even returned to the farmers. Misery, plenty of it, remained in Bihar near Nepal and the Himalayas, but unquestionably a beginning had been made: all India knew that Mohandas Gandhi and the indigo workers in Bihar had won some money for the poor, had effected a change in the law, had managed to persist in the face of severe intimidation, and not the least, had emerged with a moral as well as material victory.

Even as Gandhi (sick with malaria) was in Champaran working on behalf of the peasants, his attention was being called to troubles right in his own backyard. His devoted friend, Anasuyaben Sarabhai, had been writing him of troublesome conditions in Ahmedabad's textile mills; and in late December 1917, her brother Ambalal received a letter from Gandhi in which he ever so innocently asked "why should not the mill owners feel happy paying a little more to the workers?" He asked to be forgiven, of course, for intruding in Ambalal's business, but anything affecting anyone in India was becoming his business. Erikson comments upon "Gandhi's charming and intuitive" way of being assertive, of "meddling — while denying the wish to meddle — in the affairs of his friends in general and in their familial relations in particular."

The friends and their involvements with Gandhi are again taken up. Introduced at some length in the first part of *Gandhi's Truth*, at last they are to be seen "on stage," as it were: aiding the Mahatma and resisting him; bargaining with him and reproving him and going along with him and following his lead unequivocally, all depending upon which "friend" (and what *kind* of friend) he or she was.

Erikson brings them all back in order to give us conclusions rather than descriptions; that is, he tells us gently and respectfully, but as clearly and accurately as he can, just what went on between these various individuals and the Mahatma. He was becoming that, Gandhi was. To some degree what "went on," as we so brazenly put such complicated matters, had to do not only with Gandhi and his particular manner of talking and doing things, but with the presence of the Mahatma, and with what that presence could set in motion among "the masses" and their rulers.

So, although Ambalal didn't want to increase the wages of his workers, he also didn't want to offend a prominent and much-loved man — not out of crafty calculation, but because they shared certain things. (A Mahatma does that, brings out in various people what they and he have in common.) Erikson takes note of Ambalal's "sense of comradeship with a *manly voluntarist* of a high order and a *maternally concerned* man of universal dimension." The italics are his, and the words he chooses are also characteristically his — reflecting a desire to avoid the usual stereotypes, the pat expressions, the ideologically tinged phrases. And then, there was Ambalal's sister, who was close to Gandhi and gave herself completely to the poor; she lived, in Erikson's description, "a virginally maternal life." Now known in India as the "mother of Labor," she was once a beautiful and sensitive girl. Shy and retiring, she would eventually show that such a description simply would not do. The shy and retiring Anasuyaben was also a woman who worked boldly and forcefully among the poorest and most wretched of India's families, the Untouchables.

Also close to Gandhi as the "event" began to take place was Shankerlal Banker, whom Erikson met, and Mahadev Desai, Gandhi's beloved secretary and constant companion, who died in August 1942. Gandhi had his match in Mahadev; some twenty years younger, his mind was sharp and exceedingly subtle. When he died, Kasturba is reported to have said, "Bapu has lost his right and his left hand! Both his hands Bapu has lost!" Such was probably not the case; Gandhi had a legion of what Erikson nicely calls "sons and followers." He was exceptionally close to Mahadev, but he was also exceptionally close to Shankerlal and Anasuyaben and Pyarelal and indeed any number of men and women for whom he was not a distant "Bapu" but a thoroughly close one. In any event it was Mahadev who wrote the only extended account of the Ahmedabad "event," and it was Shankerlal who worked with great zeal at Gandhi's side during the "event."

Before we get "the event retold" Erikson asks us to stop for one brief and luminous moment and consider Gandhi as the leader of those men, among others, and also Gandhi as a father; consider, that is, whether something very crucial about the Mahatma cannot be learned from a knowledge of how he got along with both his spiritual kin and his blood kin. Erikson has gone over with particular care everything that Gandhi wrote immediately before and during the Ahmedabad event. He gives the reader a remarkable view of a psychoanalyst at work with a man's literary and psychological heritage, not to mention a view of Gandhi about to become a leader and trembling a little at the prospect. "We owe to *The Collected Works*," Erikson writes, "a series of intimate letters, culminating in the report of a dream to his son, which will permit us for once to observe a leader fight a life-crisis on two fronts at once: his battle for supremacy in historical actuality and his conflict with the personal past that marks every man as a defined link in the generational chain." Apparently Gandhi did not become totally distracted by the larger, more abstract issues that increasingly took up his time as he grew older. Under pressure he became if anything more personal, more concerned with those close to him. And again: "On the verge of becoming the father of his nation, he did not (as he has been accused of doing) forget his sons, although the way in which he did remember them was not without tragic undertones and consequences."59

What does Erikson have in mind — about what was on Gandhi's mind? There is ample evidence in Gandhi's correspondence that as things in Ahmedabad became more tense Gandhi became anxious in a very particular way. His letters recite the possible dangers ahead. His letters also show him in a "passionate search for sons who would be worthy disciples and for disciples who would be ideal sons." In one letter from Gandhi to his son Devadas a dream is mentioned, and its substance reveals that a courageous man was nevertheless afraid, even as the interpretation of the dream in *Gandhi's Truth* reveals how possible it is for an analyst to look long, hard and deep at such a man and not lose sight of the fact that, for all the sadness and turmoil he experienced while asleep (and no doubt when awake, too), he could also lead thousands toward a better, more honorable life. Here is Gandhi's description of his dream:

I keep thinking of you all the time. I know you have plenty of zeal and can interest yourself in anything. Had you been here, you would have every moment observed the supreme wonder and power of truth. This is all the legacy I can leave for you. As I believe, it is an inexhaustible legacy. For him who knows its worth, it is priceless. Such a one would ask to have or desire no other legacy. I think you have realized its worth and will cherish it with love. I dreamt last night that you betrayed my trust in you, stole currency notes from a safe and changed them. You spent the amount on vices. I came to know about it. I took alarm; felt very miserable. Just then I awoke and saw that it was all a dream. I thanked God. This dream bespeaks my attachment to you. You, of course, want it. You need not fear that it will ever disappear altogether during this present life. I am making a supreme effort to bear equal love to all, but from you I do hope for something more.[60]

Erikson then notes that "this is certainly a short dream, but it nevertheless manages to harbor betrayal, thievery, and vice, as well as alarm and misery." Gandhi loves his son, and says so emphatically in his letter — yet in the dream turns on him accusingly. In Ahmedabad, Gandhi was in a way also turning on people he knew and very much respected (such as Ambalal) and no doubt expected to be called a few names by them. Dreams like Gandhi's don't "explain" his almost messianic leadership, but they do show that those who challenge powerful industrialists and even whole empires can at a crucial moment get nervous indeed, and hark back to earlier days, when a father seems to have all the world's power. Here is a section of Erikson's remarks on the dream:

That Devadas was Gandhi's youngest son, as Gandhi was *his* father's, and that he was still in his teens, as Gandhi had been at the time of *his* theft, only underlines his identification with his son in the dream. At the very moment, then (so I would conclude), when Gandhi was about to be tested as a prophet of nonviolence in his homeland, the childhood antecedents of this new weapon were reactivated with sufficient strength to make him re-dream that old memory: how he had indulged in vice and had confessed to his stunned father, and how in his way of confessing he had disarmed this violent father with the truth. If this was the youthful antecedent of Satyagraha in his life history, he was now getting ready to test it on a scale vastly greater, thus proving to be a greater leader than his father in both essence and extent. Thus, as he was about to become with a vengeance what his father — the erstwhile passive resister to princely despotism — had been on a smaller scale, he identified himself sufficiently with him to dream of himself as the betrayed father.[61]

Thus did the Gandhi who once had taken money from his father in order to smoke (as reported in his autobiography) now fear that his son would do likewise; and all of that happened in the sleeping brain of a man trying to wrest some cash from mill owners, who didn't want to give it, and obviously had a lot of power behind them in the stand they took. We all have devils to exorcise; and we all go through moments when the devils seem close upon us, and even likely to overtake us. Few of us, though, live lives in which the fearful and anxious situations we had to face as children somehow come to be almost and incredibly exact prototypes of large-scale historical moments, in which again we are involved as protagonists.

Maybe Gandhi's dream cleared his head for action; certainly there was plenty of it in Ahmedabad. Erikson chronicles the entire "event," incident by incident, day by day almost, in a fine chapter, full of narrative power. We learn everything: details about the plague that struck the city, the economic condition of the mills, the mood of the workers and their bosses, the attitude of various other segments of the city's population. *Gandhi's Truth* becomes for some forty pages a political and psychological "thriller," a first-rate history book, and really, something that could be called "India's Truth." The author may say that "one needs to have seen the slums of Indian cities" to appreciate what a monsoon can do, and to understand how an epidemic of plague can get going — but he actually does bring it all to us in strong, clear, simple but skillful prose, larded with enough facts to accredit him as an Indian social historian. Here, for example, is what Ahmedabad was like before the strike at the mills:

In the midst of this grim story of polluted water and rat-fleas, of municipal failure and mortal superstition, one finds the civic-mindedness of an Ambalal and the humanity of the stretcher-bearers from Rajputana. But one also finds the following item, characteristic of the isolation, geographic and psychological, of the city's élite circles. During a week in early September, when 400 city dwellers contracted the plague and 350 died, the theater critic of the *Praja Bandhu* also reported an "Allies Tableau" to be presented by a number of ladies to raise money for the British war effort:

"The Allies Tableau is bound to be immensely appreciated. The heart of every patriotic person will pulsate with emotions at the scene presented. Each of the Allied Nations will be personified by a young lady. You will see Belgium crushed but dignified — hopeful for the future. You will see Servia trampled upon but undaunted — unbroken in spirit. Of course, you will cheer England and her brave friends — cheer with all your might. But, you are entitled to bring down the roof of the Theatre with your shouts of joy when you see India (personified by a young Parsi lady) marching proudly in the procession of Nations. The other scenes will be equally attractive. There will be a scene episode, which Hindus will specially welcome; the representation of the court of Jehangir and Noorjahan will dazzle you with its grandeur; and you will be conveyed to the historical past of your city by the scene representing King Ahmedshah in his beautiful garden."[62]

While some shouted with joy at the sight of that young Parsi lady, hundreds died and panic seized the city. Almost everything shut down — schools, colleges, many businesses. The mills wanted to stay open, however, and in order to do so offered bonuses, "plague bonuses" to workers who did not flee Ahmedabad, as many were doing, and instead came to work every day. The bonus immediately antagonized other workers — warpers they were, better paid and more skilled and settled enough in fine enough homes to be less tempted to flee. They were offered no bonus. Their continuing presence at the mills was simply taken for granted. They were offended, and demanded a "dearness allowance," an increase in wages. Anasuyaben felt their demand justified, to the chagrin of the mill owners, Ambalal excepted. He may not have agreed with her argument, but he defended her right to express it — while at the same time Anasuyaben herself was rather naturally made nervous by her position as an outspoken advocate of the workers. She wrote to Gandhi and asked for his advice. A little later, when the plague subsided, her letter became outdated, because the mill owners decided to renege on all bonuses. Ambalal himself at this point turned to Gandhi. He was aware that his colleagues, also owners of textile mills, were going to stop the bonus payments, and in addition, he worried over his sister's increasing involvement in what was beginning to be a serious and dangerous conflict. Gandhi listened. He talked with other mill owners. He talked with Anasuyaben and with the workers. He saw the trust the workers had already given to Anasuyaben. He made up his mind. He would stand with her, stand with the workers, help formulate and work on a position which would achieve the widest possible support for a substantial wage increase.

Once he had made up his mind he was into everything. A "ceaseless moralist," in Erikson's apt phrase, he gently reminded the workers that money was only part of the story: they should be concerned with their living conditions, with the education of their children, with the things they ate and should eat and should not eat. At the same time, he kept in touch with the mill owners; indeed he was the one person they somehow (if only somewhat) trusted. He also talked with the city's authorities. Nevertheless, the situation steadily worsened. The mill owners closed most of their mills. Only those who would take a twenty percent raise were to be accepted back at work. The workers were asking for fifty percent. Gandhi had decided that a thirty-five percent raise was badly needed by the workers, and could be sustained by the owners, who admittedly had to wage their own struggle for survival in a fiercely competitive industry. Finally, and most important in Gandhi's calculations, the general public would most likely rally round to the workers if they indicated a willingness to compromise.

Things did not quite work as Gandhi surmised. The owners were unyielding; the workers became restive and fearful. Meanwhile, every day Gandhi, Anasuyaben, Shankerlal and others worked with the workers. They visited homes, made inquiries about various problems, brought with them medical assistance, suggested a number of temporary jobs that would ease matters. Every day Gandhi also wrote a leaflet, issued over the name of Anasuyaben and distributed to the workers, and every evening the workers gathered around him "under the famous babul tree on the banks of the Sabamati outside the Shahpur Gate." Erikson "wanted to find the tree, of course. But a great flood had washed it away." The Gate is no more, either — the city's flood of traffic caused it to be torn down. But in *Gandhi's Truth* the whole scene most definitely comes back: the crowd of five to ten thousand; the 1915 Overland roadster, bearing Anasuyaben and "the little man in the loin cloth"; the leaflets, "so well printed that they are still clear and clean today in the ashram's folders"; the nervous police nearby; the almost religious spirit that came upon the daily meetings. The heart of the scene is conveyed through an analysis of those leaflets; one by one they are summarized, quoted from, commented upon, and fitted into Gandhi's overall effort to educate the workers and also himself; to toughen people but also to restrain them; to exhort the poor and the fearful; to buoy up their spirits and give them a larger perspective, a sense of God's will and man's past and India's possible future, a sense of the world's inequities but also a sense of the never-ending effort that people all over the world have made and must keep on making if things are to change for the better. And as if all that was not enough, the leaflets contained in addition an uncanny mixture of practical advice and discussions of particular political alternatives.

For some thirty pages "the event" unfolds before the reader's eye. The presentation is clear-cut: first leaflet, second leaflet, third leaflet and so on. Erikson's writing is sharp, alternately restrained and emphatic. And there is pace to the narrative; the event moves along, and the reader is carried along — just slowly enough to read Gandhi's words and Erikson's observations, but fast enough to experience the flow of things as they must have happened, as they almost seem to happen again. One thinks of the power certain historians can mobilize — for example, Southerners such as C. Vann Woodward and David Potter — as they present facts and analyze ideas, but also reveal themselves to be essayists of the first order, sensitive to the problems of exposition, possessed of a dramatic touch, desirous that their words have both clarity and life. Particularly impressive is the way, in the interests of economy and tempo and force, a brief summary gets joined to comment and analysis:

> If the workers, then, are admonished to be *truthful,* this is not merely a matter of not telling factual lies, but also an exhortation against the spread of rumors by which an undisciplined group can easily become a delusional mob. If they are told to be *courageous*, it is because their previous state of near-slavery always opens them to the dread of total abandonment if they arouse anger in the "masters" to the point of being considered expendable: here, too, panic can release senseless violence — or surrender.[63]

Again and again Gandhi warns the workers that their suffering may not be redeemed, that they may lose rather than win — but again and again he seems literally to breathe hope into them. His ability to walk a tightrope, to inspire and admonish and advise and educate and entertain, comes across strikingly, as does the keen mind of the man who has excerpted the various passages and used the occasion to explain many things indeed. It all comes across like a duet performed by two men who do very well together. Gandhi says, "Happiness follows suffering voluntarily undertaken." Erikson knows that dozens and dozens of his readers, Western materialists of one kind or another, will ask exactly what "happiness" is, and will lift their eyebrows at the idea of "suffering voluntarily undertaken" — and from the likes of him will most certainly expect some "interpretations." Hopefully those Westerners will not be disappointed: "To take active charge of senseless suffering by deliberately choosing to court meaningful suffering can be experienced as one exhilarating mastery over fate within a new ritualization such as Satyagraha."

Gandhi knew that words like "happiness" and "anger" and "suffering" and "disappointment" and "fear" are for some people concepts endlessly fitted into large-scale psychological or political theories. When those same words become something real and alive, that is, experiences gone through by a particular person or group of persons, they simply cannot be examined and judged categorically, as this or that, as good or bad, as evidence of health or sickness. That simple adverb "voluntarily" has wrapped up in it a whole world of what others call "ego psychology," a whole world of "will" and "intentionality" and "cognitive growth" and mental "structuralization." As for Satyagraha, Gandhi saw it as something shared, as something (again) voluntarily taken up by a number of men and women, and something that makes connections for people, ties together ideas, ideals and emotions — not to speak of acts — in such a way that words like "happiness" and "suffering" take on a fresh and different meaning. And such things would perhaps be easily understood by a man who sees "identity" as, among other things, the mind's effort to affirm itself, to find for itself purpose and coherence in a particular world.

In the fourth leaflet a fast is anticipated by what Erikson calls "a fateful promise." Gandhi says, "We shall not ourselves eat or dress without providing food and clothing to such of the workers as are reduced to destitution in the course of the struggle." Erikson in response comments:

Before this statement, Gandhi, with his equal tolerance of the wealthy and the poor, had not shown that he fully comprehended what class differences the workers would perceive in the simple daily fact that while they were beginning to starve, their leaders would arrive in an American-built car after — as far as the workers knew or imagined — a good meal at Anasuya's well-stocked house. For the moment, he would only encourage the workers to come, confront, and censure the advisers "whenever you see us committing mistakes or slackening in our efforts to carry out our pledge."[64]

Gandhi could be stubborn and opinionated, but he also could in a flash see his own failures and failings. He wanted the workers to worry not only about their bosses but about themselves, too. In the sixth leaflet he declares most emphatically a viewpoint many can easily misunderstand as hopelessly utopian, until Erikson points out its practical implications, both psychological and political. *"That action alone is just which does not harm either party to a dispute,"* Gandhi said. Erikson writes:

I have italicized the last sentence because it is the very soul of any Satyagraha struggle. It is fair to assume that at this point relations between Gandhi and Ambalal became rather strained; for it is almost a rule that powerful opponents, in their stubborn bewilderment over being faced with this new nonviolent kind of struggle, become more ruthless. That this bewilderment induces them to use means not entirely in accord with their traditional and personal values provides a critical moment in any Satyagraha struggle, because it shows up the moral weakness of the powerful.[65]

The powerful may be morally weak, but they do not always give in on that account. They may have to be coaxed and cajoled and pushed and confronted — by the strong, unremitting, insistent concern of those who petition them out of weakness but also out of strength, the strength the weak can have. On March 15, 1918, Gandhi began the first of seventeen fasts "to the death." "But the time for leaflets, and even for those with a biblical ring, was passing," Erikson notes. "Gandhiji obviously felt that he himself would have to be the one person to hold out and also the one not to forsake himself." (In the fourteenth leaflet Gandhi had ended with this: "Even if only one person holds out, we shall never forsake him.")

Gandhi's Truth is not about "fasting" per se; indeed, it would have been all too easy for a psychoanalyst to become preoccupied with such a topic, and in a way that ignores the historical situation, the political struggle going on, the cultural and religious traditions of the people involved. Erikson describes what those fasts came to mean to India, and pointedly refuses to go after what some may want to call "the psychodynamics of fasting." As for India: "In later years, all of India would hold its breath while the Mahatma fasted, and whole cities would leave their lamps unlit in the evening in order to be near him in the dark."[66] And as for the rest of us:

And since then, many others have followed the Mahatma's example, though their reasons have often been impulsive, vindictive, or faddish. It is, therefore, especially important to understand what motivated Gandhiji's decision in this first instance and why he came to regret it as not quite worthy of his cause. But it should be clear that there cannot really be any "pure" decision to starve oneself to death, for such determination can only emerge from a paradoxical combination of a passionate belief in the absolute vitality of certain living issues and the determination to die for them: thus one "lives up" to a principle by dying for it. A martyr, too, challenges death, but at the end he forces others to act as his executioners. The decision to let oneself die is of a different and admittedly more obscure order.[67]

Gandhi put it this way when Anasuyaben and others wanted to fast with him, "Leave this to me. Fasting is *my* business." A man who talks like that has taken his personal "motives" and made them part of life's events, history's story — even as those who have other "businesses" do, be they men who run governments or banks, or treat patients, or defend clients in courts. Now, in the course of that "business" of fasting Gandhi went through "extreme mood-swings." At one point he saw the fast as terribly important, a real and decisive beginning in his overall campaign on behalf of all India; at other moments he felt he was betraying his own principles by forcing the mill owners to reckon with him rather than the workers, to yield on his account, out of fear that he might die, out of fear of his influence and reputation, rather than in response to the merits of the issue. Erikson is as candid with the reader as Gandhi was with himself:

As I pointed out at the beginning of this book when I justified my interest in the Event, the intensity of these feelings agreed ill with the tentativeness with which this whole episode is treated in the Autobiography as well as by some biographers. The reason for this treatment, we can now see, is identical with the paradox intrinsic to the Event itself. In trying to use his homeland as a platform from which to ascend to national leadership, he suspected he might have slipped into the muck of Bania bickering.[68]

Thus does it go in politics, where the saintliest of men have to meet the Devil head-on — and in themselves as well as in others. Gandhi "won"; the Ahmedabad mill owners basically acceded to the conditions he set forth when the strike began. But he was too honest and decent to hide from himself the fact that his "weak condition left the mill owners no freedom." He said that, and when others rejoiced he was, in Erikson's graphic phrase, "sad to the bone." Meanwhile India and the world saw nothing. Yet by now it comes as no surprise to the reader that a significant event could take place in obscurity, and cause a measure of despair in a man who had seemingly accomplished his aim.

In any event, the world would soon enough pay attention; and equally important, Gandhi would soon enough be on his way again, no longer moody, a fighter with enormous energy, but one determined not to hurt anyone if at all possible. The final sentence in the chapter that describes "the event" is a reminder that a man's despair, his conflicts and tensions, do not have to undo him, as those who deal with such things certainly ought to know, but sometimes seem to forget. Maybe psychiatrists — almost by definition — never do deal with people whose conflicts work *for* them, rather than against them; and maybe the two groups require a separate language, a separate set of myths, images, theoretical constructs: "This, then, is the difference between a case history and a life-history: patients, great or small, are increasingly debilitated by their inner conflicts, but in historical actuality inner conflict only adds an indispensable momentum to all superhuman effort."[69]

It is left for Erikson to deal with the immediate aftermath of Ahmedabad, and more important, pull together conceptually and reflectively what Satyagraha "is" or "means," or better perhaps, proposes to do. Within days of the strike's end Gandhi had left Ahmedabad and was working in nearby Kheda on behalf of peasants who had also been devastated by the monsoon of 1917. In Kheda the problem was not so much the plague and its consequences, but the devastation brought to thousands of poor farmers, who were asked to pay taxes even though their crops had failed — a policy that made already marginal families penniless. Gandhi, like others before him in history, was considered an "outside agitator," but not by the peasants, of course; they adored him and followed his lead. The campaign ended, in Gandhi's words, "without grace." True, it was the beginning of something; the peasants did protest, and did obtain some acquiescence on the part of the government, in the sense that the poorest farmers were not, after all, taxed, while the richer ones agreed to pay more. But Gandhi could not but note how grim and reluctant and stingy and mean-spirited the government officials were. He wanted to help the poor; but he wanted to change the climate between antagonistic people, so that further changes would follow without, at each stage, costly and exhausting demonstrations. He wanted, in other words, a beginning at least of trust — not metaphysical trust, but concrete, practical (political, it can be said) trust. He did not see that kind of result emerge in Kheda, and so he was honest enough with himself to feel disappointment.

Meanwhile the First World War was dragging on mercilessly in

Europe, and Great Britain had no real idea in the spring of 1918 when the end of it all might come. Even as the Kheda affair was being settled, Gandhi agreed to attend a conference in Delhi summoned by the Viceroy for the obvious purpose of obtaining Indian men for a European war. India's peasants found Gandhi's agreement to work with the British, to help them raise men, at best confusing and a lapse of sorts; many of them were hurt and angered, as were some of his supporters. Erikson wants to understand what happened:

As he embarked on nationwide ambitions, he was once more drawn into that strange complexity of emotions and ideas which had characterized earlier confrontations involving the necessity of fighting the British giant: he first had to offer his help and his succor to the parent body while it was in danger.[70]

The point is that the man was "half troubled and half challenged" in his attitude toward the British. In "fear and trembling" he agreed to help, but he did agree and he did try to help — and failed. The peasants would follow him for redress of their grievances but not to a distant war. And, anyway, how could he, the apostle of non-violence, dare come before them or anyone else as a military recruiter?

The man's struggle is documented, as best it can be, from his writings and letters and the replies he received to letters. He was emotionally and physically exhausted. He was also deeply involved in a most important personal and philosophical struggle. His oldest son Harilal was in trouble, was always in trouble, it seemed, but then in fresh trouble. The campaign in Kheda was in trouble. England was in trouble. Gandhi was torn by all sorts of conflicts and admits it, says in fact that he had a "nervous breakdown." He felt loyal to the crown; he even expected that if India were to prove itself loyal during the war, independence would be granted soon thereafter. He refused to go along with the many advisors and friends (a number of them not Indians) who felt he was compromising himself and his ideals. It turns out that he was grappling with those ideals, testing out what he did believe, and yes, showing himself as mixed-up and inconsistent as life itself is. Erikson draws heavily upon the Mahatma's words at this point and explains why. Gandhi's words are lucid, suggestive, utterly compelling:

I have come to see, what I did not so clearly before, that there is non-violence in violence. This is the big change which has come about. I had not fully realized the duty of restraining a drunkard from doing evil, of killing a dog in agony or one infected with rabies. In all these instances, violence is in fact non-violence.[71]

On the same page one reads this from Gandhi: "We shall learn military discipline as we help the Empire, gain military experience and acquire the strength to defend ourselves. With that strength, we may even fight the Empire, should it play foul with us." And this:

What am I to advise a man to do who wants to kill but is unable owing to his being maimed? Before I can make him feel the virtue of not killing, I must restore to him the arm he has lost. . . . A nation that is unfit to fight cannot from experience prove the virtue of not fighting. I do not infer from this that India must fight. But I do say that India must know how to fight.

Gandhi knew, in Erikson's concise summary of decades of the Mahatma's life, including its tragic end, that he would have to "face the danger of disorganized violence in a people ready neither for violence nor for nonviolence." Gandhi said repeatedly that the path of nonviolence is difficult; and so he could hardly follow that path himself without difficulties, both ideological ones and emotional ones. Meanwhile, at every step of such a man's journey there are the critics — not only the strong and uncompromising ones who really help a man, but those others who set him up in order to knock him down, or use him as a foil for all sorts of single-minded, dogmatic purposes. Erikson's effort to understand Gandhi at times reaches out to those critics; and what is more, the effort reveals a good deal about the mind and character of the man who makes the effort — and nowhere more revealingly than in these observations:

In the meantime, the utterances of this period show how uninformed are the casual criticisms with which even some of the best educated among us declare Gandhi to be so one-sided and visionary as to be irrelevant; or to have been unable to foresee the riots which, indeed, eventually scarred the face of independent India. What, they ask, would he have done about or against the invasion of the Chinese hordes? Well, he *did* foresee disorganized violence in India and elsewhere; and as to the Chinese, nobody can know what a man of such complexity *would* have said or done.

But it is equally important to acknowledge that he did not envisage a possible triumph of Satyagraha on a national or international scale with a naive "peace of mind," or, indeed, without severe symptoms of inner conflict. To deny this by declaring him only physically exhausted as his adherents do would seem to do an injustice to the stature of the man. He himself does not mind reporting as a "nervous breakdown" what others make out to be a physical crisis followed by recovery. All that it was, too; but is it not high time to do away with the categorical constructs of purely physical, mental, or spiritual disturbance when we speak of the inner struggles of one of the wholest of men and one of the most miraculously energetic — most energetic, in fact, when inspired by the very momentum of recovery from temporary self-doubt and inactivation?[72]

He did, of course, recover. There is space in *Gandhi's Truth* to discuss only briefly the Mahatma's later Satyagrahas: the one in 1919 against the British antisedition law, meant to cripple all nationalist opposition; the fast undertaken in response to rioting and murder done by Indians (mostly) against Indians; the famous Salt Satyagraha, the "march to the sea" of 1930, in protest against the Salt Act, which provided that all salt should be taxed, and struck hardest at the poorest of the poor. *Gandhi's Truth* is not Gandhi's biography, and for that matter "the event" is not meant to be *the* event in Gandhi's life, but rather a particular "moment" which, when carefully explored, helps us understand at once a man, an ethical ideal, and a means of political and social action. The later Satyagrahas are mentioned to remind the reader what a long and hard and by no means satisfactory or conclusive struggle Gandhi continued to wage, until at the age of seventy-nine he was felled by an assassin. It was in many ways an ultimately tragic life, but it was also an exemplary one, and one by no means void of joy. As he briefly takes up the Satyagrahas that came after Ahmedabad and Kheda, Erikson seems to want for us what he must have felt over and over again as he wrote the book: an awareness of the work it took, the energy, the devotion, the imagination and resourcefulness, and too, an awareness of how high the stakes were, how vicious the police, the army, the government eventually became, as a man and his companions and followers step by step took on an empire which considered itself civilized, but could in the clutch resort to awful violence, even as could the frightened, hungry and uneducated "masses" of India.

In the book's last chapters Erikson makes clear his own conviction that the stakes were even higher than Gandhi himself realized, could possibly have realized. Gandhi was seventy-five when two atomic bombs were dropped, ironically, on another Asian land. Since Gandhi's death the world has accumulated quite enough weapons to destroy every nation, to end life of all kinds on this planet. In this

way has one man's feverish desire to curb violence become everyone's cause, the furthest thing from a casual matter, an abstract, intellectual exercise.

To Erikson, Gandhi was above all a *religious actualist*, the kind of
man who can sense in his bones a universal danger and will try to end
it. He calls Gandhi that seriously but also ironically, because he really
does not wish to "call" him anything: "If, for the sake of the game, I
should give his unique presence a name that would suit my views, I
would call him a *religious actualist*." In this century Gandhi has been
called just about everything; and God knows the world is as full of
people who like to label other people as it is with violence, and perhaps the two "phenomena" are not unrelated. The Mahatma was
more than the sum of those claims, those miscellaneous labels, more
than the sum of any new ones an analyst might be tempted to use.
But "if, for the sake of the game," one tries, one struggles with
words, a brief and suggestive description can be worth dozens of
technical terms. "I think the man was right who said that Gandhi,
when he listened to his inner voice, heard the clamor of the people."

Gandhi had another side to him, a tormented and bitter side; he
could be deaf to the cries of his own sons, and no doubt about it,
those sons may have enabled millions of other Indian sons to feel
some hope about life. Yet, despite all the suffering Gandhi went
through and put others through, he struggled hard to end suffering,
real and awful suffering, and most of all he struggled to realize for
himself and others — exactly *who* is without any meanness? — a
world substantially kinder than the one he knew. Perhaps he *more*
than struggled; perhaps that is the point: "Therefore I would interpret, and interpret with humility, the truth-force of the religious
actualist thus: to be ready to die for what is true now means to grasp
the only chance to have lived fully."[73]

This he did; literally die for what he believed true, having lived
not one but many lives. But in all of those lives, spent on three continents, the man's ability to combine tenderness with firmness, gentleness with sturdiness, keeps on coming across, unwittingly in his own
writings, and certainly in this psychological and historical study of
him by a scholar who obviously shares some of the religious and ethical concerns his "subject" had — all of which may explain why
Gandhi's worries and fears, so openly and abundantly written down
in his various letters and books, are treated with a degree of care that
is itself an example, maybe even a kind of "presence." "In his re-

vealed life," Erikson says of Gandhi, "the abnormal and the super-
normal vie with such disarming frankness that whatever we could
diagnose as his neurosis simply becomes part of his personal *swaraj*,
the home ground of his being — and a man must build on that."

Gandhi did so build. In another sense Erikson does, too: by seeing
a man like Gandhi in that way, he emerges with a study that is
straightforward and free of either affectation or animus — no mean
achievement in an age dominated by grandiose, bickering ideologies.

Gandhi was obviously no ideologue; he was for much of his life
racked with self-doubt. His mind gave him little rest in that regard,
little rest in general — because always he was thinking, praying, writing his thoughts down, changing his mind, calling himself mistaken,
adding a twist or turn to an idea, qualifying what before had been
stated a bit categorically. "I have taken things as they have come to
me and always in trembling and fear," he said once in a letter. He was
trying to make the point that, thoughtful as he was, his life was not
thought out in advance, not self-consciously planned and punctuated
in accordance with some program. He knew how to ride, ride with
the flow of events, with changing circumstances, with the accidents
and incidents that daily take place, with dozens of swift and sometimes
swiftly changing currents, with history itself. It is fitting, and not a
little encouraging, therefore, that a study of his "truth" should end
with a discussion of what he has done rather than what he thought
— or feared. "We have reported Gandhi's saying that God appears
to you not in person but in action," says Erikson in his last chapter.
There follows another sentence, a warning it is, but really an act,
one that hopefully may inspire others to watch their thinking, watch
their tongues, watch the way they jump — *to* conclusions and *on*
people: "But this also means that the full measure of a man — and
that includes his unconscious motivation — can never be comprehended in isolation from his most creative action."

It is just such "creative action" that Erikson has wanted to understand. The "unconscious motivation" he found in Gandhi is not so
different from the urges and forces, the rages and compulsions we
all contend with, express, carry with us. But what Gandhi, the intelligent, kind and honorable man, did with those demons! Whatever
his "problems," whatever the punishment he felt worthy of, there
was in him something that seemed to say enough. That is, we have
had enough of the blind leading the blind, enough of the hurt inflict-
ing more hurt. Somehow such cycles have to end, so that life can go

on more decently and surely, so that the lives of millions are no longer tragically interrupted and destroyed.

One feels that *Gandhi's Truth* is itself part of the history it describes, the long and by no means ended struggle man has waged to live ethically, to forgo the fist, the sword, and yes, the dubious pleasure and outright danger of the raised, self-righteous voice. Toward the end of *Gandhi's Truth* the reader comes across a series of "associations," quite reasonable ones, and altogether clarifying ones. A sentence is quoted from Joan Bondurant's *Conquest of Violence*: "The only dogma in the Gandhian philosophy centers here: that the only test of truth is action based on the refusal to do harm." To which Erikson adds that Gandhi showed "a determination not to violate another person's essence." Then he recalls his own effort to find values that make sense and (just as important) lead to the commitments, the deeds a world desperately needs. He recalls his lecture on medical ethics to a graduating class of medical students at Harvard, and paraphrases what he tried to say then:

I suggested that (ethically speaking) a man should act in such a way that he actualizes both in himself and in the other such forces as are ready for a heightened mutuality. Nothing I have read or heard since has dissuaded me from the conviction that one may interpret Gandhi's truth in these terms. In fact, Gandhi made a similar assumption when he viewed Satyagraha as a bridge between the ethics of family life and that of communities and nations.[74]

He next goes back to Joan Bondurant and Gandhi:

What Bondurant calls "veracity," then, must have actuality as well as reality in it, that is, it depends on acting passionately as well as on thinking straight; and acting passionately would include acting upon and being guided by what is most genuine in the other. Truth in Gandhi's sense points to the next step in man's realization of man as one all-human species, and thus to our only chance to transcend what we are.[75]

Gandhi wanted men to respect one another, not with lip service or convenient phrases, but out of the heart-felt knowledge that we are together human above all, above all man-made categories, above all the distinctions we choose to make, and make others pay for dearly — skin color, boundary lines, amount of yearly income, and on and on to the point of absurdity, to the point of banality. In 1966, in his paper on "The Ontogeny of Ritualization in Man," Erikson has spelled out the trouble we are in: billions of us separated from one another by divisions we not only subscribe to, but virtually worship — as if "we" are saved, whereas "they" are condemned, and worth only that, condemnation, and if need be, extinction. By one of those strange twists of history, men like Erikson and Konrad Lorenz now have come to realize how far we have to go if we are to be as "civilized" as many animals, who have yet to "learn," as we have, the ability and willingness to commit wholesale murder. Many critics of Gandhi, and even those drawn to him, have wondered whether man can ever really be "nonviolent." They suggest that we are "instinctively" violent or "aggressive" or whatever. Yet there are concrete observations that should make us wonder about animals, let alone human beings. Animals who supposedly are far more "driven" than we, far more "aggressive" and "primitive," in fact display the kind of restraint which our nations, and particularly our "civilized" nations, had better well have, if any nation is to be around much longer:

The inhabitants of an Indian jungle live face to face with "beasts" in their domain; but even they consider an occasional "killer" among tigers something of an outlaw or a deviant, a creature whom one cannot come to terms with, and who, therefore, must be singled out and hunted down. A normal lion, however, when ready for the kill (and he kills only when hungry) shows no signs of anger or rage: he is "doing his job" — or so he appears to be when his physiognomy can be studied in the wilds through long-range lenses. Nor is there any pervasive tendency for mass annihilation in nature's book — except, apparently, in rodents such as rats, under particular conditions. Wolves on the chase (Dante's *bestia senza pace*) do not decimate healthy herds but pick out the stragglers who fall behind. Among themselves, they are capable of devoted friendship; and it is reported that when two wolves happen to get into a fight, there comes a moment when the one that begins to weaken bares his unprotected neck to his opponent, who, in turn, is instinctively inhibited from taking advantage of this now "nonviolent" situation.[76]

Gandhi saw, as anthropologists have, as child psychoanalysts have, how significantly we become what our social and political institutions prompt us to become: greedy and murderous members of a given country, or reasonably quiet and gentle members of one or another community. He saw that somehow we will have to meet the challenge offered by a child's potential range of responsiveness: a child can learn to feel part of a wide world, indeed, or learn to find almost everyone hateful and worthless. And when societies play on the latter, fatefully and deliberately do so, thousands and thousands of children grow up "ready" to kill upon a command. Add to that what man's technological genius has given to us, a button that can destroy a planet, and one arrives at where we are today. Of course, those who press buttons have always dismissed the Gandhis of this world as dreamers — as if to dream is somehow less "practical" than to kill. But Gandhi was even "practical," we now know; and by the same token what he saw as "right" and important was also natural for animals certainly, and for us potentially — *if*, as he kept on saying and demonstrating, each of us takes upon himself certain responsibilities. And what are those responsibilities? Gandhi wrote about them and wrote about them, and in the West others have also written about them. Here, simply and directly, is what Gandhi and Freud, certainly from the West, agreed upon as man's task, his central responsibility — as described by another Western man in a book that brings together a "truth" which was one man's but must become ours if we are to survive:

Gandhi's and Freud's methods converge more clearly if I repeat: in both encounters only the militant probing of a vital issue by a non-violent confrontation can bring to light what insight is ready on both sides. Such probing must be decided on only after careful study, but then the developing encounter must be permitted to show, step by step, what the power of truth may reveal and enact. At the end only a development which transforms both partners in such an encounter is truth in action; and such transformation is possible only where man learns to be nonviolent toward himself as well as toward others. Finally, the truth of Satyagraha and the "reality" of psychoanalysis come somewhat nearer to each other if it is assumed that man's "reality testing" includes an attempt not only to think clearly but also to enter into an optimum of mutual activation with others. But this calls for a combination of clear insight into our central motivations and pervasive faith in the brotherhood of man.[77]

After that there is little more to say, except, perhaps, for a brief but almost stunning autobiographical remark:

When I began this book, I did not expect to rediscover psychoanalysis in terms of truth, self-suffering, and nonviolence. But now that I have done so, I see better what I hope the reader has come to see with me, namely, I felt attracted to the Ahmedabad Event not only because I had learned to know the scene and not only because it was time for me to write about the responsibilities of middle age, but also because I sensed an affinity between Gandhi's truth and the insights of modern psychology. That truth, and these insights, are the legacy of the first part of this century to its remainder. A concrete event has served to illustrate their origins in all the complexity of historical actuality. I did not undertake to do and could not do more than that. But as we historicize more consciously, we also assume some of the burden of tradition. Even one past event, seen in the light of a new awareness, must make it apparent that man denies and abandons the visions and the disciplines he has already acquired only at the risk of historical and personal regression.[78]

In fact, *Gandhi's Truth* offers no more than that — but that it does offer, perhaps to the reader's eventual surprise as much as the author's. And "that," that achievement, may be more than enough for us to have, and hold on to as an example not only of how a psychoanalyst can think and write, but what he can come to do. The Mahatma's truth, his "truth force," his Satyagraha, has been brought to the West that Gandhi so long admired, emulated, importuned, struggled against, tried to win over, wanted to change; a West that needs "truth force" rather than a million jealous truths, and rather than megatons upon megatons of force. A man who writes a book, admittedly, cannot thereby change the world. But the man who wrote *Gandhi's Truth* at least has gone all over that world in order to see and hear and listen, and in general put his profession "on the line," which means to put it at the service of urgent ethical tasks. He has also rescued from various kinds of pedantry and idolatry the living spirit of two immensely worthwhile men, Gandhi and Freud, men whose ideas, so often chewed over and picked apart, do not need yet another interpreter, but a responsive listener who will use what was once said by others to help us today understand what is, and what hopefully may someday be. Maybe no one should want to do more than that; maybe when each of us tries to do that, very little more will have to be done. Gandhi's "truth force" becomes — modestly and affectingly — Erikson's "truth force." In other words, the two men and their ideas came together with no loss of dignity to either. All over the world human beings need to go through something like that, need to be won over to each other, need to be won over not to points of order and articles of faith but to ways — to more kindly and respectful ways of thinking about each other and getting along with each other, to liberating, redemptive ways.

XII

Epilogue, Interlude and Prologue

WHAT next, one asks — as if always a life can be fitted into
some methodical narrator's desire to point out everything,
indicate all possible directions. I write this in 1970. Erikson is to be
sixty-eight this year. At times when I look at him and watch him,
I see a man who is like a child — direct and smiling and lively. At
other moments he is a thoughtful man who has lived a long time and
seen a lot, and like many others today feels troubled and uncertain
about the future. Nevertheless he is an energetic man, not much
given to despair. The white hair, the full face, the reddish complexion, the open blue eyes, the tall and sturdy body, the erect carriage —
one searches in vain through those physical characteristics for an "explanation" of the man's "presence." Can such a quality, what we
call "presence," ever really be pinned down and spelled out in
words? And can it be that some artists, writers or scientists, however well they understand themselves, never know what they *will*
do until they find themselves doing it, mysteriously at work again?

In any event, whatever the man does in the coming years, it is
safe to say that children and young people will continue to be
very much on his mind. In 1968, he went to South Africa in order
to give the T. B. Davie Memorial Lecture at the University of Cape
Town. The month was August, and news dispatches reported rising protests by South African students against the nation's apart-
heid laws. Erikson was finishing his book on Gandhi, and was not
unaware of the Mahatma's years in that country. It is the *students*
of Cape Town who invite the T. B. Davie Memorial Lecturer, the
same students who had invited Robert Kennedy to South Africa in

1966, and who talked day and night with Erikson about something quite real, quite actual in their lives, perhaps best summarized by a news report of mid-August 1968: "Students massed outside the gates of Witwatersrand University near the center of the city in a defiant demonstration against the government's veto of the appointment of Archie Mafeje, an African, to the staff of Cape Town University."[1]

The lecture was called "Insight and Freedom," and included some of the lecturer's thoughts about Gandhi and nonviolence. Before the lecture was delivered, the president of the university Student Representative Council read the following "Dedication to Academic Freedom," and invited the audience to repeat with him the final paragraph:

We are the members of a University which since its foundation has always been free to decide whom to admit to its fellowship.

In exercising this freedom our University has acted in the belief that the only valid criterion for entry to a University is academic merit.

Nevertheless, without consultation with our University, without its consent, and, in our view, for no sufficient reason, a law has been passed authorising the Government to impose restrictions based on colour.

We wish to testify from our own experience that relations in our University have been harmonious, that mutual understanding has been fostered, and that our very diversity has enriched our academic life and helped us to contribute to the advancement of knowledge.

We dedicate ourselves to the tasks that lie ahead: to maintain our established rights to determine who shall teach, what shall be taught and how it shall be taught in this University, and to strive to regain the right to determine who shall be taught, without regard to any criterion except academic merit.[2]

Then, after a brief introduction, came Erikson's first words:

To stand before you as a T. B. Davie Lecturer means to link arms with those men who have previously demarcated, at your request, the irreducible line of academic freedom. This is a momentous task, to be assumed with all humility, and demands from each of us a statement as to where he stands and where he comes from.

My country must be marked in your minds as it is in mine by the fact that so recently a vital young statesman who was your guest two years ago was shot to death — as was his brother, who had already taken his place in history — and also Martin Luther King, unforgettable for his understanding of militant nonviolence. I come from a country, then, which in all its wealth and power, freedom and talent, is at the mercy of armed psychopathy and riotous revenge. (And today is the day of Hiroshima.) But my country is also — in spite of all the politics-as-usual of a campaign year — vigorously reassessing the ethical basis of its national policies abroad and at home, and this, if for no other reason because our academic youth insists on it with all manner of deep involvement and of non-violent (and occasionally violent) challenge.[3]

Nor has he been able to retreat from the challenge he mentions — the challenge his own country's youth is making. In a paper written for the *International Journal of Psychoanalysis*, and also published in the Winter 1970 issue of *Daedalus*, Erikson reflects upon "the dissent of contemporary youth" in a way noticeably at variance with the approach some of his colleagues have taken. He refuses to label young activists with clinical terms. He refuses to call them "regressed" or "neurotic" or in need of "treatment." He also refuses to be intimidated by mean and vulgar and cruel and arrogant behavior, on the part of young people or on the part of their elders. Moralistic self-righteousness, whether in the hands of youthful protesters or aging defenders, sets the stage for bitterness, malice, spite; and no particular generation is without danger of falling into that psychological sequence.

The essay is a relatively short one, and perhaps a prelude to a future effort to answer a question put to the reader: "What, really, *is* an adult?" Certainly the author will not shirk looking at teachers as well as students, doctors as well as young "patients." At one point we are reminded that "we who know so much about the child in the adult know so much less about the fate of the adolescent in him; and yet it is eminently clear that adults of ethical stature retain their ideological involvements as well as their punitive moralism and can fall back on both." And he points out that if the young are driven by something that has to do with "parricide," then "filicide" also drives men to obvious and sly kinds of brutality and arrogance, if not murderousness. In his "mostly 'diagnostic' paper," free of sweeping generalizations that proclaim complicated social and political problems to be the "result" of certain "child-rearing" practices or the "expression" of certain psycho-pathological processes, one "therapeutic" suggestion is almost apologetically made — and a sensible and welcome suggestion it is:

If the older young people could find the courage in themselves — and encouragement and guidance from their elders — to institutionalize their responsibility for the younger young, we might see quite different images of both youth and young adulthood emerge than those we now know. New models of fraternal behavior may come to replace those images of comradeship and courage that have been tied in the past to military service and probably have contributed to a glorification of a kind of warfare doomed to become obsolete in our time; and they may come to continue the extraordinary work, both inspired and concrete, done in the last few decades by pioneering youth groups on a variety of frontiers. This, in turn, would make it possible for adults to contribute true knowledge and genuine experience without assuming an authoritative stance beyond their actual competence and genuine inner authority.[4]

Yes, at twenty or fifty, men can be mean and small-minded, which means that we have to take notice not only of youthful irrationalities but elderly ones, not only crazily indignant students (and those who craftily manipulate them) but the "display of that brittle dignity which is supposed to protect occupational identity and status." The latter is something to which many young people react with scorn and even a sense of horror: "to them a career that is not worth sacrificing for professed ideals is not worth having."

There is much of Gandhi in that way of looking at things: insistently fair-minded, sharp but also generous, and above all hopeful in spite of fears and worries that are acknowledged, indeed carefully discussed. As a matter of fact *The Times of India* (December 19, 1969) in a review of *Gandhi's Truth* caught the tone in the paper on youth's dissent rather well when mention was made of the "affection and respect [that] mark Erikson's attitude." I quote now a little more of that review because I believe that the Mahatma's nonviolence, comprehended and brought to life by Erikson, needs to be absorbed not only by "the young" or their "elders," but by the rest of us, the self-appointed critics and observers and commentators who use various kinds of sociological and psychiatric "constructs" to hurt and slander and kill rather than understand and illuminate:

Scores of good, bad and indifferent books have been written about Gandhiji in the past and no doubt many more of the kind will be written about him in the years to come as his living image is gradually transfixed into an icon. But few are likely to improve on Erik Erikson's immensely rewarding and clinically competent study of the Mahatma and his methods.

And toward the end of the review: "What this modest scholar whose first visit to Ahmedabad in 1962 set off this search for

Gandhiji's truth has done is to reveal to us, his countrymen, many of whom have seen him in flesh and blood, the full extent of Gandhiji's greatness."

The important word is "reveal." Where are the many, many *revelations* we so badly need now, not sublime or apocalyptic ones, but ones concrete and immediately to the point of our lives, our daily experiences, our existence as men and women surrounded by injustice and on the brink of a dozen or so awful wars? Under such circumstances to "reveal" Gandhi was to reveal what we ache to have in greater numbers, the Gandhis we so very much need.

Meanwhile children are born and grow up. Every day they try to make sense of a world all too often senselessly mean and harsh. Over thirty years have elapsed since Erikson went to visit the Sioux and tried to understand how their children came to terms with a grim life indeed. Still, in the late sixties, he was asked to return to South Dakota and see what (if anything) had happened to the tribe and especially its children. In fact, the "play constructions" described in *Childhood and Society* are once again being done by a wide variety of children. Mrs. Erikson and a friend of hers have asked black and white children in New York City to do them, build what they see fit to build, and the Eriksons have gone to the South and the Southwest in hopes eventually of working with Navaho children and rural black children. Nearing seventy, they could perhaps be forgiven if they decided such hard, demanding "field work" is too much for them; but apparently they feel that is not the case.

And in Chicago under the sponsorship of Loyola University there is now the Erikson Institute for Early Childhood Education; its chief concern is training teachers to work with small boys and girls who live in the ghettos of our cities or in grim rural settings. Teachers come there from all over the country for training, and those who teach the teachers come from all over the world — and in recent years have included Anna Freud, René Spitz, Konrad Lorenz, Jean Piaget, not to mention the man whose name the institute bears. That kind of distinction Erikson proudly accepts, and tries to remain worthy of — even as he year after year turns down an astonishing number of invitations and offers of honorary degrees.

I suppose it can be said that Professor and Mrs. Erikson and their children are demonstrating in many ways the kind of "generativity" a book like *Childhood and Society* describes and one like

Gandhi's Truth illustrates. Now that the book on Gandhi is done, and his years as a professor at Harvard are nearing their end, one senses the man feeling himself in the midst of an interlude which is at the same time a prologue, a time of questions which ultimately demand answers, hence more work, another span of heightened activity. Meanwhile, they will live in Massachusetts — in Stockbridge during the winter and during the summer in Cotuit. Their son Kai Erikson with his wife and two boys lives relatively nearby, in New Haven, where he is master of Yale's Trumbull College and a professor of sociology. The *Yale Alumni Magazine* in November 1967 had this to say about him:

Kai T. Erikson, professor of sociology, has won the Robert M. MacIver award of the American Sociological Association, the highest research honor that can be awarded any sociologist. Erikson received the prize for his book, *Wayward Puritans: A Study in the Sociology of Deviance*, which was cited "for its sharpness and clarity of focus, for its incisive relating of social theory and historical materials, and for the elegance of its writing."

Another son, Jon, is a photographer and lives in California; and the youngest child, Sue, takes care of her son in New York City, where her husband teaches at New York University. The mother of those three grown children is also the author of two published books and several articles. The books are unusual in both content and design. *The Universal Bead* (1969) has a substantial text and a wide variety of drawings and photographs, both in black and white and color. One learns about beads, necklaces, and earrings from all over the world, and one finds psychology joined to history — and done so in prose that is direct, unaffected and suggestive:

I work with gold and silver, precious and semiprecious stones. I design and make jewelry. At my work bench planning, dreaming up a pair of earrings or a necklace, I have become aware of the special attraction of what are probably the simplest forms I work with — beads. . . . With curiosity as my guide I began to visit museums and libraries to ask questions and listen to the experience of others. And I was astonished at the sparseness of catalogued information on this subject. A wealth of material is hinted at in the accounts of ancient and modern travelers, in the reports of archeologists, anthropologists, and historians. But no book devoted to beads alone or to the special role they have played in human affairs was to be found. . . . In historical writings beads have been treated as objects of slight importance, even when they could be used to buy men and countries, were manufactured by the ton, and filled the holds of ships. But we shall try to piece this history together: where and how beads have been made and of what materials; how and where they have been transported and to what purpose.[5]

The reader learns that men have used beads for "decoration, as insignia of rank and status, as bearers of magic power, as universal currency and as durable wealth." He learns of the ancient trade routes, which extended across the world, from the edges of Asia to points in Africa and Europe. He learns how utterly, beautifully, handsomely tangible a bead can be; and he also learns what beads can embody — man's ability and need to turn the concrete into the symbolic. Mrs. Erikson's second book, *Mata Ni Pachedi* or "The Pachedi of the Mata," continues in the direction set by *The Universal Bead*. The book was published by the National Institute of Design in India and offers Mrs. Erikson's text along with dozens of photographs, all in an effort to further the reader's understanding of

the pachedi of the Mata, the cloth of the mother goddess, the goddess of a hundred names and as many attributes — that prevailing deity of India since time immemorial. Worshipped by the poor of low caste, of which there are so many, her cloth is dyed and handprinted by a guild of her devotees. On the banks of the Sabarmati River, surrounded by great textile mills, the age-old process is meticulously carried out in the dazzling sunlight.[6]

While the Eriksons were in Ahmedabad, and near the Sabarmati, intent on learning about Gandhi, they truly did take in the sights and sounds of India. Erik Erikson describes them in one way all through the first section of *Gandhi's Truth*, and Joan Erikson does so again in rich and sensual language, a worthy accompaniment to page after page of pictures:

The city is a clamour of sounds — whistles, sirens, the shriek and rumble of trains and more immediate and nagging, the insistent high pitched horns of bicycles, taxis, and cars. The river sounds are of a different order and since the bed of the river lies below the city level they maintain their more intimate and individual qualities. The bleating of goats being led down in a flock to water — the occasional braying of donkeys and mooing of cattle, and the swish of air sound that marks the swift passing of a flock of birds, form a muted background to the noises of working people. Voices call to one another and the ever present two wheeled snack cart piled with small sweets, toasted, spicy foods and nuts rings its tinkling bell. But the sound of the river is, above all, the constant rhythmic banging of cloths on large stones in the water, for this is how things are made clean in India. The washermen stand holding the cloth by one end and beat it firmly and noisily letting out a great gasp of breath with each stroke. Sometimes this gusty accompaniment emerges as a song — not very melodic but consistently rhythmic, and if words become distinguishable a breathy "Sita" and "Rama" may be heard. Even work songs retell the much loved stories from the epic of Ramayana. How the cloth survives is a wonder, but it is woven to meet this test too, and this is one proof of its quality.

The river bed sings with colour. It spreads out like a great palette with areas of blue, yellow, purple, green — for these hand printed and hand dyed fabrics are set by the burning, blinding glare of sun on sand. But predominantly there is red. Red is the colour on the shores of Sabarmati — red is the colour on the streets of Ahmedabad — red is the colour of India — brick red — ruby red — vermillion — scarlet — crimson — bougainvillaea and blood red.

Village women swish their full, brick red or scarlet patterned skirts as they pull their heavy carts and the enormous turbans of the cowherds display flamboyant reds of every imaginable shade. Red is the preferred colour for saris and when another colour is chosen it is often banded with red or dotted with reddish spots. The peasant women wear long black veils bordered with brilliant crimson and splashed with a sun burst of the same colour at the back of the head. Red is everywhere.

Red is an auspicious colour they say — the very essence of energy, of joy, of life itself. It is the colour for festive occasions. Wedding invitations are written with red ink; the bride wears a red sari, red sandals and many red bangles of glass or lacquer. The tiladi mark on the forehead of women is red and in Bengal where women wear their hair parted, the part is marked with red after marriage. The gods are worshipped with red marks made with kumkum and red powder is thrown on everyone at the festival of Holi.

In ancient times a mother actually marked the forehead of her son with blood drawn from her own hands before sending him off to battle. Red is warm, red is pure, red is life and vitality. Blood red, black and white are the colours of the pachedi, blood sacrifice is still a sacred feature of the worship of the mother goddess.[7]

The book tells us not only how a certain cloth is made, but how it is used and why — by people whom we can see in striking photographs, and get to know through a warm-blooded writer's words.

Another project of Mrs. Erikson's aims to tell us about the nature of sainthood: the meaning saints have had for generations of Western Christians, the character and temperament of the saint — who is a person and yet a little more than a person. All of that will be done through St. Francis, whose life and ideals will be approached unconventionally — through what Joan Erikson calls his "four ladies": his mother, the lady Pica; the bride he assumed as a monk, the Lady Poverty; the Lady Clare, the first abbess of an order of nuns who still proclaim their allegiance to St. Francis by calling themselves Poor Clares; and finally, of course, Mary, "Our Lady Queen of Heaven." St. Francis was a master of the parable; he was a poet, a dramatist, a lively and warm and colorful man. Moreover, he was very much one who knew what some of our young people today have in mind when they want to live together in "communities" and be freed of the tyranny a glut of possessions can exert. St. Francis figures in *Gandhi's Truth:* a man of the West's Christian tradition, he no doubt helped Erikson cross the bridge to Asia, where he would have to understand a Mahatma not unlike that itinerant preacher who lived among the poor of Italy hundreds of years ago. And Erikson wrote *Gandhi's Truth* in Italy, in Perugia actually, within sight of Assisi.

In 1936 Paul Tillich introduced the first volume he wrote as an émigré from Germany (*The Interpretation of History*), with an autobiographical sketch, later published separately as *On the Boundary*. "The boundary is the best place for acquiring knowledge," he began. He spells out the boundaries, one after the other: between two temperaments, the meditative and conscientious, as against the romantic and carefree; between country and city; between social classes; between reality and imagination; between theory and practice; between one's own will and the obligations of the citizen, the member of a community; between theology and philosophy; between church and society; between religion and culture; between the eternal life and the immediate needs of today, particularly the needs of the least fortunate among us; between the native land (Germany) and the alien land that one comes to love (America). He talks of his "boundary-fate" and more or less makes a summary of what he means in the following paragraph:

When I was asked to give an account of the way my ideas have developed from my life, I thought that the concept of the boundary might be the fitting symbol for the whole of my personal and intellectual development. At almost every point, I have had to stand between alternative possibilities of existence, to be completely at home in neither and to take no definitive stand against either. Since thinking presupposed receptiveness to new possibilities, this position is fruitful for thought; but it is difficult and dangerous in life, which again and again demands decisions and thus the exclusion of alternatives. This disposition and its tension have determined both my destiny and my work.[8]

Erikson cited the theme of boundaries and "boundary-fate" in the remarks he made at a memorial to Tillich held at Harvard on November 4, 1965. He did so in order to pay homage to Tillich's wisdom and self-knowledge, and he does indeed have a right to feel close to Tillich. Erikson also left Germany in that fateful year of 1933, and it would seem that as artist and clinician, as psychoanalyst and historian, as Dane, German and American, as a wanderer who learned to sit still and learn from patients, he shares Paul Tillich's destiny. Both men made a home out of boundaries, and in the course of doing so, edged rather close to a new one, the kind that separates intelligent scholars from particularly inspired intellectual and spiritual leaders — in Gabriel Marcel's words, "vivifying minds."

In late February 1970, I went to Mississippi with Erik and Joan Erikson. We went first to Leake County, to a settlement called Harmony. I had been there before, knew the people. In 1964 I had watched them build a community center for themselves. They would build by day, and by night stand guard over their growing "project." Klansmen came and came but were fought off. Shots were fired, homes and churches dynamited, but men with rifles kept that center from harm. The people of Harmony are black yeoman farmers. They are proud landowners, sturdy and tough Mississippians. They are not about to leave the state, not about to stop planting, stop harvesting, stop praying, stop fighting for something. For what are they fighting? They ask themselves that, but not in order to come up with stock answers, half-meant banalities, or overcomplicated analyses of life's "meaning." They want their children to live, to have a doctor or dentist when needed, to have enough food every day, to attend schools where "the teachers be respectful to the boys and girls, and really teach and don't squelch them and squeeze all the juices out of them."

We talked with some of those children; they were three or four or five years old and taking part in a Head Start program. We also talked with teachers and with parents. The children were naturally quiet at first, wide-eyed with intense curiosity. Erikson noticed their eyes, how they kept upon us, held to us, pursued us. He also noticed the energy and enthusiasm of the children, many spared hunger, malnutrition and a whole range of diseases, if not death itself, by the good food and medical care Head Start provides. He sat down with a group of children and soon was drawing for them — horses and cars. The boys and girls looked and looked. They looked at the artist, looked at his pictures, back and forth. Later in the day we all sat around in a circle and the women of Harmony, teachers and mothers both, followed us and one another with their eyes, and talked and talked and talked. We heard of the hardships they knew and still know, but we also heard of their fierce determination to persist, to achieve things, tangible and intangible, things that in sum amount to "life, liberty and the pursuit of happiness." It was not always easy, not easy to hear the stories of violence, murder, extreme hardship. Nor was it easy to answer the questions about children, about how they grow, what they do and do not notice and believe as they get older and older. Quietly Erik and Joan Erikson responded, told the women what they are now trying to do — in fact, find the answers to some of those questions, find out how children in India and Pakistan or ghetto children in American cities or our middle-class white children or children on our Indian reservations and even our rural black children all come to look at themselves and their world. The Eriksons, working with Mrs. Arthur Penn, are doing so by asking children to use certain toys, build things, and then talk about a little world they choose to create. They are doing so not to "get data," to "find" something, but rather to see, to be shown — by children who are simply given a chance to play, to imagine, to exercise the will.

The people of Harmony asked the Eriksons to come back, and not only out of routine politeness. And in the Delta other parents and children were no less interested, no less curious, no less hospitable. We moved across a wide arc of the Delta, through Yazoo City, through Louise, through Midnight and Belzoni. We stopped at various Head Start centers. We visited with children and their teachers. We talked with the children. We listened to them sing. We watched them play. We were fed good food. And toward the end of our stay, as we drove along, past cotton fields and the cotton gins, past the cabins, past the little Delta towns that in a flash appear and disappear, I noticed Erik Erikson looking out the window, observing — but in his face also responding, trying hard to make sense of what he saw, and just as important, trying hard to learn what he believed, where his ethical concerns would require him to go. I reminded myself that he needn't have been there, needn't have been in that car, on the particular road; yet he had wanted to be there, had come there. I reminded myself that he was getting old, that he was perhaps tired. But a few moments later he was no longer tired; he had napped briefly and so was wide awake. I thought of a line in Robert Penn Warren's *Audubon:* "He walked in the world. Knew the lust of the eye." I thought of a line in T. S. Eliot's "East Coker": "Old men ought to be explorers." Then we came upon yet another fork in the road, and there was no more time for thoughts. We had to decide where we were going next, and by God, hope we would find our way there.

Notes

PREFACE

1. Anna Freud, *Difficulties in the Path of Psychoanalysis* (New York, International Universities Press, 1969), p. 20.

I. PHILOSOPHICAL ROOTS

1. Regis Jolivet, *Introduction to Kierkegaard*, W. H. Barber, trans. (New York, Dutton, 1952). Walter Lowrie, *Kierkegaard* (New York, Oxford University Press, 1938); also *A Short Life of Kierkegaard* (Princeton, N.J., Princeton University Press, 1944).
2. Gabriel Marcel, *Creative Fidelity* (New York, Farrar, Straus, 1964).

II. PERSONAL AND PROFESSIONAL ROOTS

1. Walter Z. Laqueur, *Young Germany* (New York, Basic Books, 1962).
2. Philippe Ariès, *Centuries of Childhood* (New York, Knopf, 1962).
3. Ernest Jones, *The Life and Work of Sigmund Freud* (New York, Basic Books, 1953).
4. Erik Homburger, "Psychoanalysis and the Future of Education," *Psychoanalytic Quarterly*, IV (1935), 50–51.
5. *Ibid.*, p. 67.

III. TO AMERICA

1. Erik H. Erikson, "Dramatic Productions Test," in *Explorations in Personality*, by Henry A. Murray and others (New York, Oxford University Press, 1938), p. 552.
2. *Ibid.*, p. 552.
3. Erik H. Erikson, "Observations on Sioux Education," *Journal of Psychology*, VII, first half (January 1939), 102–103.
4. *Ibid.*, pp. 123–124.
5. *Ibid.*, p. 129.

IV. TO CALIFORNIA

1. Erik H. Erikson, "Sex Differences in the Play Configurations of Preadolescents," *American Journal of Orthopsychiatry*, XXI (October 1951), 671.
2. *Ibid.*, p. 671.
3. *Ibid.*, p. 688.
4. *Ibid.*, p. 691.
5. Erik H. Erikson, "Observations on the Yurok: Childhood and World Image," University of California Publications in American Archaeology and Ethnology, Vol. XXXV, No. 10 (1943), p. 257.

6. *Ibid.*, p. 258.
7. *Ibid.*, p. 260.
8. *Ibid.*, p. 274.
9. Sigmund Freud, "The Claims of Psychoanalysis to Scientific Interest," Standard Edition, Vol. XIII (London, Hogarth Press, 1955), p. 188.
10. A. A. Brill, *Basic Principles of Psychoanalysis* (New York, Doubleday, 1949), p. 48.
11. Erikson, "Observations on the Yurok: Childhood and World Image," p. 296.

V. BUILDING A NEW POINT OF VIEW

1. Erik H. Erikson, "Sex Differences in the Play Configurations of Preadolescents," p. 424.
2. Erik H. Erikson, *Young Man Luther* (New York, Norton, 1958), p. 18.
3. See Erik H. Erikson, "Problems of Infancy and Early Childhood," in *An Outline of Abnormal Psychology*, G. Murphy and A. J. Bachrach, eds. (New York, Modern Library, 1954).
4. Anna Freud, *Normality and Pathology in Childhood* (New York, International Universities Press, 1965), pp. 4-5.
5. *Ibid.*, pp. 5-6.
6. *Ibid.*, pp. 6-7.
7. *Ibid.*, pp. 7-8.
8. Erikson, "Problems of Infancy and Early Childhood," pp. 4-5.
9. *Ibid.*, p. 7.
10. Erikson, *Childhood and Society*, pp. 72-73.
11. *Ibid.*, p. 75.
12. *Ibid.*, p. 76.
13. *Ibid.*, p. 81.
14. *Ibid.*
15. Erikson, "Observations on the Yurok: Childhood and World Image," p. 301.
16. Erikson, *Childhood and Society*, p. 86.
17. *Ibid.*, pp. 91-92.
18. Erikson, "Problems of Infancy and Early Childhood," p. 13.
19. Erikson, *Childhood and Society*, p. 92.
20. *Ibid.*
21. *Ibid.*, pp. 96-97.
22. *Ibid.*, p. 259.
23. Erikson, "Problems of Infancy and Early Childhood," p. 24.
24. *Ibid.*, p. 25.
25. *Ibid.*, p. 29.
26. Quoted in Erik H. Erikson, "Hitler's Imagery and German Youth," in *Personality in Nature, Society, and Culture*, Clyde Kluckhohn and Henry A. Murray, eds. (New York, Knopf, 1948), p. 486.
27. Erikson, "Hitler's Imagery and German Youth," p. 486.
28. *Ibid.*, p. 487.
29. *Ibid.*, p. 488.
30. *Ibid.*, p. 489.
31. *Ibid.*, p. 490.
32. *Ibid.*, p. 491.
33. *Ibid.*
34. *Ibid.*, p. 492.
35. *Ibid.*
36. *Ibid.*, p. 493.
37. *Ibid.*
38. *Ibid.*
39. *Ibid.*, p. 496.
40. *Ibid.*

41. *Ibid.*, pp. 500–501.
42. *Ibid.*, p. 503.
43. *Ibid.*, p. 504.
44. *Ibid.*, p. 505.
45. *Ibid.*
46. *Ibid.*
47. *Ibid.*, pp. 506–507.
48. *Ibid.*, p. 510.
49. Erikson, *Childhood and Society*, p. 358.
50. Erik H. Erikson, "Ego Development and Historical Change," in *The Psychoanalytic Study of the Child*, Vol. II (New York, International Universities Press, 1946), p. 359. This article has been revised in chapter 2 of Erik H. Erikson, *Identity: Youth and Crisis* (New York, Norton, 1968).
51. *Ibid.*, p. 359.
52. *Ibid.*, pp. 359–360.
53. Quoted in *ibid.*, p. 360.
54. *Ibid.*, p. 360.
55. *Ibid.*, p. 365.
56. *Ibid.*, p. 369.
57. *Ibid.*, pp. 371–372.
58. *Ibid.*, p. 373.
59. *Ibid.*, p. 374.
60. *Ibid.*, p. 378.
61. *Ibid.*, pp. 382–383.
62. *Ibid.*, p. 383.
63. *Ibid.*, p. 384.
64. *Ibid.*, p. 387.
65. Erik H. Erikson, "Ruth Benedict," in *Ruth Fulton Benedict, A Memorial*, A. L. Kroeber, ed. (New York, Viking Fund, 1949), pp. 14–17.

VI. *CHILDHOOD AND SOCIETY* ACHIEVED

1. Erikson, *Childhood and Society*, pp. 16–17.
2. *Ibid.*, p. 17.
3. *Ibid.*, p. 192–193.
4. *Ibid.*, p. 193.
5. *Ibid.*, p. 202.
6. Quoted in *ibid.*, pp. 209–210.
7. *Ibid.*, pp. 210–211.
8. *Ibid.*, pp. 213–214.
9. *Ibid.*, p. 214.
10. Quoted in *ibid.*, pp. 220–221.
11. *Ibid.*, pp. 235–236.
12. *Ibid.*, p. 261.
13. *Ibid.*, pp. 262–263.
14. *Ibid.*, pp. 267–268.
15. *Ibid.*, p. 274.
16. *Ibid.*
17. *Ibid.*, pp. 270–271.
18. *Ibid.*, p. 277.
19. *Ibid.*, pp. 283–284.
20. *Ibid.*, pp. 291–292.
21. *Ibid.*, p. 293.
22. *Ibid.*, p. 361.
23. *Ibid.*, pp. 362–363.
24. *Ibid.*, p. 390.

25. *Ibid.*, p. 390.
26. *Ibid.*, p. 403.
27. *Ibid.*, pp. 423-424.
28. *Ibid.*, p. 17. (See note 1.)
29. Personal communication.
30. Personal communication.
31. Erik H. Erikson, "Statement to the Committee on Privilege and Tenure of the University of California Concerning the California Loyalty Oath," *Psychiatry*, XIV (May 1951), 243-245.

VII. BACK EAST

1. Sigmund Freud, "Leonardo da Vinci and a Memory of His Childhood" (1910), Standard Edition, Vol. XI (London, Hogarth Press, 1957), p. 131.
2. Quoted in Erik H. Erikson, *Identity: Youth and Crisis* (New York, Norton, 1968), p. 19.
3. Erik H. Erikson, "The Problem of Ego Identity," in *Identity and the Life Cycle*, Vol. I, No. 1 of *Psychological Issues* (New York, International Universities Press, 1959), p. 101. This paper was originally published in the *Journal of the American Psychoanalytic Association*, IV (1956), 54-121; it has been recently revised in "Identity Confusion in Life History and Case History," chapter 4 of *Identity: Youth and Crisis*.
4. See "Some Psychoanalytic Comments on Culture and Personality" in *Psychoanalysis and Culture*, G. B. Wilbur and W. Muensterberger, eds. (New York, International Universities Press, 1951).
5. Erikson, "The Problem of Ego Identity," p. 116.
6. *Ibid.*, p. 129.
7. *Ibid.*, pp. 152-153.
8. *Ibid.*, pp. 156-157.
9. *Ibid.*, p. 158.
10. *Ibid.*, pp. 163-164.
11. Erik H. Erikson, "The Dream Specimen of Psychoanalysis" in *Psychoanalytic Psychiatry and Psychology*, Robert P. Knight and Cyrus R. Friedman, eds. (New York, International Universities Press, 1954), p. 133. This paper is also published in the *Journal of the American Psychoanalytic Association*, II (1954), 5-56.
12. *Ibid.*, p. 134.
13. *Ibid.*, pp. 139, 140.
14. Quoted in *ibid.*, p. 135.
15. *Ibid.*, pp. 137-138.
16. *Ibid.*, pp. 152-154.
17. Sigmund Freud, "Address to the Society of B'nai B'rith" (1926), Standard Edition, Vol. XX (London, Hogarth Press, 1959), p. 273.
18. Erikson, "The Dream Specimen of Psychoanalysis," p. 170.
19. Sigmund Freud, *The Origins of Psychoanalysis* (Letters to Wilhelm Fliess, Drafts and Notes: 1887-1902), Marie Bonaparte, Anna Freud, Ernst Kris, eds. (New York, Basic Books, 1954).
20. Erik H. Erikson, "Freud's 'The Origins of Psychoanalysis,'" *International Journal of Psychoanalysis*, XXXVI (1955), 4.
21. *Ibid.*, p. 15. The quote attributed to Pythagoras may be found in "The Harmony of Spheres," in *The Unwritten Philosophy*, Francis Cornford, ed. (Cambridge, Oxford University Press, 1950), p. 26.
22. Erik H. Erikson, "The First Psychoanalyst," chapter 1 in *Insight and Responsibility* (New York, Norton, 1964), pp. 19-20.
23. *Ibid.*, pp. 22-23.
24. *Ibid.*, p. 27.

VIII. LUTHER AND HISTORY

1. Erikson, *Young Man Luther*, p. 8.
2. *Ibid.*, p. 10.
3. *Ibid.*, pp. 21-22.
4. *Ibid.*, p. 27.
5. *Ibid.*, p. 29.
6. *Ibid.*, p. 36.
7. *Ibid.*, p. 38.
8. *Ibid.*, p. 53.
9. *Ibid.*, p. 56.
10. *Ibid.*, p. 67.
11. Quoted in *ibid.*, pp. 74-75.
12. *Ibid.*, p. 77.
13. *Ibid.*, p. 83.
14. Quoted in *ibid.*, p. 97.
15. *Ibid.*, p. 96.
16. *Ibid.*, pp. 99-100.
17. *Ibid.*, pp. 108-109.
18. *Ibid.*, p. 132.
19. *Ibid.*, pp. 139-140.
20. *Ibid.*, p. 141.
21. *Ibid.*, p. 146.
22. *Ibid.*, p. 151.
23. *Ibid.*, pp. 151-152.
24. Quoted in *ibid.*, p. 161.
25. *Ibid.*, p. 162.
26. *Ibid.*, p. 171.
27. *Ibid.*, pp. 171-172.
28. *Ibid.*, p. 174.
29. *Ibid.*, pp. 174-175.
30. *Ibid.*, p. 182.
31. *Ibid.*, p. 194.
32. *Ibid.*, p. 196.
33. *Ibid.*, p. 206.
34. *Ibid.*, p. 212.
35. *Ibid.*, pp. 212-213.
36. *Ibid.*, p. 213.
37. *Ibid.*, p. 228.
38. *Ibid.*, p. 228.
39. *Ibid.*, p. 234.
40. *Ibid.*, pp. 234-235.
41. *Ibid.*, p. 239.
42. *Ibid.*, p. 253.
43. *Ibid.*, pp. 266-267.

IX. FROM CLINICIAN TO PROFESSOR

1. Julian Huxley, in *Discussions on Child Development*, Vol. III, J. M. Tanner and Barbel Inhelder, eds. (New York, International Universities Press, 1958), pp. 197-198.
2. Erikson, *Identity: Youth and Crisis*, pp. 15-16. These remarks were originally made at a "Workshop on Identity" held at the San Francisco Psychoanalytic Institute in January 1966; they were later included in edited form in chapter 1 of *Identity: Youth and Crisis*.

X. ETHICS AND THE PREPARATION FOR GANDHI

1. Erikson, "The Nature of Clinical Evidence," in *Insight and Responsibility*, p. 50.
2. *Ibid.*, pp. 51–52.
3. *Ibid.*, pp. 54–55.
4. *Ibid.*, pp. 56–57.
5. *Ibid.*, p. 59.
6. *Ibid.*, pp. 61–62.
7. *Ibid.*, p. 64.
8. *Ibid.*, pp. 72–73.
9. *Ibid.*, p. 78.
10. Erikson, "Identity and Uprootedness in Our Time," in *Insight and Responsibility*, p. 87.
11. *Ibid.*, p. 107.
12. Erikson, "Human Strength and the Cycle of Generations," in *Insight and Responsibility*, p. 111.
13. *Ibid.*, p. 133.
14. *Ibid.*, pp. 139–140.
15. Erikson, "Psychological Reality and Historical Actuality," in *Insight and Responsibility*, p. 162.
16. *Ibid.*, pp. 199–200.
17. *Ibid.*, pp. 201–202, 208–210, 212.
18. Erikson, "The Golden Rule in the Light of New Insight," in *Insight and Responsibility*, p. 233.
19. *Ibid.*, p. 239.
20. Erik H. Erikson, "Youth: Fidelity and Diversity," in *Youth: Change and Challenge*, E. H. Erikson, ed. (New York, Basic Books, 1963), p. 23. This paper is also included as chapter 6 in *Identity: Youth and Crisis*.
21. Erik H. Erikson, "Womanhood and the Inner Space," chapter 7 in *Identity: Youth and Crisis*, pp. 277–278.
22. *Ibid.*, p. 282.
23. Erik H. Erikson, "Psychoanalysis and Ongoing History: Problems of Identity, Hatred and Nonviolence," *The American Journal of Psychiatry*, CXXII (September 1965), 243–244.
24. Erik H. Erikson, "The Ontogeny of Ritualization in Man," in *Philosophical Transactions of the Royal Society of London*, Series B, Vol. CCLI, No. 772 (1966), p. 338.
25. *Ibid.*, p. 339.
26. Erik H. Erikson, "On the Nature of Psycho-Historical Evidence: In Search of Gandhi," *Daedalus* (Summer 1968), Philosophers and Kings: Studies in Leadership, 695–730.
27. *Ibid.*, pp. 721–722.

XI. THE MAHATMA

1. Erik H. Erikson, *Gandhi's Truth* (New York, Norton, 1969), pp. 9–10.
2. *Ibid.*, p. 12.
3. *Ibid.*, p. 19.
4. *Ibid.*, p. 20.
5. *Ibid.*, p. 22.
6. *Ibid.*, p. 31.
7. *Ibid.*, p. 36.
8. *Ibid.*, pp. 38–39.
9. Quoted in *ibid.*, p. 51.
10. *Ibid.*, pp. 51–52.

11. Pyarelal Nayar, *Mahatma Gandhi*, Vol. I, *The Early Phase* (Ahmedabad, Navajivan, 1965), and *The Last Phase* (2 vols.) (Ahmedabad, Navajivan, 1956, 1958).
12. Erikson, *Gandhi's Truth*, p. 91.
13. *Ibid.*, p. 92.
14. *Ibid.*, pp. 98–99.
15. Quoted in *ibid.*, p. 98.
16. *Ibid.*, p. 110.
17. *Ibid.*, p. 113.
18. *Ibid.*, p. 116.
19. *Ibid.*, p. 121.
20. *Ibid.*, p. 122.
21. *Ibid.*, p. 144.
22. *Ibid.*, p. 153.
23. *Ibid.*, p. 155.
24. Quoted in *ibid.*, p. 170.
25. *Ibid.*, p. 176.
26. *Ibid.*, p. 178.
27. *Ibid.*, p. 181.
28. *Ibid.*, p. 205.
29. *Ibid.*, p. 219.
30. *Ibid.*, p. 229.
31. Quoted in *ibid.*, p. 230.
32. Quoted in *ibid.*, p. 230.
33. Quoted in *ibid.*, p. 230.
34. *Ibid.*, pp. 230–231.
35. *Ibid.*, p. 231.
36. *Ibid.*, p. 233.
37. *Ibid.*, p. 234.
38. *Ibid.*
39. *Ibid.*, pp. 243–244.
40. *Ibid.*, p. 244.
41. *Ibid.*
42. *Ibid.*, pp. 244–245.
43. *Ibid.*, p. 245.
44. *Ibid.*, p. 246.
45. Anna Freud, *Difficulties in the Path of Psychoanalysis* (New York, International Universities Press, 1969), p. 21.
46. Erikson, *Gandhi's Truth*, p. 247.
47. *Ibid.*, p. 248.
48. *Ibid.*
49. *Ibid.*, pp. 249–250.
50. *Ibid.*, p. 250.
51. *Ibid.*
52. *Ibid.*, p. 251.
53. *Ibid.*, p. 253.
54. *Ibid.*, p. 254.
55. *Ibid.*, pp. 257–258.
56. *Ibid.*, pp. 260–261.
57. *Ibid.*, p. 278.
58. *Ibid.*, p. 290.
59. *Ibid.*, p. 316.
60. Quoted in *ibid.*, p. 319.
61. *Ibid.*, p. 320.
62. *Ibid.*, pp. 324–325.
63. *Ibid.*, p. 334.
64. *Ibid.*, p. 339.

65. *Ibid.*, p. 342.
66. *Ibid.*, p. 351.
67. *Ibid.*, p. 352.
68. *Ibid.*, pp. 355–356.
69. *Ibid.*, p. 363.
70. *Ibid.*, p. 366.
71. Quoted in *ibid.*, p. 374.
72. *Ibid.*, pp. 377–378.
73. *Ibid.*, p. 399.
74. *Ibid.*, p. 413.
75. *Ibid.*
76. *Ibid.*, p. 425.
77. *Ibid.*, p. 439.
78. *Ibid.*, pp. 439–440.

XII. EPILOGUE, INTERLUDE AND PROLOGUE

1. *The New York Times*, August 20, 1968.
2. Erik H. Erikson, "Reflections on the Dissent of Contemporary Youth," *Daedalus* (Winter 1970), 174.
3. Erik H. Erikson, "Insight and Freedom," T. B. Davie Memorial Lecture (1968). Unpublished.
4. *Ibid.*
5. Joan Mowat Erikson, *The Universal Bead* (New York, Norton, 1969), pp. 13, 14.
6. Joan Mowat Erikson, *Mata Ni Pachedi* (Ahmedabad, National Institute of Design, 1968), p. 3.
7. *Ibid.*, pp. 12–13.
8. Paul Tillich, *On the Boundary* (New York, Scribner's, 1966), p. 13.

The Writings of Erik H. Erikson

Die Zukunft der Aufklaerung und die Psychoanalyse. *Z. psychoanal. Paedag.* 4:201–216, 1930.
  In English: Psychoanalysis and the Future of Education. In *Psychoanalytic Quarterly* 4:50–68, 1935.
Bilderbuecher. *Z. psychoanal. Paedag.* 5:13–19, 1931.
Triebschicksale im Schulaufsatz. *Z. psychoanal. Paedag.* 5:417–445, 1931.
Book Review: *Psychoanalysis for Teachers and Parents* by Anna Freud. In *Psychoanalytic Quarterly* 5:291–293, 1936.
Configurations in Play — Clinical Notes. *Psychoanalytic Quarterly* 6:139–214, 1937.
  In German: Traumatische Konfigurationen im Spiel: Aufzeichnungen. *Imago* 23:447–516, 1937.
  Short version: Traumatische Konfigurationen im Spiel, *Z. psychoanal. Paedag.* 11:262–292, 1937.
  In Spanish: Configuraciones en el Juego. *Revista de Psicoanálisis* VI, 2, 1948.
Dramatic Productions Test. In *Explorations in Personality* by Henry A. Murray and others, pp. 552–582. New York, Oxford University Press, 1938.
Section on Play Therapy: A Panel Discussion with Maxwell Gitelson and Others. *American Journal of Orthopsychiatry* 8:449–524, 1938. Especially pp. 507–510.
Observations on Sioux Education. *Journal of Psychology* 7:101–156, 1939.
Problems of Infancy and Early Childhood. In *The Cyclopaedia of Medicine, Surgery and Specialties,* pp. 714–730. Philadelphia, Davis and Company, 1940. Also in *Outline of Abnormal Psychology,* edited by G. Murphy and A. J. Bachrach, pp. 3–36. New York, Modern Library, 1954.
Studies in the Interpretation of Play: 1. Clinical Observation of Play Disruption in Young Children. *Genetic Psychology Monographs* 22:557–671, 1940.
On Submarine Psychology. Committee on National Morale (for the Coordinator of Information), 1940. Unpublished.
On the Feasibility of Making Psychological Observations in Internment Camps. Committee on National Morale (for the Coordinator of Information), 1940. Unpublished.
Concerning the Interrogation of German Prisoners of War. Committee on National Morale (for the Coordinator of Information), 1940. Unpublished.
Further Explorations in Play Construction. *Psychological Bulletin* 38:748, 1941. Abstract.

Comments on Hitler's Speech of September 30, 1942. Council on Inter-Cultural Studies, 1942. Unpublished.

Hitler's Imagery and German Youth. *Psychiatry* 5:475–493, 1942.
Revised in *Personality in Nature, Society and Culture,* edited by Clyde Kluckhohn and Henry A. Murray, pp. 485–510. New York, Knopf, 1948.

Observations on the Yurok: Childhood and World Image. Monograph, University of California Publications in American Archaeology and Ethnology 35:257–301, 1943.

Plans for the Veteran with Symptoms of Instability. In *Community Planning for Peacetime Living,* edited by Louis Wirth. Stanford, Calif., Stanford University Press, 1945.

Childhood and Tradition in Two American Indian Tribes. In *The Psychoanalytic Study of the Child.* Vol. I, pp. 319–350. New York, International Universities Press, 1945.
Revised in *Personality in Nature, Society and Culture,* pp. 176–203. 1948.

Ego Development and Historical Change. In *The Psychoanalytic Study of the Child.* Vol. II, pp. 359–396. New York, International Universities Press, 1946.
Revised in *Identity: Youth and Crisis.* 1968.

Ruth Benedict. In *Ruth Fulton Benedict: A Memorial,* edited by A. L. Kroeber, pp. 14–17. New York, Viking Fund, 1949. Includes Erikson's portrait sketch of Ruth Benedict as frontispiece.

Childhood and Society. New York, Norton, 1950. Second, enlarged edition, 1963.

Growth and Crises of the "Healthy Personality." (With Joan M. Erikson.) In *Symposium on the Healthy Personality,* edited by Milton J. E. Senn, pp. 91–146. (Prepared for the White House Conference, 1950.) New York, Josiah Macy, Jr., Foundation, 1950.
Revised in *Personality in Nature, Society and Culture,* pp. 185–225. 1948.
In German: *Wachstum und Krisen der gesunden Personlichkeit.* Stuttgart, Ernst Klett, 1953. Also in *Psyche* 7:1–31, 112–139, 1953.
Revised in *Identity: Youth and Crisis.* 1968.

Statement to the Committee on Privilege and Tenure of the University of California Concerning the California Loyalty Oath. *Psychiatry* 14:244–245, 1951.

Sex Differences in the Play Configurations of Preadolescents. *American Journal of Orthopsychiatry* 21:667–692, 1951.
Revised in *Childhood in Contemporary Cultures,* edited by Margaret Mead and Martha Wolfenstein, pp. 324–341. Chicago, University of Chicago Press, 1955.

Book Review: *Children Who Hate* by Fritz Redl and David Wineman. In *Basic Book News and Bibliography,* pp. 1–3. May 1952.

Cross-Cultural Patterns in the Adjustment and Maladjustment of Children: 1. Deviations from Normal Child Development with Reference to Cross-Cultural Patterns. 2. Etiology of Maladjustment in the Environment of the Child. *Scandinavian Seminar on Child Psychiatry and Child Guidance.* Geneva, World Health Organization, 1952. Abstract.

Remarks Made at an Interagency Conference at Princeton, New Jersey, September 21–25, 1951. In *Healthy Personality Development in Children: As Related to Programs of the Federal Government.* New York, Josiah Macy, Jr., Foundation, 1952.

The Power of the Newborn. (With Joan M. Erikson.) *Mademoiselle* 62:100–102, 1953.

On the Sense of Inner Identity. In *Health and Human Relations*, pp. 124–143. Report of a Conference Held at Hiddesen, Germany, August 2–7, 1951. New York, Blakiston Company, 1953.

In German: Uber den Sinn der Inneren Identitaet. In *Gesundheit und Mitmenschliche Beziehungen*, edited by M. von Eckhardt and W. Villinger, pp. 137–152. Munich, Ernst Reinhardt, 1953.

Revised in *Identity: Youth and Crisis*. 1968.

Wholeness and Totality – A Psychiatric Contribution. In *Totalitarianism*, edited by Carl J. Friedrich, pp. 156–171. Proceedings of a Conference Held at the American Academy of Arts and Sciences, March 1953. Cambridge, Mass., Harvard University Press, 1954.

Revised in *Identity: Youth and Crisis*. 1968.

The Dream Specimen of Psychoanalysis. *Journal of the American Psychoanalytic Association* 2:5–56, 1954. Also in *Psychoanalytic Psychiatry and Psychology, Clinical and Theoretical Papers*. (Austen Riggs Center.) Vol. I, edited by Robert P. Knight and Cyrus R. Friedman, pp. 131–170. New York, International Universities Press, 1954.

In German: Das Traummuster der Psychoanalyse. *Psyche* 8:561–604, 1954–1955.

Revised in *Identity: Youth and Crisis*. 1968.

Identity and Totality: Psychoanalytic Observations on the Problems of Youth. In *Human Development Bulletin*, pp. 50–82. Fifth Annual Symposium. Chicago, The Human Development Student Organization, 1954.

Freud's 'The Origins of Psychoanalysis.' *International Journal of Psychoanalysis* 36:1–15, 1955.

In German: Zu Sigmund Freud 'The Origins of Psychoanalysis.' *Psyche* 9:90–116, 1955.

The Problem of Ego Identity. *Journal of the American Psychoanalytic Association* 4:54–121, 1956.

In German: Das Problem der Identitaet. *Psyche* 10:114–176, 1956–1957. Also in *Entfaltung der Psychoanalyse*, edited by Alexander Mitscherlich. Stuttgart, Ernst Klett, 1956.

Revised in *Identity: Youth and Crisis*. 1968.

The First Psychoanalyst. *Yale Review* 46: 40–62, 1956. Also in *Freud and the Twentieth Century*, edited by Benjamin Nelson. London, Allen and Unwin, 1957.

In German: Sigmund Freuds Psychoanalytische Krise. Festvortrag zu Freud's 100 Geburtstag. In *Freud in der Gegenwart*. Lectures Given at the Universities of Frankfurt and Heidelberg. Frankfurt, Europaeische Verlagsanstalt, 1957.

Revised in *Insight and Responsibility*. 1964.

Ego Identity and the Psychosocial Moratorium. In *New Perspectives for Research on Juvenile Delinquency*, pp. 1–23. Washington, D.C., U.S. Department of Health, Education and Welfare, Children's Bureau, 1956.

Revised in *Identity: Youth and Crisis*. 1968.

Confirmation of the Delinquent. (With Kai T. Erikson.) *Chicago Review* 10:15–23, 1957.

Revised in *Identity: Youth and Crisis*. 1968.

Trieb und Umwelt in der Kindheit. In *Freud in der Gegenwart*. 1957.

Identity and the Psychosocial Development of the Child. In *Discussions on Child Development*. Proceedings of the Third Meeting of the Child Study Group, World Health Organization. Vol. III. New York, International Universities Press, 1958.

Young Man Luther, A Study in Psychoanalysis and History. (Austen Riggs Center, Monograph No. 4.) New York, Norton, 1958.

On the Nature of Clinical Evidence. In *Daedalus* 87:65–87, 1958. Also in *Evidence and Inference*, pp. 73–95. The First Hayden Colloquium. Cambridge, Mass., M.I.T. Press, 1958.
Revised in *Insight and Responsibility*. 1964.

Identity and the Life Cycle: Selected Papers. In *Psychological Issues*. Vol. I. New York, International Universities Press, 1959.
Revised in *Identity: Youth and Crisis*. 1968.

Late Adolescence. In *The Student and Mental Health*, edited by Daniel H. Funkenstein. The World Federation for Mental Health and the International Association of Universities, 1959.

Youth and the Life Cycle, an Interview. In *Children*, Vol. VII, no. 2. Washington, D.C., U.S. Department of Health, Education and Welfare, 1960.

Identity and Uprootedness in Our Time. Address Before the Eleventh Annual Congress of the World Federation for Mental Health. Vienna, 1958.
In German: Identitaet und Entwurzelung in unserer Zeit. *Psyche* 13:1, 1959.
Revised in *Insight and Responsibility*. 1964.

Psychosexual Stages in Child Development. In *Discussions on Child Development*, Vol. IV. World Health Organization Study Group, 1959.

The Roots of Virtue. In *The Humanist Frame*, edited by Sir Julian Huxley, pp. 145–165. New York, Harper & Row, 1961.
Revised in *Insight and Responsibility*. 1964.

Childhood and Society. In *Children of the Caribbean*, pp. 18–29. San Juan, P.R., Printing Division, 1961.

Introduction. In *Emotional Problems of the Student* by Graham B. Blaine and Charles C. McArthur. New York, Appleton-Century-Crofts, 1961.
Revised in *Identity: Youth and Crisis*. 1968.

Youth: Fidelity and Diversity. *Daedalus* 91:5–27, 1962.
Revised in *Identity: Youth and Crisis*. 1968.

Reality and Actuality. *Journal of the American Psychoanalytic Association* 10:451–473, 1962.
Revised in *Insight and Responsibility*. 1964.

The Golden Rule and the Cycle of Life. (The George W. Gay Lecture on Medical Ethics, 1963.) *Harvard Medical Alumni Bulletin*, Vol. XXXVII, no. 2, 1963. Also in *The Study of Lives*, edited by R. W. White. New York, Appleton-Century-Crofts, 1963.
Revised in *Insight and Responsibility*. 1964.

Youth: Change and Challenge, edited by Erik Erikson. New York, Basic Books, 1963. Also in paperback: *The Challenge of Youth*. New York, Doubleday, 1965.

The Inner and the Outer Space: Reflections on Womanhood. *Daedalus* 93:582–606, 1964.
Revised in *Identity: Youth and Crisis*. 1968.

Insight and Responsibility. New York, Norton, 1964.

Memorandum on Identity and Negro Youth. *Journal of Social Issues*, Vol. XX, no. 4, pp. 29–42. 1964.

Psychoanalysis and Ongoing History: Problems of Identity, Hatred and Nonviolence. *Journal of the American Psychiatric Association* 122:241–250, 1965.

Concluding Remarks: In *Women and the Scientific Professions*, pp. 232–245. M.I.T. Symposium on American Women in Science and Engineering. Cambridge, Mass., M.I.T. Press, 1965.

The Concept of Identity in Race Relations: Notes and Queries. *Daedalus* 95:145–170, 1966.
> Revised in *Identity: Youth and Crisis*. 1968.

The Ontogeny of Ritualization in Man. In *Philosophical Transactions of the Royal Society of London*. Series B, no. 772, vol. 251, pp. 147–526. 1966.
> Revised in *Psychoanalysis — A General Psychology*. Essays in Honor of Heinz Hartmann, edited by Rudolph M. Loewenstein, et al. New York, International Universities Press, 1966.

Concluding Remarks, Discussion on Ritualization of Behavior in Animals and Man. In *Philosophical Transactions of the Royal Society of London*. Series B, no. 772, vol. 251, pp. 513–524. 1966.

Gandhi's Autobiography: The Leader as a Child. *The American Scholar*, Autumn 1966.

Book Review: *Thomas Woodrow Wilson* by Sigmund Freud and William C. Bullitt. *The New York Review of Books*. Vol. VIII, no. 2, 1967. Also in *International Journal of Psychoanalysis*, Vol. 48, no. 3, 1967.

Memorandum on Youth for the Committee on the Year 2000. *Daedalus*, Summer 1967.
> Revised in *Identity: Youth and Crisis*. 1968.

Memorandum on the Draft. In *The Draft: A Handbook of Facts and Alternatives*, edited by Sol Tax. Chicago, University of Chicago Press, 1967.

The Human Life Cycle. In *International Encyclopedia of the Social Sciences*. New York, Macmillan, 1968.

Psychosocial Identity. In *International Encyclopedia of the Social Sciences*. New York, Macmillan, 1968.

Identity: Youth and Crisis. New York, Norton, 1968.

On the Nature of Psycho-Historical Evidence: In Search of Gandhi. *Daedalus*, Summer 1968.

Insight and Freedom. The Ninth T. B. Davie Memorial Lecture, University of Cape Town, August 6, 1968. Unpublished.

Gandhi's-Truth. New York, Norton, 1969.

Reflections on the Dissent of Contemporary Youth. *Daedalus*, Winter 1970. Also in *International Journal of Psychoanalysis* 51: part 1, 1970.

Autobiographic Notes on the Identity Crisis. *Daedalus*, Summer 1970.

Index